THE SPANISH RESURGENCE,

1713–1748

THE LEWIS WALPOLE SERIES IN EIGHTEENTH-CENTURY CULTURE AND HISTORY

The Lewis Walpole Series, published by Yale University Press with the aid of the Annie Burr Lewis Fund, is dedicated to the culture and history of the long eighteenth century (from the Glorious Revolution to the accession of Queen Victoria). It welcomes work in a variety of fields, including literature and history, the visual arts, political philosophy, music, legal history, and the history of science. In addition to original scholarly work, the series publishes new editions and translations of writing from the period, as well as reprints of major books that are currently unavailable. Though the majority of books in the series will probably concentrate on Great Britain and the Continent, the range of our geographical interests is as wide as Horace Walpole's.

THE SPANISH RESURGENCE, 1713-1748

Christopher Storrs

Yale

UNIVERSITY PRESS

New Haven & London

Published with assistance from the Annie Burr Lewis Fund.

Published with assistance from the foundation established in memory of Henry Weldon Barnes of the Class of 1882, Yale College.

Yale University Press books may be purchased in quantity for educational, business, or promotional use. For information, please e-mail sales.press@yale.edu (U.S. office) or sales@yaleup.co.uk (U.K. office).

Set in MT Baskerville and MT Bulmer types by IDS Infotech Ltd.
Printed in the United States of America.

Library of Congress Control Number: 2016934660
ISBN 978-0-300-21689-9 (cloth : alk. paper)

A catalogue record for this book is available from the British Library.

This paper meets the requirements of ANSI/NISO Z39.48-1992 (Permanence of Paper).

10 9 8 7 6 5 4 3 2 1

For all Catz men and women

CONTENTS

CONTENTS

ACKNOWLEDGMENTS

The despatch of this book to the publisher brings with it the delightful task of thanking those who have helped in their different ways to complete something which has been far too long in the making. I must first acknowledge the support given by the Arts and Humanities Research Council in the form of a grant of matching research leave, under the now-defunct scheme of funding projects close to their completion, and by the University of Dundee for matching that award. Unfortunately, my expectation that the book was like ripe fruit just waiting to be picked proved very far from the reality. Equally important have been the many small grants received over the years from the Carnegie Trust for the Universities of Scotland, for which all thanks. At the University of Dundee, my colleagues have contributed to a sense of community and general good humour which has been a great help. I want particularly to single out Jim Livesey because he it was who, having kindly agreed to read my typescript, suggested I send it to Yale University Press. How perceptive, bingo! At Yale, Chris Rogers responded so enthusiastically and promptly to my proposal and chapters, while Erica Hanson has been enormously helpful in seeing the book through to publication; thank you both. I am likewise greatly indebted to Yale's anonymous readers; their suggestions have surely improved the final version of the book. My copy-editor at Yale University Press, Lawrence Kenney, made an initially daunting task much easier than I could have expected, as did Jeff Schier; thank you also. Many colleagues, fellow Hispanists, and others have expressed an interest in this book along the way, too many to be named individually. However, I must thank Julio Muñoz for his gift of a copy of his excellent book on Murcia in the War of the Spanish Succession. The Oropesa club moves on. I am much obliged also to those whose friend-ship and occasional hospitality have contributed to the successful conclu-sion of this project, including Lorraine Goodhew, Nick McGill, and Richard Beville in London, and my former student, now my peer, Nicola—now Dr.—Cowmeadow. Much of the introduction was pub-lished as "The Spanish Risorgimento in the Western Mediterranean and Italy 1707–1748" in volume 42 of the *European History Quarterly* in 2012 and is reproduced with the permission of SAGE publications. Finally, but in fact first and foremost, I want to thank my best—my kindest—reader, critic, and editor, my wife and now also my peer, Anne-Marie—now Dr.—Storrs. Without her remarkable generosity, kindness, affection, and patience this book might well never have been completed. Many authors take this opportunity to observe that their children make clear what is really important to them in life; for me it is Anne-Marie.

NOTE ON MONEY

General

1 *real* = 34 *maravedís* (the maravedí being the lowest denomination in circulation),

    10 *reales* = 340 maravedís = 1 *escudo* (coin of account) or crown = just over 1 German florin

    11 reales = 1 *ducado,*

    15 reales = 1 *peso,* and

    60 reales = 1 *doblón*

    1 pistole = 6 escudos

    1 florin (= 20 stivers) = 6.66 *vellón reales* (because 9 florins = doblón [1725])

    1 piastre = 27 maravedís

    1 *peso fuerte* = silver 8-real piece = piastre (increasingly known as dollar)

Sources: Henry Kamen, *The War of Succession in Spain 1700–1715* (London: Weidenfeld, 1969), 168–69, 398; Eugenio Larruga, *Memorias políticas y*

económicas sobre los frutos, comercio, fábricas y minas de España, 45 vols. (Madrid, 1787–1800), 1:73; José I. Aparicio, *Norte fixo y promptuario seguro para la más clara y breve inteligencia del valor de todas las monedas usuales y corrientes del continente de España* (Madrid, 1741); Gerónimo de Uztáriz, *Theory and Practice of Commerce and Maritime Affairs*, translated by John Kippax, 2 vols. (London, 1752), 1:88, 164; John J. McCusker, *Money and Exchange in Europe and America, 1600–1775, A Handbook* (London: University of North Carolina Press, 1978); *Diplomacia Secreta y Paz: La correspondencia de los embajadores españoles en Viena Juan Guillermo Ripperda y Luis Ripperda (1724–1727) / Geheimdiplomatie und Friede; Die Korrespondenz der spanischen Botschafter in Wien Johan Willem Ripperda und Ludolf Ripperda (1724–1727)*, edited by Ana Mur Raurell, 2 vols. (Madrid: Ministerio de Asuntos Exteriores y de Cooperación, 2011) 1:161, 2:333, 367; Antonio M. Bernal, *España, proyecto inacabado* (Madrid: Marcial Pons, 2005), 297; José de Santiago Fernández, *Política Monetaria en Castilla durante el Siglo XVII* (Valladolid: Junta de Castilla y León, 2000), 249–61.

Examples

1722: 2,101,255,529 maravedís (net value of the Castilian *rentas provinciales*) = 6,180,163 crowns (escudos)[1]

1724: 1,200 pistoles = 7,200 escudos de vellón[2]

1732: 6 million reales = 100,000 pistoles[3]

1737: the Castilian revenues put 209,671,221 reales (vellón) = about 13,978,081 piastres [pesos], or 28 million florins, and just over 2 1/2 millions sterling[4]

THE SPANISH RESURGENCE,

1713-1748

INTRODUCTION

The war, we have with Spain, seems more likely to be determined in Italy,
than in America.
—*Viscount Bolingbroke, September* 1743

The first half of the eighteenth century was a momentous period in the
history of Spain and its global empire, or Monarchy. The last Spanish
Habsburg, Charles II, died in 1700 and was succeeded by the first
Spanish Bourbon, Louis XIV's grandson Philip V.[1] Thereafter a war of
succession engulfed Spain in a way not seen for more than two hundred
years. Philip won that struggle but lost territories in Flanders and in Italy
that Spain had held for two centuries and more in some cases, with major
implications for Spain's domestic history. The Spanish presence in north
Africa also shrank, with the loss of Oran and Mazalquivir in 1708.
Besides this imperial contraction, which to many later commentators was
simply the culmination of a long Spanish decline, the war meant major
internal changes.[2] The Aragonese territories (Aragon, Catalonia,
Majorca, and Valencia), which had acknowledged Philip's rival, the
Austrian Habsburg "Charles III"—the future Holy Roman Emperor
Charles VI—suffered the loss of the quasi autonomy they had enjoyed

1

largely unaltered since the unification of "Spain" by the Catholic Kings, Ferdinand and Isabella, at the end of the fifteenth century.

Not surprisingly, the War of the Spanish Succession has attracted a great deal of attention from historians. So, too, has Philip V himself, or the more bizarre aspects of his behaviour—his mood swings and his marked uxoriousness. Unfortunately, such studies help ensure that other developments during Philip's long reign (1700–46) have been largely ignored, such that despite a considerable volume of work published on the period in recent decades, Henry Kamen's observation, made more than a generation ago, that the years 1665 to 1746 represent a "dark ages" in modern Spanish historiography still has some force.[3] Among the many aspects of Philip's reign which have not been properly explored is the impressive revival of Spanish power after 1713, above all in north Africa and Italy, where in the 1730s and 1740s Philip's forces appeared to be resurrecting the extensive dominion carved out there by Ferdinand and Isabella and Charles V.

Successful aggression in the Mediterranean was part of a wide-ranging Spanish resurgence, or *risorgimento*, as it was so aptly described in 1725 in his end-of-mission report, or *relazione*, by a Venetian diplomat, a resurgence that was evident also in the Atlantic and the Caribbean. Philip V detested the Utrecht settlement of 1713, which he had been obliged to accept in order to end the succession struggle with Britain and with all of the allies except the emperor, a conflict which formally ended only with the conclusion of the peace (treaties) of Vienna in 1725. Utrecht had ratified the dismemberment of the Spanish Monarchy in Europe, confirmed British possession of Gibraltar and Menorca, and given the British privileged access to Spain's American empire in the form of the infamous *asiento*, or contract to supply African slaves to Spanish America, of the South Sea Company. Philip wished to reverse all of these concessions, and in focusing, as this study does, on the Mediterranean we should not lose sight of the Atlantic or of Philip's determination to erode British penetration of the Spanish Indies. This policy culminated in the War of Jenkins' Ear from October 1739, a conflict subsumed from 1741 onwards in the War of the Austrian Succession, whose conclusion triggered the winding up at last of the asiento.[4]

Nevertheless, the preoccupation of historians with the early modern Atlantic world in recent decades and an accompanying neglect of the Mediterranean world should not obscure the fact that Philip's efforts to reverse the 1713 settlement across the Atlantic cannot be compared in type, scale, or impact with those made in the Mediterranean. In addition, once war broke out, Spain's American empire was largely invulnerable: witness the British failure to have any impact there after the initial success at Portobello in 1739, a failure which facilitated focusing on Italy thereafter. Spanish America was valued by the Spanish court primarily for the resources it supplied for the pursuit of ambitions in the Mediterranean, where the Spanish revival had its greatest success. As Steve Pincus has observed of a different polity, England, in an earlier period, the 1690s, we need to be wary of focusing exclusively on the Atlantic.[5]

Philip V made surprisingly little attempt to restore the old Spanish Monarchy in northern Europe by recovering Flanders. He had not himself visited Flanders, which had been effectively handed over to Max Emanuel of Bavaria early in the War of the Spanish Succession and been conquered by the allies from 1706 onwards. Philip had by no means abandoned all hope of recovering some or all of Flanders after 1713 (see chapter 5), but Italy—above all the territories which had been part of the old Monarchy—was Philip's priority, and well before his second marriage. More will be said about Philip (see chapter 4), but it must be made clear at the start that policy was his and not that of his second wife, Isabel (Elisabeth) Farnese. Philip's marriage to Isabel largely confirmed and only to a degree modified his Italian ambitions, which also included the restoration of his allies, the dukes of Guastalla and of Mirandola. The first Bourbon already had two sons, Luis and Ferdinand, by his first marriage, to Marie Louise of Savoy, and thus it was highly unlikely that any of Isabel's sons, Don Carlos, Felipe, or Luis, would succeed in Spain. Since in Spain the Infantes did not, unlike the princes of the blood in France, receive substantial endowments, or *appanages*, she sought to place them in the Italian states on which she had dynastic claims: the Farnese duchy of Parma (and Piacenza) and the Medici grand duchy of Tuscany. As the niece of the reigning duke of Parma, Francesco (1694–1727), who had no sons and only an elderly, unmarried brother, Isabel had a strong claim to that duchy. In Tuscany the grand duke, Cosimo III (1670–1723), had a son, Giangastone (1723–37), but the latter had no male heirs. Isabel, a descendant of the sister of Grand Duke Ferdinand II, was one of a number of female claimants, including Cosimo's daughter, the Electress Palatine.[6]

As for north Africa, historians of early modern Spain too often ignore Spanish concern with that region, a concern which underpinned Charles V's expeditions against Tunis (1535) and Algiers (1541) and the interventions there of Philip II and Philip III. This preoccupation, shared by Philip V, was a blend of secular, strategic, and religious anxieties. Twentieth-century historians tended to doubt the extent to which the foreign policies of most sovereigns were influenced by religious considerations after 1648. This rather simplistic view is now being challenged, a revisionist approach which is particularly appropriate in the case of Philip, for whom the title of Catholic King seems quite appropriate, as he was personally very devout (see chapter 5), while his triumph in the succession struggle had owed much to his being depicted as a religious warrior, combatting Muslims as well as the Protestant Christian allies of his Austrian Habsburg rival. Philip sometimes clashed with Rome, while he frequently deployed religious arguments in pursuit of essentially secular policies. But we cannot ignore a religious, even crusading, element in Spanish policy in north Africa, where it might be difficult, even misleading, to try to distinguish the religious from the secular. Philip's African inheritance—a number of fortified posts, or *presidios*, strung out along the north African coast—had been depleted during the succession conflict. At the same time, Philip was unable to devote the necessary forces to the relief of Ceuta, which had been under siege since 1694 and which on inheriting the throne he had declared to be his first priority but which was still beleaguered in 1714. The following year, in response to a remarkable circular from Philip to all Spanish bishops inviting suggestions on how to relieve Spain of its difficulties by appeasing an angry divinity, Cardinal Luis Antonio de Moncada y Belluga, the bishop of Cartagena and one of Philip's leading clerical supporters in the succession struggle, urged the king to prioritise the recovery of Oran and intervention in Africa rather than in Italy.[7]

Besides pointing out the religious benefits of such a policy, Belluga, whose diocese was among those most threatened by the north African corsairs, argued that it would end that danger; he also argued that conquests in Africa would be a source of timber for the king's fleets and of grain, thus making good the loss of Sicily. Indeed, to Belluga, expansion in Africa would compensate for the loss of Flanders and Italy, which had anyway been a burden. Last but by no means least, expansion in north Africa would in part be funded by the church. A few years later, in 1717, another ecclesiastic, Philip's chief minister, Cardinal Giulio Alberoni, urged an expedition to north Africa rather than the invasion of Naples being pressed by the Neapolitan duke of Popoli: Alberoni claimed it would be easier to mount, would fulfil promises made by the king to the pope, would be in Spain's interests, and would be a source of honour or glory to the king.[8]

Philip's subsequent conduct suggests he was not insensitive to the arguments of Belluga and Alberoni, who were making a strong case for a strategy which was neither Atlantic nor Italian. Within Christian Europe the Catholic King was less obviously a champion of the faith after 1713. This was evident in his continuing quarrel with the emperor, which he did not set aside to allow Charles VI to harry the Ottomans in the Balkans. Nevertheless, the religious impulse continued to draw Philip, like his Habsburg predecessors, to Africa. So did more secular concerns, such as the powerful Moorish presence just across the strait (which the Moors might cross and again overrun Spain, as in the eighth century) and the possibility that an advance in north Africa might facilitate an attack on, or at least counter and to a degree isolate, the British garrison in Gibraltar, which was often supplied from north Africa. Philip may also, like Ferdinand of Aragon before him, have seen Africa as a basis for intervention in Italy. Finally, Philip may not have had much choice: there is a marked contrast between his policy in north Africa, where in some respects Spain was on the defensive against an Islamic jihad which had begun circa 1680, and that in Italy, where it was far more clearly on the offensive.[9]

Whatever the inspiration, these various preoccupations underpinned a striking resurgence of Spanish activity in the Mediterranean. Following Philip V's recovery of Aragon, Valencia, and Catalonia between 1707 and 1714, his forces reconquered the islands of Majorca and Ibiza, and in 1716, at the request of the pope, he sent a flotilla of 5 warships and 5 galleys to the defence of Corfu against the Turks. In 1717 a Spanish expeditionary force comprising 9,000 troops aboard some 100 transports and escorted by 12 warships of various types invaded the island of Sardinia and, to widespread astonishment, conquered it in little more than two months. In 1718 a much larger force, an armada of 439 ships including at least 276 transports and carrying 36,000 men, began the conquest of the larger, neighbouring island of Sicily. Fear that the Spanish court would overturn the Utrecht settlement in the South prompted a concerted response by some of the other powers in the guise of the Quadruple Alliance. The war which followed (1718–20) saw the almost complete destruction of the Spanish fleet in Sicily, stranding Philip's forces in Sardinia and Sicily, while British and French forces invaded northern Spain. Philip reluctantly joined the Quadruple Alliance in January 1720, evacuating Sicily and Sardinia. He then turned his attention to north Africa: 16,000 men were convoyed to Ceuta, ending the siege begun there more than twenty years before.[10]

Philip hoped not just to build on the success at Ceuta but also that his troops might occupy Tetuan and Tangier. Unfortunately for these African ambitions, the commander of the Ceuta expedition, the marqués de Lede (who had also led the invasions of Sardinia and Sicily), believed this was beyond his forces. Indeed, the Spanish court was curiously quiescent in the 1720s, although the diplomatic revolution represented by the peace and alliance with the court of Vienna in 1725 triggered a cold war—as well as a real, if brief, one with England, during which Philip's forces besieged Gibraltar in 1727. Peace with Britain and the treaty of Seville which followed (1729) facilitated renewed intervention in Italy. In October 1731, in accordance with that treaty, an Anglo–Spanish expeditionary force, including 23 Spanish warships plus 7 galleys and 48 transports carried almost 7,500 Spanish troops to Italy to install the Infante, Don Carlos, in the central duchies.[11]

Having reestablished a Spanish presence in central Italy, Philip switched his efforts once again to north Africa, where he was being drawn into the regional power struggles. In 1731 a Moroccan prince sought Philip's support in his quarrel with the king of Morocco, promising, if successful, to restore Oran. For his part, Philip's disgraced former chief minister, the Dutch baron Jan Willem van Ripperda, was urging on the king of Morocco against Philip. Whatever Philip's motives, in June 1732 an expeditionary force of more than 600 vessels—warships and galleys escorting hundreds of transports with almost 27,000 men aboard—left Alicante, reconquering Oran and then Mazalquivir. Like so many of

Spain's foreign adventures in this period, this one attracted widespread foreign interest.[12]

Spain's north African presidios continued to preoccupy Philip V and his ministers: in 1740, for example, following the outbreak of war against Britain, it was feared the British might incite an Algerian attack on Oran. But 1732 saw Philip's last major expedition across the straits: henceforth Spanish efforts in the Mediterranean focused almost exclusively on Italy. In the autumn of 1733, in alliance with the French court (the first Family Compact), Philip intervened in the War of the Polish Succession, sending a convoy of 16 warships and 150 transports carrying almost 36,000 troops to Italy, with more following. José Patiño's claim, in January 1735, that Philip had 56,000 troops in Italy no doubt exaggerated, but there were nearly 50,000 troops in Philip's pay in Italy at the end of 1735. By then they had conquered Naples, Sicily (another ambitious amphibian operation involving the shipping of about 18,000 troops in more than 200 transports escorted by warships and galleys), and the component fortresses, namely, Piombino, Orbitello, Porto Ercole, Santo Stephano, and Tellemone, of the Tuscan presidios, which had formed part of Spanish Italy. After 1713 Philip ceded these conquests, along with Porto Longone, the only part of the presidios complex he retained and his only foothold in mainland Italy, to Don Carlos, who was crowned king of the Two Sicilies in Palermo in July 1735.[13]

Victorious in southern and central Italy, Spanish troops headed for Lombardy to complete the expulsion from Italy of the Austrian Habsburgs. However, disagreement over Mantua, which the Spanish court intended should form part of a Milanese state destined for another of Isabel Farnese's sons, the Infante Felipe, and fears at the court of Turin of Spanish domination of Italy divided the allies. The French court therefore negotiated separately with the emperor a settlement which ruled out further Spanish gains in Italy and which was imposed on Louis XV's allies. The peace of Vienna (1738) which ended the conflict confirmed Don Carlos's possession of Naples, Sicily, and the Tuscan presidios but obliged him to surrender Parma, Piacenza, and Tuscany to the Austrian Habsburgs, who also retained Mantua and Milan.[14]

Despite these successes the Spanish court was not at all satisfied in Italy. After the death of Philip's former rival, Emperor Charles VI, in October

1740, its ambitions there were crucial in extending to Italy the War of the Austrian Succession. Already at war with Britain since October 1739, between November 1741 and March 1742 about 40,000 Spanish troops headed for Italy in three expeditions, the first two convoyed by Philip's fleet to central Italy to join about 10,000 men offered by Don Carlos, the third marching overland through France under the Infante Felipe. This intervention in Italy, in alliance with the kings of France (the second Family Compact, 1743) and the Two Sicilies, the duke of Modena, and later the republic of Genoa, enjoyed remarkable success. It also helped ensure that the war against Britain in the Caribbean, which largely fizzled out after the British failure at Cartagena in 1741, was soon eclipsed by that in Europe, and not least by the struggle in Italy. By the end of 1745 the Bourbon forces had secured Parma, Piacenza, and, at last, Milan, which the Infante Felipe entered in triumph in December 1745. They had also occupied Nice and the duchy of Savoy, thereby alarming Protestant Switzerland, and much of Piedmont. At the start of 1746, when Philip may have had as many as 56,000 men in Italy, he had almost entirely restored the Spanish Italy which he had inherited in 1700, overturning the Utrecht settlement of 1713.[15]

But the winter of 1745–46 was the peak of Spanish fortunes in Italy, which collapsed thereafter, as María Theresa temporarily abandoned her efforts in central Europe to recover Silesia from Frederick the Great of Prussia in order to give priority to the reconquest of Italy, sending 30,000 men there at the end of 1745. This reinforcement had its effect. The Spanish forces were expelled from Milan and Parma, and they and their French allies suffered a crushing defeat at Piacenza on 2 July 1746, one that may have contributed to the death of Philip V in July 1746.[16] The Spanish and French forces escaped complete disaster only by fighting their way to the Riviera and making their way along the coast into France, abandoning their ally, the republic of Genoa, to its fate. Only Savoy was still occupied by Philip's forces, while a triumphant María Theresa had hopes of recovering Naples and Sicily. The accession in the summer of 1746 of Ferdinand VI, who was far less committed to his father's policy in Italy and determined to end a war so damaging to his Spanish subjects, might have further threatened Bourbon prospects there except that Ferdinand wished to settle the Infante Felipe in Italy in order to remove him from Spain. Thus Spain fought on, and the peace treaty ending the conflict, which was concluded at Aix, in October 1748, confirmed Don Carlos's possession of Naples and gave Parma and Piacenza to the Infante Felipe. Four years later the Austrian Habsburgs and Spanish Bourbons guaranteed each other's territories in Italy in the treaty of Aranjuez, ending the generation-long cycle of Spanish military intervention in Italy and helping ensure that the latter was untroubled by war for four decades thereafter.[17]

For over thirty years, then, in decades when Europe is generally thought to have been tranquil, the peace was either broken or menaced by a resurgent Spain. During this time it mounted operations which merit comparison with other seaborne expeditions, such as William of Orange's invasion of England in 1688 and the abortive British assault on Cartagena in 1741, "the most formidable force ever assembled in the Caribbean." The other courts of Europe were almost constantly alarmed by fears of new Spanish adventures and aggression in a period in which the Spanish court was the single greatest threat to peace in Europe. The neglect of this remarkable resurgence—and more specifically of Philip V's African and Italian adventures—by recent historians of international relations and, more narrowly, of Spain is understandable. For one thing, the diplomacy of the period has become a byword for complex, indulgent, and at times almost pointless negotiation, although in large part it simply represented the efforts of other powers to respond to the court of Madrid's revanchism. For another, there is a sense that the rise of Prussia and Russia in north, central, and eastern Europe was regarded, both at the time and later, as being of far greater importance than other developments, including a Spanish revival in the south which was only partly successful. There is a widespread belief, too, inside and outside Spain, that a more important development in modern Spanish history was the collapse of the *antiguo régimen* in the early nineteenth century and that the key to this lies in the immediately preceding era, that is, the later eighteenth century, and in the failure of Charles III, the former Don Carlos of Naples, to save the Bourbon monarchy in a bout of "Enlightened Despotism."[18]

This is not to deny the importance attached by historians to Philip's reign as a period which saw the first steps towards the necessary creation, after a sustained seventeenth-century crisis and decline, of a modern, centralised, unitary, and national Spain, with Philip V playing the part of "patriot king." The supposed centralised, national unity was in large part a consequence of the succession struggle and the suppression of Aragonese particularism, a development which has spawned a largely negative "Aragonese" historiography (see above). Among the weaknesses of that historiography is a failure to see that Philip's recovery of the Aragonese realms must also be understood as part of a rather different historical conjuncture, the Spanish resurgence in the western Mediterranean. Seen from a narrowly Spanish perspective, Philip's Italian and African adventures have been criticised as a distraction from and irrelevant to the supposedly more important creation of a modern Spanish state and have been largely attributed to the selfish ambitions of Philip's second wife, in Thomas Carlyle's lapidary phrase the "termagant of Spain." And as we have seen, although they enjoyed some success and impressed contemporaries, those adventures were not completely successful. Certainly the promise of 1735, when the Spanish Bourbons seemed unstoppable in Italy, and that of 1745 were not sustained. In consequence, Spain emerged in 1748 with less than had earlier seemed possible. Perhaps not entirely surprisingly, after 1748 Spanish ministers turned their backs on the Mediterranean and instead focused upon what some Spaniards thought was a proper national concern, Spain's American empire and a more effective exploitation of its resources by and for Spain.[19]

Yet this is to underrate the Spanish success in the Mediterranean after 1713. Philip V had recovered lost ground and reasserted himself in north Africa, something which is unduly neglected in the historiography. As for Italy, by 1748 one Spanish Bourbon dynasty was entrenched in southern Italy and would remain so until Giuseppe Garibaldi's expedition to Sicily in 1860 and the creation of the Kingdom of Italy in 1861. The same was true of the other Spanish Bourbon dynasty, which had been installed in Parma and Piacenza. Italy, whose future in 1713 had seemed to lie with the Austrian Habsburgs and the House of Savoy, was now once again predominantly Spanish. Indicative of the shift were enduring Savoyard fears after 1720. The new distribution of power in Italy in 1748 was one factor in the decision of King Charles Emanuel III of Sardinia to marry his son and heir, the future king Victor Amadeus III, to a Spanish Infanta. The military successes which created this new situation, particularly those in the War of the Polish Succession, represented a reversal of military fortune abroad for Spain after decades of apparent failure in the later seventeenth century and echoed the achievement of both Ferdinand and Isabella and Charles V (see above). The British presence at Gibraltar and Menorca was certainly a fly in the ointment, but a stronger Spanish presence on the opposite shore of the straits represented some sort of a counterweight to Gibraltar and might even be exchanged for it.[20]

These developments have major implications with regard to our understanding not only of Italy but also of international relations in the generation after the War of the Spanish Succession, when Spanish revisionism was one of the most powerful forces driving European diplomacy. The period between 1713 and 1739 was one in which the two great rivals of the eighteenth century, Britain and France, were relatively weak because of domestic difficulties, including dynastic and financial ones. These problems and a desire not to offend the Spanish court, which might visit its displeasure on those of their subjects trading, whether directly or indirectly, with Spanish America, reinforced a reluctance to go to war so soon after the conclusion of the War of the Spanish Succession and even brought the two states together, as allies. The Spanish court exploited that reluctance with some success by threatening and at times waging war and was sometimes appeased, as in the treaty of Seville (1729) and the Anglo–Spanish expedition to Italy of 1731. When France and Britain drifted apart in the thirties and forties Spain benefitted by securing the invaluable military and naval support of France. Whatever its basis, Philip V and Isabel Farnese clearly went some way towards achieving their objectives: in 1735, following the conquest of Naples, Philip's representative in London, the conde de Montijo, declared, with justifiable hyperbole, that the Utrecht settlement was dead.[21]

International relations in this period have not been entirely neglected, Alfred Baudrillart's multivolume study of Philip V and the French court being, despite its age, perhaps the most striking evidence to the contrary. Nevertheless, Spanish ambitions and policies and their impact have not attracted the attention they merit, especially in recent decades. Thus, despite the work of Guido Quazza and others, the War of the Polish Succession, in which the Austrian Habsburg Monarchy came close to collapse and in consequence of which Italy was restructured, has been largely neglected, as has the Italian theatre in the War of the Austrian Succession. Spanish preoccupation with the Mediterranean and the response of other powers to Spain's ambitions there ought also to call into question the commonplace that the Mediterranean was an international backwater. On the contrary, Spanish ambitions in Italy could have serious knock-on effects elsewhere: in 1745 some of Philip's ministers anticipated that the Spanish military presence in north Italy might influence the imperial election at Frankfurt. Until the Spanish resurgence in the western Mediterranean is restored to its true place in the history of international affairs in Europe, relations between the European powers in that generation will not be properly understood.[22]

While acknowledging the relevance of what might be termed non-Spanish factors in explaining the revival of Spain, we cannot ignore the contribution of Spain's own resources to its recovery, exemplified in Philip V's Mediterranean adventures, which impacted upon the king's subjects far more in this period than did the defence of the Americas. This book therefore largely ignores the Americas, which are the main interest of Anglophone historians preoccupied primarily with the origins of the War of Jenkins' Ear, except insofar as their wealth funded operations in the Mediterranean. These decades saw critical changes within Spain, changes which cannot be separated from the demands of the forward policy in Africa and Italy. The near-constant state of alert in peninsular Spain, above all in the 1730s and 1740s, is crucial to explaining the transformation of early eighteenth-century Spain in the direction of what has been termed the "fiscal-military state," one in which the demands of war shaped the state, not least in its distinctive fiscal policies. Philip's frequent wars and preparations for war mean that in some respects his Spain fits the bill better than that of his son Charles III.[23]

Unfortunately, the historiography has not always properly acknowledged these things. For one thing, as I have already noted, historians have tended to take the view that these Italian ambitions had nothing to do with Spain or Spanish interests and that they represented little more than the appropriation of Spanish resources by Philip V's second wife in order to secure thrones in Italy for sons with few prospects in Spain itself. Associated with this is the view that the expeditions represented little more than adventurism. But criticisms of Philip's Mediterranean policy also reflect another historiographical strand, one which sees the new Bourbon dynasty as synonymous with enlightenment, reform, and the modernisation of Spanish and Spanish American state and society. It is almost a cliché that Philip's reign was characterised by innovation and that Philip was a moderniser, although historians debate the sources of and inspiration for his innovations, whether they were of native, Spanish origin or, as many argue, a foreign, French import, such that the arrival of Philip V marked the first real wave of *afrancesamiento* experienced by Spain.[24]

Criticisms of Spanish Mediterranean policy in this period reflect the view held by some historians that empire had been a burden which Spain was well rid of in 1713. In fact, it is arguable that Philip V's Italian policy had more support within Spain than has been acknowledged. Perhaps the most positive Spanish assessment of the Spanish court's Mediterranean policy is that of Bethencourt Massieu, for whom the architect of success in Italy was Patiño. To Bethencourt, Patiño was pursuing a national policy, one which was certainly more in the interest of the country at large than is generally allowed and which was also much broader in conception than has been recognised. Bethencourt's insight is salutary, not least because of the persistence of the older, negative view, in the work of Antonio Domínguez Ortiz and Didier Ozanam, and because his appreciation of Patiño has rescued from obscurity an unjustly neglected contemporary of Robert Walpole and André-Hercule de Fleury. Exactly what constituted a national policy and Spanishness is also an issue which, although highly contentious in contemporary Spain, has hardly been addressed apart from Philip V's suppression of the distinctive institutions of the crown of Aragon. While the possibility that Spain might constitute a plurality of nationalities rather than a single nation well into the eighteenth and even the nineteenth century has long been recognised, the possibility that there might be a lingering supranational sense of identification of Philip's Spanish subjects with Italy, inherited from the Habsburg era, rooted in and inseparable from an identification with the ruling dynasty, has hardly been acknowledged.[25]

However, while Bethencourt does see things more positively and while there may well have existed a domestic constituency for a forward policy in Africa and Italy, he does not sufficiently explore all aspects of the domestic mobilisation of resources implied or necessitated by this policy. Equally neglected is a proper assessment of the impact on Philip's Spain: mobilisation may have created more stresses and tensions within Spanish society than has been recognised. Indeed, we need to consider the extent to which intervention in Italy, especially in the 1740s, triggered on the one hand some resistance and in part, by way of response, an assertion of royal authority which might be thought of as an archetypal expression of royal absolutism. The episode was not serious enough to undermine the "construction of loyalty" achieved by Philip in the War of the Spanish Succession, but it triggered, or rather confirmed, a reaction against the monarch's Italian ambitions such that 1748 was more of a watershed in ending a deep-rooted Spanish interest in and commitment to Italy than was the peace of 1713. The challenges of the 1740s suggest that historians have not sufficiently acknowledged the extent to which the War of the Austrian Succession—as much as the War of the Spanish Succession which preceded it and the Seven Years' War which followed—tested the participants.[26]

As for modernisation and reform, here, too, we must be cautious. For one thing, we need to understand both of these concepts in eighteenth-century terms rather than in nineteenth-century ones. In this guise, *modernise* might mean the introduction of what were regarded as the most up-to-date and effective institutions and practices, their effectiveness demonstrated, for example, by the success of contemporary states, allies and enemies, on the battlefield. More important perhaps, we need also to bear in mind that Philip V's essential objective, namely, the preservation or reconstruction or both of Spanish north Africa and Italy, was essentially conservative, even backward looking. This implies important elements of continuity across 1700 rather than the sense of fracture which informs most writing on the change of dynasty. Early Bourbon Spain was emphatically a dynastic, patrimonial state, one in which inherited claims, not mercantilist aspirations, largely determined policy; but it arguably also had more affinities with its predecessor than has been acknowledged or recognised by historians who tend to be scholars either of Habsburg Spain or of Bourbon Spain and rarely of both. Philip V not only sought to resurrect the Spanish Habsburg Monarchy in Africa and Italy but also made much greater use of its institutions and practices than has been admitted, as my book will show. As for the social impact of this remarkable effort, Spain remained a society of orders or estates: Philip, rather than rewarding a bourgeoisie which had backed him, as some have claimed, reinforced this older structure by advancing in rather traditional ways those who served him.[27]

The following chapters seek to explain the significant revival of Spanish fortunes and power in the generation following the conclusion of the War of the Spanish Succession and to identify its impact on Spain. They further explore the essential paradox of Philip V's reign: that in seeking to rebuild the composite Monarchy in Africa and Italy he created a much more obviously Spanish state. The source materials for an exploration of Spain's revival and its consequences are extensive. They include the records of the new central administrative agencies which emerged in this period. Some of the materials generated by these Secretariats of War, Navy, and Indies and Finance perished in the fire which consumed the old Habsburg royal palace, or *alcázar*, in Madrid in 1734.[28] Nevertheless, abundant documentation relating to the army, the navy, and the finances survive in the Archivo General at Simancas and in the Archivo Histórico Nacional in Madrid. In addition to these records are those of the municipal authorities, who were called on to supply men and money for Philip's Mediterranean adventures. Furthermore, within Spain there are the papers of noble and other families and private correspondence, although these are the most problematic, not least because they are scarce and often difficult to access. Official publications such as the *Gaceta de Madrid* are also of some use. Last but by no means least, there is the correspondence in non-Spanish archives of the many foreign diplomats in Madrid and, between 1729 and 1733, in Seville, whose presence made the Spanish court again one of the great centres of diplomatic activity and whose job it was to find out and report on Spanish policy and resources to sovereigns frequently alarmed by Spain's warlike preparations and aggression. Highly valuable in this respect are the reports of successive representatives of the dukes of Savoy, later the kings of Sicily (1713–20) and Sardinia (from 1720), Victor Amadeus II (d. 1730) and Charles Emanuel III. Not only was the court of Turin among the most obvious victims of Spanish revanchism in the Mediterranean but Victor Amadeus was the grandfather (and Charles Emanuel the uncle) of the future Ferdinand VI, while the house of Savoy had a reversionary interest in the Spanish succession should Philip V's line die out, a claim enshrined in the Utrecht settlement. Savoyard diplomats therefore took a very close interest in developments in Spain these decades, as, of course, did the representatives of most other states, large and small.

Chapter 1 discusses Philip V's army, chapter 2 his navy. Chapter 3 examines the funding of Philip's foreign adventures, while chapter 4 explores the administrative challenge they posed and how they affected Spanish political life. Finally, chapter 5 focuses on the way in which one of the most central developments in Spain after 1707, that is, the greater integration of Aragon, Catalonia, and Valencia into the Spanish state, was affected by the interventions in Africa and Italy, and on the nature of relations with the recovered Italian territories and Italians. It also hints at a connection between the two, bridged by the presence in what had been Spanish Italy of so-called Austrian exiles from the Aragonese territories, and addresses the issue of identity. In this way the chapter seeks to relate Philip's Mediterranean revanchism to recent debates in Spain about patriotism and national identity in the country during the eighteenth century.[29]

CHAPTER ONE

THE ARMY

It is incredible the joy of this Court . . . at the recent success in
Puglia . . . . [T]he entire nation has not failed to demonstrate its pleasure
at recognising in this action the old valour of the Spanish troops.
—*Papal nuncio, Madrid, June 1734*

In the sixteenth and early seventeenth centuries Spain was Europe's
foremost military power. By the later seventeenth century, however, it had
lost that primacy. The War of the Spanish Succession represented a nadir
of Spain's military fortunes as war engulfed the peninsula and the
Monarchy lost the territories which had hitherto housed two of its three
main, permanent fighting forces, the Army of Flanders and the Army of
Lombardy, the third being the Army of Catalonia. Indeed, Philip V's triumph in the succession struggle owed much to the military support of his
grandfather, Louis XIV.[1] After the conclusion of that conflict, however,
Philip's Spain reemerged as a significant independent military power.

Spain's military revival after 1713 owed much to the fact that Philip's opponents in Europe, notably the Austrian Habsburgs, both were weak and
prioritised other theatres of war. Those successes also owed something in
the 1730s and 1740s to the support of allies, above all, France, who not
only diverted Philip's opponents in those other theatres, the Rhine and

Flanders, but also collaborated with his forces in Italy. Yet Philip could not always find allies, fighting alone between 1717 and 1720, while allies had their own priorities, Louis XV ending the War of the Polish Succession before the Spanish court had achieved all of its objectives in Italy. Philip therefore needed an independent military capability rooted in Spain. He had gone some way towards achieving this in the succession struggle, during which Spain's Habsburg military inheritance was transformed. The multifaceted overhaul included the replacement of the distinctive *tercios* by regiments; the introduction of a new hierarchy of ranks and the assertion of greater royal control over appointments; the adoption of new weaponry; the establishment of new corps, including that of engineers; the elaboration of a structure of royal commissaries; and last but by no means least, a marked expansion of the army, which by 1713 was not only larger than that which Philip had inherited but also a standing force stationed in Spain rather than in Flanders and Lombardy.[2]

Unfortunately, however, while much attention has rightly been paid to these initial reforms, Philip V's army *after* the War of the Spanish Succession is in many respects terra incognita. Spanish historians have enhanced our understanding of that army in recent decades. But other historiographical trends, including the prevalence of prosopographical studies, mean that they have largely ignored it as the fighting instrument abroad which so impressed contemporaries. They also neglect the sheer extent of the military effort represented by major operations in Africa and Italy and the impact of that effort not only on the army itself, in terms of additional reform and the way this contributed in turn to further progress in the direction of modernisation and state formation, but also on Philip's subjects.[3]

I address these issues in this chapter, drawing primarily on the abundant surviving documentation in the series generated by the newly created Secretariat of War in the Archivo General de Simancas and the Archivo Histórico Nacional in Madrid. I exploit as well other sources, including rare military memoirs, in order to clarify the extent of Spain's remarkable military activity in the decades between the end of the War of the Spanish Succession and the conclusion of that of the Austrian Succession, the ways in which the challenge of activity on this scale was met, and the extent to which the demands of war and the military establishment shaped the state. How far was Philip building on as well as overhauling the legacy of the Spanish Habsburg state? Just how he and his ministers responded to the logistical challenge of major operations and how far they innovated in preferring public, state administration over the private sector asiento favoured by the Habsburgs offer one area of comparison. For many later commentators Philip's Spain was not only a fiscal-military state but also a nation-state, but it is not at all clear that the composition of his army fully justifies the claim. As for the impact of Philip's military adventures on his subjects, some have suggested that early Bourbon Spain, echoing developments elsewhere, was militarised, but this too is questionable.[4]

Commitments and Numbers

Philip V oversaw a substantial increase in the size of his army in Spain in the course of the War of the Spanish Succession, during which large numbers of his subjects were mobilised, to a total of 100,000 men in 1714. He continued to maintain large, permanent forces thereafter. As is true in the case of all armies in early modern Europe, it is not easy to be precise about the size of those forces. It is not always clear whether the figures given in contemporary sources or those used by later historians are complete: there was frequently a difference, for example, between a unit's establishment, that is, the number of men when it was complete, and the number of effectives. This helps explain the widely varying figures sometimes given for the same forces.[5] Nevertheless, as long as we recognise that the official figures, often derived from the periodic musters or reviews, do not always represent the true picture, they remain a useful indicator.

Philip V had lost Flanders and Italy by 1713, but his defence commitments thereafter continued to span the Atlantic. Before the reign of Charles III there was no permanent Army of America. Instead, apart from scattered garrisons in key fortresses there, men were despatched to the Indies as and when required. In 1726 troops were sent to Havana as Anglo–Spanish relations deteriorated between the alliances of Vienna and Hanover and following the departure of an English squadron to the Caribbean, while the outbreak of the War of Jenkins' Ear in 1739 triggered the departure of more units to Spanish America. Within a few years, however, the war in Europe—in Italy—was once again centre stage:

Spanish troops no longer fought in Flanders, but in terms of military priorities Europe came first for the Spanish court, as it had before 1700.[6]

In Europe, Spain's land frontiers and extensive coastline required constant defence, the new British presence at Gibraltar adding to Philip V's commitments in this respect before, during, and after the siege of 1727. But the disposition of Philip's troops in Spain itself was not determined just by external threats; a substantial military presence in the territories of the Crown of Aragon mirrored the fact that the exercise of greater royal authority from 1707 onwards rested on Philip's assertion of a right of conquest (see chapter 5). Throughout the reign large numbers of troops were deployed in Aragon, Valencia, and above all Catalonia. In the summer of 1717, 43 of 81 infantry battalions in Philip's pay were stationed in the crown of Aragon, 35 of them in Catalonia. Twenty years later it was claimed that there were rarely fewer than 20–30,000 troops in Catalonia, in part to contain its population.[7]

Philip could not neglect either the islands or the garrisons beyond the peninsula. After its reconquest in 1715, a large garrison was also stationed on the island of Majorca, whose strategic importance was increased by the British occupation of neighbouring Menorca and the threat it posed. Indeed, in 1740, following the outbreak of war with Britain, an expedition against Menorca was discussed in Madrid but was abandoned in favour of intervention in Italy. What was left of empire in north Africa and Italy, that is, the coastal garrisons, or *presidios*, also had to be manned. In Africa these included Alhucemas, Ceuta, Melilla, el Peñón, and, from 1732, Oran. In Italy the presidios meant Porto Longone, off the Tuscan coast. In 1734 Philip, as we have seen, ceded Porto Longone, along with Naples and Sicily, to Don Carlos, but it continued to be garrisoned by Philip's troops.[8]

The concentration of troops on Spain's eastern seaboard also reflected the military thrust into the Mediterranean after 1713. Apart from the achievement of a large standing army in Spain itself, the most striking feature of Spanish military activity between 1713 and 1748 was the occasional expeditions overseas, which often triggered a more substantial military commitment. They also helped to determine the size of Philip's army, which expanded and contracted with his changing commitments in Africa and Italy (table 1). In 1715, following the conclusion of the War of the

Spanish Succession, Philip effected a substantial reform, or reduction, but the first cycle of intervention in the Mediterranean triggered the recruitment of about 33,000 men between the summer of 1717 and 1720, an increase of almost 50 percent. There was another bout of cost cutting after 1720, in which most of the new units disappeared. But the War of the Polish Succession and Spanish intervention in Italy meant renewed expansion. In February 1734 José Patiño envisaged raising the number of troops in Philip's pay by just over 40,000, an increase of 50 percent, to give an army of 123,900. In fact, 20 new regiments were raised, while existing ones were increased in size, such that this target was exceeded, the Spanish army peaking at more than 130,000 men. The end of the Polish succession struggle was followed by another round of reductions, so that war in the Caribbean from 1739 and in Italy from 1741 prompted another expansion. Initially, in 1741, this involved adding a third battalion to existing regiments of just 2 battalions—10 battalions in all, a total of 6,500 men—although all were disbanded by the end of 1744. By means of various separate agreements concluded throughout the war, other units were taken into service. Peace in 1748 was followed by the usual reform.[9]

These wartime totals merit comparison with those achieved in late Habsburg Spain. At their height Philip V's forces, deployed above all in Italy, matched the largest achieved under Philip IV and Charles II. Philip

TABLE 1. Philip V's and Ferdinand VI's Forces, 1714–48[a]

	1714	1716	1721	1724	1734	1739	1748
Infantry	63,000	56,000	64,160	58,370	112,840	103,660	88,963
Cavalry	37,000	10,058	15,531	12,300	18,160	12,960	8,310
Total	100,000	66,058	79,691	70,670	131,000	116,620	97,273

[a] Ozanam, "Política," 521, unless otherwise indicated. From 1734 the infantry includes the militia; Andújar Castillo, "Privatización," 131; Martínez Shaw and Alfonso Mola, *Felipe*, 248. Concepción de Castro, *A la sombra de Felipe V: José de Grimaldo, ministro responsable (1703–1726)* (Madrid: Marcial Pons, 2004), gives 70,000; Hellwege, *Provinzialmilizen*, 35. For a higher figure in 1734—140,206—which assumed all units were complete but omitted the new militia regiments, Keene to Newcastle, 7 April 1734, NA, SP 94/119. For a total in 1739 of 127,348 (82,490 infantry, 10,200 cavalry, 10,158 dragoons, and 24,500 militia), cf. Estado General, 20 June 1739, BN Mss 12950/6. Conde de Clonard, *Historia Orgánica de las Armas de Infantería y Caballería Españolas*, 16 vols. (Madrid: Francisco del Castillo, 1851–59), 5:231, mentions just 67,000 infantry in April 1739.

V's achievement is the more striking in view of the fact that his Habsburg predecessors were able to recruit far more widely, in the Europe-wide Monarchy, than the first Bourbon.[10]

Wastage

To maintain forces of this size Philip V needed to recruit large numbers of men, both to complete, that is, bring up to strength, existing regiments and to form new ones, especially given the constant loss of men through desertion and illness and in action as they were wounded, killed, and captured. Desertion was not a problem peculiar to Philip's army, but that did not lessen its seriousness. In the autumn of 1720 desertion greatly reduced the expeditionary force despatched to Ceuta. Two decades later, in July 1742, Cardinal Fleury feared that José Carrillo de Albornoz, duque de Montemar's expeditionary force, recently arrived in Italy, was already so weakened by desertion that it could not engage the enemy. Later in that same conflict Juan Buenaventura Dumont, conde de Gages, was said to have lost 5,000 deserters on his retreat to Naples in 1743–44. Men deserted anywhere and everywhere and for all sorts of reasons, including arrears of pay and lack of proper provision of food and shelter, and was particularly pronounced among foreign troops. It did not help that men were often lured from one unit to another, reflecting the fact that Philip's army was not a monolith but a collection of battalions and regiments with different, even competing, interests.[11]

King and commanders adopted various countermeasures. Harsh penalties were repeatedly imposed against deserters and those who aided them. Men who fled and were captured often suffered severely. In Italy in 1744 Gages hanged one-fifth of all deserters from the Spanish forces found among the Austrian troops on the surrender of the town of Nocera. The effectiveness of such draconian measures must be questioned, however, given their frequency and the equally frequent pardons offered to deserters who returned to their units. In July 1717 an amnesty was seen as one means to boost numbers against the background of intervention in Sardinia, and almost thirty years later a similar measure was seen as a means to reinforce the army in Italy for the campaign in 1745.[12] Better pay and conditions (see below) might also reduce desertion. But just how effective any of these intended correctives were is not clear, as desertion continued to weaken Ferdinand VI's forces.

Casualties in action were also sometimes serious. In February 1743 the drawn engagement at Camposanto may have cost the Spanish forces 3,464 men, or 23 percent of the total force. The debacle at Piacenza in 1746 was far more deadly. The joint Spanish and French army incurred about 12,000 casualties, almost 25 percent of the entire army, the Spanish losses alone totalling well over 7,000: 3,220 dead, 3,516 wounded, and 915 taken prisoner. While a major engagement generally meant great losses, the cumulative effect of a succession of lesser actions might also be grave.[13]

The third major reason for loss of men, sickness, was sometimes the most serious. In July 1717 during the conquest of Sardinia 500 men were lost, most of them victims of the island's malarial climate. As for the War of the Austrian Succession, according to one review of the army in Savoy in 1744, of a total force of 16,056 men, 4,356, or more than 25 percent, were declared to be ill, and a further 785 wounded. Men fell ill for all sorts of reasons, including contagious diseases and all the other ailments to which the civilian population was vulnerable. The troops also succumbed to the exertions of army life, especially if new to them and if inadequately provided for. Veterans were more robust, one of the reasons they were so highly valued, but new recruits were likely to fall sick in Spain itself on the march to the ports where they were to embark for Africa or Italy. In 1747, for example, D. José Meléndez was at Valladolid with 214 men levied in Galicia, having left 34 men behind, ill, en route. Campaigning abroad was even more gruelling. During the War of the Austrian Succession Philip's forces suffered on reaching Italy, where they were bottled up in the Tuscan presidios, and thereafter by campaigning in trying conditions. In his military memoirs D. Antonio de Alós y de Riús described how men froze during the alpine fighting in poor weather in late 1743, while in 1746 the long retreat from Piacenza to the Riviera severely depleted the Spanish forces. Effective medical services (below) might stem the flow of losses of this sort but could not halt it completely. There was thus a constant demand for new recruits, above all before a major expedition and in wartime: between 1717 and 1720, 1732 and 1735, and 1741 and 1748.[14]

Recruitment of Foreign Troops

Philip V and Ferdinand VI found men in a variety of ways, some abroad, some at home, preferring volunteers but also using compulsion. Whereas the cavalry was levied almost entirely within Spain, simply because it was easier to recruit, the infantry was much more cosmopolitan. In general, more than 50 percent of the infantry were Spanish, as in 1716 and 1724, but these were years of peace, and the foreign component tended to expand and sometimes to predominate when overseas operations were undertaken. In 1731, for example, of 8 infantry battalions which were to accompany Don Carlos to Italy, just two were Spanish. The foreign component continued to loom large but may have fallen in the course of the War of the Austrian Succession. In 1745 Spaniards contributed 32,500 of the 49,000 infantry in the Infante's army in Italy, while in the spring of 1747 the marqués de la Mina thought Spain's contribution to an allied total in Italy of 75,000 infantry would comprise 591/2 battalions, of which 47 were Spanish and the rest, just 20 percent, were foreign. Whatever the explanation for the decline, in the latter stages of the Austrian succession conflict, the Spanish monarch may have been recruiting more of his own Spanish subjects.[15]

Foreign troops were attractive for various reasons, the most important being Spain's limited manpower. Establishing the population of Spain in the early eighteenth century is no easy matter. Nevertheless, the basic trends are clear and were positive. Spain's population may have grown by two million between the late seventeenth century and the middle of the eighteenth to a total of about eight million around 1713 and to just over nine million by 1768. Certain areas were more populous, including Galicia, in the northwest, the capital, Madrid, which drew immigrants from the rest of the country, and Andalusia, making these attractive recruiting grounds. Nevertheless, Philip V's Spain could not boast the demographic resources of France and this fact, as Spanish and foreign commentators made clear, limited the number of Philip's Spanish subjects who could be diverted into the military without disrupting Spain's economy and antagonising those same subjects. Foreign troops, on the other hand, were less likely to desert in Spain, where they had fewer kin and friends to shelter them, and, while costly, they might be easily raised in wartime close to where they might have to serve and just as easily disposed of, that is, be demobilised, at the end of a conflict. These factors helped ensure that, like his Habsburg predecessors, Philip relied on a substantial minority of foreign troops rather than on an entirely Spanish army drawn from the Iberian peninsula and islands: 15 of the 18 new infantry regiments levied for Italy in 1717–20 were raised in Italy and Switzerland. While Spaniards may have loomed larger between 1741 and 1748 (above), thereafter Ensenada saw the taking on of foreign units, 28 battalions, as a key part of the solution to the problem of recruitment.[16]

Foreign troops included entire units such as companies, battalions, and regiments as well as individuals, some of them drawn from foreign communities long resident in Spain. There had long been a substantial French contingent in Spain, one swelled during the succession conflict, and this was one source of men. Portuguese, too, were frequently recruited, in large part along the frontier with that state. Another source of foreign recruits was the Irish resident in Spain. Their numbers grew in the early eighteenth century with the influx of many of those who had abandoned Ireland following the Williamite conquest in 1689–91 and who, often after a brief residence in France, moved to Spain during and after the War of the Spanish Succession. For some of these Irish exiles military service was a stepping-stone to high office in Spain. Exemplary in this respect was the career of Ricardo Wall: having fought in the marine corps on the Sicilian expedition in 1718, he served in the army in Italy in the War of the Austrian Succession before being appointed secretary of state by Ferdinand VI.[17]

Some of the foreign units in Philip V's service were essentially the inheritance of the past and served a nonmilitary as well as military purpose. Thus units of both the Flemish, or Walloon, Guards and the Italian Guards (below), which helped maintain the connection between the Spanish court and the elites of the former Flemish and Italian territories of the Monarchy throughout the century, fought in most of Philip's African and Italian campaigns. So, too, did various units raised in Italy in the War of the Spanish Succession, units which followed Philip to Spain when Spanish Italy collapsed. Some other Italian units were raised during the later Italian expeditions, between 1718 and 1720 (above), from 1734, and in 1741–42.[18]

Other foreigners served in whole units which Philip V took into pay for a fixed period. This meant above all the Swiss Catholic regiments, whose attractions included the proximity of their recruiting ground(s) to the theatres, notably Italy, where they would serve. In 1720 a capitulation for such a regiment was agreed with one Charles Ignacio Niderist and was renewed in November 1724, and in May 1725 another, for 3,200 men in 16 battalions of 200 men each, with one Charles Alfonso Besler. In 1732 more agreements of this sort were agreed with a number of Swiss officers. The Swiss could be problematic: they were expensive and sometimes effectively went on strike until paid their arrears, as happened on campaign in Italy in 1735. However, the advantages outweighed the disadvantages, and in 1737 Philip renewed the capitulation with Besler for ten years. In the summer of 1742 a number of Swiss officers already in Philip's service agreed to raise a further 10 battalions, most of which served in Italy. This helped ensure that in the summer of 1745 there were at least 14 battalions of Swiss in Spanish service in Savoy and Nice, totalling about 3,500 men. Spanish commanders and ministers continued to debate the value of the Swiss, but they remained an essential ingredient of Spain's fighting machine.[19]

The distinction between Spanish and non-Spanish troops should not be exaggerated: between 1717 and 1720 some of the supposed Spanish regiments in Sardinia and Sicily were, necessarily, recruited locally, either from the population of those islands or in adjacent mainland Italy. By the same token non-Spanish units include Spaniards. In 1717 Philip allowed his Irish, Italian, and Walloon regiments to recruit in Spain, in view of the difficulties they faced in recruiting in their home territories, and he did so again during the War of the Austrian Succession. In 1745 all 4 battalions of the Milan and Brabant (Walloon) infantry regiments were recruiting in Spain and Italy. As for the Irish regiments, which, according to privileges granted to the Irish community by earlier Spanish monarchs, were treated as native Spaniards, they recruited more widely in Britain. In 1733, for example, Colonel Raimundo Burk was allowed to complete his Limerick regiment by recruiting English and Scots as well as Irish. Those Irish units also included many Spaniards by 1748.[20] War had thus facilitated, even accelerated, the hispanisation of some of the foreign units in Spanish service.

Whatever their nationality and arguably more important in giving the army of Philip V, the Catholic King, an identity was that it was over-whelmingly Christian and, above all, Roman Catholic. The association of Philip's cause with Roman Catholicism had played an important role in his winning the succession struggle and remained influential after 1713. In October 1746 deserters from the Irish Ultonia regiment were condemned to the galleys, but that sentence was commuted to perpetual military service following their conversion to Roman Catholicism.[21]

Recruitment of Spanish Troops

Despite Philip V's reliance on foreign troops, his army was largely Spanish, that is, recruited from among his subjects in Spain. This is hardly surprising. Spaniards had long been prized for their endurance, their fighting qualities, and their supposed loyalty as well as for the fact that they were cheaper and less likely to desert than foreign troops. In addition, the loss of the non-Spanish European territories restricted recruiting opportunities in those areas after 1713. In any case, Spanish efforts to recruit abroad were not always welcome: in 1736 the activities of Spanish recruiters in Rome prompted riots there and the expulsion of all Spanish residents.[22] Practical necessity, then, ensured that Spain itself would see much recruiting activity, especially in 1717–20, 1732, and 1735 and again between 1741 and 1748.

Before 1700 recruitment in Spain had been overseen by the Council of War, guided by the Comisario General. However, the War of the Spanish Succession and its aftermath saw important changes in the role of the council, whose executive role largely passed to the newly established office of Secretary of State for War (below), while in 1704 the office of Comisario General had been replaced by that of Director General of Infantry. In the localities, however, recruitment was still largely left to the bodies and officials who had been responsible for it before 1700, namely, the *alcaldes*, or magistrates, of the numerous settlements inhabited by a largely scattered population, *corregidores*, and, where they existed, the officials of the Chancillerías and Audiencias, which in Spain as in the Americas were as much administrative as judicial bodies. Briefly, between 1718 and 1721, and, not coincidentally, at the height of Philip V's first bid for Italian dominion, there was an abortive experiment with intendants, or *intendentes*, of the army *and* provinces; but between 1721 and the full-scale reintroduction of a network of provincial intendants in 1749, the only intendants were those of the army, in the three realms of the Crown of Aragon, Majorca, and the other frontier provinces, Andalusia, Castile, Estremadura, and Galicia, plus the intendants who accompanied each overseas expeditionary force (see below). Local recruitment in Spain during the Wars of the Polish and Austrian Successions was thus largely the responsibility and achievement of an older, effective administrative setup.[23]

Most historians of the Spanish military in the eighteenth century have focused largely on involuntary recruitment and the Bourbon state's imposition of an obligation to serve. There is good reason for this (see below), but it ignores the preference of monarch and ministers for, and the continued importance of, voluntary enlistment, as many men responded willingly to the recruiting captain or sergeant. Evidence of this is provided by both royal legislation and the discharge certificates given to those leaving the army. In June 1745 one Antonio de Plata, a soldier in the Lisbon infantry regiment, was discharged. When he was press-ganged almost three years later in 1748, his certificate was produced by his wife in support of her petition for his release; according to that document, Antonio had enlisted voluntarily in 1736. Volunteers still accounted for the largest number of recruits in the Spanish army towards the close of the War of the Austrian Succession, when recruiting captains were still expected to find men of this type.[24]

Explaining why men in a society which does not appear to have held the soldier in high regard enlisted is not easy, not least because little evidence survives as to why they did so. However, many of the reasons which have been identified for earlier periods no doubt continued to apply in the early eighteenth century: camaraderie, a desire to escape family, village, or town and embarrassing entanglements there, and, not least for those hoping to escape poverty, enlistment money and army pay: in 1731 recruits in Murcia were offered eight and even sixteen pesos on joining up. Enlistment money, pay at a time when wages were falling in real terms, and the guarantee of food in hard times, as in the thirties and early forties, when harvests were poor and mortality rates high, might also attract volunteers. Some others may have been attracted by the *fuero militar,* the distinctive military jurisdiction or privilege, the proliferation of which triggered occasional confrontations between the civil and military authorities. Such spats necessitated the imposition of limitations by the crown, not least when the fuero was abused, as it had been under the Habsburgs, to cover fraud. Whatever drew them, volunteers could always be found.[25]

A variant on the system of voluntary recruiting just described, in which all the costs of the levy were borne by the king, was the practice whereby the monarch accepted an offer to recruit a company or even a whole regiment from an individual. The recruiter would then bear those costs before the men entered the royal service in return for various benefits, including the right to appoint officers, otherwise a royal prerogative. This privatisation or devolution of recruitment by means of an *asiento* agreed with a contractor was not entirely new, having been practiced in the Habsburg era. In some respects it simply represented a variant on the so-called military entrepreneurship of an earlier age. It also manifested a venality which was widespread in Philip V's Spain. For the applicant, or *asentista,* it often meant buying promotion within the army or a fixed post or both and also offered the prospect of social advancement. Typically, in 1719 D. Felipe Serrano y Contreras, a "reformed" lieutenant colonel of cavalry, offered to raise at his own cost a company of 100 infantry. To fund this operation he sought permission to burden his entail with loans, to the value of 4,000 *ducados.* Philip V referred the request to the Council of Castile and its adjunct, the Cámara de Castilla, which monitored and protected entails. The Cámara expressed concern, wanting to consult the heir to the entail, whose interests would be affected by the grant. Philip, however, while acknowledging these misgivings, insisted that the petition be granted, immediately, given his urgent need of troops, implying that the demands of war underpinned the assertion, if only briefly and episodically, of greater royal authority, absolutism, at the expense of traditional practices and constraints.[26]

The speed and economy involved in this method of raising men had great attraction for the king and some of his ministers, but such offers were not simply rubber-stamped by them. Some bargaining was always necessary, as when, in 1719, the Sicilian duke of San Blas offered 300 cavalry. Sometimes, too, the agreement required subsequent adjustment.

In 1748 D. Jayme Torrijos was granted the captaincy of a company in the Lisbon infantry regiment in return for raising 70 men, to be delivered to Badajoz in Estremadura. Upon his arrival in Valencia to recruit the men, however, the captain general of that realm, the duque de Caylus, thought the original destination inappropriate. The distance the recruits must travel was too great, with potential loss through desertion and sickness, and the duke urged instead that Torrijos give his recruits to a captain in the Murcia regiment who already had the king's commission to recruit in Valencia. Last, units raised privately had to be approved by royal officials before being accepted into the king's service and pay.[27]

Recruiting in this way was both cheap and speedy and highly attractive at the start of a conflict; it may have been the largest single source of new regiments under Philip V. Between 1718 and 1720, 40 battalions of infantry of 13 companies each, 6 cavalry squadrons of 4 companies, and 40 squadrons of dragoons of 3 companies—a total of 664 companies—were raised by this means. During the War of the Polish Succession, of 20 new regiments levied in 1734–35, just 3 were raised at royal expense; as for the War of the Austrian Succession, privatisation of this sort raised 10 new battalions in 1742.[28]

But voluntary recruiting, despite efforts to make the army more attractive by, for example, reducing the length of service (as in 1741, to three years), did not always yield sufficient men. In these circumstances, compulsion of some sort was the answer. Impressment took various forms. It had long been usual to condemn convicted criminals and other malefactors to the African garrisons, which men were reluctant to volunteer for, and the practice continued. In 1701 penalties imposing presidio service laid down in 1684 for the defrauding of the royal tobacco monopoly were confirmed, in 1724 five men condemned after anti-seigneurial disturbances in Galicia were sentenced to service in an African presidio, and in July 1741 the captain general of Catalonia despatched thirty-four convicts to Oran, condemned to presidio service by the criminal court of the royal Audiencia and by the *auditor general* of the Army of Catalonia. Other convicted offenders might themselves elect such service as an alternative to prison or have it chosen for them by local communities eager to be free of the threat they posed and the cost of their incarceration. In 1748, following the arrest of one Joseph Madrid for defrauding the king's salt revenues, his community requested that he and two accomplices serve with the army for four campaigns. The courts supplied a steady trickle of men for the African garrisons and for other, regular units throughout Philip V's reign. Other criminals might seek a pardon in return for military service.[29]

Another tried-and-tested means of forcible recruitment, one which could claim to be trying to solve the problem of delinquency at a more general level, was the impressment of the rootless poor, as had happened before 1700 and during the War of the Spanish Succession. Roundups of this sort were ordered in July 1717, July 1718, 1732, December 1733, December 1744, and in April and June 1745. Philip's periodic drives against vagabonds coincided with and were driven by his need for troops for operations in Africa and Italy.[30]

Rounding up of this sort was often designated a levy, or *leva*, to distinguish it from another method of impressment, the so-called *quinta*. Originally signifying, as its name suggests, the imposition on communities of an obligation to provide one-fifth of their eligible menfolk, the quinta, another tried-and-tested method, inevitably attracted a monarch needing men for his Mediterranean adventures. A quinta was an integral part of the preparations for the Oran expedition in 1732, and, following its departure, another was expected as part of a larger recruitment drive which would both supply more men for Oran and replace 25,000 men recently despatched to Majorca, Italy, and the other African garrisons. In fact, a quinta of 7,153 men was ordered in December 1732, justified as a last resort on the grounds of the king's failure to find sufficient volunteers. It is no coincidence that the major eighteenth-century Spanish work on this subject, Francisco de Oya y Ozores's *Tratado de levas, quintas y reclutas de gente de Guerra*, was published a couple of years later, in 1734, at the height of the War of the Polish Succession. These two means of the forcible recruiting of men remained the poles around which discussion and practice revolved. In 1741 the president of the Council of Castile, which in some respects spoke for the Castilian towns (see chapter 4), vetoed a quinta proposed by the secretary for war, but a forcible levy to raise 7,919 men was ordered in December 1741, as Philip V prepared to intervene in Italy. As the Austrian succession struggle progressed, the need for men meant further drives of this sort. In December 1746 Ferdinand VI ordered a combination of quinta and levy to secure 25,000 men for 1747, the largest such mobilisation throughout this period, more than three times the number of men ordered to be levied in 1741–42.[31]

How did it work? The king and his ministers having decided upon the number of men required, the total was broken down into provincial quotas which bore some relationship to demographic capacity. The largest quota in the quinta levy ordered in December 1732, for example, was that assigned the populous Galicia, 878 men, or just over 10 percent of the total number the levy was intended to yield. In Old Castile, by contrast, the province of Burgos, with a much smaller population, was expected to give 367 men, or just under 5 percent of the total, and the city of Burgos, the assembly point for the quotas of that province and for those of Toro, Palencia, Soria, Avila, Segovia, Salamanca, and Valladolid, just 19 men. Quotas remained fairly constant. In December 1741, following Philip V's decision to impose another quinta, of 7,919 men, the province of Burgos was asked for 400 men and the city itself just 17, a proportionate increase on the number requested towards the slightly smaller overall levy of 1732. Individual quotas were communicated to the provincial officials responsible for their implementation. In December 1746, for example, the intendant of Galicia was informed of that realm's share (1,181) of the 25,000 men Ferdinand VI hoped to find, and he in turn assigned quotas to the realm's seven principal cities. The intendant would also contact the local magistrates. The magistrates oversaw the lottery, or *sorteo* (below), which was increasingly the method used to identify those who should fulfil the community's quota, and arranged for the men selected to be sent to the assembly point. Captains would then escort the men to the ports where they embarked for their destination.[32]

It was rarely so simple in practice. Quinta levies were unpopular with those called up, and observers were often pessimistic about their likely yield. In 1726 the introduction of quintas provoked riots in Catalonia. Their unpopularity was one reason they were not the first resort of the king and his ministers, who often justified other measures to raise men on the grounds of their reluctance to impose a quinta. Those who could exploited any relevant privileges to avoid being taken. In December 1732 the town of Solera in Cuenca, which was expected to find 76 men, successfully petitioned for exemption from both quintas and levas, pleading its obligation to maintain the royal sheepwalk along which the flocks of the Mesta moved. The following year one of the directors of the tobacco revenues, D. Jacobo Flon, complained that the corregidor of León had included in the sorteo employees of the tobacco monopoly, despite a royal order exempting them. The king ordered the release of any of these men who had been levied and who had been employed in the monopoly fifteen days before the publication of the quintas. Reflecting the unpopularity of levies of all types, new grants of privilege in these decades frequently included exemptions from them.[33]

Not all claims of exemption succeeded. In December 1741 the corregidor of Burgos demanded 3 men of the town of Torrecilla of a total of 82 men assigned the district, or *partido*, of Logroño. In response, the magistrates of Torrecilla pleaded a royal exemption, granted for ten years, from January 1735, but to no avail. Those unable to plead a privilege sometimes simply fled. Some of those unlucky enough to win this lottery purchased substitutes, resulting in accusations of collusion by officials. In 1735, following an extensive investigation, charges were prepared against the prince of Campoflorido, the captain general of the realm of Aragon, the intendant, and others responsible for the execution of the quintas of 1733–34 there. The charges included allowing those who had been selected in the lottery to buy themselves out. Others who were forcibly levied might be rescued by more violent means: in 1733 a diplomatic incident was triggered when the Dutch ambassador's servants forcibly freed men who had been impressed in Seville.[34]

Not all resisted, and many fugitives were recovered or replaced, to an extent that although the yield of the forced levies was sometimes poor they did contribute large numbers of men to the various expeditions to Africa and Italy. In January 1742, for example, the corregidor of Burgos delivered up 180 *quintados* of that province, almost half of its quota of 400 men, who then left for Barcelona and Italy. Two weeks later D. Joseph López Colmenero, the captain of the Burgos infantry regiment, led another 142 quintados to Barcelona, so that just 78 men remained to be found to meet the quota. A week later, the recruiting captain D. Joseph Alberto Bonnet reported the arrival from Soria of 71 men, although he had to dismiss seven of them as ineligible or incapable. From the announcement of the quinta in December 1741 it had taken less than two months for Burgos to raise 96 percent of its quota. Burgos was by no means exceptional, as other cities and provinces too fulfilled their quotas, even if belatedly. Quotas might even be exceeded: in January 1748 Juan Francisco de Urdainz despatched 109 men from Salamanca, more than the 100 demanded from that city and its district. Not surprisingly, local magistrates involved in quintas and levies cited their services and their success when petitioning for royal favours.[35]

Provincial Militias

One means of mobilising men without making undue demands on Philip V's subjects or disrupting the economy was the overhaul and reestablishment of the militia in 1734. This was the most significant military innovation of Philip's reign after the Spanish succession struggle. It has been posited recently that, given their disappointing performance, militias have received disproportionate attention from historians. Yet they cannot be simply dismissed, not least because contemporary governments were so inclined to resort to them and because of the implications for those of their subjects who were affected. Philip inherited a militia from the Habsburgs, and in 1703–4 he sought to use it to yield 100 regiments (50,000 men) following the outbreak of the succession struggle, but the confused circumstances of that conflict helped frustrate the attempt. Following the succession struggle the militia was largely neglected, although local units were occasionally deployed to the African presidios. It was the outbreak of the War of the Polish Succession in 1733 and the need thereafter to recruit the expeditionary force in Italy from among the regular troops in Spain which prompted the landmark measure of 1734.[36]

The reform of Spain's militia was in part influenced by that in neighbouring France, although it was not the only available model. In January 1734 Philip decreed the creation of 33 new provincial militia regiments. Each regiment would comprise 700 men, creating a reserve of 23,000 men which was required to assemble for training for three days each quarter. This was not a universal obligation: the Aragonese realms were excluded, at Philip's insistence, as were the Basque territories and Navarre. More surprisingly perhaps, most of Castile was also exempt, supplying only

8 regiments. This signalled the intention that the militia would defend the coasts and frontiers, leaving the interior, Castile, to supply recruits for the regular units which would serve abroad. Most affected were Andalusia, which was expected to raise 14, or almost half, of the new regiments, and Galicia, which was to provide 6. In the provinces or realms (*reinos*) which were to raise militia regiments, each district was assigned a quota of men. At the same time, a new administrative superstructure comparable to that overseeing the regular troops was established, headed by the inspector general of militia.[37]

Some observers thought the scheme too ambitious. This was too pessimistic, not least because there were volunteers, some perhaps attracted by the privileges, the fuero militar, attached to militia service. But certainly there was some reluctance to serve, which expressed itself, as ever, in the exploitation of loopholes to secure exemptions. In Galicia, for example and no doubt elsewhere the privileges attached to the *matrícula de mar* (see chapter 2) were often asserted. The real testing time, however, was the War of the Austrian Succession, when, besides being used for home defence to replace regulars in garrisons in Spain itself, entire militia regiments were despatched abroad to take part in offensive operations in Italy. In early 1743 the grenadier companies of all militia regiments were sent to reinforce the Infante's army, followed soon after by 7 whole militia regiments: Burgos, Murcia, Palencia, Logroño, Sigüenza, Toro, and Soria.[38] At the end of that year, 200 men were taken from each of the 26 militia regiments remaining in Spain to form 4 new regiments, which also headed for Italy. In October 1744 the army of the Infante included 2,624 men in the 7 militia regiments just mentioned. A month later, looking ahead to the needs of the Infante's army for 1745, which he put at 8,000 recruits, the inspector general of militias proposed that besides completing the militia regiments already in Italy, the remaining 5–6,000 men be found by creating 17 new militia regiments in Spain. That move would bring the total to 50 and include territories hitherto excluded, such as Aragon and Valencia, and draw the required recruits from the new units. This ambitious proposal was not implemented, perhaps a sign of the extent to which the deployment of the militias abroad was increasingly contentious (below), but about 18,000 militiamen served in Italy in the Austrian succession conflict.

These were striking developments, reviving older military obligations, imposing new ones, eroding or modifying existing privileges, introducing a new privilege in the form of exemption from the new service obligations, and elaborating an equally new organisation and jurisdiction. The inspector general and subinspector oversaw the whole, enforcing a growing corpus of relevant orders and the quotas demanded of local communities. But, typifying the way in which agencies of the ancien régime were not merely instruments of sovereign authority, the inspector and subinspector defended the interests of militias and of militiamen. While some militiamen were willing to serve in Italy, however, the growing use of the militia and its deployment abroad, in breach of traditional understanding of the role of the militia, created increasing disquiet. Efforts by whole communities and individuals to evade militia service are one indicator of this, desertion was another. In the spring of 1743 one militia regiment lost more than 200 men en route to Barcelona, where there was a mutiny, the men claiming that the conditions of militia service meant they should not serve outside Spain. Philip sought to ease the burden in October 1743 by distinguishing three classes of liable adult male: (1) bachelors, (2) married men and widowers without children, (3) married men and widowers with children, who would be called on in that order. The response, fathers marrying their sons off to escape militia service, led the king in November 1744 to substitute four classes: (1) single men, (2) men married before the age of eighteen; (3) married men and widowers without children and unemployed young men; and (4) married men and widowers with children and employed young men. The demographic patterns revealed in the postwar *catastro,* or survey, of 1753 may have been shaped by these developments.[39]

Reluctance to serve underpinned a dynamic tension in the War of the Austrian Succession, the king's efforts to close loopholes exploited by his male subjects to avoid militia service contributing to the further development of the militia as both military and social institution—and as obligation on those subjects. Equally revealing in this regard is the preamble to the second addition to the militia regulations of April 1745, in which Philip V referred to criticisms of this type and sought to rebut them, declaring that when *urgencias* obliged the king to deploy militiamen abroad this was not outside the original remit of the militia. The king declared

further that militia service differed from levas and quintas and from service in the pre-1734 militia and that all privileged exemptions from older
military obligations were invalid in respect of the new militia. In effect,
Philip was suppressing all earlier grants of exemption from militia service, cutting a swathe through existing privilege. This was a remarkable
assertion of royal authority.[40]

Philip V's arguments may well not have convinced his subjects or si-
lenced critics. In Galicia, where earlier levies had already provoked resistance of all sorts, including flight into neighbouring Portugal, the king's
order in the summer of 1745 that 1,200 militiamen from the realm—
which had supplied men in 1743 and 1744—should join a squadron preparing for Havana caused some consternation. Towards the end of the
next year, potential recruits in Galicia were still absconding. It was
reported that the authorities there were taking harsh measures against
their families by way of reprisal in an attempt to raise that realm's militia
quota for 1747; the authorities were also said to be arresting those who
had talked or written on this subject in a reflecting, that is, a critical,
manner and to have given orders at the post offices to open letters in order to determine who should be arrested. Here, then, was another sign of
growing unease within Spain triggered by the demands of war in Italy
(see chapter 5), prompting what might be called an absolutist response on
Philip's part. His subjects' obvious disquiet would contribute to Ferdinand
VI's wish to bring the war to a close. Nevertheless, new obligations had
been imposed, with important implications.[41]

Recasting the Officer Corps

Military success depended upon the recruitment not only of large numbers of men but also of officers to lead them. Philip's reign witnessed an
increase in the number of junior and senior officers, markedly so during
his overseas adventures, and in addition a reordering of the officer corps,
as the old Habsburg hierarchy was remodelled along French lines. Philip
also asserted his right, as king, to appoint and promote officers, thus ensuring his was a royal army, and, especially where this affected the militia,
encroaching on the patronage of local elites. Philip used that power to
attract into his army large numbers of nobles, in that way sealing a new

alliance between crown and nobility. Historians emphasise the extent to which the first Bourbon "tamed" a Spanish nobility, and more precisely an aristocracy of titled nobles and grandees, which had become over-mighty under Charles II and whose loyalty was suspect during the succession conflict.[42] There is some truth in this, but it is not close to the whole story. In fact, Philip successfully nurtured loyalty among the nobility during and after the War of the Spanish Succession (see chapter 4), and the army was one of the instruments whereby he achieved this.

Another was his forming of a personal relationship between himself and those nobles serving in the expanded military establishment at court. In 1704 Philip established four companies of guards, two of Spaniards and one each of Italians and Walloons, although the latter was briefly suppressed between 1716 and 1720. Thereafter, the bodyguard comprised three companies (Italian, Spanish, Walloon) of 300 men each and 2 infantry regiments (Spanish, Walloon) of 4,800 men each, plus a company of halberdiers. These units, whose number grew as additional corps were added to the royal household, including, in 1735, a Company of Grenadiers which had taken part in the Oran expedition and the conquest of Naples and Sicily, enjoyed extensive privileges. Among these were accelerated promotion prospects, which set them apart from the rest of the king's forces, emphasising that Philip's army, like so many in the ancien régimes of Europe, was less a monolith than a mosaic. The royal bodyguard was also dominated by the aristocratic elite. The Walloon and Italian Guards were also a means of retaining a connection with the territories lost during the Spanish succession conflict and boosted the presence of non-Spaniards in the highest echelons of the army (below).[43]

Philip also encouraged young nobles to serve in his army by means of a privileged cadet officer entry and promotion scheme (1704), modelled on that of France. Cadets were expected to prove their nobility and were not expected to do the tasks of the common soldiers. For those whose noble status was less clear-cut, military office, even if purchased, might confirm that standing following the king's order in 1722 equating the rank of captain with that status (above).[44]

The nobles who did serve in Philip V's army could look forward to various rewards, including membership—and with it with the distinctive cape, or *hábito*—and, for some, an estate, or *encomienda*, of the Military

Orders, Alcantara, Calatrava, Montesa, and Santiago. It is possible that more of these dignities were bestowed on soldiers in this period, suggesting that Philip's reign may have seen a remilitarisation of the Military Orders; many were certainly given to those who distinguished themselves in action in Africa and in Italy. D. Sebastian Eslava was just one of many who served on the Sicilian expedition and were rewarded with an encomienda. Philip also encouraged nobles to serve as officers in the refurbished militia from 1734: as an incentive, militia officers too could aspire to hábitos after ten years' service. Military service could lead to promotion within the nobility.[45]

Philip's African and Italian operations and the accompanying expansion of the army enabled him as well to reward those loyal to him in Catalonia during the succession struggle and to stimulate loyalty among the Catalan nobility thereafter. Thus two Catalan dragoon regiments raised in the War of the Spanish Succession survived the reform of 1715, one becoming the Sagunto dragoon regiment in 1718, when new units were raised in Catalonia, and supplying men to the new company of mounted grenadier guards formed in 1731 (above) in part to benefit faithful Catalan nobles. In 1734–35 the Aragonese marchese di Arigno (or his son and heir) and the Valencian marqués de Sumacarcel were each allowed to raise a new dragoon regiment for the king at their own expense. Individual Catalans who pursued successful military careers included Antonio de Alós y de Riús, first marqués (1736) de Alós; the scion of a family loyal to Philip in the War of the Spanish Succession, he served on many of the Italian expeditions, among them the invasion of Sicily in 1718, the conquest of Naples and Sicily in 1734–35, and with the Infante from 1742, subsequently recording his experiences in invaluable *mémoires* written for his sons.[46]

The nobility responded positively to Philip V's encouragement, judging by their presence throughout the officer corps. In 1718 all colonels of regiments were nobles, most of them titled, while in 1733 the titled nobility represented a higher proportion of the high command than two decades earlier (above). At the same time, the officer corps was increasingly drawn from within Spain. This and the readiness of various nobles to raise troops at their own expense for the king imply that his noble subjects continued to see themselves as, in part at least, a military estate. But they hint as well that service in the king's army, in Bourbon Spain as in Bourbon France, was as much an instrument of noble family strategy—a means to provide a niche for younger brothers and sons—as of royal authority. For some individuals military service came at a high cost. The duque de Arcos and his eldest son both died in action in Italy in the War of the Austrian Succession.[47]

Yet this positive discrimination, privileging noble entry into the officer corps, carried risks and might compromise the effectiveness of Philip V's army. The sale of military office ensured that military commands, including that of colonel, were often secured by men with little or no military experience. The favoring of distinguished birth could have the same result. So, too, could appointments which were effectively royal favours, or *mercedes*, in a system of so-called distributive justice in which these rewarded and cemented loyalty (see chapter 4) and in which petitioners cited the services of relations and ancestors. These defects were apparently compounded by another: an excess of senior officers. The Junta de Medios complained about this in 1737; so did José Campillo at the start of the War of the Austrian Succession in his wide-ranging critique of Spain's ills, *Lo que hay de más y de menos en España* (What Spain has, more or less) (1742): not only were there too many senior officers but also too many of them had not been appointed on good military grounds. Similar criticisms were made by the marqués de la Mina following the disastrous campaign of 1746.[48]

Certainly some commanders were not able or effective, with sometimes serious consequences, as was evident in the War of the Austrian Succession. In 1746, that annus horribilis for Spanish arms, neglect on the part of General Francesco Pignatelli y Aymerich was said to have endangered the retreat of the Bourbon army after the defeat at Piacenza. More broadly, in an army which was a collection of units each aware, and jealous, of its distinctive status, individuals and entire units were inclined to compete for rank and precedence. Sometimes commanders were so jealous of their own rank and perceived slights that it affected their relations with other commanders: in 1734 Ignacio Francisco Glimes de Brabant, conde de Glimes, apparently refused to serve under Montemar for this reason. At the lower levels there was evidently fraudulent practice by officers seeking to profit from the posts they or their families had often invested in. Absenteeism was cause for concern as well.[49]

But the picture is not so dark. There were poor officers in Philip V's, as in all armies, but they were not simply tolerated. Officers committing fraud were pursued, while those thought culpable were subject to investigation. Those who abused the system of licensed absence were also brought to heel. Efforts were made to improve training where appropriate. In 1720, after it had long been urged by Philip V's chief engineer Jorge Próspero de Verboom, a Real Academia Militar de Matemáticas was established at Barcelona for the education of military engineers. There were efforts to make experience and merit the path to promotion and to limit any negative consequences of the play of influence. In 1734, for example, the director general of infantry intervened on three occasions in promotions in the Castilla infantry regiment in favour of the candidates with greatest seniority and at the expense of those being preferred for their family connections. Equally, although some senior officers started their military careers with the purchase of a command, not all did so, and any harmful effects could be offset by appointing more experienced officers to serve with a colonel who had bought his commission, as when the Itálica dragoon regiment was raised in 1734. As for the influence of favouritism and patronage, while these could have negative consequences, it was also important, if an operation was to succeed, for commanders to enjoy the confidence of ministers, as the chevalier Vieuville, one of the senior officers on the expedition to Italy in 1733 had that of Patiño.[50]

Such reliance might create other problems. Spanish commanders invariably received precise and pressing orders, generally to take the offensive and to secure specific objectives, from the court and were likely to be recalled if they did not comply, as were both Montemar in September 1742 and Glimes in December 1742: the former was replaced by Gages, and the latter, following his retreat from the duchy of Savoy, by Mina, who promptly invaded the duchy again. But this issue apart, favour, venality, and high birth were by no means incompatible with ability and merit. Indeed, many of Philip V's commanders were intelligent, capable men who did good service. Garcia Ramirez de Arellano, marqués (1727) de Arellano, for instance, was an avid reader of books about war and a successful, practical soldier.[51]

The example of Arellano suggests that Philip V's reign witnessed some progress towards a more clearly defined career structure and greater professionalism within the officer corps. The change wrought by the new dynasty, however, should not be exaggerated. To do so may understate the commitment and professionalism of that same cadre before 1700. Indeed, many of those who led Philip V's army, including the conde de Montemar and the marqueses de Bedmar, de Lede, and de Valdecanas, the director general of infantry in 1712, had all begun their military careers in Africa, Flanders, and Italy under Charles II.[52] Here, too, was continuity across the change of dynasty, and we should not underestimate the importance of the earlier service in preparing the men who led Spain's military resurgence after 1713.

For most of these men a successful career after 1713 included participation in one or more of Philip V's Mediterranean adventures. Lede demonstrated his abilities in Sardinia and Sicily and at Ceuta between 1717 and 1720, while Montemar was the hero of the successful Spanish intervention in the War of the Polish Succession. The marqués de la Mina commanded the dragoons on the Sardinia expedition in 1717 and was promoted brigadier in 1720. After further promotions, including as director general of dragoons in 1741 and captain general in 1743, he replaced Glimes as effective head of the Infante's force in Italy in 1746 following the accession of Ferdinand VI. Frequent promotions were made in the wake of major operations and rewarded real ability, zeal, courage, and success. In 1743, for his part at Campo Santo, the Walloon Juan Buenaventura Gages Dumont was promoted captain general; other promotions included those of four lieutenants general, sixteen field marshals, and seventeen brigadiers. Many more promotions followed in 1744 and again in 1745, when Gages's crossing of the Apennines contributed enormously to the Bourbon success in Italy that year, for which he was promoted conde de Gages.[53]

Militarisation?

These developments raise the question, referred to earlier, about the extent to which Philip V's ambitions and reforms involved the militarisation of his state and his subjects. This is a complex question, one by no means confined to Philip's Spain, and one which should not be confused with later understanding of militarism. The issue undoubtedly provoked contemporary debate. Military men were increasingly appointed to what had been civilian posts, viceroys were superseded by captains general, and in some areas civilian authorities were to some extent simply bypassed. These developments were highly evident in the former foral territories of the Crown of Aragon, but they were not limited to them. In addition, troops were used to quell dissent on occasion. As for society at large, the new militia meant that more of Philip's male subjects were under military jurisdiction, while his order of 1722 that the rank of captain was equivalent to noble status had implications in the meshing of civil and military society.[54]

However, the militarisation of government was limited, even within Aragon. More important, the term *militarisation* suggests a society in which attitudes, values, and practices associated with the army and army service itself are not only accepted but also define that society and self-define individuals within it. Yet just as in other states, for example, Prussia, where historians are questioning a supposed militarisation identified by earlier historians, so in Philip V's Spain it is difficult to see militarisation of the population at large. Philip was in many respects a warrior king for whom war offered an opportunity to overcome a natural melancholia; but he did not wear uniform at court. He frequently resorted to war after 1713, but it was often as a last resort, following the failure of diplomacy. Nor was the Secretariat of War (see chapter 4) a self-contained office run by and for soldiers or ex-soldiers. As for society at large, certainly there was a greater military presence in the peninsula after 1713 than before 1700, but in some respects developments after 1713 represented a *demilitarisation* of a society mobilised in a remarkable way for war during the succession conflict. While more noble and nonnoble males were increasingly drawn or coerced into the military, the majority still had no experience of the army, and the evidence of desertion rates (above) implies that they were far from willing participants when they did join up. As for those who did serve, growing professionalism did not mean that all of them were defined only by or as the military; something true of noble and nonnoble alike. The fact that barracks began to be built only rather late in the reign ensured that soldiers and civilians did not become separate estates, isolated from and unsympathetic towards each other (although closer contact did not inevitably make for good relations). Philip V's Spain was emphatically not what has been called a garrison state. Nor would it be correct to think of it as militarised or militarist.[55]

Supply: The "Contractor State"

Military success depended as much on effective supply as on the performance of the troops in the field and might affect the latter, as all recognised. Major operations abroad like those in Africa and Italy represented an enormous challenge in this respect. The hinterland of the African garrisons was dominated by hostile forces, and although the surrounding population did sometimes supply them and the troops mounted raids to seize livestock, it was difficult for those garrisons to live off that backcountry: they had long depended upon supply from Spain and continued to do so. As for Italy, whereas before 1700 there was a local administrative structure in Spanish Italy which could provide for Spain's forces there, this was not the case before the reconquest of Naples and Sicily in 1734–35. Philip V's high command was deeply concerned about logistical issues when considering any operation, while the need to protect vital supply lines could determine the way the troops were deployed abroad. In 1741 it was decided to send the expeditionary force heading for north Italy to the Tuscan presidios because there they could be supplied from Naples; later, in the winter of 1744–45, the Spanish forces in north Italy were assigned quarters which should ensure their communications with those same presidios. Defeat in the summer of 1746 created severe logistical problems for Philip's troops in Italy.[56]

The supply needs of even the smallest expedition were substantial, those of a large one enormous. They included uniforms, arms and equipment, food, transport, accommodation, and various services. At least 6,000 pairs of shoes were ordered in preparation for the Oran expedition in 1732. As for weapons—muskets, bayonets, bullets, powder, grenades, and so on—in 1720 almost 20,000 *fusiles* with bayonets were thought necessary for the 16,000-strong Ceuta relief force. Twelve years later the Oran expedition departed with 20,000 grenades and 12,427 *quintales,* or hundredweights, of powder plus a great quantity of muskets and bayonets. The infantry consistently outnumbered the cavalry in Philip V's army (above), but Spain's military operations in these decades required a great number of horses and equipment. Besides small arms, every major expedition needed an artillery train of field and siege guns and draught animals to pull it. The Sardinian expeditionary force of 1717 embarked

32 cannon and 14 mortars besides 737 quintals of powder and 33,000 cannon balls. Once on campaign, men and animals naturally had to be fed. In 1732 it was calculated that the Oran expeditionary force needed 26,212 daily rations of bread for the men and the horses 5,426 rations of barley. Some thought had to be given to the accommodation of the troops, not least because this was one way of preventing illness. On campaign this meant tents to give shelter against the cold and wet and, in Africa, the heat. For those who did fall ill or were wounded medical services were necessary. Such provisioning all added up to an immense challenge for administrators.[57]

Overseeing the supply of this crucial war materiel was a radically reformed central military administration. The extent to which the agents of the monarch or state, anywhere in Europe, were in effective control of supply is increasingly questioned, but they cannot be ignored. Directing all, after 1717, was the new Secretariat of State for War, the Habsburg Council of War being effectively sidelined and restricted to a judicial function (see chapter 4). The secretary was flanked by a new cadre of senior officials charged with monitoring the effectiveness of the various arms: the inspectors and directors of infantry, cavalry, militia, and artillery. Answerable to the secretary of state and more directly responsible for coordinating logistics and supply was a network of army intendants and their subordinate commissaries. In some parts these were increasingly ousting local bodies which before 1700 had at the least been consulted about and had their consent sought for local levies. Thus, whereas in the seventeenth century the king had asked the Junta of the Reino of Galicia for money and men when he needed them, after the arrival of the intendant in 1712 that body was never summoned for this purpose and could only make representations on royal orders.[58]

For a very few individuals, notably Patiño, Campillo, and Ensenada, these posts helped them to advance to the highest offices in the state. Others did not rise so high but still carved out a niche for themselves in military administration. Francisco Salvador Pineda (1670–1743), for example, was appointed intendant of occupied Sardinia in 1718 but was named intendant of Sicily (1718–20) before he could occupy that post, subsequently served as intendant on the Ceuta expedition in 1720, and ended his career as intendant of the army in Galicia. Indicative of the extensive responsibilities of the intendant were the lengthy instructions prepared before the Oran expedition in 1732 for Jose Contamine (c. 1675–1763), who had hitherto served as *comisario ordenador* in Catalonia and would later occupy the intendancy there.[59] Contamine, assisted by a phalanx of other administrators, was to oversee all aspects of the financing and supply of the expedition and was expected to collaborate closely with the military chief, Montemar.[60]

During the succession conflict Philip's forces had depended greatly on munitions supplied from France, but the struggle had also stimulated Spain's own arms industry in Navarra, Vizcaya, and Cantabria. Alberoni and others continued to nurture this activity after 1713. In 1720 it was calculated that nearly 4,000 of the almost 20,000 fusiles with bayonets required for an African expedition (above) could be obtained from the arms manufactory at Plasencia, but this was only 25 percent of the total required. For his part, the mercantilist author Gerónimo de Uztáriz, writing in the early 1720s, thought Spain's arms industry in Cantabria and Catalonia produced 18,000 to 20,000 firearms annually, although in wartime the demand might be twice that.[61]

Heavy guns like cannon, mortars, and so on could be produced in the arsenals of Barcelona and Seville, where, in 1732, 24 big artillery pieces were assayed prior to the Oran expedition. The pressure of demand and cost cutting may have affected quality, but artillery was being produced in such quantity that Spain was better able than during the war of succession and even before 1700 to meet its own needs. Nonetheless, as late as the eve of the war of 1739 it was claimed there was a serious shortfall in production that left Spain's military short. The explanation appears to be the result of two closely related factors: the reliance on contractors and the failure to pay them (see chapter 3). Whatever the explanation, it did not augur well for the challenges of renewed war on a large scale in the 1740s. Philip sought to ease the demand in 1743, broadly repeating the regulation issued in the summer of 1718 (above) reducing the number of types, or calibre, of cannon to just five, as in France, to good effect. Some of the products of this native arms industry were highly regarded abroad.[62] The abandonment and loss of war matériel in the disastrous campaign of 1746 exacerbated Spain's problems in this sphere.

As for grain, great quantities were shipped from Spain with and for its expeditionary forces throughout this period. In 1717 the Sardinian expedition embarked 1,680 sacks of flour (8,400 *arrobas*, 4 arrobas being equivalent to a hundredweight) and 2,300 *fanegas* (a fanega being equivalent to 11/2 bushels) of barley for the horses and mules and was said to have baked 10,000 rations of bread daily. In the War of the Austrian Succession large consignments of grain were despatched to Italy in the spring of 1745 in preparation for that campaign, while defeat in 1746 and the withdrawal of the Spanish forces to France did not lessen its supply needs.[63]

Horses, too, could be obtained in Spain. Many of those raising cavalry units at their own cost supplied mounts. Otherwise, the crown would purchase horses. In January 1718, in a move echoing practice before 1700, Philip V ordered that the left ear of all horses purchased for the army be cut to prevent loss by theft and improper sale; and in January 1726 he revived the *junta* to encourage horse breeding established by Philip IV in 1659. In 1746, during the Austrian succession conflict, Philip renewed the latter order, although responsibility soon passed to the Council of War. Just how successful this initiative was is not clear, but horses were certainly carried from Spain to Oran in 1732 and to Italy in the Wars of the Polish and of the Austrian Succession.[64]

By the end of the War of the Spanish Succession, Spain was less dependent than hitherto on outside supply. Nevertheless, the demands of mobilisation and a sustained conflict sometimes necessitated the purchase of matériel abroad. In 1720 of the almost 20,000 fusiles with bayonets needed for an African expedition, it was suggested that 7,000, almost one-third of the total, be obtained in Holland. Unfortunately such purchases were vulnerable to interception: earlier, in 1718–19, the Dutch authorities had seized arms and munitions bought for Philip V in the republic.[65] Philip and his ministers continued to purchase abroad, but mishaps of this sort pointed to the importance of developing domestic sources of supply of war matériel.

Where medical services were concerned, Philip V inherited from the Habsburgs a network of permanent military hospitals. He issued new hospital regulations in 1721, following the expeditions to Sardinia, Sicily, and Ceuta, and again in 1739, after the War of the Polish Succession. The permanent hospitals were supplemented by field hospitals as required. In 1720 a field hospital was established at Tarifa in connection with the expedition to Ceuta. Similarly, in January 1732 Philip ordered the intendant of Barcelona, D. Antonio de Sartine, to establish a field hospital there for 1,000 sick and 500 wounded, with beds, bedding, tents, chapel, senior staff, and medicines for three months; that summer another hospital was being prepared at Málaga for the casualties of the same expedition, and it was proposed that another with accommodations for 800 men be established at Cartagena both because of its proximity to Oran and because use could be made of the facilities there for the sick of the fleet. The departing Oran expedition took 1,000 hospital beds; if the sick surpassed that number, the intendant was to send them to Alicante, Cartagena, and Málaga.[66]

The facilities in Spain itself were cut back in 1741–42, as Spanish forces headed for Italy. Campillo closed more than twenty establishments and drastically reduced a number of others. This left just three hospitals in Spain, in Barcelona, Gerona, and La Coruña, and six in the African garrisons. More important was the provision in Italy, where hospitals were ordered to be established in major centres in Savoy during the Spanish occupation. The Spanish troops also sometimes benefitted from the medical facilities of a nearby town: after the battle of Campo Santo many of the wounded were cared for in a house adjacent to the battlefield which was converted into a field hospital as well as in the hospitals of nearby Bologna, where Spanish troops had also been looked after in the Polish succession conflict. These facilities and those in Nice and Savoy ensured that many of the hospitalised returned to the ranks.[67]

The system of procurement overseen by intendants and commissaries was little different from that of the Habsburgs, who depended very largely upon the private sector, that is, on various contractors, or *asentistas*. In 1717, for example, D. Jose García de Asarta contracted to supply uniforms for all the infantry regiments for four years. Nearly two decades later, in December 1734, D. Mathias de Valparda bid successfully to provide nearly 15,000 infantry uniforms for 1735, the total value of the contract being nearly 8 million reales. Contractors supplied many other services as well. In 1732 D. Francisco Paredes agreed to furnish draught animals for the artillery train and Salvio Torres to supply bread and barley for the Oran expedition. Later that year Catalan asentistas agreed to deliver 2,000 mules for the artillery train going to Italy in 1733. The fiscal–military state of Philip V remained in key areas of its operation a "contractor state."[68]

The system was not without its defects, as had long been apparent. Contractors were sometimes negligent, especially when not paid. In December 1720 the troops at Ceuta were short of wine, and it was discovered that the asentista had not been paid for some time; in 1733 those responsible for uniforms, provisions, and magazines apparently refused to fulfil their contracts when the treasury would or could not pay. Neglect and corruption were not always tolerated, but as long as Philip V and his ministers benefitted from the credit allowed them by contractors, who often continued to provision the king's forces despite not being paid, there was little to gain from fiddling with this primitive industrial-military complex, in which those who farmed the revenues also often supplied services which were beyond the capacity of the royal administration (see chapter 3).[69]

Some ministers did, however, seek to sideline the contractors. In the 1730s Patiño pioneered a state-run system of provisioning the army which depended upon the intendants, but this did not long survive his death or the demands of the War of the Austrian Succession, the contractor Francisco Mendinueta assuming the work from 1744. In another initiative, ministers devolved responsibility to individual units. In Italy during the War of the Austrian Succession the intendant with the army in Savoy, Ensenada, arranged that 20 battalions there should effectively negotiate their own contracts for new uniforms. According to Ensenada, this scheme was much cheaper than if the royal treasury assumed responsibility, negotiating provision from Lyon or Geneva, whether by *administración* or asiento; the regiments would also insist on good quality. Unfortunately, the deal fell foul, first, of the fact that the asentista had already purchased the materials to execute his contract, and, second, of the king's order to not only buy those materials but also to manufacture the uniforms in Spain (below).[70]

However arranged, the demands of war inevitably affected Spain's economy. The Italian ambitions of Philip V and his wife have been frequently condemned as not being in Spain's interests. But it is arguable that in many respects the economy was stimulated by the need to supply war abroad. Certainly Philip's declared wish and his order, in October 1719, to outfit his forces from Spain with Spanish manufactures encouraged the textile industry there, which produced great quantities of uniforms.[71] Some Spaniards undoubtedly did profit from Philip's Mediterranean adventures.

Operations overseas involved substantial supply from Spain, but Spanish forces also, necessarily, helped themselves locally. In 1741 Campillo urged that the expeditionary force then being prepared should find what it needed in Italy. This might mean appropriating enemy stores. In 1720, when evacuating Sardinia, the Spanish forces carried off much of the island's artillery, the question of their return dogging Spanish–Sardinian relations thereafter. Yet such windfalls could meet only a tiny proportion of any expeditionary force's needs, while defeat, notably that at Piacenza in 1746, worked the other way. Allies might more amicably supplement Spain's resources. During the War of the Austrian Succession the Spanish war effort in Italy was aided by the republic of Genoa but above all by the kingdom of Naples. Don Carlos supplied the Spanish forces with an artillery train, with horses, and with grain: in 1746 he allowed the export of 20,000 *tomoli* of grain for the Spanish army (a *tomolo* being equivalent to fifty kilograms). Philip V also relied on local asentistas to supply his troops. In 1734, for example, a number of contracts were concluded in Italy for the provision of the Spanish forces which conquered Naples and Sicily, including the first of many with duke Ignazio Barretta, who was also used in the War of the Austrian Succession, when the Spanish expeditionary forces in Italy again depended on local contractors.[72]

The materials necessary for a major expedition were so numerous and diverse that almost inevitably—Carl von Clausewitz's "friction"—there was confusion, delay, and shortage In 1732 Montemar, the commander of the Oran expedition, was said to be critical of the want of supply; Philip V expressing annoyance with the minister responsible, Patiño. A few years later a damning report lamented the inability of Spain's arms industry to meet the country's needs in peacetime, let alone in war. During the War of the Austrian Succession, too, there were failings in this respect. In 1744 the late delivery of uniforms for recruits newly arrived in Italy from Spain delayed the opening of the campaign. The Oran expedition, however, was on a scale much greater than, for example, the Sicilian expedition of 1718 and was a success, as was the War of the Austrian Succession before 1746. Nor were these problems new in the Spanish Monarchy or peculiar to Spain in the early eighteenth century. Generally speaking, there was little real incentive yet to overhaul the familiar asiento system.[73]

Philip V's ability to threaten the peace of Europe after 1713 depended in large part upon his ability to deploy large numbers of troops. His success clearly owed much to non-Spanish factors, including the military weakness of his opponents and the availability of allies. But success also depended in part upon the remarkable overhaul and improvement—modernisation, in the sense of bringing Spain into line with best, most effective, and successful practice elsewhere—of Spain's own military resources. Much of the innovation represented the adoption of French models. Nevertheless, innovation, frenchification, and the extent to which these developments represented a radical break with the past should not be exaggerated. Militia reform built upon Habsburg foundations, while Philip also followed Habsburg practice in relying on contractors to both recruit troops and supply them. Those changes which were introduced in Philip's Spain represented the further elaboration of what has been termed the fiscal-military state. But it would be wrong to conclude that Philip and his collaborators had state formation, or the creation of a distinctive, new type of Spanish state, in view, as opposed to simply maximising his authority and ability to mobilise resources for the pursuit of dynastic objectives in Italy. Philip's army, recruited from his subjects in the Iberian peninsula and the islands, was more Spanish than that of his predecessors, but, indicative of Spain's relatively small population, the foreign element remained sizeable and critical at all levels. Even so, major operations abroad necessitated an extraordinary mobilisation of men and materiel in Spain itself and were accompanied by efforts, on the one hand, to attract and, on the other hand, to coerce more of Spain's adult male population into serving in the royal army. Philip's Mediterranean expeditions were crucial in triggering this and other innovations. However, the pressure to serve, and above all Philip's use (for some of his subjects, abuse) of the militia, sparked growing resentment of and even opposition to this burden in the Austrian succession struggle. By the time of his death Philip had reached the limit of what Spain itself could do, what his subjects would bear, what he could recruit abroad, and what his allies could or would do, as the last years of the War of the Austrian Succession made clear. By the same token, it is by no means clear that Spanish society was transformed. Philip's military needs resulted in both the creation of new privileges for militiamen and the limitation or virtual abolition of older ones. Similarly, more nobles may have been serving as army officers, but this was not novel. It cannot be said that Philip's Spain was militarised. What was clear, however, was just how successfully Spain had adapted militarily to the losses of the War of the Spanish Succession. Spain continued to depend upon troops recruited abroad, but what had been a European monarchy was now more markedly a Spanish one.

Appendix: Contributions to Levies 1742–47

Year	Total of levy	District	Quota (and % of whole)
1742 (ordered 5 December 1741)	7,919		
		Galicia	966 (12.1)
		Catalonia	823 (10.39)
		Granada	650 (8.20)
		Seville	620 (7.82)
		Asturias	170 (2.1)
		Córdoba	280 (3.53)
		Burgos	400 (5.05)
		Madrid	70 (0.88)
1747	25,000		
		Córdoba	546 (2.1)
		Burgos (including partido of Laredo but not that of Aranda)[a]	818 (3.272)
		Galicia	1,181
		Asturias	499 (2.00)

[a] Certification of the quota of men due (32) from the partido of Laredo, calculated according to the 560 households (*vecinos*) there of the *estado general*, 8 January 1747, AHPC, Corregimiento de Laredo, leg. 271-1/2.

CHAPTER TWO

THE FLEET

To maintain the interests of his majesty in Italy . . . cannot
be done with land forces.
—*Gerónimo de Uztáriz*, 1724

Spain's resurgence after 1713 depended in part upon an impressive demonstration of sea power, while throughout this period policy makers everywhere in Europe were alarmed by reports of Spanish naval preparations. Yet most historians are reluctant to acknowledge this remarkable naval effort. Such unwillingness owes much to an enduring negative image of Spanish sea power deriving largely from earlier Spanish disasters at sea, notably the defeat of the Armada in 1588, that off the Downs in 1639, and that sustained at Trafalgar in 1805. This perception was reinforced in respect of Philip V's reign by the destruction of his fleet at Cape Passaro off Sicily in 1718 and by the virtual disintegration of his rebuilt naval strength in the Mediterranean during the War of the Austrian Succession: his galley squadron was almost annihilated in 1742, while from 1744 until the end of the war Spain's Mediterranean squadron was blockaded in Cartagena by the British. Ensenada's programme of naval reconstruction after 1748, which helped ensure that, before Trafalgar, Spain was second only to Britain as a naval power in western

Europe and the Atlantic, has reinforced this negative image through its implication that the Spanish navy had reached its nadir before Ensenada revitalised it.[1]

Certainly Spain could be weak at sea, above all when facing the British fleet. Indeed, Spain was able to confront the British with any hope, and no guarantee, of success only when supported by France. This fact was most clearly demonstrated in the Mediterranean in January 1742, when the second Spanish expeditionary force headed to Italy following the death of Charles VI. That convoy risked interception by a stronger British squadron, which would at the least have disrupted Spanish intervention in Italy. However, the British force was inferior to the Spanish when the latter was joined by the Toulon squadron, whose appearance ensured that the convoy reached Italy unhindered. But at sea as on land, allies were not always to be had and not always reliable when they were. Indeed, the mutual recriminations of Spanish and French crews after the engagement with the British off Toulon in February 1744 stymied further Bourbon cooperation at sea and may have helped turn opinion in Spain against the alliance and the war (see chapter 4). Philip V needed both to build a fleet of his own and to strengthen the one he inherited in 1700.[2]

Historians have not neglected the Spanish navy in the early eighteenth century. On the contrary, the programme of naval reconstruction associated with Alberoni, Patiño, and Ensenada has attracted considerable attention. Most accounts of Spain's fleet in the eighteenth century, however, emphasise developments after 1748 and are more concerned with organisation than with what the fleet actually did. This focus reflects the fact that changes in the way the war at sea was fought demanded the elaboration of an ever more complex and expensive infrastructure, such that the navy was an important component in the state structure elaborated by Philip V and his successors. Indeed, like Britain and France, eighteenth-century Spain was as much a fiscal-naval as a fiscal-military state. That focus reflects as well a preoccupation of historians with Philip's innovative, supposedly modernising agenda and achievement. In fact, however, while there was innovation, many of the naval institutions of Habsburg Spain survived the change of dynasty. They included not only aspects of forest policy (below), but also the use of the galleys, which, although a minor component of Philip's naval strength, nevertheless continued to have a role in the Mediterranean and were not suppressed until November 1748. Changes in naval warfare had certainly rendered galleys less crucial, France also suppressing its galley fleet in 1748. However, Charles III reinstated Spain's galleys in 1785 to counter the Algerian corsairs, and their use was abandoned for good only in 1803.[3] Most studies of Philip's navy, when they do discuss operations, focus overwhelmingly on the Atlantic rather than on the Mediterranean. This, too, is understandable, given the importance of the Indies (below), but, in contrast with a broadly defensive Spanish naval strategy across the Atlantic, in European waters or, rather, the Mediterranean Philip's fleet was more aggressive and more successful than historians have allowed. I draw here on the records of the new (below) Secretariat (or ministry) of the Navy and on the reports of worried foreign diplomats to clarify the naval contribution to the post-1713 resurgence, what underpinned it, why it faltered, and how it had a broader impact on the Spanish state and society. It has been suggested that the development of navies, or the "turn to the sea," encouraged progress towards consensual and market-oriented polities. This thesis has been questioned with specific reference to eighteenth-century Spain, but I will point out here that the mobilisation of resources for the war at sea in Philip V's Spain was accompanied by, and in part did depend upon, a degree of bargaining and cooperation.[4]

Attitudes to Sea Power

Spanish policy makers had long recognised and debated the importance of sea power, and Philip V and his ministers were no different. As early as 1713 Philip's ambition to rebuild Spain's depleted naval strength was evident in plans to acquire French ships, a project which briefly threatened the peace process. Thereafter, Alberoni sought to convince Philip that Spain should become a naval rather than a military power. This debate about priorities persisted throughout the reign. Uztáriz's mercantilist treatise *The Theory and Practice of Commerce and Maritime Affairs* (published in 1742 but written around 1724), argued that sea power was the best means to achieve the king's Italian ambitions and urged a reduction of the army to pay for a permanent fleet of fifty ships of the line and twenty frigates. Admiral Juan José Navarro also pressed the importance of the fleet. Philip had some sympathy with these views. In 1729, at Cádiz, he visited the galleys and the warship *San Felipe,* inspected the dockyards, and attended the launch of the seventy-gun *Hercules.* No previous Spanish monarch had done this. Another minister who believed that more should be spent on the fleet and that Spain deserved greater consideration as a sea power was José de Carvajal y Lancaster, councillor of the Indies from 1738 and its head in 1742–44. In his *Testamento Político* (1745) Carvajal deplored the fact that Spain was not considered a maritime power when it dominated more tracts of ocean than the two states usually described as such, Britain and the Dutch Republic. Like Uztáriz, he thought Spain needed at least fifty well-armed warships and twenty-five to thirty frigates. At precisely this time a far larger proportion of the budget than ever before in the reign was allocated to the navy (see chapter 3). Following the conclusion of the War of the Austrian Succession and in response to Carvajal's complaint that the fleet had consumed vast sums but had performed poorly in that conflict, the duque de Huéscar articulated what was by then a commonplace, that Spain would not be taken seriously until it had a strong navy. Some among Spain's ruling elite, not only the marqués de Ensenada, recognised the need to be effective at sea. Despite great efforts, much remained to be done in 1748. But what was achieved thereafter built on foundations laid under Philip V.[5]

Organisation

Operations overseas represented a considerable administrative achievement and were associated with a radical overhaul of naval organisation. Hitherto, the fleet had often been known by the name of its component, regional squadrons, reflecting Habsburg devolution of responsibilities, but from 1714, by the king's order, the whole was a royal navy. This and other changes wrought by Philip showed the influence of French administrative models. They included, as was true of the army also (see chapter 1), the expansion and restructuring of the officer corps (below) and the relinquishment by the Council of War of responsibility for the navy, which passed to a separate Secretariat of State with its own minister, or secretary, who dealt with the king. That office was sometimes held with other portfolios of state, notably the Indies, mirroring the role of the fleet in the defence of those territories; it was also occupied by some of Philip's ablest ministers, some of whom, including Patiño, Campillo, and Ensenada, had accompanied, as administrators, the expeditions to Africa and Italy. Equally important was the earlier institution (1705) of the Intendencia General de Marina, a post occupied from 1717 by Patiño, who, as intendant and, from 1726, as secretary of state, has been credited as the real driving force behind the creation of an effective Spanish navy by the time of his death in 1736. Seventeen seventeen was a significant year for naval reorganisation: the instructions issued on the eve of the invasion of Sardinia were a founding code for the royal navy and were part of a growing body of official regulation which, from 1723, included instructions for the administration of naval arsenals.[6]

A more wide-ranging ordinance of 1725, issued against the background of the threat of war between the rival alliances of Vienna and Hanover, led to the establishment in 1726 of three naval departments, each of which was the home, starting in 1732, of one of the three squadrons which henceforth made up the royal fleet: the newly founded Ferrol, adjacent to La Coruña (Galicia), for the northern Atlantic; Cádiz, for the southern Atlantic and Americas but also well placed for intervention in the Mediterranean; and Cartagena, for the Mediterranean. The galleys, based at Cartagena, received their own code in 1728, remaining the responsibility of the Council of the Cruzada, within a strategy framed by the secretary of state.[7]

The regulation of 1725 instituted, under the secretary of the navy and intendente general de marina, a new civilian administrative cadre. In each naval department a captain general oversaw military, that is, naval, matters and an intendant the administrative and financial ones. Subordinate to the intendant was a network of *comisarios*, one in each district of the department, and their lower-ranking subdelegates. In theory at least this was a more hierarchically structured and effective system than what preceded it, with a more defined career structure for those within it. The opportunities the new administrative hierarchy offered are demonstrated by the career of D. Zenón de Somodevilla y Bengoechea (b. 1702). In 1720 he joined the naval bureaucracy as supernumerary, with the aid of Patiño, who had been impressed by his abilities in preparing the Ceuta expedition of that year. In 1724 he was promoted second official and in

1725 first official and *comisario de matrículas* (see below) in Cantabria. In 1726 the future marqués was despatched to the shipyard at Guarnizo (below). In 1728 he was promoted, again at the instance of Patiño, to *comisario real* and subsequently (1730) passed to Cartagena as principal accountant of that naval department, only to be redirected to Ferrol as comisario real under the naval intendant there. In 1731 he accompanied the squadron which installed Don Carlos in the central Italian duchies and in 1732 was involved in the preparation of—and accompanied—the Oran expedition, for which he was rewarded with promotion to *comisario ordenador* at Ferrol. In 1733 Ensenada was the senior naval administrator on the expeditionary force sent to Italy at the start of the War of the Polish Succession; his contribution to the conquest of Naples and Sicily brought him the Neapolitan title of marqués de Ensenada (1736). In 1737 Ensenada, not surprisingly given his ability and expertise in the workings of the naval administration, was appointed secretary of the new Admiralty (below) and in effect administrative head of the navy.[8]

Ensenada's career was unique, but others also advanced up the naval administrative hierarchy. However, the novelty, effectiveness, and uniformity of the new structure or the extent to which it was a meritocracy should not be exaggerated. While army and fleet had both been the responsibility of the Council for War before 1700, each had had its own secretariat, in which the number of officials was expanding and becoming more professional under the last Habsburgs.[9] The office of comisario had been created long before, by Philip IV in 1625, while there were anomalies in the Bourbon bureaucracy. Thus, D. Antonio de Sartine, a French financier who was appointed intendant of the army in Catalonia in 1726, was also intendant of the navy there, effectively depriving the naval intendant of the department of Cartagena, which included Catalonia, of authority in the principality. There were good reasons for this arrangement: the personal standing of Sartine, in an age when the man could shape the scope of his office; the special status of Catalonia following its conquest in 1714; and the fact that so much of the traffic associated with intervention in Italy passed through Barcelona. As for Ensenada's success, it undoubtedly marked his ability, but that had been demonstrated above all in expeditions to which the monarch himself attached enormous importance; Ensenada also enjoyed the patronage of the all-powerful Patiño.

These administrative developments were accompanied by the demise of an older office, that of hereditary Admiral, or Almirante, of Castile, created in 1248. The last almirante, the grandee D. Juan Tomás Enríquez de Cabrera, had joined Philip V's rival for the throne, Archduke Charles, in 1703, dying childless in exile in 1705. In 1726 Philip declared he would not appoint a successor. In 1737, however, Philip created a new Spanish admiralty, or *Almirantazgo*. To many historians this represented the substitution of a more modern institution, one similar to the admiralty board in Britain, for one which was antiquated and little more than a fiefdom of one of the grandees. For Vargas Ponce, for example, the biographer of Navarro, the Almirantazgo was the culmination of Philip's rebuilding of the navy after its virtual collapse under the last Habsburg. There is something to be said for this view. In some respects, however, the new body was less progressive and reflected rather the dynastic, patrimonial character of Philip V's Spain. The measure effectively hived off the fleet to provide a fief within the state for the Infante Felipe, now grand admiral, aided by a *junta*, or board, composed of the secretary of the navy and a trio of admirals: D. Francisco Cornejo, who had commanded the fleet on the Oran expedition of 1732, the marqués de Mari, and D. Rodrigo de Torres y Morales (below). The Infante enjoyed a special jurisdiction over the seafaring population via the registration scheme for seamen, the *matrícula de mar* (below), extensive patronage in the form of the appointment of naval officers, although appointments were still the king's, and a substantial income derived from a levy on all vessels entering Spanish ports. This arrangement and the fragmentation of jurisdiction it implied were a powerful incentive to Ferdinand VI to establish his half brother the Infante in Italy: having achieved this goal, he promptly suppressed the Almirantazgo in October 1748. In that sense, completing the Italian policy of his father enabled Ferdinand to reknit a state structure fragmented by Philip V.[10]

The administrative cadre, which totalled more than 250 officials in 1742, was a crucial component of Philip V's revamped navy. In 1732, for example, the naval intendant at Cádiz arranged the despatch of arms from Cádiz to Alicante for the Oran expedition. But it was not enough to create an administrative structure: there had to be resources to organise, deploy. In addition, tensions between administrators and naval officers might undermine the effectiveness of the fleet. In 1741 the conde de Vegaflorida, the commander of the *San Fernando,* threw one of the civilian administrators overboard. Nonetheless, being the instrument of a policy which was determined to use Spain's resources to pursue, often aggressively, clearly identified objectives, the new administration did much to ensure the availability of fighting ships, transports, and crews which contributed so greatly to Spain's revival after 1713.[11]

Strategic Commitments and Numbers

Historians have exaggerated the collapse of Spanish sea power in the last Habsburg decades, to 1700. Nevertheless, in terms of the number and strength of fighting ships, Spain was weaker at sea on Philip V's accession than it had been at the death of Philip IV in 1665, and its maritime strength declined further during the War of the Spanish Succession, when Philip was unable to replace ships lost, was deprived of the galleys of Spain's former Italian territories, and was largely dependent on the fleet of his grandfather Louis XIV. After that conflict, however, Spain's strength at sea revived considerably, albeit erratically. Counting ships can be as problematic as counting troops (see chapter 1) because lists are not always complete, some listing only major fighting ships, *navíos,* and frigates, and they do not always make clear whether the ship could or would put to sea. Yet from fewer than thirty vessels—ships and frigates—in 1716 the number increased to thirty-five in 1718 before plummeting, the impact of the disaster in Sicily in 1718, to a low of just over twenty in 1722 (table 2). Thereafter, the total rose to forty-five ships of various types in 1728 and to fifty-four in 1737, while the naval code issued by the Admiralty in 1738 provided for a fleet of sixty vessels. The numbers declined after that, primarily owing to losses during the War of the Austrian Succession, to a level in 1748 below that in 1716. Another bout of rebuilding would be needed after 1748. This was somewhat short of Uztáriz's suggestion of a standing fleet of seventy ships and could not compare with the fleets of Britain or France. Nevertheless, Philip's navy had more than doubled between 1720 and 1740, whereas other naval powers were disarming following the conclusion of the succession struggle in 1713, and was certainly stronger than those of most other states. Given that almost the entire fleet

TABLE 2. Spain's Fleet, 1716–48[a]

Year	1716	1720/1725[b]	1728/1730	1735	1740[c]	1745	1746	1750
Navíos and frigates	28	25	45	55	57	38	37	22

[a] Ozanam, "Política," 467, Stanhope to [?], 18 April and 6 June 1718 and enclosed lists, NA, SP 94/88; Poyntz to [Newcastle], 16-27 February 1729, and enclosed list, NA, SP 78/190; Cayley to Norris, 2 July 1735, and enclosed list, NA, SP 89/38; Alcalá Zamora, "Aportación," 40; Muhlmann, *Reorganisation*, 30, 339; Black, "Anglo-Spanish," 235; Fernández Duro, *Armada*, 6:224-25 (1737), 382 (1746), the latter also online at http://.todoabor.es/datos_docum/estad_1746.htm. The galley squadron, omitted by Ozanam, remained stable at six or seven galleys.

[b] For just twenty vessels in 1725, only eight of them fit for service, plus two vessels recently launched in Galicia, cf. "Relation de l'Espagne" (1726), Mur Raurell, *Diplomacia Secreta y Paz*, 2:355-71 (at 367).

[c] Vargas Ponce, *Vida de Navarro*, 134, identifies just fifty-one ships on the outbreak of war with Britain in 1739.

had been built since 1720 and over half of the ships since 1730 it was in some respects more modern than its rivals. It was also supplemented by the galleys.[12]

The grand strategy within which these ships fitted was not so different from that of the Habsburgs. Following the loss of Flanders during the succession conflict, Philip V did not maintain a naval presence in north European waters, but otherwise his naval commitments were much the same as those of his Habsburg predecessors. Spain's most pressing obligation remained the defence of the Indies, of the Atlantic routes between Spain and America, and of the transport to the Indies of the mercury crucial to silver production and from there of the crucial specie. In December 1747, for example, the *León* and two frigates were preparing at Cádiz to carry mercury to the Indies. These functions were filled by means of a permanent force in the Indies, the revamped Barlovento fleet, and in the Pacific the *armada del Sur*, by the new paramilitary coastguard, or *guardacostas*, by the regular (less so than before) transatlantic convoys, the *flota* and *galeones*, and by despatching squadrons and individual vessels on an ad hoc basis from Spain.[13]

The Mediterranean generally took second place to the Indies. This hierarchy of strategic priorities was reflected in the concentration of ships at Cádiz at any given moment, a distribution which was enshrined in the

general regulation of 1738: of sixty vessels of all types, fifty-four, including the most heavily armed, were to be based at Cádiz (forty-two) and
Ferrol (twelve) and just six at Cartagena. The outbreak of the War of
Jenkins' Ear confirmed these priorities, the British success at Portobello in
October 1739 and the subsequent attempt on Cartagena prompting the
despatch of reinforcements to the Indies. In July 1740 Admiral Rodrigo
de Torres left Ferrol for the Caribbean with a flotilla of twelve ships of
the line and almost two thousand soldiers, and in October of that year
Admiral José Pizarro left Santander to oppose George Anson's attempt to
carry the war into the Pacific. Indeed, Emperor Charles VI's death in
October 1740 came very inopportunely for Philip V given that the bulk
of his fleet was absent from Europe, thereby delaying a seaborne intervention in Italy for another twelve months. All that could be done in the
short term was to reallocate seven ships preparing to leave for America at
Cádiz to an Italian expedition being prepared at very short notice.[14]

In fact, however, the Mediterranean had not been neglected hitherto. It
could not be. Spain's extensive coastline needed to be defended against
the ever-present threat of the Barbary corsairs, who not only raided
Spain's Levant coast but also sometimes advanced into the Atlantic, raid-
ing as far as Galicia, and even apparently threatened the fleets passing between Spain and the Indies. Indeed, for many of Philip's subjects who had
little or no interest in the Indies, protection of this sort was the main purpose and justification—what some historians seeking to explain processes
of state formation and loyalty label "political interest integration"—of the
royal navy. It also constituted a lifeline to the north African presidios, that
outer bulwark against the Moorish threat, regularly carrying men, matériel, money, and provisions to these isolated outposts.[15]

These were permanent defensive commitments, echoing the role of the
fleet before 1700. More striking in many respects was the fleet's offensive
role in the Mediterranean expeditions launched from Spain between 1713
and 1748 (see the introduction). The seaborne offensives launched against
Africa and Italy by Philip V do not compare with the great armadas of
his Habsburg predecessors, the contribution to the Lepanto campaign of
1571, the Armada of 1588, or that which came to grief off the Downs in
1639.[16] They did represent, however, a substantial mobilisation of Spain's
sea power.

The Role of the Fleet

As under the Habsburgs, Spanish naval power under Philip V had three main functions within this larger strategy: combat, escort, and transport, and the maintenance of the royal reputation, or *gloire*. Thus the size of Philip V's contribution to the Anglo–Spanish force sent to Italy in 1731 in part reflected Patiño's determination that no unfavourable comparison should be made between the British and Spanish contingents, mirroring in turn both ministerial amour propre and the role of the fleet in projecting Philip's reputation. The following year Philip's galleys forced those of the king of Sardinia to salute their master's standard off La Spezia, triggering a diplomatic row.[17]

Spats over salutes rarely led to combat. In fact, combat meant many things. Major engagements such as artillery duels and close encounter between battle fleets were rare; there were only two of note in this period. The first was that at Cape Passaro in 1718, when the British fleet captured eleven and destroyed three of the original twenty-one Spanish ships present. The second was the engagement off Toulon in 1744, after which the British fleet retreated briefly to Port Mahon for repairs. The Spanish court seized the opportunity to order the transport by sea of between six and eight thousand men to Monaco for the conquest of Nice, for which Navarro, the Spanish squadron commander, was rewarded by Philip with the title marqués de la Victoria. To facilitate engagement, ships carried both guns (below) and troops, including the marines created in 1717. This corps doubled in size from five battalions in 1728 to ten in 1741 but was reduced to eight in the general reform, that is, the reduction, which followed the peace of 1748.[18]

At sea, however, as on land, far more typical than the major encounter between rival battle fleets were the minor engagements involving a few, generally small vessels. Dog fights of this sort were the essence of the struggle against the Moors. In 1728 the galleys captured a Moorish frigate in such an encounter. Demonstrating the web of interests connected with these operations, the dean and chapter of the cathedral of Santiago de Compostela later complained that their privilege, a medieval grant confirmed by Philip V of a share of the prize equivalent to a cavalryman's ration had not been respected. Philip ordered that they receive their due.

But such clashes were not confined to the struggle against Spain's Islamic foe, as was shown in 1735, when, during the War of the Polish Succession, the galleys *San Felipe* and *Soledad* captured two enemy corsairs.[19]

Philip V's fleet, reflecting his revanchist policy and the need this implied to take the fight to the enemy, played, as noted earlier, a much more offensive role than that of his Habsburg predecessor Charles II. But there was far more to offensive operations at sea than combat. In the Mediterranean the fleet contributed to the success of operations in a variety of ways. On occasion the arrival of naval forces in strength rendered further military operations unnecessary: thus the appearance in 1734 of the conde de Clavijo's squadron off the Neapolitan coast triggered declarations in favour of Philip V and Don Carlos by the neighbouring islands of Ischia and Procida, contributing in this way to the rapid conquest of Naples and Sicily. Where operations were necessary, the fleet could both defend Spanish supply lines and disrupt those of the enemy. In 1717, for example, the galleys prevented the landing of Austrian reinforcements in Sardinia, in 1719 they captured a Neapolitan troop transport, and in 1734, during the War of the Polish Succession, D. Gabriel Pérez Alderete's squadron intercepted in the gulf of Taranto reinforcements intended to shore up the collapsing imperial position in Naples, Pérez Alderete being rewarded for his operations in the Adriatic with a Castilian title. The fleet also aided the war on land in other ways: in Sardinia in 1717 the Spanish naval forces isolated Alghero by sea while the army laid siege to it, and in 1718 blockaded the Sicilian towns of Siracusa and Trapani; almost two decades later, in 1734, D. José Alfonso de Pizarro's squadron cut off Messina, as Sicily was again conquered.[20]

Of far greater import, however, in terms of the fleet's contribution to successful intervention in Italy and Africa, was its role as convoy or escort. Uztáriz understood this function. Of his suggested force of seventy ships (above), twenty (twelve ships of the line and eight frigates) were to be employed in the Indies trade, that is, as Atlantic escort. Such activity included the regular supply by sea of the presidios of north Africa and Porto Longone, for whom the maritime link with Spain was crucial. But the fleet really came into its own in this respect in Philip's major amphibian operations, when troops and supplies had to be ferried to their overseas destination and put ashore; and, should operations continue, to carry on transporting reinforcements, provisions, and so on until the end of the conflict, when they would ferry men and matériel back to Spain. The first cycle of intervention in Italy and Africa between 1717 and 1720 saw the royal fleet scurrying around the western Mediterranean on escort duties. In 1717, for example, the landing in Sardinia was made under cover of the guns of the naval escort, as was that in Sicily the next year. In the succeeding years the occupying Spanish forces on those two islands depended enormously on supply from Spain and elsewhere by sea and were left stranded by the destruction of the fleet at Cape Passaro. The Oran expedition of 1732 was another major naval enterprise, the Spanish success there owing a great deal to the speed with which the naval forces put men and matériel ashore. As for the War of the Polish Succession, after the initial seaborne intervention in Italy in 1733 the troops were continually supplied from Spain with reinforcements, provisions, and money. Transportation was among the chief concerns of the intendant general of the expeditionary force, José Campillo, throughout the conflict. In the War of the Austrian Succession, too, following the initial convoy of expeditionary forces there in 1741–42, each succeeding spring saw the carriage by sea to Italy of recruits and of war matériel. There was a massive supply operation like this one before the successful campaign of 1745.[21]

Most of this transferral was the achievement of numerous small craft, many from France and Naples.[22] The main Spanish Mediterranean force, bottled up in Toulon from 1742 and from the spring of 1744 in Cartagena, played virtually no part, not seeking again after Toulon to confront the British fleet or to convoy a major force from Spain to Italy, not even when the British fleet was temporarily weakened or when, as in 1746, the allied invasion of Provence and the Genoese revolt offered incentives and pressures to send out the fleet. Instead, men continued to go overland or on small craft, while both the Spaniards and the British—the latter in part influenced by the inactivity of the former—reduced their presence in the Mediterranean, in this sense reverting to an earlier pattern of priorities: three vessels were despatched from Cartagena to Cádiz in late 1746 to escort the returning Caracas fleet. Changes in Spain's political direction, among them the accession of Ferdinand VI earlier that year, may also have played some part in the failure of the Cartagena squadron to exploit its opportunities. Other, structural factors affected Spain's strategy at sea as well.

Ships and Shipbuilding

Philip V's maintenance of a substantial fleet was all the more remarkable in view of the losses sustained in the naval operations described above, an achievement in part obscured by the fact that new ships were often given the names of those they replaced: there were, for example, three ships named the *San Felipe* operating between 1716 and 1748. Most of the rebuilding of Spanish sea power to 1718 was reversed at Cape Passaro when, as noted, of the original twenty-one ships three were destroyed and eleven, including the seventy-four-gun *San Felipe el Real*, were captured by the British. In addition, a number of vessels then under construction as well as dockyards were the victims of the English and French incursions into the Basque country, Cantabria and Galicia, in 1719, reducing Spain's shipbuilding capacity. In 1741 more Spanish ships were sunk, this time at the hands of Philip's own commanders, as they sought to hinder the British fleet's assault on Cartagena de Indias. As for the galleys, in 1742 virtually the entire squadron was destroyed off Saint Tropez (above). That same year the *San Isidro,* pursued by British warships, was scuttled off Corsica. But, as in the past, most losses at sea were due to the elements, not to enemy action. Built at La Carraca in 1730, the sixty-gun *Andalucía,* which had been part of the convoy taking Don Carlos to Italy in 1731, participated in the Oran expedition and carried Spanish troops back from Italy after the conquest of Naples and Sicily, sank in 1740 in a storm off Puerto Rico. The *Invencible* was destroyed by fire after being hit by lightning off Havana in July 1741. Wear and tear also played a part. Whatever the cause of loss, ships did not last forever, and Philip's overseas adventures added to the pressure to acquire more and new ships.[23]

Occasionally, if ships were needed speedily they were purchased abroad, as in the Habsburg era. This was most likely to happen at the start of a war or in expectation of one and was facilitated immediately after 1713 by the reduction of the fleets of other powers at the conclusion of the War of the Spanish Succession. The core of the newly created fleet in 1713–14 and most of the vessels sent to Sardinia and Sicily in

1717–18 were obtained in this way. In 1718, after Cape Passaro, the Irishman George Camocke, formerly in the British but now in the Spanish service, sought to bribe senior British officers to join Philip, with their ships. In 1724 Peter the Great offered to sell Philip up to sixty ships, while from 1725, as war threatened between the alliances of Hanover and Vienna, Ripperda was said to be buying ships in both Italy and northern Europe and to have offered to purchase three Russian ships then at Santander. Ships continued to be bought abroad thereafter if need be: the *Brillante, Oriente,* and *Poder,* all of which fought off Toulon in 1744, were among six ships bought in France in 1740.[24]

Alternatively, ships could be obtained by seizing Spanish merchant vessels, as in 1744, when half of the twelve Spanish vessels engaged off Toulon were merchantmen diverted from the Carrera de Indias and not properly speaking the king's ships. The demands of war in the 1740s meant that the royal navy was possibly less than completely royal.[25]

A long-term solution to the need for ships, and almost a sine qua non for any realistic programme of naval reconstruction, was to have them built in Spain and Spanish America. The Indies meant above all Havana, where timber of excellent quality was abundant and construction relatively cheap; the arsenal there, built around 1725 as part of the larger overhaul of the navy at that time (above), was perhaps the most prominent source of Spain's fighting fleet in the second quarter of the eighteenth century. More than one-third of naval vessels constructed in Spanish yards between 1720 and 1739 were built at Havana. Among these were the *America* (1736) and *Constante* (1732), both of which fought off Toulon in 1744.[26]

In Spain, too, new shipyards were established early in the reign. Indeed, fifty-one ships of the line were built in Spanish shipyards between 1716 and 1740. The most vital centres of shipbuilding were, in northern Spain, Pasajes and Santoña, and from 1719 onwards Guarnizo in Santander. Campillo served as superintendent of shipbuilding at Guarnizo from 1722 until his appointment as intendant general of the expedition to Italy in 1733, where his colleagues included the future marqués de Ensenada. In 1741 Campillo claimed that most of the king's ships had been built under his direction The capacity of these northern yards was seriously reduced in 1719 by deliberate enemy action (above), but they continued to build ships. In all, twenty-four ships were built at Santander between 1716 and 1732. In 1731 five newly built ships from Santander participated in the expedition to Italy. At Guarnizo twenty-five ships carrying 1,420 guns were built there between 1722 and 1740, including the *Santa Isabel* and the *Real Felipe* (1732), the navy's biggest vessels. Outside Navarre and the Basque country, other shipbuilding yards—some developed in place of those on the northern coast, which were vulnerable to attack—were located at the ports of Galicia (Ferrol), Catalonia, and Andalusia, above all in the vicinity of Seville and Cádiz. The facilities of the Andalusian yards were expanded in the later stages of the Austrian succession conflict at the express order of the king. Galleys continued to be built at Barcelona until the employees of the Atarazanas yards were removed in 1745 to Cartagena, which only later acquired the infrastructure appropriate to its role as headquarters of one of the three naval departments created in 1726.[27]

It has been posited that the "reforming early Bourbon state" gradually tilted the balance in favour of the state and against the private sector in respect of naval supply. Certainly the development of facilities, above all, at Cádiz, Ferrol, and, later, Cartagena, was a substantial expansion of state activity into ship construction and maintenance, exemplifying the elaboration of a fiscal-naval state. However, development was still relatively limited outside Cádiz by 1748, while most of the ships constructed in Spain were built, as in the past, by both the crown and private contractors. As before, which method was preferred depended on various factors, such as how many ships the king needed and how urgently, whether there were contractors ready to do the work, and the cost. It would be wrong to describe the crown's approach as a consistent policy. In the summer of 1718, as confrontation with Britain loomed, the Spanish court ordered the building of nine new ships, eight in Vizcaya and one in Catalonia, and, in order to have them by the following spring, advanced some of the money to the builders. But contractors could not always be relied upon. In 1741 the recently established Havana Company agreed to build for the king three or four ships annually for ten years, thus promising an increase across the decade of thirty to forty ships; but the company could not fulfil the contract and surrendered it in 1749.[28]

To build just one ship might require the felling of thousands of trees: in the spring of 1728 the naval comisario at Málaga arranged the transport five thousand tons of local timber to Cádiz. Thus, whoever was responsible for construction, a successful domestic shipbuilding industry depended in part upon the availability of vast quantities of timber in a world in which the fleet was just one of many competitors for the country's wood. Philip V inherited a forest policy of planting and felling trees from the Habsburgs which was policed by a network of regional *superintendentes* and which had in some respects been enhanced under Charles II. The *montes de Marina*, that is, the forests and woodlands designated to supply the navy, were subject to a distinctive jurisdiction, that of the *juez conservador de montes*, the magistrate who conducted occasional inspections, or *visitas*, to ensure the various obligations regarding felling and planting were obeyed and who fined offenders: between 1713 and 1748 three such visitas were carried out, in 1719, 1724, and, the most wide-ranging of all, 1737–39. These magistrates were now subject, however, to the three departmental naval intendants, who themselves sometimes held the office. Despite the failings of this system, it was the one in place in the War of the Austrian Succession: in the spring of 1745 the interim naval intendant of Cartagena, acting as juez conservador, sent to Murcia, Orihuela, Valencia, and Alicante to have cut 100 walnut trees, 150 white poplars, and 150 oaks needed to fit out Navarro's squadron at Cartagena. However, the experience of that conflict and Ensenada's determination to remedy the weakness at sea it had exposed and exacerbated—and the implications in regard to timber needed—prompted the overhaul of the system. In January 1748 the Admiralty issued new orders respecting the montes de Marina. This measure, "Spain's first national forestry code," was less radical in the broad range of duties it detailed and in the administration of the montes than it was in embracing far more of Spain's forests, and more systematically, than before. The measure met with some local resistance but was broadly successful, triggering both a wave of new planting to replace felling for the construction of new ships and further surveys, which provide invaluable insights into both the ownership of the montes and the continued struggle over access to and exploitation of them. The postwar *catastro* of Ensenada recorded much of the new planting, underlining the fact that the findings of that survey in some respects were the product of very recent developments sparked by Spain's experience in the War of the Austrian Succession. The new

regime remained in force until the overhaul of administration and jurisdictions initiated by the Cortes of Cádiz during the Napoleonic Wars.[29]

Spanish sea power in the Habsburg era had been distinguished in the
Atlantic by the large galleon, which was getting bigger as the seventeenth
century progressed, and in the Mediterranean by the galley, although
there was some movement towards the construction of ships more akin to
those found in other fleets before 1700. This trend became much more
pronounced under Philip V. At the same time, greater uniformity was introduced into Spanish ship construction, with the despatch in 1722 of
José Antonio Gaztañeta to Guarnizo to implement it, after his construction methods were given official backing in the ordinances of that year.
Thereafter the types of ship which comprised the Spanish fleet were not
so markedly different from those in other fleets: they included warships,
or navíos, frigates—the fighting vessels, instead of the now-outdated
galleons—and a variety of smaller, lighter vessels. On the whole, however, Philip's ships were not as large or heavy as their main competitors.[30]

The Spanish ships were also more heavily armed than before, but not
as heavily as their leading opponents at sea. There was often a difference
between a ship's formal establishment, that is, how many guns it should
have, and how many it in fact carried, complicating any attempt to count
the number of guns mounted by individual ships and the entire navy.
Nevertheless, the armada of twenty-nine ships which sailed to Sicily in
1718 appears to have carried 1,360 guns, the heaviest armed being the
74 gun *San Felipe,* while a list of Philip V's ships of December 1728 identified forty-nine vessels bearing a total of 2,586 guns. A few years later, in
1731, the twenty-five ships accompanying Don Carlos to Italy carried
1,422 guns, the most heavily armed being the newly built *San Felipe* and
Santa Isabel, both of 80 guns. Subsequently, the admiralty regulations of
1738 provided that the anticipated sixty vessels of the fleet should bear
a total of just over 3,000 guns, including thirty-two navíos with a total of
2,134 and twenty frigates carrying 800 guns; in 1744 the twelve ships
which fought at Toulon carried a total of 812 guns, most of them 60 or
64); in 1746 the thirty-seven vessels (above) carried 2,016 guns, including
sixteen (the largest group) of 60 and one, the *Real,* 114. No British ship
in this period matched the *Real,* but it was unique. Throughout this period the Spanish fleet was no match for the British fleet when it came to

numbers of ships and total firepower. The largest category was, as in other navies, of 4th rates (50–64 guns): thirty-one of the forty-nine Spanish ships were in this group. It was not entirely surprising that in the two encounters at sea between the rival fleets, in 1718 and 1744, the Spaniards suffered sizeable losses.[31]

Philip V's African and Italian adventures, like most combined operations, required large numbers of transports and other auxiliary vessels, far more indeed than warships (above). These were invariably hired from local, Spanish private contractors for as long as was necessary: fifty-eight of the two hundred and fifty vessels hired for the Sicilian expedition in 1718, for example, were contracted in Alicante. The preparations for the Oran expedition reveal the challenge posed by the need to assemble sufficient transports for a major overseas expedition. In March 1732 officials were freighting transports of between 60 and 110 tons and detaining for this purpose foreign vessels in Spanish ports and even looking abroad, in French and Italian ports. By early April the total contracted had reached eighty, and more were being hired. It was not always easy to co-ordinate what was a frantic search: the marqués de Risbourg, the governor of Barcelona, asked the marqués de Campoflorido, captain general of Valencia, to find transports, but they arrived too late, by which time alternatives had been found, the latecomers being returned to Valencia. In the autumn of 1733, too, large numbers of transports were freighted and seized in preparation for the despatch of the expeditionary force to Italy.[32]

These demands placed such a strain on and caused such a disruption of Spain's mercantile marine that, as we have seen, foreign ships were as likely to be hired or seized as Spanish ones for a major overseas operation. English vessels were hired for the Oran expedition and during the War of the Polish Succession. The hire and seizure of the ships of Philip's own subjects and those of other sovereigns were again resorted to in the War of the Austrian Succession. Even so, there was still a shortage of transports in 1741–42. This no doubt explains why the troops Philip then sent to Italy travelled in a succession of smaller expeditionary forces, and some overland, rather than as one large convoy, as in 1588 and 1639, although the experience of these earlier operations also hints that risking all in one giant convoy had its drawbacks.[33]

Manning the Fleet

Finding men to crew his ships was another of the challenges facing Philip V if he was to maintain an effective force at sea. The most conse-quential development of his reign in this respect, the matrícula de mar, has often been dismissed, not least because of its collapse in the very challenging circumstances in which Spain's navy found itself at the end of the eighteenth century. Nevertheless, it enjoyed some success and went some way towards solving the recruiting challenge which faced all would be naval powers in this period.[34]

Just how many men were needed depended on the size of the ship, and in Spain the number was calculated according to a well-established for-mula which laid down that for every 100 *toneladas*, or tons, a ship should carry 26 seamen, or *plazas de marinería*, and 26 fighting men. In 1732 D. Antonio Serrano, the commander from 1733 of the Mediterranean squadron, applied this rule when reporting on the *Princesa* (1,700 tonela-das) and the *Real Familia* (1,200) at the end of the campaigning season. By that point both vessels were short of their complement of both seamen and infantry, highlighting the difficulty in reaching precise figures in this as in so many other respects regarding the navy and army. Inevitably, a major expedition, one involving many ships of large tonnage, required a great number of men. In 1718, for example, the armada of twenty-nine ships which sailed to Sicily had a total of 10,110 crew; in 1731 the twenty-five ships accompanying Don Carlos to Italy carried 10,050 crewmen; and in 1744 the twelve Spanish ships in action off Toulon had a total complement of 8,450 men. According to the Admiralty regulation issued in 1738, the sixty warships envisaged in that order required a total of 2,474 plazas de marinería.[35]

Great numbers of mariners were mobilised for the big overseas expedi-tions: in February 1741, 400 seamen were said to have arrived at Cádiz, with another 2,000 expected from Vizcaya, to crew the squadron prepar-ing for Italy. This was still not enough, causing a delay in the squadron's departure. Similar problems explain the failure of the Cádiz squadron to accompany the first convoy to Italy in November 1741.[36]

Like land forces, ships' crews were reduced by losses in action, deser-tion, and illness. There were just over 600 casualties, dead and wounded, in the engagement at Toulon in 1744. In November 1731 it was reported that the ship *Rubí* could not go to Cartagena for want of both equipment and seamen, 38 of whom had already been sent to hospital and another 20 on board waiting to go; the frigate *Atocha* was in a similar situation. A year or so later the fleet, then at Alicante, was said to be suffering comparable difficulties. The problem continued to dog the Spanish fleet in the War of the Austrian Succession: by the end of 1743 Navarro's squadron at Toulon had lost 26 percent of the 8,159 men who had sailed from Spain: 180 of the missing 2,124 men were in hospital.[37]

Something could be done both to prevent illness in the first place, by ensuring proper supply of clothing and food, and to cure those who did fall sick with effective medical provision. Steps were taken toward instituting more independence, better training, and greater professionalism of the naval medical corps, exemplified by the establishment in 1728 of a corps of naval surgeons and culminating in 1748 in royal approval for the founding of the Royal College of Surgery at Cádiz for the training of naval surgeons. More specifically, in 1732 a hospital was said to be preparing at Málaga for the wounded and sick of the forthcoming Oran expedition, and it was proposed that another be opened at Cartagena, where a hospital already existed, because of its proximity to Oran. Many wounded and sick would pass that way en route to Málaga, and the sick could occupy quarters being prepared for the Marina y Galeras battalions that served with the fleet. These facilities could apparently accommodate 800 sick. Hospital was also a place to recruit those who had recovered after being left behind: in November 1731 Sartine gave the *Rubí* 55 of the 274 seamen deposited in the naval hospital at Barcelona by the squadron which had recently sailed to Italy.[38]

Desertion, too, reduced crews. In 1731, when the frigate *San Francisco Xavier*, which was carrying troops to Italy, was detained in the Gulf of Spezia, 16 of its crew seized the opportunity to desert. Deserters might be amnestied in some circumstances, as in the summer of 1742, when a pardon was offered to all deserters from the fleet then at Toulon on condition they returned within sixty days. But king and ministers were rarely so indulgent. To counter the problem of desertion the authorities issued those mariners who were on leave or who had completed their period of service licenses which they could show if necessary. In 1743 one Manuel

Garcia, a deserter from the *León*, appears to have stolen the license of another seaman, Domingo de Arago; unfortunately for him, he did not match the physical description in the document, and he was found to be on the matrícula, or register of seamen (below) in Málaga—and thus a deserter.[39]

Spain's extensive coastline and large seafaring population meant the fleet faced competition as a recruiter from other maritime activities. These included the Indies trade, or Carrera de Indias, which was a magnet for sailors in the vicinity of Cádiz and Seville and from other parts, too, who preferred the better terms of service to those offered by the royal fleet. In other parts of Spain the fishing industry and other trades also competed with the royal fleet for scarce manpower.[40]

Seamen were recruited for the fleet in various ways.[41] As in the case of soldiers, there were always volunteers. In March 1733 the official responsible for recruiting men in Majorca reported that he had obtained 60 volunteers in less than two weeks, many of whom had already served with the Spanish fleet and were therefore veterans. Volunteers continued to present themselves thereafter: in the autumn of 1744 of 45 men transferred from the ship *Real* to the frigate *La Paloma* 7 were identified as volunteers, including 2 shoemakers, 1 tailor, 1 deserter from the army, and 1 labourer. Those responsible for finding sailors were alert to measures which might make the service more attractive to men inclined to sign up: in April 1733 D. Bernabé de Ortega Sanz sent Patiño an account of the number of seamen recruited so far and urged that more would come forward if promised exemption from the ongoing forced levies for the army.[42]

Yet volunteers were not always so easily found, not least because conditions of service aboard the king's ships were often unattractive and certainly not as attractive as service on board the fleets sailing to the Indies (above). In the spring of 1744 men from the *Hércules* and *Constante*, recently returned with Navarro from Toulon, where both had been blockaded since 1742 and both having participated in the engagement there a few months earlier, rioted outside the house of the naval intendant of Cartagena. They were seeking their discharge, many claiming that they had not seen their families in four or five years and that none of the promises made to them by the authorities about paying the families a portion of their wages had been kept. The resentments of the men and consequent desertion, much easier ashore than at sea, threatened the manning of the fleet. It did not help either that the men themselves were sometimes not paid for long periods. When the fleet reached Cartagena in March 1744 the crews were owed more than 12 million reales. The fact that casualty rates were among the highest of the century for Spain's fleet also dampened enthusiasm among potential recruits.[43]

As with the land forces, the king received offers to recruit seamen at the recruiter's cost, in return for some reward, or *merced*. In the summer of 1733, for example, Philip V's representative in Genoa, D. Bernardo Ezpeleta, forwarded to Madrid an offer received from the Genoese D. Carlos Grillo, a lieutenant, or *alférez*, in the Spanish navy, to raise at his own expense 300 seamen; in return he sought promotion to the rank of captain. Ezpeleta supported the proposal, saying it would save him having to find men and would be less costly to the royal treasury.[44]

When volunteers could not be found, force was used, as in the past and as elsewhere.[45] In 1731, in view of the want of sailors to complete the expedition carrying Don Carlos to Italy, the authorities detained ships in Spain's ports and by mid-August were said to have seized more than 1,100 men from among those who worked on the river in Seville; further pressing was expected, causing great consternation. In fact, seamen were being recruited for the fleet by generalised levies, much as were men for the army in 1731 and again in 1732, to crew five warships whose departure had been delayed by the lack of men. In the spring of 1733, too, it was reported from Cádiz that there were only enough seamen to crew two of nine ships which had been ordered to be prepared there, seven of them destined for the Mediterranean; and from Alicante came news that despite great efforts to recruit on that coast only 40 of 500 men ordered to be levied had been found and that two-thirds of those collected had deserted. The situation was aggravated by the fact that the ships already in the Mediterranean were hit by epidemic. It became clear that the Spanish authorities would not secure the requisite number of seamen without resort to the violent remedy of the previous year, impressment. A few weeks later men were being seized in the night in Seville and adjacent ports.[46]

Two years later, in 1735, during the War of the Polish Succession, there was another general levy at several ports and towns in the coastal districts east of the Strait of Gibraltar and on the island of Majorca, prompting seamen at Cádiz to either sign on with the regular fleet to the Indies or go into hiding to escape being taken forcibly for the royal navy. According to one report, following the arrival of orders from Madrid to speed the departure of the fleet, all boatmen, fishermen, and stragglers of any kind found at Cádiz, Puerto Santa María, and so on were pressed into service. One of the defects of the system was soon evident in the poor quality of a consignment of almost 500 men from Majorca in August 1735. Nevertheless, this method of recruitment continued to be used: in September 1744, 32 of the 45 men transferred from the *Real* to the *Paloma* (above) were said to have been effectively conscripted by levy.[47]

But this expedient was not entirely satisfactory: in April 1733 the naval intendant at Ferrol reported that only 377 of the 2,000 men ordered to be levied in Galicia had arrived there. Two years later, in the summer of 1735, the town of Xavea declared it could not fulfil its quota because many of the seamen resident there had fled to escape the levy. There was some recognition of the need to put something more effective in its place. Hence the imposition of quotas, or *repartimientos*, comparable to those being imposed to recruit the army (and echoing earlier, Habsburg practice). There were attempts to spread and hence to ease the burden: in 1731 the community of San Vicente del Grove in Galicia was included in a levy of this sort, following a survey of the coast and ports of the realm in 1729–30. The survey had revealed the presence there of 110 *vecinos*, including 25 seamen, 20 of them capable of serving. Inevitably there was resentment and resistance: the community protested by petitioning against its inclusion in the levy in 1733, as preparations were made for another expeditionary force for Italy. The naval intendant urged rejection of the petition, arguing that to allow it would be harmful to both the royal service and to the public, that is, to the other ports who must bear a greater share of the realm's quota. That same year the seven communities of Somorrostro in Vizcaya successfully complained to the king that their share of the quota of 300 men demanded of the territory for the squadron then fitting out at Ferrol did not fairly reflect the number of their inhabitants. The success of their petition created difficulties with the other Basque communities and escalated into a broader discussion of Vizcaya's relationship with the crown. Communities were often reluctant and slow to meet their quotas, although resistance and failure were not inevitable: in 1735, for example, the coastal districts of the kingdom of Valencia and of Murcia were assigned a quota of 452 seamen, most of which had been fulfilled by early September, although by then the fleet should already have put to sea.[48] Clearly, something more was needed.

As noted earlier, the most striking development with respect to recruitment was the matrícula de mar, introduced in 1726 as part of the major overhaul of Spain's naval organisation that year. This system had been anticipated by a registration scheme in Guipúzcoa worked out between the senior naval officer, Gastañeta and the Diputación of that province in 1717–18 and was extended in August 1726 and again in 1727. That year Philip V ordered the compilation of registers of seamen, declaring that all those who signed up—registration was voluntary—would enjoy certain privileges, including exemption from the *quintas* for the army.[49]

The matrícula echoed the French maritime classes, Jean-Baptiste Colbert's solution to the problem of recruiting seamen for Louis XIV's navy. This may be further evidence of the extent to which reform in Bourbon Spain in the early eighteenth century represented little more than the introduction there of the innovations of late seventeenth-century Bourbon France. However, it also represented the reactivation of an older Spanish institution established by Philip IV in 1625, although one which had not proved successful for want both of an effective administrative framework and of the advantages which should attract mariners. It had to all intents and purposes collapsed.[50]

Unfortunately, as is true of so many elements of the Spanish naval revival in this period, just how the matrícula worked in practice before 1748 is not entirely known. But it was not always welcomed by Spain's seafaring population. In December 1732 the naval intendant at Ferrol, D. Bernardino Freyre, forwarded to Patiño a request from the governing body of the port of Camarinas in Galicia, on behalf of the local fraternity of San Jorge, seeking exemption from the matrícula. For his part, the intendant valued the measure, both as clarifying the obligations of communities such as San Vicente del Grove (above) and as a means whereby he would know the number of seamen in his department, although as late as October 1733 the registers ordered to be compiled in 1726 still had not been completed in his department.[51] There were, as ever, anomalies:

after fierce local opposition founded on their traditional *fueros,* Guipúzcoa and Vizcaya were exempted from the royal registration scheme on condition that they maintain their own register.[52]

The inadequacies of the voluntary scheme of 1726, exemplified in the disappointing results of a levy of 600 men in Catalonia in 1735, resulted in the further elaboration of that scheme in the landmark decree of October 1737 during the Polish succession conflict. The matrícula now became more obviously compulsory. Creating a *fuero naval* paralleling the fuero militar (see chapter 1), the decree bestowed various privileges upon Spain's coastal, seafaring population, but made their enjoyment, and in effect employment in most maritime occupations, including fishing, dependent on being registered. The new decree also offered those privileges to foreign Catholic seafarers ready to serve Philip, reflecting that his navy, again like his army, had or was intended to have a distinctive religious identity as well as targeting a potentially rich recruitment seam in other Catholic states and in Protestant states with Catholic minorities.[53]

There were just over 39,000 registered seamen in the three naval departments in 1739 and just over 36,000 by 1748. The number of those actually fit for service was much smaller, about 17,000 in 1737, 25,000 in 1739, and 27,000 in 1749. More important perhaps was the fact that ministers soon took the matrícula into account in naval planning: in 1739 just over one-third of all those registered in Galicia (1,953 men of a total of 5,570 men able to serve) were destined to serve in the fleet preparing at Ferrol for the Indies on the eve of war with Britain.[54]

But not unexpectedly, as with the imposition of military service and despite the additional privileges, the obligation, even after the amendments of 1737, remained unattractive to many. In 1739 the directors of the king's tobacco revenues successfully requested the same privileged exemption of the seamen they employed as was enjoyed by those working the ships of the contractors who supplied the presidios. Others resorted to alternative, more violent forms of resistance: in the summer of 1744, when the naval intendant's *subdelegado* at Vera in the naval department of Cartagena despatched 19 *matriculados* to seize those registered mariners of the town of Mojacar who were to serve in Navarro's fleet after more peaceful methods had failed to get them to fulfil their obligation, rioting broke out.[55]

In fact, the registration system did produce seamen: in 1744, for example, of the 45 men transferred from the *Real* to the *Paloma* (above) 8 were
said to be matriculado. One of the men, registered at Ayamonte, had
been levied in Cádiz, as had another, registered in Mogel. Just 2 of 11
mariners transferred at the same time from the *Real* to the *Brillante* were
identified as matriculado. However, the sailors yielded by the matrícula,
as by all types of recruitment, were often found wanting. In 1744 the marqués de la Victoria complained about the poor quality of a batch of
83 seamen recently sent to Cartagena: the men had been secured by various means, matrícula, levy, volunteers, but too many were either in bad
health or had never been to sea, in part because the authorities were now
calling up men who had registered only to obtain the related benefits.
The scheme of 1726, which had been reformed at the close of the War of
the Polish Succession (1737), was overhauled again, in 1748 and 1751, following the experience of the War of the Austrian Succession, the new
regulations answering to and exposing many of the difficulties encountered during that conflict.[56]

When Spanish seamen were wanting, especially when crews were needed
urgently, foreigners were recruited. As early as 1715–16 the project for a fleet
of twenty-four ships (above) assumed the recruitment of foreign seamen
and proposed they be enrolled as naturalised Spaniards after so many
years service. It was claimed that the Spanish fleet at Cape Passaro carried
more than 1,000 English sailors, and that Dutch and French sailors
were bribed to join the Spanish fleet in 1727–28. One especially favoured
recruiting ground was the Ligurian riviera in Italy. In the summer of 1731
D. Gregorio Espinosa in Genoa recruited seamen along that coast at the in-
stigation of the intendant of Catalonia. Later that same year the Spanish
minister in Genoa supplied 30 seamen to the frigate *San Francisco Xavier*, am-
ply replacing those lost by desertion. Genoa continued to be fertile ground
for naval manpower during the War of the Polish Succession: between
March and July 1734 Philip V's envoy in Genoa recruited and sent to
Barcelona a number of sailors, the vast majority of them Genoese. But
Liguria was not the only source of men. The Spanish presence at Leghorn
from 1731 enabled the fleet to pick up men from the many foreign ships
which put into that major port: as early as July 1731 the British consul there
reported that the Spaniards were busy lifting sailors and had recruited 15

British deserters from merchant vessels. British and other foreign seamen were also lured into the Spanish service from ships putting into port in Spain itself. Foreign seamen continued to swell Spanish crews in the War of the Austrian Succession.[57]

Men also had to be found for the galleys. The galleys needed on average between 250 and 300 oarsmen each: in late September 1744, for example, the galley *San José* had 283 men at the oars, 41 officers and officials, and a complement of 24 soldiers. Six galleys thus required between 1,500 and 1,800 men at any one time. The understandable lack of volunteers meant that oarsmen had been drawn from Spain's convict population for as long as the country operated galleys at sea. *Forzados* were a highly prized asset: when in 1715 Philip V decided to dispense with the services of the duque de Tursi, whose galleys at Genoa had long been a part of Spain's galley fleet, he triggered a dispute with the duke about possession of the forzados of those galleys.[58]

In Spain itself, there was, as in the past, a close link between the pursuit and punishment of offenders and the marginalised and the needs of the galleys, such that penal policy continued in some respects to be driven by those needs. A whole range of offences, old and new, were punished by a term on the galleys. In 1717, for example, Philip V ordered a census of Spain's gypsies; those who evaded it risked despatch to the galleys. The following year some of those convicted after the alleged revolt of 1718 in Vizcaya were condemned to the galleys, as were some of those condemned in 1724 after anti-seigneurial disturbances in Galicia. An edict of 1725 condemned nonnobles carrying banned weapons to six years in the galleys.[59]

In consequence, forzados continued to supply the bulk of the oarsmen. In 1721, for instance, of the 291 men on the *San Felipe*, 256 were forzados; more than a decade later the *Santa Theresa* had 256 rowers, of which 184 were forzados, and in September 1744 such men contributed 160 of those manning the oars aboard the *San José*. Sometimes, too, forzados who had completed their sentences were detained for want of men to replace them.[60]

The other major source of oarsmen were Moorish slaves, who numbered 38 of the 291 oarsmen on the *San Felipe* in 1721, 61, a rather higher proportion, of those aboard the *Santa Theresa* in 1732, and 94, or one-third, of those aboard the *San José* in the autumn of 1744. In February 1734 one of the Spanish galleys took on board 60 slaves at Málaga. The slaves were usually either captured in war or purchased. Thus, all but 1 of the 20 Moors captured in one engagement (1728, above) were sent to the galleys. When these sources yielded insufficient oarsmen, alternatives had to be found, including, during the War of the Austrian Succession, enemy prisoners of war.[61]

The effectiveness of the Spanish fleet was at times undermined by a serious shortage of mariners, which was perhaps the single greatest obstacle to Spanish effectiveness at sea. It was not always so: in the War of the Polish Succession the fleet seems to have had the men it needed, enough to man the ships required to contribute to the conquest of Naples and Sicily, although a shortfall may have emerged by 1737. The shortage of manpower was particularly apparent, however, during the War of the Austrian Succession. In 1744, when the Franco–Spanish fleet sailed out to confront the British, Navarro was obliged to leave behind in Toulon three frigates and one smaller vessel (25 percent of his entire force) for want of men to crew them and to complete the crews of the ships which sailed out to fight. The issue was not that men were not being despatched from Spain but that they were travelling overland, leaving late, and delayed by, among other things, snow in the Pyrenees. Yet the enemy superiority on that occasion was just four ships. On other occasions thereafter a lack of seamen may also have played a part in the failure of the Spanish fleet to challenge its British opponent more successfully. But the manning shortage was not a problem peculiar to Spain: it faced all maritime powers. In attempting to meet this challenge the Bourbon state had fashioned a new institution, or reshaped an older, Spanish one, the matrícula, a maritime militia, in which the crown was obliged to balance coercion with rewards in a manner implying the limits of a wholly authoritarian approach. The matrícula was not a complete solution to the problem of naval manning; other measures included giving diplomatic support to the efforts of Spanish fishermen to press their claims to access the fisheries of Terranova, which had been undermined by the peace of 1713. The matrícula also required subsequent tweaking, but it was a solution of sorts, one with enduring consequences for Spain's seafaring population.[62]

Supply, Facilities, and Funding

As well as being built, ships had to be fitted out with rigging, sails, and countless other necessities and to be patched up after months at sea and following engagement with the enemy, as in 1718 and 1744. Crews had to be fed, the Spanish fleet, like that of other states, requiring vast quantities of rations prepared in advance. In 1731 the contractor responsible for supplying the fleet was expected to provided 600,000 sea rations for that year, while a further 146,000 rations were sent to Leghorn for the vessels which had carried Don Carlos to Italy. The various convoys to Italy in 1741–42 likewise required a prodigious effort of provisioning: in February 1742 orders went to Barcelona to send 900,000 rations to Toulon for the Spanish fleet, that is, the escort of the first and second expeditionary forces, which were now in the French port. If these needs were not met, a fleet could be immobilised or at the least seriously weakened, as happened to the Barlovento fleet in 1738. The administrative and financial challenge of supply was even greater when ships were operating outside Spain.[63]

To equip his ships with cannon, as he did his land forces with artillery, Philip V could resort to the established centres of production in Spain, notably Lierganes and La Cavada in Santander, helping to ensure that the period after 1713 was one of expansion. He also ordered the construction of an arsenal adjacent to Graña in Ferrol in December 1726. As for naval stores, some of the raw material necessary to their production could be produced in Spain, including hemp for ropes and rigging. There were efforts, as in the Habsburg era, to promote domestic production of these crucial commodities but, as before, with little success. As a result, the Spanish fleet had to compete for a limited domestic product whose price fluctuated: in 1745 the cost of hemp rose in Catalonia after large purchases were made the previous year to refit Navarro's squadron following the action off Toulon. Philip could buy materials abroad, although this was not entirely satisfactory, being subject to political and other complications.[64]

As before 1700 king and ministers preferred to use private contractors not just to build ships but also to provide equipment, such that in the naval as in the military sphere Philip V's state was a contractor state. Typically, in 1741 the Catalans Ignacio and Juan Buxo (or Boxo) contracted to supply rigging for the naval departments of Cádiz and Cartagena for ten years, and in 1744 D. Carlos Lasarte did the same to supply the fleet with masts and rigging, planking, and pitch for twelve years. Even if produced in or supplied from Spain these materials might have to be delivered where the fleet was serving, overseas. At such times the fleet enjoyed the services of Philip V's diplomats: in 1743–44, for example, the Spanish resident at Genoa pressed the authorities there to allow the duty-free import of materials for Spain's galleys.[65]

Philip V might rely on allies and sympathetic neutrals to purchase naval supplies abroad, as in the War of the Austrian Succession. But on the whole Philip's fleet was outfitted by Spanish contractors. The contract for the supply of provisions to the fleet, generally for three years at a time, was held for most of this period by the Navarrese Norberto Arizcun (1722–25, 1725–30) and his nephew Miguel, later (1741) marqués de Iturbieta, who besides the navy supply contracts (1730–35, 1735–40) also farmed the *rentas provinciales* of Galicia from 1729 onwards and the wool revenues of Castile and Aragon from 1731. When Miguel died in 1741 his cousin Ambrosio Agustín de Garro secured the contract (1741/42–44, 1745–48) for the duration of the War of the Austrian Succession. In some respects the staying power of the Arizcun family simply signaled the weakness of the state, that is, its inability to pay the contractor and its dependence upon him. In 1739 the royal bankruptcy (see chapter 3) saw the king owing Arizcun more than 17 million reales on the supply contract. In this sense, a naval-fiscal complex paralleled the military-fiscal complex, with tax farmers and financiers also deeply involved in provisioning.[66]

Contracting worked reasonably well, at least in peacetime. There were, inevitably, problems, but few of these, including fraud, were new. According to Ensenada, the failure of the English contractor Burnaby to fulfil his agreement, concluded in June 1732, to supply the fleet with essential materials meant delay, additional expenditure for the crown, and a deterioration in the quality of what was dispensed, which affected the performance of the fleet in Italy in the War of the Polish Succession. There were delays in concluding contracts because of misgivings about the viability of the contractor, doubts exaggerated by royal officials associated with rival contractors. However, not all contractors defaulted.

Josep Basora, for instance, having fulfilled his own contract, stepped in when Burnaby failed in 1738, and the system was really tested and found wanting only in wartime. During the War of the Austrian Succession, with the Spanish fleet engaged on two fronts, the Mediterranean and the Caribbean, the demand for ships' stores proved too much for some contractors. Urgent need, in part owing to lack of planning, meant that materials of poor quality were sometimes supplied. This was one very good reason to reform the system of provision after 1748. Thus in 1751 a state rigging factory was established at Cartagena. In fact, in a succession of contracts from the 1720s onwards the crown had been shifting the balance in its own favour and at the expense of the *asentistas*, or financiers, such that developments after 1748 were not such a radical innovation. Already during the Austrian succession conflict, the crown had purchased a foundry at Júzcar in Ronda to manufacture ships' anchors.[67]

The acquisition and fitting out of ships, their maintenance, and the supply and pay of crews were enormously expensive, as in all states with any pretensions to naval power. The first ship built in the new facilities at Cádiz in 1731 cost 4.5 million reales, while the *Real Felipe*, the most expensive ship built in Spain in this period, cost 11 million reales. Reliable figures are elusive, but Uztáriz calculated a fleet of seventy vessels, fifty ships plus twenty frigates, to cost almost 5 million crowns a year, whereas just 2 million were assigned in 1724. Annual spending on the navy did increase substantially. It almost doubled between 1714–16 and 1717–20, to just over 20 million reales on average; it continued to rise, and between 1723 and 1736 again almost doubled, from 28 million reales to 51 million, more than 15 percent of total spending; between 1737 and 1741, when spending on the fleet absorbed almost 20 percent of all expenditure, and 1741–46 it rose by nearly two-thirds to an average of almost 88 million reales a year. Spending on the fleet had thus increased more than eightfold between 1713 and 1748, reflecting the fivefold increase in the size of the navy in the same period. Budgeted spending according to the naval ordinance of 1738 put the salaries and wages of all 8,236 individuals employed in the fleet at over 1 million escudos, or 10 million reales, a year. Indeed, at the height of the War of the Austrian Succession spending on the fleet outstripped that on the army, such that during this conflict Spain certainly merited the label, fiscal-naval state. The reality, however, was that funds were not always available, which unavoidably impaired the effectiveness of the fleet. Philip V never spent or allocated anything like the sums devoted to their fleets by Britain and France.[68]

Officer Corps

Funding was possibly the most vital factor in achieving success at sea, but it was not the only one. The capacity of the Spanish fleet to do what was asked of it depended as well upon the quality of the officer corps, which was in effect recreated in 1714 and almost quintupled in size from 98 in 1719 to 478 in 1741, in line with the expansion of the fleet. The corps was also restructured, becoming more clearly defined, hierarchical, and professional and thereby creating a career ladder. The future secretary of state for the navy, Julián de Arriaga, joined the navy as *alférez de fragata* in 1728, rising to *alférez de navío* (1731), *teniente de fragata* (1732), *capitán de fragata* (1737), *capitán de navío* (1745), and *jefe de esquadra* (1749). The naval officer corps was more clearly distinguished from the land service: Cornejo, one of Spain's most distinguished mariners, and Navarro had both transferred from the army to the navy in the 1710s, but such transfers were far less common a generation later. The corps also became more Hispanicised and an attractive new niche for many among Spain's lesser nobility.[69]

In 1747, in a wide-ranging memorial on the deficiencies of the Spanish fleet, as revealed by its poor performance in the War of the Austrian Succession, Spain's most distinguished mariner, Navarro (now marqués de la Victoria), explained the earlier catastrophe at Cape Passaro in terms of both the inferior construction and firepower of the Spanish ships and the inability of commanders to manoeuvre those vessels and to fight capably at sea. The Spanish naval high command certainly had its imperfections, and Gaztañeta was not alone in attracting criticism. The Genoese marqués de Mari, the senior officer on the Italian expedition of 1731, was said to have endangered his fleet and was investigated, but it appears that the protection of Isabel Farnese's entourage saved him from disgrace. The following year, 1732, after the Algerian fleet returned home with many Spanish prizes, there was criticism of the inaction of the commanders who had failed to stop it. For his part, Navarro himself related in later life how, as a frigate captain in 1729, he attracted the attention of the king and queen during their visit to Cádiz by his ability to dance and draw and thus secured his promotion to ship's captain. On a darker note, Navarro was later accused of cowardice by the French in the recriminations which followed the Toulon engagement of 1744. He was the champion of the serving officers in a bitter struggle between the corps and the growing naval bureaucracy, whose interference was resented by those serving at sea. Operations were not always helped by such tensions or by the rivalries of senior naval officers, such as that between Gaztañeta and Mari, which may have contributed to the disaster at Cape Passaro in 1718. The play of interest and influence could also ensure that less capable men were promoted at more junior levels. Thus one D. Joseph de Brea, who was reformed because he was thought to be incompetent and no captain would have him, was nonetheless promoted frigate captain.[70]

But the defects of the high command or of the officer corps in general, many of whom served on one or more of Philip V's Mediterranean expeditions, should not be overstated. Gaztañeta was in fact able and experienced, the author of influential works on navigation and shipbuilding (see above); in 1727 he showed real skill in evading the British fleet, which was seeking to intercept the fleet returning from the Indies. Another proficient, competent individual was Blas de Lezo, the senior officer on the Oran expedition and hero of the defence of Cartagena de Indias in 1741. Navarro, who had served on the Sardinian, Sicilian, and Oran expeditions, also wrote intelligently on naval matters. French criticism of his conduct in 1744 cannot be either separated from the backbiting which followed that disappointing engagement or taken at face value. The memorial he wrote for Carvajal in 1747 on the performance of the Spanish ships in 1744 demonstrated both critical intelligence and a recognition that if Spain was to do better at sea it must have better, larger, more heavily armed ships than it had on that occasion.[71]

In fact, poor standards were not indulged. Officers shirking their duty by failing to engage the enemy, being tardy in reporting negative outcomes, and so on were called to account. In the wake of the destruction of the galley squadron in 1742, the senior officers concerned were court-martialled, although they were exonerated. Previously the conde de Vegaflorida had been tried for abandoning his ship but was also pardoned. Yet not all those who were tried by court-martial were acquitted, while the system of appointments, one intimately associated, like that of the army, with the play of patronage and connection, was by no means peculiar to Spain, nor was it incompatible with ability and merit.[72]

In fact, serious efforts were made to improve the standards and quality of the expanded and more clearly defined naval officer corps by way of training. Crucial to that project was the establishment at Cádiz in 1717 of the Academia de Guardias Marinas, which was seen by Patiño as a school for young noblemen and which attracted students from abroad. Like the army cadet scheme (see chapter 1), entry to the naval academy as a *guardia marina* was a royal merced and restricted to those of proven noble status, thus meeting the challenge of merging the social and technical requirements of an officer corps; the graduating cadets entered the fleet and, applying the skills they had acquired, climbed the official hierarchy.[73]

Some encouragement was given to the production of useful technical materials: besides the writings of Navarro, in 1732 D. Blas Moreno y Zabala, an alférez de fragata, was licensed to publish his *Práctica de la Navegación*. Indeed, the contribution and role of the Cádiz academy and of naval institutions and personnel more generally have intimated that scientific activity experienced some militarisation in early eighteenth-century Spain.[74]

These developments indicated a real preoccupation with improving the quality of Spain's naval officer class. The overall performance of those officers suggests the effort was not entirely wasted. Some reaped substantial rewards: after the engagement off Toulon in 1744 various naval officers were promoted, some received *hábitos* in the Military Orders, while Pérez Alderete and Navarro together with Rodrigo Torres Morales, who brought home the treasure fleet in 1745, evading British efforts to seize it, all received titles. Such rewards were not unknown before 1700, but the social standing of naval officers seems to have improved in Spain in these decades, along with their growing professionalisation and the enhanced status of the navy itself.[75]

Unlike the army, the navy saw very few officers drawn from the ranks of the grandees. In that sense little had changed since Luisa de Padilla advised her sons against service at sea a century before. One exception, Pedro Fitz-James Stuart, the brother of the duque de Berwick, entered the service at age sixteen in 1736 and was promoted ship's captain in 1745. The naval officer corps was another sphere in which the lesser nobility, *caballeros* and *hidalgos,* particularly but not only along Spain's lengthy littoral, formed a niche for themselves in the state. Cornejo (b. 1675), who rose from frigate captain to command of the Ferrol department and membership of the Almirantazgo and Council of War, came from a family of hereditary *regidores* of Valle in Burgos; he was one of that generation which, while holding senior commands under Philip V, had reached maturity in the reign of Charles II, Clavijo (b. 1676) being another. As for the younger generation, the sailor and scientist Jorge Juan (b. 1713) was a younger son of a lesser noble family from Elche in Alicante, while his colleague, D. Antonio de Ulloa (b. 1716), who entered the academy in 1733, was the son of one of Seville's ruling elite and had two brothers in the army. In this way, the revamped navy, along with the army, facilitated the emergence of a Bourbon service nobility: later, all three brothers of the reformer Baltasar Jovellanos (b. 1744) who reached adulthood, members of the lesser nobility of Asturias, one of the most impoverished parts of Spain and offering few other opportunities, entered the naval college at Cádiz, becoming junior officers, one falling ill and dying off the Americas and another being killed in action.[76]

These training institutions, especially that at Cádiz, helped ensure that Spain's naval officer corps became less dependent upon recruitment abroad. In 1713 Philip V had looked to Louis XIV for experienced officers as he sought to rebuild the Spanish fleet. As before 1700, foreigners continued to serve, among them some French officers, the Genoese patrician Stefano De Mari, and the Irish renegade Camocke. Philip also employed a number of exiles from what had been Spanish Italy before its collapse in the War of the Spanish Succession, including the Sicilian D. Miguel Reggio Branciforte, commander of the galleys. But, as noted, the corps as a whole was increasingly Hispanicised, recruited from among the king's subjects in the Iberian peninsula and islands, and among those Spanish institutions most transformed in his reign.[77]

Corsairs and Privateers

The royal fleet was not the only naval force available to Philip V. Other resources were local vessels armed on an ad hoc basis. In 1716, for example, the marqués de Lede, then governor of Majorca, ordered the fitting out of local ships against Moorish attacks. More central, however, were the privateers which all sovereigns relied on to enhance their capability at sea. Like his Habsburg predecessors[78] and his contemporaries, Philip licensed privateers to prey on enemy shipping during the succession struggle, in 1718 against Britain, in 1724 against the Barbary corsairs threatening Spain's eastern shores—on both occasions seeking to encourage privateers by surrendering his regalian right to the fifth of prizes—in 1726 and 1738 against the Moors, and from 1739 against Britain again.[79]

Privateers were a useful auxiliary. Their crews might help recruit the royal fleet, and they also sold captured naval stores to it. On occasion they might be even more critical as a means of striking at the enemy, especially when the royal battle fleet could not do this, for example, after the debacle at Cape Passaro and in the War of the Austrian Succession. The Spanish presence at Ceuta and Oran offered the corsairs additional bases from which to operate and to which to carry their prizes. The exploits of individual corsairs were recorded in the official gazette throughout this period. In July 1719, it carried the story of Juan Bautista Masi of Vigo, who had captured a number of English ships that year, and in 1743 that of D. Juan de Zubarán, who seized an English vessel carrying a cargo worth 21,000 pesos from Dublin to Leghorn.[80]

It is not easy to arrive at a reliable total of the number of prizes. However, the privateers disrupted enemy trade and in that way put pressure on, for example, British ministers to settle with Madrid. But, as in other states, privateers did not always cooperate with the royal fleet, with which they sometimes competed for crews. In early 1743, for instance, the crew of a new Bilbao corsair was said to comprise mainly deserters from the Toulon squadron, putting local officials into a quandary as to how to react should the vessel put into their ports. In addition, the overriding goal of the privateers was to amass prizes and prize money, and they might drive a hard bargain with the king. One consortium of would-be privateers in 1732 did just that before they would fit out three frigates at Barcelona. In pursuing prizes, privateers often created difficulties for the king by attacking neutral shipping. In December 1743, after Spanish privateers had threatened Dutch shipping at a time when it was important not to alienate the United Provinces during the War of the Austrian Succession, Philip V's ambassador at The Hague promised the restitution of the ships of subjects of the states captured by Spanish royal warships and privateers and the payment of compensation. For Carvajal, this independence was good reason to ensure that those fighting the war at sea were the king's men.[81] The privateering war in Spain, as in Louis XIV's France, was in some respects a sign of royal weakness.

A strong navy was crucial if Philip V was to reassert Spanish power overseas after 1713, and his fleet did experience a remarkable revival in the decades following the peace of Utrecht. The Atlantic and Caribbean constituted Spain's main concerns at sea in this period, as they had been before 1700 and would be again after 1748. Philip was thus able to draw on a broad consensus of support for a policy which enhanced Spain's naval strength. However, he also pursued an ambitious, aggressive naval strategy in the Mediterranean. He was not always successful. Defeat in 1718 aborted a happy intervention in Italy and necessitated the rebuilding again of a Spanish fleet only recently reconstructed. Equally striking was the collapse of Spanish sea power during the Austrian succession struggle, when Spain's Mediterranean fleet was confined to Cartagena, seriously hindering the war effort in Italy. Being a fiscal-naval state did not guarantee success at sea, while the overhaul of the Spanish fleet after 1748 was made more necessary by the weaknesses exposed in the previous years.

However, while acknowledging Spain's failures at sea, Philip V's Spain was far more obviously a sea power—and respected and feared as such—than was that of his immediate predecessor, Charles II. His fleet had enabled Philip to achieve some of his objectives in Africa and Italy and across the Atlantic, not least by transporting thousands of men and great quantities of war matériel overseas. As was true of the struggle on land, success owed much to the weakness of Spain's opponents, above all, the Austrian Habsburgs. They owed a great deal, too, to the inaction, even cooperation, of those states which *could* challenge Spain at sea, above all, France and Britain, whose presence in the Mediterranean was the single greatest obstacle to the realisation of Philip's ambitions in Italy. But Spain's revived strength at sea, the first phase of a flowering of Spanish sea power in the eighteenth century which was abruptly terminated at Trafalgar, also owed much to the reform of its own naval organisation and to an expensive programme of rearmament, which stimulated, deliberately, Spain's economy (perhaps more than the revamping of the army).[82] The problems facing Philip's efforts to assert himself at sea, namely, lack of ships, guns, crews, and especially men, were a real want of resources (men, money, timber) but were not unique to Spain, nor were many of the solutions he adopted. Philip did not overcome all of these dilemmas, but by 1748 Spain was better able than in 1713 to meet its needs at sea from its own resources. Philip did not militarise Spain's seafaring population any more than he did the population of the interior (see chapter 1). Nevertheless, those seafarers shouldered a burden of obligation by the end of his reign which they had not done at its start. But those charges were accompanied by privileges. Spain therefore remained a society marked by a multiplicity of corporate, geographical, professional, and social privileges which Philip's naval reforms reinforced. This suggests that while Thompson, referring to Bourbon Spain, rightly questions the assumption that a "turn to the sea" was associated with the development of representative institutions, nevertheless the absolute monarchy was more likely to succeed by bargaining, by offering privileges in exchange for service, than merely by decreeing new impositions on his subjects.

CHAPTER THREE

FINANCES

A power as great as Spain, which has no other goal but Italy . . . and all
the resources of a vast monarchy and the wealth that it furnishes.
—*Charles Emmanuel III, September* 1743

The Spanish resurgence after 1713 was enormously expensive. Indeed,
Philip V's African and Italian adventures were probably the single most
important factor driving the increase in spending and associated growth of
revenues between 1713 and 1748, which far outstripped the growth of
Spain's economy in that period. Yet, despite their importance—not least in
triggering radical reform of the Spanish finances during the war years between 1739 and 1748—and widespread criticism of Philip's Mediterranean
enterprises as a costly self-indulgence, the financial implication of these
operations has been largely ignored. This is part of a larger neglect: there
is no general survey of the finances of Philip's reign comparable to those
of the finances of his Habsburg predecessors or of his Bourbon successors.
Excellent work exists on financial aspects of the War of the Spanish
Succession, Navarrese financiers, corruption, and the place of the reign in
the broad evolution of Spanish state finance. But until recently the broader
fiscal history of the reign has languished in relative obscurity.[1]

In part, such neglect signals difficulties which dog all financial history. The proliferation of agencies meant that some payments and receipts effectively by-passed the central administration. They were recorded, but the complexity could justify those who claimed, as did Campillo, appointed secretary of state for finance in 1741, that the fiscal system was opaque. Whether revenue figures are gross or net is also problematic. Diverse systems of classifying the various revenues also create confusion. Another difficulty arises from the different units in use—*maravedís, reales, escudos,* or crowns, *ducados, pesos* (and *pesos fuertes* or *pesos de a ocho reales*), *doblones,* and piastres (see note on money); yet another problem is the use of both *plata* and *vellón,* and still another is the manipulation of values in 1726, 1728, and 1737. Last, the accounts of those handling royal revenues could take decades to finalise: the account for one tax farm, which ended in 1714, was not closed until 1789. It is often virtually impossible to reconcile figures derived from different sources.[2]

Despite these difficulties, historians, who may have a better idea of the condition of state finances in the early modern era than did contemporaries, are now paying greater attention to the broad pattern and evolution of government finance in Philip V's Spain. Unfortunately, much of this work, particularly those macro studies influenced by the so-called New Institutional Economics which seek to relate the ability to mobilise resources, including credit, to particular political systems, focuses on the later eighteenth century; it also largely ignores the real impact of royal demands on Philip's and Ferdinand VI's subjects. There is a tendency, too, to ignore or underplay the immediate and crucial context of war when explaining innovation.[3]

In fact, the evidence of the expenditure necessitated by Philip V's Mediterranean projects suggests we need to revise our understanding of Spain's finances after 1713. It is widely held that the fiscal pressure was very great during the succession struggle but relaxed thereafter. In 1724, most notably, various extraordinary impositions dating from the war of succession were abolished or reduced, along with the older *servicio de milicias.* It has also been posited that after 1713 Philip was unable to expand state revenues, as he had during the succession struggle, because of the weakness of the state. Yet in reality Philip spent great sums on his African and Italian projects, and to raise them he imposed substantial obligations upon his subjects. In this sense Philip's Spain was a fiscal-military state of the type familiar to historians elsewhere in contemporary Europe, one in which at its most basic fiscal policy was driven by the needs of war. Indeed, Philip's Spain was at least as much a state of this type as that of his son, Charles III, in whose reign, it has been proposed, war was the first call on spending. When Philip appointed Campillo as secretary of state for finance in 1741 he particularly recommended to him Spain's imminent military intervention in Italy. The most successful finance ministers, Patiño, Campillo, Ensenada, were those who secured the necessary wartime funds, often using the same expedients as their Habsburg predecessors. Those who failed in this respect might be vulnerable: in 1724, during the factional struggle between the two former *tesoreros mayor,* Fernando Verdes Montenegro and Nicolás Hinojosa, the latter was accused of failing to pay the troops in Sicily between 1718 and 1720. These things mattered because Philip prioritised them and, like his Habsburg predecessors, expected his ministers to find the funds come what may. In that sense, Rafael Torres's remarks regarding the fiscal-military state of Philip's son Charles III are relevant to Philip's own: political will was more important than the money itself, while the means of funding might, reflecting political cultures, differ from one fiscal-military state to the next. However funded, the sheer cost of Philip's Mediterranean adventures and the demands made of his subjects stimulated both resentment and fiscal reform by exposing the inadequacy of existing arrangements, stimulating the process of Spanish state formation.[4]

War Expenditure

Spending had risen markedly during the succession struggle between 1700 and 1713 and continued to grow after the war (table 3).[5] When considering the broad evolution of expenditure and income we need to bear in mind price inflation, although this was on the whole less pronounced between 1713 and 1748 than before or after. In addition, these decennial averages mask some striking fluctuations. Spending peaked at 345 million in 1737 during the War of the Polish Succession (1733–35) and at around 375 million at the height of the War of the Austrian Succession (1741–48). Growth was fuelled by various costs, including those associated with a

TABLE 3. Average Annual Expenditure by Decade 1721–50[a]

Period	Average annual expenditure (vellón reales, current prices)
1714–20	230,742,501
1721–30	250,518,972
1731–40	294,002,178
1741–50	325,175,478

[a] Jurado Sánchez, *El gasto,* 48.

growing royal family, the royal households absorbing over 40 million reales annually circa 1740, about 20 percent of revenues; the building of the royal palace at San Ildefonso and of a new royal residence in Madrid after the destruction by fire in 1734 of the old *alcázar;* the royal *jornadas,* or seasonal removals from one palace to another; and the longer-term transfer of the court from Madrid to Extremadura and Seville between 1729 and 1733.[6]

Nonetheless, war and its instruments were the greatest charge on revenue. Between 1713 and 1716, the culmination of the succession struggle in Spain, the Secretariat for War absorbed an annual average of almost 180 million reales, little short of 80 percent of net revenues of almost 230 million, while the Junta de Medios, or committee of means (1737, below), calculated that expenditure on the army had totalled 13.7 million escudos before and 11.5 million after the army reform of 1715, and 12.8 million after that which followed the end of intervention in Italy and Africa between 1718 and 1720. The army and navy both required less funding in peacetime, the budget for 1724 assigning the secretary of war just 51 percent of total spending and the navy almost 7 percent. Thereafter, however, Philip's Mediterranean campaigns triggered sizeable hikes in spending, while actual expenditure invariably exceeded that budgeted, exacerbating the financial pressure: the years between 1717 and 1720, those between 1732 and 1735/37, and above all those between 1742 and 1748, when Spain was also at war in the Caribbean, saw the steepest increases in expenditure for the entire period.[7]

The cost of intervention in Sicily (1718–20) was put by the marqués de la Mina at 22 escudos, equivalent to an entire year's revenue. The Ceuta expedition, too, proved expensive. As for the Oran expedition, by the time the treasurer prepared his accounts in September 1732 he had received and spent 11,676,028 reales. Thereafter, Philip V may have spent 28 million escudos (or 280 million reales) establishing Don Carlos in Parma and Tuscany and on the thrones of Naples and Sicily. The expedition to Italy in 1733 may initially have cost over 7 1/2 million reales a month in 1734, that is, as much as 40 percent of Spain's annual budget, while at the end of 1735 Patiño claimed the Spanish court was remitting 600,000 piastres a month to Italy. By 1737 the Junta de Medios reported that the army had spent 20,849,126 and the fleet 5,100,000 of total spending of 21,100,758 escudos at a time when ordinary revenues amounted to just 34,595,296 escudos (table 4). It is not surprising, then, that in 1737 it was asserted the war in Italy had drained Spain of silver. But the War of the Austrian Succession proved even more expensive. In 1741, on the eve of Philip's intervention in Italy, Campillo, who had

TABLE 4. Sums Remitted to/Spent in Italy, 1741–49[a]

Period	Treasurer	Amount received (reales/maravedís)	Amount spent (reales/maravedís)
1/11/1741–31/7/1745	Pedro Gordillo, Treasurer of Army of Italy	178,023,006/29	178,023,006/29
1/4/1742–30/9/1746	Francisco de la Rea, Treasurer of Army of Infante	484,728,364/128	484,733,495/130
1/10/1746-30/9/1747	Pedro Gordillo, Treasurer of Army of Infante	91,668,425/9	91,671,297/11
1/10/1747–31/3/1749	Francisco Nuñez Ibáñez, Treasurer of Army of Infante	93,264,692/20	93,264,692/20

[a] "D. Pedro Gordillo . . . libro único de cargos y datos," AGS/TMC/4458; "Relación jurada y cuenta . . . D. Franc de la Rea" and "Relación jurada y cuenta . . . D. Pedro Gordillo . . .," AGS/TMC/4475; and "Relación jurada y cuenta . . . D. Franc Nunez Ibanez," AGS/TMC/4540. There is some overlap, one treasurer's receipts including sums recorded as spending by his predecessor.

served as intendant general with the Spanish forces there in the last conflict, calculated that the funding of an expeditionary force of 30,000 men, including artillery, hospital, and so on, required 470,000 escudos a month. In 1747, according to Ensenada, the war absorbed 60 million escudos annually, almost equivalent to three years' income.[8]

Spending on the army generally exceeded that on the navy, but the fleet was also costly. In 1717–18, when Philip launched his invasions of Sardinia and Sicily, naval expenditure was almost 41 million reales a year, compared with just under 15 million in 1713–17. Spending on the fleet declined thereafter but continued to absorb large sums during its rebuilding after 1720 and during the War of the Polish Succession. However, as was the case with the army, spending on the fleet peaked during the War of the Austrian Succession: whereas between 1727 and 1739 naval expenditure had amounted to just over 40 million reales annually, between 1739 and 1750 it totalled twice that, more than 80 million reales a year. Between 1742 and 1746 more than 80 percent of the increase in total expenditure on the previous five years was due to the growth of the navy budget. Simply making money available to the army or the fleet was no guarantee that either would achieve what was hoped of it, but it is no wonder the ministers were disappointed in 1748 at the poor showing of a navy which had been so generously funded (see chapter 2).[9]

It was not simply the cost of campaigning that Spain carried. Philip V was, initially at least, obliged to subsidise some of the reconquered overseas territories. The Spanish forces in Sardinia, for example, depended upon funding from Spain between 1717 and 1720 because the island itself was too poor to support them. Don Carlos's establishment in Italy between 1731 and 1734 also required financial assistance from the Spanish court. Patiño hoped that Carlos's acquisition of Naples and Sicily would end his need for help from Spain, but their initial conquest depended on Spanish funding, and the court of Madrid continued to aid Carlos thereafter.[10]

Besides maintaining his own forces Philip V resorted to another, traditional means to achieve his foreign policy objectives, namely, the payment of subsidies to allies in wartime. In 1725 Philip promised subsidies of 3 million florins a year to his new ally, Emperor Charles VI. Large sums were sent to Vienna between 1725 and 1728, including at least 4 million escudos in 1725, at least another 300,000 dollars in 1726, and an additional 3 million florins, or 24 million reales, in July 1728. This subsidy fuelled the ministerial struggle in Madrid, Patiño resenting the export of sums better spent, he thought, on naval reconstruction (see chapter 4).[11]

Philip V continued to accumulate obligations of this sort, subsidising both Louis XV of France and the elector of Bavaria during the War of the Polish Succession. Philip paid subsidies in the War of the Austrian Succession as well. The largest was that given to his son, the king of the Two Sicilies, which amounted to 50,000 escudos (or 500,000 reales) a month from July 1744, while the duke of Modena received 5,000 doblones (or 300,000 reales) a month from 1742. Other recipients or targets of Spanish money were the imperial electors. In 1741 an annual subsidy of 960,000 florins (or 7,680,000 reales) was promised to the elector of Bavaria, the future Emperor Charles VII, to enable him to raise 15,000 men who might be deployed in Italy in support of the Bourbons. In 1745 Philip was expected to help buy the backing of the elector of Cologne before the imperial election following Charles VII's death, and at French insistence paid a subsidy to Charles Edward Stuart, whose invasion of England might topple George II. In Italy Philip promised the republic of Genoa a monthly subsidy of 3,000 piastres (or 45,000 reales) from January 1746, although, as often happened with subsidies, each party felt the other was failing to fulfil its obligations. Following the brief Austrian occupation of Genoa in 1746, the Genoese again sought assistance. A regular subsidy was refused, but in 1747 a one-off payment of 200,000 escudos was agreed.[12] Philip V's pursuit of his Mediterranean goals, in short, was costly, especially in his last years. But how did he pay for these operations, and what were the implications for his subjects?

Ordinary Revenues

Philip V inherited a fiscal structure which had been elaborated in the preceding two centuries, taking final shape under Philip IV (1621–65). The process was overseen by the Council of Finance, headed by the one major innovation of his immediate predecessor, Charles II, the *superintendente general de la Real Hacienda*. Both council and superintendente survived the War of the Spanish Succession but were effectively eclipsed by the secretary of state for finance after 1714. The succession struggle had also prompted the transformation of the existing Tesorería Mayor into a war treasury at the expense of the older Tesorero General. The Tesorería Mayor continued to rival the Tesorero General, complicating efforts to calculate total income and outgoings, but was effectively abolished in 1726; thereafter all receipts were paid into the Tesorería General, and only the Tesorero General could authorise payments from them. A number of other fiscal agencies persisted, inside and outside Castile. The galleys continued to be funded from the Cruzada revenues administered by the council of that name, expenditure on the galleys being recovered from the administrators of the Cruzada, while the foral territories (see chapter 5) retained their own treasuries. Nevertheless, financial administration was more tightly controlled from the centre after 1713, a control which intensified with Campillo's reinforcement of the roles of the secretary of state and the treasurer general in 1743 during the War of the Austrian Succession.[13]

Philip V inherited a complex revenue structure. The royal revenues in 1700 comprised the *rentas provinciales*, paid only by the twenty-one provinces of Castile, that is, by the territories within the jurisdiction of each of the towns with a vote in the Castilian Cortes, and the *rentas generales*, which extended beyond Castile and included the customs and monopolies, such as that of tobacco, established in 1636. These revenues were further broken down into (1) the so-called *regalias*, impositions which belonged to the crown by right and included the customs, the *alcabala*, or sales tax, the *media anata*, or the obligation on newly appointed officeholders to advance half of their first year's salary to the crown, and the stamp duty on paper; (2) *servicios*, or grants, voted by the Cortes, above all, the so-called *millones*, or millions raised from impositions upon essential consumer goods; (3) the *gracias apostólicas*, or ecclesiastical levies, that is, the *cruzada*, *subsidio*, and *excusado*, which depended upon periodic papal grant and which gave Philip a financial incentive for a forward policy in Africa, as the struggle against Islam justified appeals for donations from the church; and (4) the revenues derived from the Indies. These were the core of Philip's ordinary revenues, although the remarkable near doubling in royal revenue during the War of the Spanish Succession, to an annual average of about 230 million reales circa 1713, was due mostly to the exploitation of various extraordinary impositions, none of them entirely new. In 1713 the then superintendente of the finances, the Fleming count Bergeyck, sought to simplify the tax system, but his initiative was opposed by most of Castile's Cortes voting towns and by the tax farmers whose advances were crucial to the royal finances (below) and ultimately failed. This meant that the system remained much as it was in 1700, apart from one major innovation. Following the so-called reconquest of the Crown of Aragon from 1707 onwards, far more was extracted from the territories of that realm than before 1700 (see below). Thus, despite the failure of some other of the more radical reforms implemented during the succession struggle, the finances of the Spanish crown were in better shape in 1713 than in 1700.[14]

It was by making the most of this structure that Philip V sought to keep abreast of rising expenditure after 1713. Both the *rentas reales* and what the king received from all other sources increased markedly: the former more than doubled from just over 100 million reales to little more than 236 million between 1713 and 1742, while the latter more than trebled from just over 114 million in 1711–13 to just under 370 million in 1744–47. A snapshot of those revenues in 1725, totalling 19,881,540 escudos, is provided by the imperial ambassador in Madrid, and another in 1737 by the British minister in Madrid, the latter no doubt originating in the Junta de Medios of that year (below). According to the latter, the king's ordinary revenues, that is, those which, with some fluctuation, he received year on year, amounted to 226,855,672 reales. This was little different from the total at the end of the War of the Spanish Succession, although some items were in fact missing from the list, including the ecclesiastical revenues and those derived from the Crown of Aragon (below). The Castilian rentas provinciales remained the largest contributor, yielding 39,270,930 reales, or 69,159,145 including the millones. Next in importance were the rentas generales, at 33,511,993 reales, the largest single items being the customs (23,764,799 reales) and the wool revenues (6,764,706 reales). Various revenues which were not farmed and which included the tobacco monopoly (49 million reales) and what was received from the Indies (40 million reales) yielded an annual average of 97,430,641 reales. Geographically, Andalusia—above all, Seville and Granada—gave the most. Deducting the annual interest on loans, which amounted to just over 17 million reales, or almost 8 percent of the total, left a net income of 209,671,221 reales. Another source, one probably also derived from the junta, states that the gap that year between revenues (excluding those from the Indies), just over 21 million escudos, and expenditure, just over 34 1/2 million reales, was almost 13 1/2 million reales.[15]

There were various ways in which the ordinary revenues could be maximised, the effectiveness of collection of existing taxes possibly offsetting the need to impose new ones. Administrative changes intended to improve collection and yields included the establishment of a network of provincial intendants, in 1718 against the background of war in Sardinia and Sicily, the first step in a more ambitious shake-up of management of the finances. However, the experiment proved short-lived, the victim of a combined assault by various interested groups and institutions, against whom, particularly following the end of the cycle of intervention in Italy and Africa between 1717 and 1720, king and ministers were not inclined to press the case for the new network (see chapter 4). Some decades later, in 1743, during the War of the Austrian Succession, receipts in Castile were ordered to be paid directly to the treasurers of the army in an attempt to speed up the passage of funds to the latter. But more radical reform aimed at increasing revenues could provoke resentment. An attempt was made during the War of the Austrian Succession to end the practice of compounding, or *encabezamiento*, whereby communities negotiated with the treasury to compound for some of their tax obligations (that is, the rentas provinciales), which generally meant a reduction of the burden. Furthermore, the reform insisted on payment of the full amount of tax, thus increasing the total yield. The two changes triggered rioting in at least one community in the province or realm of Granada in 1746, at the height of the War of the Austrian Succession.[16]

But, as in the past, policy makers swung between two basic options: whether the crown should administer the revenues directly, using its own paid employees, or *administración*, or whether it should contract out, that is, privatise, collection to tax farmers, who, in accordance with their contract, or *asiento*, would pay an advance, absorb the costs of collection, and keep any profit. Philip inherited a structure in which farms were the norm, and in 1713–14 his ministers preferred to improve rather than undermine the system of tax farming. They did so by consolidating farms in the hands of a small number of individual financiers or companies, which farmed as a single block (although they might themselves subfarm) all of the revenues of individual provinces which had hitherto been farmed to a plethora of individuals and companies. The plan met with some success: by 1722 there were just fifteen or sixteen farmers for the farmed revenues of the twenty-one Castilian provinces.[17]

Intervention in the War of the Austrian Succession stimulated a marked shift away from farming towards administración. This might suggest that the reigns of Philip V and Ferdinand VI witnessed a fundamental, long-term transition from one system to the other. Certainly there were earlier moves towards collection by royal officials. Thus, in 1731 the tobacco monopoly, which hitherto had been partly privatised, was taken into full administration, its yield increasing markedly during the War of the Polish Succession and reaching new heights in the War of the Austrian Succession, due in part simply to charging the consumer more. The tobacco revenues rose from 70 to 74 million in 1745. Nevertheless, reflecting the great increase in other, extraordinary revenues in that conflict, they fell as a proportion of the total from 33 percent in 1740 to 25 percent in 1745. The later conflict also saw the taking into administration from 1742 onwards of the rentas provinciales in a number of provinces, Seville, La Mancha, Toledo, Palencia, and Córdoba, where the farm found no takers. Yields rose markedly after that, with the result that from the end of 1749 all farms of those revenues were ended in favour of administración. In some respects this signalled the triumph of a growing body of opinion hostile to tax farming, an attitude shared by Patiño and Campillo.[18]

It would be wrong, however, to hold that there was a ministerial or royal blueprint for radical change or even consistent, linear progress in one direction. Some revenues were already in administration at the start of this period, not least because the economic disruption caused by the succession struggle made some farms less attractive. In addition, the rentas provinciales of the great majority of Castile's provinces continued to be farmed between 1741 and 1749, the increase in yield under administration thereafter being very marginal in some provinces. More important, however, monarchs and ministers switched from one to the other method on the basis often of short-term financial needs and anticipated yields. Where revenues continued to attract farmers, what they produced could be increased simply by seeking higher bids. During the War of the Polish Succession, for example, ministers were able to increase the yield of the farm of the wool tax, which had been in administration between 1716 and 1731 (and would be again from 1749) and was one of the most lucrative of the rentas generales in 1737 (above): from almost 5.4 million reales a year between 1731 and 1736, the revenues derived from it rose to almost 8.4 million annually between 1736 and 1741.[19]

Farming had advantages for monarch and ministers. Among the attractions was the initial advance, especially in wartime. In 1733, for instance, in order to fund preparations for the expedition to Italy that year, Patiño sought advances from the tax farmers among a variety of expedients. The management of the customs revenues was similarly dictated by war and its needs. The customs had been in administration from 1714 to 1733, but at the end of 1733 the financier Ambrosio María Andriani agreed to farm them for six years, from 1734 to 1739, promising the king almost 900 million maravedís (almost 26.5 million reales) a year and a substantial advance. Indeed, according to the Savoyard representative in Madrid, a planned increase in Philip V's army of up to 40,000 men would be in part funded by 1,200,000 piastres advanced by the farmer general of the customs. In 1740, after the outbreak of war with Britain, king and ministers again sought to exploit to the full the system of farming, offering to extend existing farms in return for substantial advances, that is, loans. Subsequently, too, in the summer of 1745, needing money for the war in Italy, Philip decided to again farm revenues which had been in administration in recent years, attracted by the prospect of an advance; but for want of takers most of these revenues remained in administration.[20]

However administered, revenues had to be protected against fraud. This was a battle fought on many fronts, as it was under Philip V's Habsburg predecessors. In August 1717, soon after the invasion of Sardinia, the abortive suppression of internal customs barriers between Castile and Vizcaya and Navarra was justified by the need to prevent fraud. The fact that the immense growth of the tobacco revenues (above) owed so much to increasing customer prices inevitably stimulated a contraband trade, which also had to be eradicated. Those who engaged in illegal activity of this sort were many, including soldiers, necessitating occasional reminders that the *fuero militar* (see chapter 1) did not protect those caught smuggling tobacco. Offenders included foreign subjects, who took advantage of the privileges enshrined in successive treaties. In 1737, in the closing stages of the War of the Polish Succession, the zeal of the officials of the tobacco revenues at Barcelona in inspecting foreign vessels prompted protests from the British, Dutch, and French ministers, who claimed these searches breached those privileges. Other revenues, too, needed to be protected, including the stamped-paper duty. In 1744, at the height of the War of the Austrian Succession, a royal order laid down the dimensions of paper which must be used in an attempt to combat evasion of that imposition by those using larger sheets. As for the customs revenues, the foundation of privileged trading companies similar to those in Britain, France, and the Dutch republic—a subject provoking much debate in Spain, where hitherto a very different form of monopoly had been the preferred means of exploiting the wealth of the Indies— was proposed during the War of the Austrian Succession, in part as a means of combatting fraud.[21]

Philip V, as noted, enjoyed substantial ordinary revenues of recent origin, those imposed in the Crown of Aragon. In Aragon proper the new *contribución* varied between 8 1/2 and 12 1/2 million reales to 1715, when it was reduced to 8 (1716) and 5 million (1718), but after further fluctuations it stood at just over 8 1/2 million reales again in 1741.[22] In Valencia, 1715 saw the imposition there of the *equivalente,* or the equivalent of the Castilian rentas provinciales. It was originally set at 1,590,000 escudos (or 15,900,000 reales), but it was soon evident that this was too ambitious and it was reduced later that year by more than one-third to 10 million reales and in 1718 to 7,750,000 reales, at which level it remained. Other impositions, however, became linked to it, so that the total take from the realm was higher, and in the War of the Polish Succession and that of the Austrian Succession the total was raised to 8.8 million reales a year. More was secured as well from Majorca starting in 1715. Finally, the *catastro* was imposed in Catalonia from 1716. Originally set at 11/2 million pesos a year, this also proved too much and was reduced to 1,200,000 pesos (1717) and then to 900,000 (from 1718), although this, too, was supplemented by additional levies totalling another 1,100,000 pesos a year. The catastro soon became an integral part of royal finances in

Catalonia, a resource to be drawn on by those organising the many Mediterranean expeditions launched from there. In 1737 the intendant of Barcelona promised to pay two-thirds of what was owed for transports to and from Italy out of the catastro. The imposition of the new levy was not without its difficulties, triggering a clash with Rome over whether the Catalan clergy should pay. This dispute was finally settled in Philip's favour in 1732, against the background of the Oran expedition, and reaffirmed in the Concordat of 1737, which restricted clerical tax exemptions. These various impositions in the Crown of Aragon added up to over 26 million reales, or 15 percent of budgeted revenues in 1722. They stagnated thereafter, but from the monarch's point of view this was still a great improvement upon the situation before 1707. It was also in sharp contrast with neighbouring Castile, where, despite the spiralling cost of Philip V's revanchism after 1713, there was no new royal taxation. This was a matter largely of political choice; Philip and his ministers preferred instead to exploit various extraordinary revenue-raising devices which did not look like taxation and did not require formal consent by the Cortes (below). This preference for extraordinary devices did not mean that Philip's Castilian subjects were spared, but they were saved from worse by the existence of other revenue streams, including those from across the Atlantic.

The Indies

The wealth of the Indies had long been the most distinctive resource of the Spanish monarchy before 1700 and continued so thereafter. The American revenues, consisting of the king's share of the precious metals mined in the Indies, the yield of taxes on trade, and that of the ecclesiastical levies, were both an ordinary and an extraordinary source of revenue. They were not included in the budget of 1724, but in 1737 were put at 40 million reales a year on average, almost 20 percent of the total (above). Spain's aspirations and achievement in Europe continued to depend upon remittances from the Americas because of their volume, because they were unencumbered, and because of the timing of their arrival. The king and his ministers fully recognised the value of the Indies.[23]

Philip V was the beneficiary of a long-term recovery in the output of the silver mines of Spanish America dating from before 1700. The growth was particularly marked in New Spain (Mexico) where production had picked up around 1670 and by 1700 exceeded that of Peru, hitherto the largest producer and itself recovering from the seventeenth-century downturn. Soon thereafter the combined output of Mexico and Peru was greater than that of Potosí (Peru) at its peak around 1600 and production continued to grow. Gold production also boomed. Not all of the bullion of the Indies reached Philip, substantial sums being spent locally on the defence of the Caribbean, not least during the War of the Austrian Succession. During that struggle Admiral George Anson captured the so-called Manila galleon with its cargo of treasure. In addition, widespread fraud and the asiento—the slave supply contract—and permission ship granted to the English at the end of the War of the Spanish Succession undermined the monopoly system of the Habsburgs, embodied in the system of regular convoys passing between Spain and America, the *flota* and the *galeones*. The frequency of those convoys had declined before 1700 and suffered even more in the succession conflict. From then on, however, royal and ministerial awareness of the importance of their American revenues underpinned both vigorous antifraud measures and efforts to revive the regular convoys by means of Patiño's Royal Project of 1720. The reinvigorating of that system also meant, however, the resurrecting of a situation in which some foreign merchants enjoyed substantial treaty-based privileges and a right to participate in the trade. The restoration of a system massively penetrated by those who were not Philip V's subjects was thus part of the price paid for the failure of his first abortive attempts to recover Spanish Italy between 1717 and 1720. In fact, Patiño's project was not entirely successful: the galeones sailed only four times after 1720 before being suppressed, while the flota sailed only six times before being suspended.[24]

Whether aboard flotas, galeones, *azogues*—a small detachment, usually of just two ships, that carried mercury to the Indies for the mines—or the growing number of so-called register ships, which were licenced from 1739 onwards to cross the Atlantic and which were more lucrative to the crown than the big convoys, large sums were still remitted to Spain from the Indies. They reached new heights in the later 1740s, partly in response to Ensenada's efforts to increase remittances during the War of the Austrian Succession, when treasure from the Indies found ways to evade the British fleet. In December 1744 Admiral Rodrigo de Torres y Morales put into La Coruña with a reported 15 million piastres; in January 1746 D. José Pizarro reached Galicia from Buenos Aires with 1 million pesos; the summer of 1746 saw the arrival of treasure put at 15 million dollars, most of it for the king; and in the spring of 1747 a single vessel reached the Canaries carrying about 2 million pesos.[25]

Much of the bullion belonged to private owners rather than to the king, but Philip still benefitted. Increasingly significant in the later seventeenth century had been the fines, or *indultos*, imposed on the merchants trading to the Indies for supposed infractions of the regulation. These, along with simple seizures, allowed the crown to mine that part of the Indies trade which was in private hands. Philip V, too, seized private cargoes and levied indultos from time to time. In the summer of 1718, against the background of the invasion of Sicily, Patiño seized 800,000 pesos belonging to French merchants, while indultos were imposed in 1726–27, in the winter of 1727–28, and in the summer of 1729 on the galleons which had returned six months before. On the last occasion the Spanish court had delayed a settlement in order to put pressure on the French and other courts to fall into line regarding its ambitions in Italy. The War of the Polish Succession prompted greater demands of this sort. In the spring of 1734 an indulto of 18 percent was imposed on a recently arrived vessel. Some years later, in the autumn of 1737, after the arrival of the flota and azogues—bringing 14–15 millions in gold and silver, about 2 million in goods, and about 4 million unregistered piastres, of which the king's share would be 3–4 millions—ministers imposed an initial indulto of 20 percent before settling for 16 percent in "hard dollars" (pesos fuertes) or 20 percent in "small" ones. Duties and indultos increased the royal share of the total remitted from the Indies, as contemporaries recognised.[26]

Other means of tapping that trade included gifts, or *donativos*, and loans, forced or otherwise. In August 1731 the Indies trade offered a donativo of 1 million pesos if Philip V would allow the delivery of the effects aboard the flota to their owners. In the summer of 1733 the crown borrowed from the merchants of Cádiz in order to complete the preparation of the ships which were to participate in the imminent expedition to Italy. Those merchants gave 100,000 pesos that year, and in 1734 another 80,000 pesos by way of a donativo. In 1737, a difficult year for the royal finances, a donativo which was said to have been offered by the Consulado of Seville, the corporation of Seville merchant houses which effectively monopolised the Indies trade, was apparently rejected as inadequate, resulting in an investigation and the imposition of a heavy fine for fraud. Patiño indulged the merchants engaged in the Indies trade to ensure their financial cooperation. But this cosy relationship broke down in 1737, in part because government asked for too big a donativo, effectively preventing the trade from profiting from the recent revaluation (above). Ministers retaliated with an investigation of the trade, which revealed massive fraud and resulted in the imposition of a heavy fine. A few years later, at the end of 1741, it was said that the naval intendant at Cádiz had orders to use threats, if necessary, to ensure that the trade gave the 600,000 scudi needed to complete the preparations which would enable the squadron then being prepared for Italy to sail. Between 1745 and 1746, the peak years of the Spanish effort in the War of the Austrian Succession, those shipping to the Indies, the *cargadores*, gave another 340,000 pesos in donativos. Philip also raised loans from the trade, including 1,400,000 pesos in 1740–41, Ensenada later also securing funds in this way. However it was done, Philip tapped the resources of the New World to achieve his objectives in the Old.[27]

Contemporaries and later historians have tended to quantify the value of American silver, in both Habsburg and Bourbon Spain, in terms of five-yearly contributions. Contemporaries, too, often calculated annual averages (above). In fact, however, yield varied from year to year, sometimes markedly so. The use of averages is therefore seriously misleading because it obscures an invaluable feature of those revenues, namely, that they sometimes arrived just in time to fund a major overseas expedition, considerably easing short-term cash flow. Thus June 1732 saw the timely arrival of ships of the galeones fleet, in view of the ongoing Oran expedition. In the autumn of 1733, Patiño was said to be impatient for the arrival of the Indies fleet because he would then have at his disposal 2 million piastres for the imminent expedition to Italy. Likewise, in the spring of 1734, Patiño was delighted at the arrival at Cádiz of a vessel carrying about 4 million piastres, including about 1 million for Philip V, which would be useful in preparing a convoy for Italy. Later that same year four warships and one merchant ship entered Cádiz with money salvaged from the flota, which had gone down off Florida. As soon as Patiño learned this news he ordered the remittance to Naples of 2,400 escudos in the form either of coin or of bars which could be minted locally. In early 1735 nearly 4 million reales recently received from the Indies were remitted to the army in Italy. Thus remittances from the Indies on the one hand reflected varying demand—from Spain, for funds for war— and on the other hand were a crucial wartime windfall. Remittances from Mexico to Spain between 1720 and 1748 exceeded 1 million silver pesos in 1720, 1726, 1728, 1732, 1733, 1735, 1737, 1744—the highest amount throughout the period—and 1746. But the war-driven demands of the Spanish court could provoke unease in the Americas, as did the tightening of the fiscal screw there after 1726.[28]

Philip V did, as we have seen, have other revenues and did not depend solely on the Indies. In 1726 the secretary of state for foreign affairs, the marqués de la Paz, implied as much when he told the British minister William Stanhope that Philip would fulfil his subsidy obligations to the emperor even if there were no flota or galeones. Nevertheless, contemporaries rightly attached considerable weight to Spain's American revenues. The previous year Stanhope had cast doubt on Spanish assurances of a wish for peace, hinting that these were merely intended to discourage any attempt to intercept the returning flota and galeones, without whose cargo, he thought, Philip could not wage war; he even suggested a preemptive strike against them to prevent war. Stanhope was right to be suspicious: although irregular, the revenues of the Indies were vital to Spain. Many ministers and others, including Campillo, believed that the Indies could and should yield more to the crown; but lacking the wealth that Spanish America already supplied, Philip's Spain could not have enjoyed the success it did between 1713 and 1748. Not surprisingly, the king and his ministers appreciated the efforts of those who safeguarded those resources in wartime. Torres y Morales, who brought home the treasure fleet in December 1744, (above) was given a hereditary noble title and appointment to the Council of the Indies. For the same reason, king and ministers remained determined to limit foreign access to the Indies. The access permitted Charles VI's Ostend Company as part of the diplomatic revolution of 1725 was a striking, if temporary, deviation from this policy and singular evidence of the extent to which the Spanish court was prepared to make concessions in the Atlantic sphere to achieve its objectives in the Mediterranean.[29]

Extraordinary Measures

As was the War of the Spanish Succession, Philip V's Mediterranean adventures after 1713 were funded partially by a variety of extraordinary measures. Indeed, as in that earlier conflict, these were a more fruitful source of additional funds than his ordinary revenues. War itself brought opportunities. These included, outside Spain, the exploitation of occupied territories, for example, the duchy of Savoy during the War of the Austrian Succession. The Spanish occupation of Savoy between 1743 and 1748 was accompanied by at least a doubling of its peacetime tax burden of about 21/2 million livres. Commodities found in captured Savoyard fortresses were sold, while Ensenada, anticipating his later efforts to reform the royal finances in Spain itself, hoped to consolidate the duchy's taxes into a single imposition. Other revenues derived from war included confiscation of the goods of those supporting Philip's enemies: in 1734, during the War of the Polish Succession, he embargoed the property and revenues of those who in his dominions backed the emperor. Another well-tried extraordinary wartime expedient which targeted his own subjects was the minting of private silver, which Philip ordered in the autumn of 1717.[30]

Identifying extraordinary sources of revenue in wartime was a major challenge, one met by various ad hoc bodies. Among these was the traditional resort to a Junta de Medios, like that appointed in April 1737 in the wake of Spain's participation in the War of the Polish Succession, the king explicitly referring to the cost of the war when establishing the body. Among the junta's members were the secretary of state for finance, the secretary of state for war, the head of the biggest-spending department, and the governor of the Council of Castile, as representative and protector of the king's subjects. The junta was to examine the royal finances, eradicate abuses and waste, and find new funds. The junta, which reported in

July 1737 and clearly did far more than simply identify extraordinary sources of revenues—the memorial it presented to the king on that occasion represented a broad survey of the fiscal history of Spain since Philip's accession—was replaced in early 1740 by a Junta de Hacienda, whose members included the governor of the Council of Castile. One of the tasks of the Junta de Hacienda was to find money for the expedition being prepared for Italy, which it did by recommending the various extraordinary revenue-raising measures of that year. In 1741 the council itself proposed various expedients as an alternative to the 10 percent levy of that year (below).[31]

Other expedients were identified by individuals, in a manner reminiscent of the seventeenth-century *arbitristas*, who outlined solutions, *arbitrios*, to contemporary economic, social and political problems. One person who offered a wide-ranging assessment of Spain's ills was Francisco Máximo de Moya Torres y Velasco, in his *Manifiesto universal de los males envejecidos que España padece* (Universal manifesto of the long-standing ills that Spain suffers) (1729). Another who offered advice was D. Miguel de Zavala of the Superintendencia General de la Pagaduría General de Juros y Mercedes, the office responsible for the payment on *juros* (below); his *Representación al rey nuestro señor Felipe V dirigida al más seguro aumento del Real Erario y conseguir la felicidad y mayor alivio y riqueza de su monarquía* (Representation to King Philip V on the most effective way to increase royal revenue and to secure the happiness, relief, and wealth of his monarchy) (Madrid, 1732) sought to identify means to increase revenues without placing a greater burden on the king's subjects and urged, as so many did, simplification of the tax system. Many of the exceptional devices posed by individuals and committees were justified in very traditional terms, that is, the unusual wartime needs of the state. In 1741, for example, the Council of Castile justified various measures, one of them being the appropriation of one-third of all alienated royal revenues (below), by arguing that all crown revenues were intended for the defence of the state and could not be exempted in a public urgency. War was unmistakably in this category.[32]

Established expedients included the sale of office, which had been practised by the Habsburgs and by Philip V himself during the War of the Spanish Succession. From early on, army commissions were effectively sold (see chapter 1). Civilian offices, too, were purchasable, in the central administration and in the municipalities. The opportunities for sale of councillorships in the Castilian towns were limited by the fact that so many of these had been sold long before 1700, but in 1738 the practice was extended to the Crown of Aragon. Venality was not limited to Spain: it was practiced in the Indies as well. Between 1700 and 1745 the crown sold eighteen appointments to the Lima tribunal of accounts and nine to the central treasury office there. Not only offices could be purchased but also noble status and titles, as before 1700. Like his Habsburg predecessors, Philip additionally sold independent town status to subordinate communities resentful of the authority, and abuse of it, of a powerful neighbouring town: the beneficiary usually "served" the king with a payment calculated according to the number of its households. The king might alienate, or sell, too, crown revenues: in Valencia in 1725, in the escalating cold war following the treaty of Vienna, various royal revenues were disposed of, raising 2 million ducats.[33]

Perhaps indicating a new conception of the state associated with the new dynasty, sales of jurisdiction were actually fewer than before 1700. Indeed, Philip V also resumed, or reincorporated, into the crown revenues which had been alienated by previous monarchs. As is the case with so many of the expedients of Philip's wars, this was not new. During the War of the Spanish Succession Philip had established the Junta de Incorporaciones to implement resumption. The junta did not long survive the end of the succession struggle, being suppressed in 1718, when its functions passed to the Council of Finance. But Philip continued to exploit this means, for example, in 1732, in the wake of the Oran expedition, when he ordered the resumption of alienated alcabala revenues, and during the War of the Austrian Succession, when recovery became the responsibility of a specific minister. While resumption was formal policy, the real concern was to generate funds, such that those whose titles were called into question were invariably allowed to compound and thus secure confirmation of their possession of those alienated revenues.[34]

Another traditional means of maximising ordinary revenues was to press the payment of tax arrears of all sorts. Arrears were an inevitable feature and consequence of the fiscal systems of most states in early modern Europe, adding to the difficulties of calculating revenues. But they presented an opportunity or resource to be tapped in times of difficulty, an easy and early target. Orders to this effect were issued in 1718, 1720, 1728, when a Junta de Quiebras (defaults or bankruptcies) was established to pursue arrears, 1734, 1737, when the Junta de Medios urge the recovery of arrears totalling more than 31 million reales), 1740, and 1741. Just how successful this policy was and how much it brought in, above all in cash rather than the surrender of credits owed by the crown, are not clear, but it did yield some revenues. In 1746 the city of Granada used money raised in excess of what it owed for the equivalent of the 10 percent levy to pay arrears due on a different charge, the *contribución de paja*, the sum paid (since 1736) to provide straw for cavalry quartered there, put at a total of 600,000 reales in 1741–42.[35]

Philip V, as noted, ordinarily refrained from introducing new general taxes, preferring instead to exploit impositions which consumers paid more or less voluntarily, such as that on tobacco. But he effectively devolved some of his military costs onto local communities, in effect charging the vassals he was supposedly reluctant to burden. Many communities responded by imposing new local taxes, or *arbitrios*, as the city of Murcia did in 1732, to fund additional military costs. Some diverted the yield of existing taxes of this sort, originally authorised by the monarch to fund local projects or needs, to military ends. In 1720, for instance, Philip effectively imposed a donativo to pay for quarters for troops, the *reino* of Murcia being assigned a quota of 150,000 reales, of which the city of Murcia must pay 36,400 reales. Having made representations regarding its inability to pay, the city was allowed to fulfil its quota over three years and to appropriate to this end the proceeds of a recently granted arbitrio. On some occasions the king simply imposed this: in 1733, when ordering the seizure of vagabonds and others for the army, Philip ruled that their maintenance should be funded out of the profits of justice or, where these were insufficient, out of arbitrios and other funds. The imposition of new or the diversion of existing arbitrios required a royal licence, or *facultad*, but this was always granted.[36]

Perhaps the most arresting illustration of this practice followed the order for the creation of militia regiments in the War of the Polish Succession. From 1734 onwards many local communities, in order to fulfil the obligation imposed upon them by the king to clothe the new units at their own cost, obtained facultades for various money-raising expedients. Typically, the authorities, or *regidores*, of Burgos requested a facultad to enable the city to pay for 150 uniforms for its militia quota, while those of Murcia were allowed to apply an existing arbitrio of one real on an arroba of wine for one year to fund their obligation. Philip also granted various arbitrios to the reino of Galicia to facilitate the purchase of uniforms for its militia contingent. Where a community had no arbitrios or *propios*, the property owned by a municipality that it usually leased to raise funds, the king might order a *repartimiento*, that is, the sharing of the community's quota among all households, which in some cases meant breaching the fiscal exemptions of the privileged. Off-loading the fiscal burden in this way was by no means new, but Philip's resort to it was one indicator of the extent to which his wars and Spain's international recovery after 1713 weighed on his subjects.[37]

The needs of war prompted Philip V to go further, to seek to appropriate more directly the yield of these local taxes. In April 1739 the king imposed a levy of 4 percent on arbitrios, a percentage which was dramatically increased to 50 percent from 1741. This measure, which was imposed in both Castile and Aragon and continued until December 1749, yielded more than 75 million reales between 1741 and 1747, equivalent to one-third of the crown's annual ordinary revenues; the province of Valladolid alone yielded more than 1,200,000 reales between 1741 and 1747, virtually all of it paid by the provincial capital.[38]

Local communities were the victims as well of what was possibly the most contentious expedient of the reign, adopted towards the end of the War of the Polish Succession: the selling off of so-called *baldíos*, or *tierras baldías*, common lands or wastelands previously belonging to the crown, and of other usurped crown lands, or *tierras realengas*. Once again, this device was not entirely new, having been used by Philip II and Philip IV and by Philip V himself in the succession struggle. In 1735 the governor of the Council of Castile proposed that the king recover usurped commons and crown lands. A pilot scheme was implemented in the marquisate of Estepa, in which an official identified usurped crown land which was then resumed or sold off or both. According to the magistrate who oversaw the implementation of the scheme in the province or realm of Seville between 1735 and 1738, it raised just over 1 million reales in

Estepa. In October 1738 the policy was extended throughout Castile, supervised by a special Junta de Baldíos until 1741, when it was abolished and oversight passed to the Council of Castile, a superintendent being appointed in 1742.[39]

The policy involved legal challenges to landowners of all types, and, one of those involved in it said it produced almost 24 million reales, some of which was diverted to the rebuilding of the royal palace in Madrid, some to pensions to courtiers, and some to the war in Italy: in the summer of 1745 Philip V agreed to supply the army in Italy with 120,000 reales obtained from the baldíos and from the levy on arbitrios. The policy was very unpopular and contentious, however, the Cortes having made it a condition of its grant of the millones in 1650 that no more licences should be granted to encroach on commons, and in 1747 Ferdinand VI halted it (see chapter 5). While it was in operation the policy benefitted local elites and some religious corporations at the expense of communities. Some leading noble families which had taken advantage of the difficulties of the crown in the previous century to extend their property at the expense of the commons were also pursued. Yet its impact should not be overstated, as great tracts were still possessed by local councils and others only to be disposed of in the great *desamortización,* or expropriation and often the sale of entailed land and other property, of the following century.[40]

Philip V also sold off other property, most notably the extensive sheep pastures known as the Dehesa de la Serena, in Extremadura. The decision to sell was made in 1744, in the middle of the War of the Austrian Succession, while 50 percent of all sales/yield transacted between 1745 and 1786 were concluded between 1745 and 1749. Not entirely surprisingly, the sell-off benefitted most the greatest, largest, wealthiest flock owners, including a number of ecclesiastical proprietors, the monks of the Escorial among them. But the greatest beneficiaries comprised a group of financiers and farmers closely connected to the court. The gains of these groups came at the expense of small local sheep owners and triggered a spate of litigation in which those who lost out sought to defend their pasture rights.[41]

On the whole this period was not as inventive and fruitful in terms of new taxation as that of the War of the Spanish Succession (above). But a radically new attempt to tap the wealth of Philip V's subjects by means of a 10 percent imposition on incomes was decreed throughout the country, including the Aragonese territories, in December 1740, although the outcome revealed the extent to which royal authority, absolutism, was negotiated. The measure was justified to Philip's subjects by the need to counter British aggression and by the lack of any alternative means of raising the necessary funds. The levy was intended to raise 65,974,317 reales, 17 million of which was to come from Andalusia—Granada, for example, contributing 51/2 million—and the Crown of Aragon 15 million—Catalonia contributing just over 8 million. However justifiable, the measure attracted widespread criticism from, among others, the Council of Castile, which was in some respects the voice of the Castilian urban elites and which proposed alternative sources of funds. In fact, the levy as originally conceived was unworkable without the cooperation of the elites, in view of the lack of information on individual wealth and of officials to enforce payment. Campillo therefore transformed the imposition into something more familiar, provincial quotas. These were determined in accordance with the ordinary tax burden of each province and could be raised as those communities thought fit. Astorga in León, Valladolid, and Murcia were among the Castilian communities which opted to meet their obligations by raising new loans, to be paid off by an additional or new arbitrio, one often levied on wine. Burgos was allowed to apply revenues from existing arbitrios originally imposed to pay off earlier *censos,* or loans, taken out by the town. In Granada the new quota, or equivalent, just over 2 million reales for the province or realm, including just 1 million for the city, was raised by additional impositions on a wide range of activities and items.[42]

Although quotas were payable in two tranches by the end of December 1741, the entire sum was often not paid for some years after. The arrearage helps explain why this innovative effort to tap the wealth of all the king's subjects was not renewed, unlike many of the other extraordinary measures of 1741. A radical fiscal device born of wartime needs had been transformed into another, more familiar expedient, one which was far from imposing a uniform 10 percent on incomes because, paradoxically, of those same needs and the resistance of the Castilian municipal elites. The crown's urgent want of money for war obliged it to compromise with those elites. They did not contest the king's right in an emergency, war, to make extraordinary demands, but the price of their cooperation was an imposition which was more palatable. While the king and his ministers might intervene to speed agreement and payment thereafter[43] they could not be too heavy-handed.[44]

Most of Philip V's expedients echoed those of his Habsburg predecessors. This was certainly true of the practice of appropriation, or *valimiento*, of a variety of funds, including the yield of local arbitrios, and that of *descuento*, or discounting, of all sorts of grants, including pensions paid by the crown. The Junta de Medios of 1737 identified a great many payments of all sorts that might be cut and acted as a court of appeal for those requesting payments of arrears of pensions, salaries, and wages. The Spanish Habsburgs, too, had used extensively the so-called free gift or donativo (above), which became very difficult for those invited to refuse to pay. Philip himself resorted to such gifts during and immediately after the War of the Spanish Succession and again in 1719, when the town of Medina de Rioseco was asked for just over 18,000 reales. On that same occasion, typically, Burgos sought to meet its quota by securing a facultad to divert some of the yield of its arbitrios. However, what was a very fruitful new income source in the seventeenth century does not appear to have been exploited by the first Bourbon after 1720, perhaps because of its too great frequency and disappointing yield in the succession struggle.[45]

Philip V inherited an extraordinary surcharge on salt, which he increased to 13 reales a *fanega*, taking the price in Andalusia and New Castile, for example, to 36 reales a fanega, at which level the additional duty remained until its abolition in 1724; it was reintroduced in 1741, in wartime, again at 13 reales. There were some other new wartime impositions, including a surcharge of 2 reales on each arroba of exported wool, which was levied in 1719, in 1741, and at the end of 1743. These were not the only expedients to which the king and his ministers resorted. Among others, by no means limited to the war years, was that allowing subjects whose properties in Madrid were subject to the *aposento*, that is, the duty of the inhabitants of the capital to lodge royal officials, a burden which had been commuted into a cash payment, to purchase release from the obligation, as proposed in 1733 and by the Junta de Medios in 1737.[46]

The vast majority of Philip's revenues derived from Castile and Aragon, but he also obtained funds from what were the only remaining foral territories, ones not jurisdictionally part of Castile, Navarre, and Vizcaya. During the War of the Austrian Succession, the Cortes of Navarre granted an unusually high servicio of 1,600,000 reales in 1743–44, most of which was remitted to the army in Italy. For its part, during that same conflict Vizcaya gave two donativos, in 1744 and 1747, both of 240,000 reales. But these were irregular and relatively small sums, not comparable with what was now received from the Aragonese territories.[47]

Philip V's Mediterranean adventures were funded in addition by special levies on the clergy: in 1717; in 1721, when the pope granted the king 2 million ducados payable by the clergy of the Indies, towards the cost of Ceuta campaign; in 1737, when he allowed Philip to tax the clergy for five years; in 1741, when he allowed Philip to levy 8 percent on ecclesiastical incomes to fund the war against Britain; and again in the spring of 1746, when Philip secured papal permission to raise an extra 150,000 ducats from the clergy. In November 1745 Philip, saying his lay subjects could not bear a greater burden than what they already carried, ordered full implementation of the provisions of the concordat of 1737 relating to the taxation of the clergy and of a papal grant to extend that taxation, although the pope had not gone as far in this direction as Philip had wished.[48]

Population growth and, setting aside the difficult years between 1735 and 1738, when poor harvests might lead the authorities to remit tax obligations, with the inevitable impact on revenues, economic recovery may have made this fiscal burden easier to bear for Philip's subjects.[49] The reality, however, was that in the face of Philip's determination to extract what he needed, those called on to pay resorted to credit. War, from 1739 and intensified from 1741 by intervention in Italy, continued, as in the Habsburg era, to shape the finances of numerous cities, towns, and communities by triggering new local levies and increasing long-term indebtedness. Valladolid's censo debt in 1750 totalled 8,663,762 reales, of which 620,617, or almost 7.25 percent, had been assumed in 1745–46 alone, the vast amount of it to fund state-imposed war-related obligations. In that sense, municipal taxation and debt should be regarded, in part at least, as covert or displaced royal taxation and debt, as demonstrating the difficulty of separating royal, or state, finance from municipal finance, and as one more manifestation of the impact of the Spanish fiscal-military state between 1713 and 1748.

Debt, Credit, and Financiers

Many of the expedients discussed above were little more than disguised loans, credit being crucial to Philip V as to so many sovereigns in early modern Europe. But credit was a complex matter, including both short- and long-term debt, funded and unfunded, and voluntary and involuntary. The king's creditors included both his own and foreign subjects.

Philip V inherited a substantial long-term funded debt in 1700, in the form of the obligation to pay interest on *juros*, bonds issued by his Habsburg predecessors, that interest being paid from, "situated" on, specific revenues, for instance, the alcabalas, rather than on the mass of crown income. Philip IV was the last monarch to issue juros, not least because his manipulation of them reduced their attraction to investors, but the formal liability, to pay interest, remained, totalling almost 110 million reales annually at the close of the War of the Spanish Succession. If paid, the interest would have absorbed most of Philip V's ordinary revenues, but it had long been subject to substantial discounting, appropriation, and taxation. After the succession conflict Philip sought both to improve the administration of what was a complex system and a substantial formal obligation and to reduce it, creating in 1715 the Pagaduría General de Juros. He also continued to supposedly discount juros, in 1718 reducing the principal by between one-third and one-half, and to distinguish between various types of juros when deciding to pay interest or not on them. In 1727, against the background of a deteriorating international situation, Philip reduced the interest on juros from 5 percent to 3 percent without exceptions; the sum saved, almost 95 million maravedís, or about 2,800,000 reales, annually, was used in subsequent years to redeem more of the juro debt. By 1737 the annual amount paid in juro interest had fallen since the start of Philip's reign by about 25 percent, to 729 million maravedís, penalising individuals, families, and institutions.[50]

War on two fronts from 1741 triggered greater assaults on juros. In 1742 an order to suspend payments to those in ecclesiastical hands was reversed in favour of an attack on the many held by financiers, which were thought to be unjustified and which were now to be investigated by a special junta—and interest due suspended. Philip V and Ferdinand VI continued to acknowledge the obligation and to pay some of the interest due, but payments had been further reduced, to just 26.7 million reales by 1748, less than a quarter of what was paid in 1713. The close of the Austrian succession struggle was the signal for new efforts by Ensenada to reduce juro obligations by buying out those willing to be bought out, the market in juros having long since collapsed, and by annulling without compensation those mainly held by financiers, or *asentistas*, deemed abusive. Juros remained a formal obligation after 1748, but many had long been effectively worthless: in 1753 the town of Tuy in Galicia maintained it had more than 3 million maravedís invested in juros on which nothing had been paid for many years.[51]

If the issuing of new juros, which had been so central in making credit available to successive Spanish monarchs well into the seventeenth century, was not possible for Philip V, there were other avenues of credit available to him to help fund Spain's revival. The king could anticipate his revenues, in effect borrowing from the tax farmer, or could borrow from others on the strength of those same revenues. In 1725, to cite one case, Philip borrowed against the tobacco revenues in order to pay some of the subsidy due to the emperor. Some years later, in October 1733, at the start of the War of the Polish Succession, the Cinco Gremios, the association of five of Madrid's main guilds that was emerging as a major source of credit in these years, crucially secured the farm of the royal revenues from Madrid for nine years, starting in January 1734—a decisive step in its rise to prominence—by advancing 150,000 doblones, or 9 million reales, to the royal treasury. In 1741 it agreed to advance the king 15 million pesos in five monthly amounts of 3 million reales.[52]

While Philip V's reign saw the reduction of the funded juro debt, the nearest thing to a national or public debt of the sort accumulated in contemporary Britain, it witnessed as well the accumulation of a substantial short-term, unfunded debt as ministers simply left obligations to contractors, officials, soldiers, sailors, and even ministers unpaid, diverting the sums due to them to the war effort. The contribution to Philip's so-called testamentary debt of his Mediterranean interventions is implied in the fact that of the total of just over 520 million reales at his death, 4 million of which was inherited from the Habsburgs, just 2 percent had been accumulated between 1701 and 1710, during the War of the Spanish Succession, 17 percent between 1711 and 1720, and a massive 75 percent since 1731.[53]

In early 1731 the artillery contractor at Eugui was owed more than 279,000 reales. In the summer of 1734, in order to fund the conquest of Naples and Sicily, Campillo did not pay either the suppliers or the troops, while by the spring of 1740 most army officers were owed two and a half years' pay. As for the fleet, already owed large sums by the mid-1730s, when Navarro's squadron returned to Cartagena after the battle of Toulon in 1744 the officers and men were owed 12 million reales. Civilian officials, too, suffered in this situation, in which public or royal debt was supported in part by—and stimulated—a network of extensive private credit upon which Philip V's creditors themselves depended. In late 1732 the members of the Council of Castile were owed forty-five months' salary and, despite a royal order to pay a year's salary on account, the councillors were still complaining on this score in 1736. Not even the royal household was exempt. Accumulating arrears there prompted a so-called reform of the system of payment at the end of 1731, which in turn caused an outcry and criticism of Philip's Italian projects. The situation did not improve, as by January 1738, when the Junta de Medios established the previous year was hearing appeals from numerous creditors seeking payment of pensions, salaries, and wages which had often not been paid for long periods, the king's household was said to have gone unpaid for five years.[54]

Philip V borrowed abroad as well as at home. In 1733 the paymaster of the Spanish troops at Livorno, the great Tuscan entrepôt, approached the merchant community there to identify some solution, perhaps a loan, to his want of funds. Some years later, at the end of 1741, the war chest with which Montemar had arrived in Italy at the start of the War of the Austrian Succession was running low, and Montemar was looking to borrow locally. Subsidy arrears also represented a form of credit in which, paradoxically, Philip's war effort was being subsidised by his subsidised ally. Those owed arrears by the Spanish court in this period included, in the 1720s, the emperor and, during the War of the Austrian Succession, the elector of Bavaria and the Republic of Genoa.[55]

Most of those whose arrears inflated the floating debt could do little about it. However, the indispensability of credit enhanced the standing and opportunities of those who could advance loans, namely, the financiers. Henry Kamen has argued that Philip V was less dependent on these men than his Habsburg predecessors. But this was far from the case. In the sixteenth and seventeenth centuries the Spanish crown had depended upon foreign financiers, the Genoese and, later, the Portuguese. But Philip V, like Charles II, relied primarily upon native Spanish asentistas. Typical was D. Mathias de Valparda, who supplied infantry uniforms from 1735 (see chapter 1) and who from 1736 farmed the saltworks of Catalonia and in 1746–49 the rentas provinciales of Toro. Some of these financiers, most notably a group of them who originated in Navarre, including, for example, Juan de Goyeneche and his associates, constituted distinctive networks or lobbies. Many of these men straddled the private and the public sectors, moving, like José Gómez de Terán and Valparda, from asiento to administración, contributing in some cases to the successful transition to public administration during and after the War of the Austrian Succession. The difference between public and private spheres was not necessarily that great. These financiers received various rewards, some gaining noble titles: in 1741, for example, Miguel de Arizcun Mendinueta, a supplier to the navy and a farmer of the wool revenues, secured that of marqués de Iturbieta, having received an hábito of the Military Order of Santiago in 1729.[56]

When all else failed, the crown was obliged to declare bankruptcy, in effect to reschedule its obligations to release funds for pressing needs, as had happened in the Habsburg era. Philip V had largely managed to avoid doing so during the succession conflict, but the gap between income and outgoings thenceforward and above all the preparations for war associated with the Vienna alliance of 1725, triggered the first bankruptcy in 1726. In 1737 the Junta de Medios suggested repudiating all debts incurred before 1736, but this was not acted upon until bankruptcy was declared in March 1739, after a couple of years in which Philip's ministers had sought to bridge the shortfall with traditional solutions that in some part depended on the asentistas. This later bankruptcy has been seen as a turning point in the management of Spain's finances and may have contributed to a loss of confidence on the part of the men the crown usually depended upon to advance it funds. It certainly worried some ministers as they contemplated how to restore public faith in—and lending to—the crown. It also increased the pressure to resort to extraordinary and radical revenue-raising measures in 1740–41, including moving away from tax farming.[57]

Philip V's wars added substantially to the debt, however it was accumulated and however repaid. The report sent by the British minister in the spring of 1738 (above) stated that the annual interest payments totalled 17,194,451 reales, or 7.5 percent of the total revenue. In the spring of 1739 it was put at just over 49 million escudos. A decade later, in 1748, Ensenada calculated that more than twice that amount, 116 million escudos, was needed if the royal debt, funded and unfunded, was to be liquidated, a clear indication of the great cost of the War of the Austrian Succession to Spain.[58]

Remittances Abroad

Operations overseas, subsidies to allies, and diplomatic salaries and expenses represented a challenge not merely in terms of the huge sums involved and the need for often substantial advances but also in that money had to be sent abroad, sometimes, as in the 1730s and 1740s, over long periods. In 1744, for example, Ensenada was arranging monthly remittances to the army in Italy of 350,000 escudos. Money might be sent in the form of coin or bullion. In May 1732, for example, three waggons carrying 700,000 piastres of Cruzada revenues arrived in Alicante for the Oran expedition, while in 1734, during the War of the Polish Succession, large amounts of coin were shipped from Spain to Tuscany prior to Don Carlos's invasion and conquest of Naples. Much the same happened in the War of the Austrian Succession. The second convoy to Italy, in January 1742, carried 500,000 pesos for the army, while in January 1744 Ensenada arranged the despatch to Italy of 60,000 doblones, followed by 400,000 escudos.[59]

However, the risks of capture or loss meant that letters of change were often preferable. Between 1718 and 1720 substantial sums were remitted for the army in Sicily in the form of both specie and letters, and in letters alone for the garrison at Portolongone. In the autumn of 1733, at the start of the War of the Polish Succession, the Spanish court remitted at least 3 million reales to Italy for its forces there by this means. Subsequently, in January 1742, at the start of Spain's intervention in the War of the Austrian Succession, the paymaster general of the expeditionary force sent by Philip V to Italy arrived there with letters of credit to Genoese and French merchants, who were to pay him 100,000 dollars monthly. Later that same year a total of thirty-two letters of change to a total value of just over 500 million reales and drawn on various merchants of Amsterdam, London, and Marseilles were also sent to the paymaster general, and more followed in succeeding years.[60]

Throughout this period the king and his ministers depended, as they did with regard to army and navy supply, on the asentistas to find letters for these and other payments abroad. The exchange and the commissions charged inevitably swelled the cost. Between 1717 and 1720, largely to provide for the Spanish forces in Sardinia and Sicily, the Tesorero General negotiated letters of change with sixteen such asentistas, for the remittance of 64.5 million reales, paying an additional 8.2 million reales (12.75 percent) in remittance costs. During the War of the Polish Succession, too, and in that of the Austrian Succession, ministers relied on asentistas, whose commissions were often again considerable. While costly, the system worked reasonably well, except when letters of change were refused or protested, as happened in January 1735 in respect of letters for the troops in Lombardy. Inevitably, this affected preparations and operations. At the start of 1744 letters drawn on a Genoese house were refused payment since the financier concerned had not made available there the funds to honour it. With preparations for the forthcoming campaign in Italy threatened, Ensenada ordered the treasurer general to suspend payment of any prior commitments on available funds in order to provide funds to back those letters. As for the exchange, in 1747 the Spanish court lost 3.5 percent under this head when remitting letters to Italy.[61]

These issues, highlighted during the War of the Austrian Succession, prompted a groundbreaking initiative at its close. In 1748 Ensenada, who hoped to exclude the British and French from the lucrative market in silver remittances, initiated the establishment of an agency which should accept deposits but also buy up letters of change payable throughout

Europe, a policy that enabled Spanish ministers not only to remit sums abroad when necessary but also to make a profit. The new body, Spain's first state bank and in part modelled on the Bank of England, proved so successful that it was refounded in 1752 as the Real Giro. Ensenada had a broad vision of the role of the Giro, but its creation should be seen not only as an integral part of his overhaul of the finances but also as further evidence of the impact in Spain of Philip V's Mediterranean adventures: the foundation of the Giro was linked by one contemporary to the costs of remittances of the sort just discussed and specifically to those for the army in Italy.[62]

Royal revenues in Spain rose markedly between 1713 and 1748 to meet the costs of Spain's remarkable resurgence as a power. But growth was far from linear. In fact, revenues rose and fell, as in Habsburg Spain, according to need and above all according to whether Spain was at war or not and whether it was waging costly, offensive war or less expensive, defensive war. Revenue expansion thus depended not simply on the possibilities of the economy but also on the priorities of the state or, rather, of the king. Rafael Torres is right to contend that while money was the sinews of war, essential too was political will. In this and in most other respects financial policy between 1700 and 1748 echoed that of the Habsburgs. Philip V did not have to subsidise Flanders at all or Spanish Italy to the same degree, but neither was he able to exploit the resources of Spanish Italy, as his predecessors did. Indeed, among Philip's achievements must be accounted the extraction of more resources from the territories that remained to him after the succession conflict to fund his revanchist policy. The pillars of royal finances were Spain—in effect, Castile and Andalusia—and the Indies, as before 1700. There were innovations, not least the extraction of far more from the Aragonese territories, which contributed about 10 percent of ordinary revenues, such that in this sphere Philip might be said to have unified Spain, except that Aragon did not pay the same taxes as Castile, diversity remaining the norm. In terms of how the royal revenues were administered, that is, collected, here too there was innovation, but again we should not exaggerate. While the end of War of the Austrian Succession saw the extension of public administration at the expense of contracting out, financiers remained crucial to the successful operation of the ordinary royal finances. In fact, the expansion of revenues in wartime depended primarily on the application of extraordinary measures. Most of these had been widely used in Habsburg Spain and by Philip himself during the succession struggle at the start of the reign, while the one truly radical innovation, namely, the 10 percent income levy of 1741, was promptly transformed into an imposition of a more traditional type and one less demanding of the Castilian elites. The plethora of extraordinary devices, especially from 1739, suggest Spain was a fiscal-military state, but the efforts of both king and ministers to identify alternatives to taxation, such as cost cutting, loans, and so on, implies that, as under Charles III, it might not be so literally fiscal. It has been posited by those influenced by the New Institutional Economics approach that Spain was hindered by lacking the political, economic, and commercial institutions which Britain uniquely enjoyed and which ensured greater access to credit. This may be true, yet Spain's institutions and the powers the king did enjoy generated large sums and underpinned Spain's revival in these decades. The large unfunded debt left by Philip V reflected both Spain's weaknesses and strengths as a source of funds. It also reveals the enormous burden of Philip's wars and in particular of the War of Jenkins' Ear / War of the Austrian Succession. The accession of Ferdinand VI relieved some of that pressure, although the war continued to 1748, and pressure for radical postwar fiscal reform, postponed until after the war because tinkering was too risky in wartime, grew. In effecting reform thereafter, Ensenada, who was determined to waste no more Spanish resources in Italy, could draw on what he had seen of other fiscal systems as intendant with the army in Savoy. As noted earlier, the major postwar survey of economic and social conditions, Ensenada's catastro, portrays a Spain deeply marked by the measures introduced since the late 1730s to fund war. Finally, while the 1740s may have been a turning point in some ways, what is most striking is just how far Spain's resurgence between 1713 and 1748 was funded by a system—if that term is appropriate—which would have been very familiar to Philip IV and Charles II.[63]

CHAPTER FOUR

GOVERNMENT AND POLITICS

I have always said that Spain, well governed, can play a great role in
the world.
—*Cardinal Giulio Alberoni, October* 1714

Spain's resurgence post-1713 had major implications for its government
and politics. The early Bourbon monarchy has frequently been identified as
a new regime in Spain, one which brought absolutism, centralisation, national unity, and modernity. Yet, as in other spheres, the extent to which
Philip's government represented a radical departure from Habsburg practice must be treated with caution. For one thing, it is doubtful whether the
early Bourbon Spanish state could simply impose its will, as traditional models of absolutism would imply, while, as, noted earlier (see chapter 2), the
creation of the Almirantazgo in 1737 suggested a return to a quasi-medieval
style of government in which public authority and revenues were a means
of providing for young royals. This chapter seeks to demonstrate that the remarkable administrative reforms for which Philip's reign has been noted and
which did mark a new phase of state formation cannot be separated from
Philip's Mediterranean adventures. My focus here will be largely on Castile,
ignoring the foral realms (see chapter 5), although innovations there offered
a model which might be applied in Castile. Effective administration was

vital to the success of Philip's Mediterranean expeditions, and participation in them was often a crucial stage in a successful ministerial career. But Philip's African and Italian ambitions and the demands they made on Spain also created political pressures. It would therefore be unwise to think of Spanish political or constitutional life as moribund following Philip's triumph in the succession conflict at the start of his reign; indeed, the spiralling demands of war in Italy in the final years of his reign may have tested the "construction of loyalty" achieved at its start.[1]

Policy and Politics

Who determined Spanish policy between 1713 and 1748? It is almost a commonplace that Philip V was not his own master. Philip had demonstrated energy and courage on the battlefield during the succession conflict, playing the part of a warrior king, but was increasingly subject to fits of depression and a debilitating lethargy. For this reason and his powerful sexual drive (and refusal to take a mistress), he depended enormously upon his two wives, Marie Louise of Savoy, and, following her death in 1713 and Philip's remarriage a year later, Isabel Farnese. Indeed, until Philip's death in July 1746 and her banishment from Madrid by her stepson, Ferdinand VI, a year later, Isabel was widely regarded in her day as the driving force behind Spanish policy, pursuing goals, above all in Italy, which were of little value to Spain and its people.[2]

Philip V certainly lacked self-confidence. He had succeeded to the Spanish throne in 1700 at the age of seventeen and had not, being a younger son, been groomed to rule. He received frequent letters of advice from his grandfather at the start of his reign. Philip's self-doubt may have explained his deep conventional piety, which may in turn have been strengthened by the importance of religion in deciding the outcome of the succession struggle. In 1725, the treaties of Vienna having reached Madrid, Philip completed his Easter devotions before reading them, while his failure to confess and attend Mass revealed his incapacity in 1728. That piety also ensured his dependence on his confessor, a post of great political importance, as it had been before 1700. In 1724 the French ambassador observed, "What in Spain is called a confessor, would elsewhere be called a prime minister." Indeed, major changes of political direction were usually accompanied by a change of confessor: the fall of the previous royal favourite, the princesse des Ursins, and, with her, Jean Orry, and Melchor de Macanaz in 1714 following the arrival of Isabel Farnese, saw the replacement of one French Jesuit, father Pierre Robinet, by another, father Guillaume Daubenton. His confessors confirmed in Philip a very traditional wish to rule justly.[3]

That concern in turn helps explain why, like his Habsburg predecessors and many other Catholic monarchs of early modern Europe, Philip sometimes submitted sensitive or contentious matters of state to informal, ad hoc committees which included ecclesiastics, so-called *juntas de teólogos*. In 1734 Philip convened a body of this sort before ceding to Don Carlos, his eldest son from his second marriage, the reconquered Naples and Sicily, which were, strictly speaking, part of the inheritance of Philip's successor in Spain, the future Ferdinand VI. In 1740 another such committee was convened to weigh extraordinary measures to fund the war against Britain (see chapter 3), Philip being anxious not to unjustly burden either his subjects or his conscience.[4]

The lack of self-assurance Philip sought to assuage by consulting his confessor contributed to his unusual uxoriousness, which contrasted with the relations of most of his Spanish Habsburg predecessors with their consorts. The influence that Philip's character offered his queen was enhanced by the fact that he was sometimes seriously incapacitated by mental illness, Isabel becoming regent in such circumstances in 1727 and again in 1732. In 1728, having abdicated once before, in 1724, Philip, during another bout of instability, sent another act of abdication to the president of the Council of Castile. Isabel, anxious for her own future and that of her sons, was determined to ensure Philip stayed on the throne and engineered the document's destruction before it could be made public. The removal of the court from Madrid to Seville between 1729 and 1733 may have been intended by Isabel to distance Philip from the Council of Castile, thereby preventing another abdication attempt and ensuring her grip on the king and on policy.[5]

Foreign observers were very clear that Philip V and Spanish policy were dominated by Isabel, who could become very agitated if thwarted in the pursuit of her goals. In the spring of 1730 she subjected the French ambassador to a fierce denunciation of his court's failure to impose the recently concluded treaty of Seville (1729) on Charles VI, while in 1735 the French considered Isabel as most likely to react violently to the proposed peace in Italy, limiting Spanish gains there. Foreign diplomats and Spanish subjects seeking advancement all sought to curry favour with her.[6] In 1734–35 verses celebrating the conquest of Naples were dedicated to her, and Campillo's critical memorandum of January 1741 on the finances and war, for example, which brought him high office, was obviously tailored to the queen's Italian ambitions.[7] Isabel's influence lends superficial support to what has been labelled a feminisation of Spanish politics in this reign, precisely because of her sway over Philip V and of Barbara of Braganza's over her own husband, Philip's equally melancholy and uxorious son and successor, Ferdinand VI. Formal politics remained a male sphere, as in most other European states, but the court was a space in which female influence had greater play, especially where a monarch was deeply attached to his wife. Almost inevitably, therefore, Philip's second wife did have a distinctive impact on Spanish policy in these decades, as did, though less dramatically, his daughter-in-law in the succeeding reign.[8]

Although Isabel's views carried great weight, however, much of the writing about her relationship with Philip was and is still simplistic, at times bordering on caricature. Some of the harshest criticisms of Philip's dependency on his consorts were made by the disaffected and cannot be taken at face value. In reality, Philip determined Spanish policy, as historians now increasingly acknowledge. His Italian ambitions and claims predated his second marriage and the birth of Don Carlos in 1716, Philip continuing to style himself king of the Two Sicilies and of Sardinia and duke of Milan after 1713. Philip had been entrusted with Spanish Italy by the terms of Charles II's will, and Philip, like his grandfather Louis XIV, was highly conscious of his reputation, or *gloire*, which had been tarnished by the loss of Spanish Italy. Such feelings were undoubtedly reinforced by Philip's sense of the mutual obligations of himself and his former Italian subjects, following the oaths sworn on both sides at the start of his reign. Philip believed he had a rightful claim to those Italian territories (much as he still had to the throne of France), despite the imposed renunciations and treaties of 1713 and his reluctant confirmation of these in 1720, when he joined the Quadruple Alliance. The initial focus of Spanish interest in Italy after 1713 was the territories which had made up Spanish Italy, Naples, Sicily, and Sardinia, not those where Isabel's claims lay, Modena, Parma, Piacenza, and Tuscany. Further, the Italian ambitions of his second wife cannot explain Philip's preoccupation with Africa, another part of his inheritance which he must conserve and, if lost since his accession, as in the case of Oran, recover and which accorded with his traditional Christian piety. Spanish policy was Philip's policy. Finally, his penchant for war meant that it was likely to rouse him from his melancholy and make him become more energetic, as he was at the time of the Oran expedition of 1732 and during the War of the Polish Succession.[9]

In fact, king and queen did not always agree on how to achieve their objectives, including in Italy. Philip's deep personal hostility towards his erstwhile rival Charles VI was not shared by Isabel, who was readier to deal with the emperor than her husband was in her efforts to achieve her goals. King and consort differed, for example, over the alliance concluded with the court of Vienna in 1725, which promised to establish Don Carlos in Italy. Philip shared some of the hostility towards the agreement of many of his subjects (below), whereas Isabel championed it, the king again considering abdication; the following year, as relations with the imperial court deteriorated, threatening the hopes founded upon the treaty, the British minister in Madrid reported Philip's daily quarrels with Isabel, "who cries morning to night." Philip had views of his own and was sensitive to any suggestion that he was not master in his own house and did not determine policy (below). He needed to be, at the least, managed by his spouse. On the whole, Isabel proved well able to manage her husband, but this only confirmed rather than determined or distorted the focus of Spanish revanchism after 1713, helping to ensure that it was most visible in the Mediterranean rather than in the Atlantic.[10]

Government and Administration

War tested administrative arrangements, then as now, while effective organisation was a vital factor in military and naval success (see chapters 1, 2). In 1700 Philip V inherited an administration which was characterised at the centre by the primacy of a multiplicity of specialist councils dating from the late fifteenth and sixteenth centuries and which combined advisory, executive, and judicial functions. Despite the many criticisms levelled against it, both at the time and later, this system had served the Spanish Habsburgs reasonably well, not least because the responsibilities of the councils reflected the fact that the Spanish Monarchy was a "composite state": the marqués de Monteleón lauded the conciliar system on precisely these grounds in 1715. However, this inherited structure was radically overhauled to the disadvantage of the councils by Philip V. To some contemporaries, including Alberoni, the organiser of the conquest of Sardinia and in Sicily in 1717 and 1718, this success would not have been possible without that overhaul.[11]

The most striking organisational innovations at the centre were not only the abolition of some of the councils and the loss of real power by those which survived but also the emergence at their expense of specialist secretariats of state. Some councils were effectively victims of the territorial and related political changes associated with the War of the Spanish Succession. In Spain itself the suppression of the foral status of the territories of the Crown of Aragon rendered the council of Aragon unnecessary, most of its responsibilities passing to the council of Castile and its adjunct, the *cámara* of Castile (see chapter 5). Similarly, the loss of the Italian territories made redundant the council of Italy, which disappeared and was not given responsibility between 1717 and 1720 for the reconquered Sardinia and Sicily. In 1726 an official counselled Philip to secure the papers of the defunct council in case he should recover his Italian territories and want to revive the body, but the king did not resurrect it following the retaking of Naples and Sicily in 1734–35, which were instead immediately given to Don Carlos. The council of State, the premier body under the Habsburgs—its members, many of them grandees, "consulting" the king on Monarchy-wide policy—fell into abeyance, although the title of councillor survived purely as an honorific distinction, later bestowed on Patiño, Campillo, and Ensenada.[12]

Royal authority was asserted at the expense of the councils which survived. This expressed itself primarily in the emergence between 1714 and 1721 from the Secretariat of the Despacho, the king's private office, inherited from the Habsburgs, of what would be six distinctive secretariats: State (foreign policy), War (the army), Marine (the navy), the Indies,

Finance, and, finally, Grace and Justice. These developed rather haphazardly, secretariats being created, associated with others, and separated often in a very short space of time before a clearer structure emerged in 1721. It is surely no coincidence that between 1717 and 1720 the Secretariats of War and Marine were combined but separated thereafter. This system overcame what had long been regarded by many in Spain itself as the great defect of the administration inherited by Philip V, the lack of an effective executive, and initially materialized to meet the administrative challenges posed by the War of the Spanish Succession. The subsequent tinkering cannot be separated from the struggle for power at court or, as in the dismissal of D. Bernardo Tinajero de la Escalera, an erstwhile creature or protégé of the disgraced Ursins, and the breakup of his combined Ministry of Marine and Indies by Alberoni in 1715, from the debate about strategy and whether to give priority to the Atlantic or the Mediterranean.[13]

But from the spring of 1717, when the crucial changes were made, ahead of the invasion of Sardinia, instead of being expedited, as before, by the relevant council, a matter would be dealt with by the appropriate secretary of state through the so-called *vía reservada*, that is, by a minister or secretary; although not always a member of the relevant council, that official would speak only with the king, and it was from his office that the orders implementing the monarch's decision were issued. The first cycle of intervention in Italy and Africa between 1717 and 1720 tested the effectiveness of this arrangement, regardless of the failure of the policy or strategy it served, and it survived. Henceforth, by and large the secretary of war alone, for example, was responsible for military and no other matters. He was assisted in Madrid by a small clerical establishment and in the localities by a network of *intendentes de guerra* and their subordinates (see chapter 1). Some of these men carved out careers as military administrators inside and outside Spain. Casimir Uztáriz rose to become *oficial mayor* in in the Secretariat of War in 1739, having received a noble title from Don Carlos following the conquest of the Two Sicilies, while Pedro Gordillo y Sánchez, later marqués (1761) de Zambrano, served as *comisario de guerra* with the Neapolitan expedition (1733–36) and as treasurer of the Army of Lombardy (1741–45). As in Habsburg Spain, alongside the new secretariats ad hoc committees, or *juntas*, were frequently established to deal with specific issues, for example, the Junta de Dependencias y Desterrados of 1715, which advised on petitions for permission to return to Spain from exiled supporters of the would-be "Charles III."[14]

Many historians see these changes as crucial to the creation of a more absolute, centralised, and unified, national Spanish monarchy. To many, they are evidence of the introduction into Spain of the institutions and practice of Bourbon France, where specialist secretariats had emerged well before 1700, although, paradoxically, Regency France experimented with polysynody after 1715. In fact, the need to remedy the supposed defects of the conciliar system had been acknowledged in Spain long before the arrival of Philip V, and French models were not the only source of solutions to those defects. Whatever its origin, the new system, with its greater emphasis on executive action, was honed and entrenched in large part by the demands of Philip's African and Italian expeditions after 1713. By 1748 the secretariats were recognised as an integral part of the administration by most commentators, including José de Carvajal, whose *Testamento Político* (1745), was an invaluable, critical reflection on the new arrangements by an insider.[15]

The king remained the lynchpin of the system, although Philip V's shyness meant that his court, whose ceremonial was reformed in 1709 in imitation of French practice, breaking with Habsburg tradition and becoming very French in terms of the serving staff, was more formal, and the king himself less visible than his predecessors.[16] This and Philip's occasional and sometimes prolonged incapacity implied the need for a chief minister to coordinate the new secretariats. Perhaps influenced by Louis XIV, Philip would not appoint or formally acknowledge such a figure, but foreign diplomats and Philip's own subjects needed to know where power lay and duly identified a succession of chief ministers. The first of these was the Italian ecclesiastic Giulio Alberoni, sent to Spain during the succession conflict by the duke of Parma and confidant of Isabel on her first arrival. He proved an able and energetic chief minister from 1714 onwards and achieved a remarkable authority. When Philip fell ill in October 1717, in a codicil to a will drawn up at that time he gave Alberoni powers to make peace and war, authority which none of his other ministers ever received. Alberoni masterminded the Sardinian and Sicilian expeditions but for that reason was also the main casualty of the failure of Philip's first attempt to restore Spanish Italy, Spain's foreign enemies insisting on his dismissal: Philip banished Alberoni in December 1719. The next chief minister was the Dutch renegade baron Ripperda, whose brief tenure (1725–26) of that role was inseparable from his negotiation of the short-lived rapprochement with Vienna. Alberoni and Ripperda were not Spaniards, but all of Philip's prime ministers thereafter were: Patiño, Campillo, and Ensenada. The emergence of an allpowerful chief minister worried some of Philip's subjects, including some of his ministers, about ministerial despotism. Carvajal, for example, appreciated the need for a chief minister but not the accumulation of ministries by one individual. However, the need to ensure that the administration was coordinated and worked effectively to achieve the king's goals, not least in wartime in the 1730s and 1740s, ensured that the role survived.[17]

There were superficial similarities between the chief minister and the seventeenth-century *valido*, but in reality the two were very different. The validos had generally been personal favourites of the monarch, most of them drawn from among the court nobility, *títulos* and grandees, but this was not true of Philip's chief ministers. This is not to say that he and Isabel did not have favourites or, rather, confidants—the unusual closeness of the monarchs arguably excluding the possibility of old-style favourites—whom the ambitious sought to cultivate. Isabel's intimates included a number of Italians: her wet nurse, Laura Piscatori, her physician, the duchesses of St Pierre (sister of the marquis de Torcy and a channel of communication between Isabel and the French court) and of Castropignano, and the marchese Annibale Scotti, who had accompanied Isabel to Spain in 1714 and represented the duke of Parma in Madrid thereafter. In 1741 Isabel told the French ambassador that Scotti would have been a minister but for Spanish resentment of Philip's use of Italians. In January 1741 Campillo submitted to Scotti the wide-ranging *mémoire* on the royal finances ahead of the intervention in Italy which led to Campillo's appointment as secretary of state for finance and soon de facto prime minister. But these favourites did not hold office in the way the validos had, whereas Philip's chief ministers enjoyed a very different relationship with the monarch and were more akin to what a later age would call technocrats. Their administrative ability, not royal affection, was their main claim on royal favour. Indeed, Philip may have disliked Patiño and was said to have struck him in 1732, the preeminence of Patiño being attributed by most observers to the favour of the queen, for whom the minister was the architect of success in Italy.[18]

The chief minister presided over a growing cadre of career bureaucrats, the *plumistas*. But the new structure was hardly a modern, Weberian bureaucracy. In the early days of the new arrangements, officials were understandably less likely to respect the emerging norms. In 1715 Patiño, who was then organising the reconquest of Majorca in his capacity as intendente of Catalonia and the army, acknowledged that he should communicate with the secretary of war, but effectively ignored him, and dealt instead with José Grimaldo, Philip's secretary of state, whom he had got to know during the succession struggle. Similarly, a powerful minister could confuse the lines of demarcation, as did Alberoni, who held none of the secretaryships. On the other hand, Alberoni's fall paved the way for the de facto premiership of the secretary of state, the self-effacing Grimaldo. Grimaldo was yet another of Philip's collaborators who, born in 1660 and having at the age of fourteen followed his father into the secretariat of the Council of the Indies, had reached maturity in the Spain of Charles II; Philip had discovered him to be a highly capable administrator during the succession struggle and somebody he could work with. For his part, Ripperda briefly occupied a secretariat without any distinctive designation or responsibility but added those of State, War, Finance, and Marine. In 1726, when Grimaldo was reappointed secretary of state, relations with Vienna were effectively hived off to Juan Bautista Orendáin, marqués de la Paz, who, along with Ripperda, was behind the rapprochement with the imperial court; thereafter, Patiño not only effectively supplanted Orendáin when the latter lost influence, while retaining the office, but went on to hold the four main secretariats. Thus when Patiño officially assumed the secretaryship of state on Orendáin's death in 1733 it made little real difference. This blurring of boundaries underlines the fact that the man was often more important than the office and structures. In that sense it was up to individual ministers to make of their offices what they would or could. Relationships were more fluid and less clearly differentiated than formal descriptions might suggest. In 1738 the secretary for war was said to be eclipsed by his *oficial mayor*. At the lower levels appointments might be sold or granted as royal *mercedes*. Last but by no means least, the accumulation of ministries by de facto chief ministers made up for the lack of any alternative means of coordinating the executive departments before the creation of the Junta Suprema de Estado, a sort of cabinet council, in 1787. The Savoyard representative in Madrid observed at the end of 1740 that the emperor's death came at a bad time for the Spanish court given its many difficulties, which included divisions between ministers; it is therefore no surprise that Campillo was soon to accumulate the key secretariats of State.[19]

In fact, most of the Habsburg councils survived alongside the new secretariats, including the councils of the Inquisition, War, the Military Orders, *Cruzada*, Finance, the Indies, and Castile. These bodies were definitely less powerful than before 1700 and in some respects restricted to a judicial function. However, this function was of some import given the continued emphasis on the role of the king as dispenser of justice, a Habsburg legacy which was not lost sight of as the first Bourbon laid the foundations of "administrative monarchy." Indeed, a new codification of the laws of the realm was projected at the end of Philip's reign. Likewise, the councils could still influence policy: Philip V's decision in October 1737 to allow the petition of the *hidalgos* of the Cuatro Villas to be exempted from the *sorteo*, or lottery, for the community's militia regiment followed a *consulta* of the Council of War. Philip's reign thus saw the adaptation of the older polysynody, not its complete destruction, and it was this hybrid structure which oversaw and underpinned Spain's resurgence after 1713.[20]

Perhaps most noteworthy was the survival of the Council of Castile (and Cámara), which was not replaced by a secretariat, and whose authority and responsibilities, already extensive before 1700, were enhanced as a result of the suppression of distinctive Aragonese institutions (above). The Council of Castile did not escape the reforming impulse of the new Bourbon regime, but its radical overhaul in 1713 proved short-lived: the council reverted to its Habsburg structure and practice in 1715, after the fall of the reform's promoters, Orry and Macanaz.[21]

The Council of Castile was an important channel of communication between the king and the realm: in June 1732, following the departure of the Oran expedition, Philip instructed the council to order public prayers for success against the infidel. The council also continued, as in the Habsburg era, to monitor local government and order in the Castilian and now the Aragonese towns. In 1744, typically, the chief magistrate, or *alcalde mayor*, of Mojácar in Almería informed the president of the council of the riot there provoked by efforts to seize men for the fleet (see chapter 2). Philip's failure to summon the Cortes (below) may therefore have enhanced the role of the council as a link between king and subjects, as his predecessor's failure to summon it had done before 1700. In consequence of these various roles, including that of arbiter of justice and of legality, the Council of Castile defended the rights of the king's subjects, as it had done in the Habsburg era, and occasionally functioned as a constitutional restraint, albeit a limited one, on the monarch. In 1712–13 individual councillors were among the chief opponents of Philip's reform of the Castilian law of royal succession, although their opposition counted for little, and in 1726 and 1728 they articulated opposition to the manipulation of the coinage.[22]

Although the council's responsibilities centred on Castile, it had a part to play in Philip V's rebuilding of Spain's Mediterranean empire. The council's legal officer, or *fiscal*, was involved in drafting the framework of government, or *planta*, of the reconquered Sardinia in 1717–19. Almost thirty years later, in December 1745, in an episode revealing of the way Philip continued to see the Italian territories as united to his crown, he ordered that the council, which, like other councils, was also a tribunal, should hear appeals from Piombino, hitherto part of the state of the Tuscan *presidios*, as the council of Italy had done; the council should therefore secure the papers of the defunct council of Italy.[23]

Janine Fayard has suggested that the head, that is, the president or governor, of the Council of Castile was a figure of reduced political importance in Philip V's reign. But the activities and role of the council hint that this is to understate the continued importance of the governors, two of whom, Miguel Francisco Guerra (president, 1715–24) and Juan de Herrera, bishop of Sigüenza (1724–27), had served in the chancery of Milan before 1707. In 1724 the then-governor, D. Luis Félix de Miraval, was appointed to the cabinet council Philip created before his abdication and to that of Luis I. The other members were the archbishop of Toledo; the inquisitor general; the conde de Santisteban del Puerto, the Spanish plenipotentiary at the congress of Cambrai and president of the Council of the Military Orders; the marqués de Lede, the hero of the Italian and African campaigns of 1717–20; the marqués de Valero, president of the Council of the Indies; and the brother of Isabel's confessor. Miraval's tenure demonstrated that the vision of the president of the council might range far beyond Castile: he opposed the marqués de Monteleón's plan to have Don Carlos installed in Italy with the backing of Britain and France and urged instead that Spain should act more aggressively towards those powers and build a fleet powerful enough to oblige them to respect Spain. A leader of the so-called Spanish party (below) and an enemy of Grimaldo, Miraval defended the Spanish system against the duc de Bourbon's criticism of government by councils, which Bourbon blamed for Spain's late Habsburg decline, and the suggestion that Spain needed a chief minister. His reluctance to agree to Philip's resumption of the throne in 1724 prompted his dismissal. He was replaced by Herrera, who had been rewarded by Philip with the see of Sigüenza for his loyalty when Spanish Italy collapsed. But Miraval's disgrace did not diminish his office. In 1732, after another crisis in Philip's mental health, Isabel proposed the creation of a Council of Regency (above) which would include the president of the Council of Castile. The other members were the prince of Asturias, the duques de Grenada and de Giovenazzo, the marqués de la Paz, the conde de Montemar, and Patiño. In 1737 the then-governor was appointed to the Junta de Medios, which was tasked with restoring the finances following a succession of expensive foreign adventures (see chapter 3). The appointment of a governor was a major event and invariably provoked comment: that of Gaspar de Molina, the bishop of Barcelona, in 1733 was widely seen as a triumph for Isabel Farnese.[24]

Administrative innovation at the centre was accompanied by new initiatives in the provinces, most notably the appearance of a network of provincial intendentes (see chapters 1, 3). It was long thought that the intendentes, first appointed during the War of the Spanish Succession, were an alien import, further evidence of the frenchification thought to be a consequence of the advent of the Bourbons. In fact, they were in part modelled on the Castilian corregidores (below), in part on a network of Castilian superintendentes dating from 1691. However, the very halting steps towards the establishment of a network of provincial intendancies before 1748 meant that, in Castile at least, the corregidores regained their traditional role and importance. In fact, many corregidores were at the same time intendentes of their town and province, for example, Bartolomé Antonio Badarán de Osinalde, briefly (1719) corregidor and intendente of the provinces of Burgos and Alava and of the *señorío* of Vizcaya. Indeed, the hostile reaction across Castile to the fact that the intendentes absorbed the responsibilities of the corregidores seems to have been a factor in their abolition in 1721–22, underlining the fact that effective government might best be achieved not by intendentes imposing absolutism but by collaborating with local elites, whose concerns they might report back to Madrid. This did not rule out reform of municipal government, where hereditary councillors, or *regidores,* had largely established a stranglehold by 1700. But the corregidores articulated that alliance, as they had done before and during the succession conflict, and they continued to do so after 1713.[25]

The corregidores chivvied those local councils when necessary: in 1745, when the regidores of Burgos declared that they could not accommodate yet another recruiting party, the corregidor insisted this be done nonetheless. As for fiscal matters, in 1741 the corregidor of Burgos pressed the city to pay its contribution to the new 10 percent imposition (see chapter 3). Throughout the reign corregidores ensured the regular renewal of the *millones* revenues by the Cortes-voting towns (below). Many of those who served as corregidores under Philip V and Ferdinand VI had already held posts of some importance, including D. Antonio de Heredia y Bazán de Parada, later marqués de Rafal, who served as corregidor of Murcia before being appointed in 1744 intendente of the army and of Aragon, together with the *corregimiento* (that is, as corregidor) of Zaragoza. Some of those who served as intendentes also served as corregidores, at the same time or later. We should not therefore underestimate the enormous contribution to Spain's revival in these decades of this older cadre of officials, whose appointments were invariably reported in the *Gaceta de Madrid;* they continued to function long after the establishment from 1749 of a network of provincial intendentes.[26]

Other older institutions still had a role as well. These included the *audiencias* and *chancillerías,* the oldest and most important being those of

Valladolid and Granada. Like those in Spanish America, they had long functioned not only as judicial tribunals but also as executive agencies of the monarchy. These bodies continued to act in this way under Philip V, who established four new audiencias, in Aragon (1707), Catalonia (1716), Valencia, (1707), and Asturias (1717). The formation of the first three was clearly part of the dismantling of the foral character of those territories, while that of the last, at the expense of the jurisdiction of the Chancillería of Valladolid, arguably reinforced foralism. Typical of the role these bodies played were the instructions which in May 1734 the president of the Chancillería of Valladolid gave to the corregidor of that town to organise celebrations following the Spanish occupation of the city of Naples. For his part, in 1741 the president of the Chancillería of Granada was instrumental in implementing in his jurisdiction the 10 percent levy on incomes. The president was ordered to intervene on this occasion because Diego Manuel de Vera Zúñiga, marqués de Espinardo, the corregidor of Granada (1739–42), was thought to be insufficiently energetic in the matter. The curriculum vitae of some of the men promoted to these bodies included participation on one or more of the expeditions to Africa and Italy: in 1736, Francisco de Salazar y Aguiro was rewarded for his service, most recently as auditor general with the army in Italy, with the post of *oidor*, or judge, in the Chancillería of Granada, a promotion which often led to appointment to the Council of Castile.[27]

For administrators, successful organisation of one of Philip V's Mediterranean adventures was a sure route to royal favour. This was how the Savoyard representative in Madrid, Doria del Maro, explained Alberoni's achievement of both "despotic" power and the backing of Isabel, against "the nation." Patiño, whose ten-year domination began in 1726, demonstrated before and after that date that he was an excellent war minister. Campillo and Ensenada both owed their rise to similar qualities: Campillo accompanied the expedition to Sardinia (1717), was intendente general of the expeditionary force sent to Italy (1733), and was rewarded by the king with the intendancy of Aragon. In 1741–42 Campillo drew on that experience and on his years in naval administration, claiming to have overseen the construction of most of the king's ships, to achieve high office (above). Many of the other honours handed out to these ministers rewarded their contribution to the success of these expeditions: when the Golden Fleece was given to Patiño in 1732, the citation referred to his role in the reconquest of Oran.[28]

The Golden Fleece was among the most prestigious rewards in the gift of Philip V. The political culture of Bourbon Spain, like that of Habsburg Spain, was founded in large part upon the dispensing of mercedes of all sorts, and one in which appointments to offices were described as the grant of a merced by the king and often made in response to the presentation of *relaciones de servicios* by those seeking preferment. Individuals petitioning for a merced would often cite either their own participation on one or more of the Mediterranean adventures or that of a relation or both. In his petition, submitted some time after 1720, Juan Gaspar Zorrilla, the alcalde mayor of Ronda and Marbella and corregidor of Tordesillas and Rioseco, cited besides his own services those of four brothers, one of whom had died on the Sicilian expedition. Francisco Ortega y Orellana, the administrator of customs and tobacco of Alcántara for fifteen years, successfully petitioned for appointment as superintendente of the *reales rentas* and millones of Talavera (1746), instancing this employment and other merits, among them the fact that four of his sons were serving in the war, a fifth having been killed at the battle of Campo Santo a few years before.[29]

Mercedes helped to bind together the various clientage groups or factions contending for power with self-confessed "creatures" gathered around a *dueño*, or patron, such as Grimaldo, Patiño, Campillo, Ensenada, and others. Orendáin rose from Grimaldo's page to be undersecretary in his office and finally himself secretary of state, the Catalan Francisco Alós addressed Patiño (1735) as his dueño and protector, while Félix Cornejo, Philip V's envoy in Genoa, declared himself to be the creature of the secretary of state. Bonds of clientage were sometimes cemented by family ties: the Patiño grouping included the conde de Fuenclara, who married Patiño's niece. Another type of bond was that of a common geographical origin. The most striking example of a network of this sort was that of the Basques who, under Sebastián de la Cuadra, marqués de Villarías, secretary of state for foreign affairs (1736–47), attained a powerful grip on his secretariat—76 percent of the employees in the secretary of state's office—provoking some resentment by the time of the accession of Ferdinand VI, under whom it was ended. For his part, Carvajal, a descendant of one of the many Portuguese nobles who had opted to remain loyal to the Spanish Habsburgs and gone into exile in Spain during the so-called Portuguese War of Restoration (1640–68), benefitted from the fact that Ferdinand's consort, Barbara of Braganza, self-confessedly favoured those of Portuguese ancestry at the Spanish court.[30]

Many of the prosopographical studies which have been such a marked feature of recent efforts to fashion a social history of power in eighteenth-century Spain have focused on things like formal, family, and other links. But another source of political bonding and the foundation of successful careers thereafter and a relatively neglected aspect of the social history of power were friendships individuals forged outside and apart from family. Participation in one of Philip V's Mediterranean expeditions was one bond of friendship for some. Personal contact did not always or inevitably make for amity, and friendships did not always endure: Campillo and Montemar, both prickly personalities, did not work easily together in Italy in the War of the Polish Succession. However, Campillo and Ensenada served together as administrators before and during that same conflict, Ensenada subsequently enjoyed the patronage of Campillo and was summoned from Italy to replace him upon his death in 1743. Among lesser figures, Manuel Antonio Terán Bustamante y Alvaro de los Ríos began his career as Campillo's secretary in Italy in 1735 and afterwards enjoyed his patronage in a successful administrative career. Similarly, the foundations of a close friendship between Ensenada and Sebastián Eslava, the future viceroy of New Granada, were laid on the Oran expedition. Agustín Pablo de Ordeñana, one of many junior officials on whom Ensenada, like Patiño and Campillo before him, depended to ensure the administration worked effectively, began his career in the Almirantazgo in 1737 under Ensenada, followed him to Italy in 1741, and became one of his closest protégés, collaborators, and friends. In 1743, on Ensenada's return to Madrid, Ordeñana succeeded him as secretary of state and war to the Infante but later that same year was himself summoned to Madrid, probably at the suggestion of Ensenada, and appointed to the Council of Finance, no doubt as a reliable backer of his dueño.[31]

The groupings which competed for royal favour, whatever their family, regional, and other connections, were not devoid of principled content.

On the contrary. Indeed, the omission of attitudes and principles, as of friendships, is one of the weaknesses of the otherwise impressive prosopographical studies which have in recent decades done so much to illuminate eighteenth-century Spain, suggesting at least implicitly that domestic politics were absent from the absolute polity. In fact, individuals were often associated with distinctive policies, and their standing and influence often rose and fell with those policies. Not surprisingly, foreign sovereigns and their representatives in Madrid sought to interfere in Spanish politics on behalf of those ministers and factions most sympathetic to their own court's interests. Thus immediately after the conclusion of the treaty of Vienna in 1725 the imperial ambassador to the Spanish court, Count Konigsegg, enjoyed wide influence there. He helped to secure for Ripperda the extensive authority supposedly requested for him by Charles VI but used his influence to topple the baron when he failed to pay the subsidies promised in 1725. In 1725–26 Grimaldo and Patiño were intriguing, Patiño, at least, secretly, with the British minister Stanhope against the Austrian alliance, while Ripperda suspected Grimaldo of intercepting his correspondence.[32] Whatever the reason for the opposition to it, the rapprochement with the emperor soon collapsed. Nevertheless, in 1731 Patiño was said to be anxious about another rapprochement between the courts of Spain and Vienna for fear his own position might again be at risk. This was by no means the end of the efforts of foreign courts to influence the struggle for power in Madrid: in 1741, prompted by Campillo, Cardinal Fleury urged the Spanish court to appoint him secretary of war as well as of finance, to ensure unity of direction.[33]

The political struggle in Madrid also affected and was affected by the conduct of military operations abroad. This was most apparent during the War of the Austrian Succession, when the long-standing differences between Campillo and Montemar (above) found initial expression in disagreement about how and where Philip V should make his initial intervention in Italy. Montemar urged a landing in Liguria, close to the objective of the operation, Lombardy, whereas Campillo preferred Tuscany; Campillo prevailed, contributing to the difficulties encountered and losses sustained by the Spanish troops bottled up in Orbitello in 1741–42; subsequently, the substitution of Gages for Montemar as commander of the Spanish forces in Italy in 1742 was attributed by some to the enduring hostility between Montemar and Campillo; Gages's own replacement by Mina later in the war also had a political resonance.[34]

Spanish Political Life: 1. The Cortes

The foreign ambitions of Philip V were politically meaningful in other respects, too, not least in the way Philip's subjects reacted to them. Unfortunately, identifying that response or those responses is not easy, primarily because of the lack of formal, public venues for their expression. Perhaps the most obvious channel was the various Cortes. However, unlike some of those of the other territories of the Monarchy, the Castilian Cortes had not been assembled since 1665 and were rarely summoned by Philip, who was thus imitating Charles II. The Cortes of the Aragonese territories no longer met after 1707. Philip was thus vulnerable to the accusation of despotism, a charge made by Spanish exiles in Vienna after 1713, notably by conde Juan Amor de Soria in his *Enfermedad chrónica y peligrosa de los Reynos de España y de Indies: sus causas naturales y sus remedios* (The chronic and dangerous illness of the realms of Spain and the Indies: its causes and cures) (Vienna, 1741). There was some foundation for this, as the administration in Madrid extended, particularly in the war years and in the sphere of military and related matters, its scope of operation at the expense of local, representative institutions like the Junta of Galicia. In 1734–35 the delay of the junta, composed of representatives from Galicia's seven provincial capitals, in arranging for uniforms for its militia regiments led Patiño to authorise negotiation of a contract in Madrid and to order the junta's dissolution. This was the end of the junta as an active partner with the crown in government. However, the charge of despotism had little real foundation. The Cortes of Castile, in which the relatively few voting towns not only represented but in fact constituted the realm, or *reino*, continued to function as before 1700 and could prove a useful negotiating ploy for the king and his ministers in dealing with other sovereigns. One British minister was told in 1728 that the alienation of Gibraltar required the consent of the Cortes. Constitutionalism was not dead: like Habsburg Spain, the Spain of Philip V cannot be understood without recognising the extent to which it was shaped by an expectation of justice and due process.[35]

The Castilian Cortes had little say in Philip's succession, apart from assembling briefly in Madrid in May 1701 to swear loyalty to their new king and to receive his oath in return. Philip summoned the Cortes to meet, again, briefly, on three further occasions; in 1709, to swear to, that is, acknowledge, the future Luis I as heir to the throne or prince of Asturias; in 1712–13, at British insistence, to witness Philip's renunciation of his claim to the French crown, Philip taking the opportunity to have approved a new law of royal succession (above); and in December 1724 following his resumption of the throne to recognise as his heir the future Ferdinand VI. The Cortes had played no role in Philip's abdication and the accession of Luis I earlier in 1724, when the Council of Castile thought it enough to consult voting towns individually, by letter, as in the reign of Charles II. The Council of Castile initially ruled that it was not necessary to assemble the Cortes because Luis had been sworn as heir in 1709, before then declaring that it should be summoned; the council finally proposed consultation by letter, which was widely regarded as equivalent to an assembly of the Cortes. That method remained the norm until the Cortes was summoned in 1789 to swear to Charles IV. In the interim, the Cortes existed in the form of two standing committees, the Diputación and the Comisión de Millones, the latter by this time in effect a branch of the council of Finance. In 1744, during the War of the Austrian Succession, Philip V appointed six ministers of the Council of Finance to the comisión, effectively packing it.[36]

Philip V's reign was of some significance in respect of the composition of the Castilian Cortes. On his accession twenty-one Castilian towns enjoyed a vote in the Cortes. (In fact, one vote circulated among the cities of Galicia and another among those of Extremadura.) In 1708–9, following the abolition of the Aragonese and Valencian *fueros* and their respective Cortes, Philip invited six Aragonese and two Valencian towns—Borja, Calatayud, Fraga, Jaca, Peñíscola, Tarazona, Valencia, and Zaragoza—to send deputies to the Castilian Cortes, increasing the number of towns represented on that occasion to twenty-nine. In 1717, after the reconquest of Catalonia and Majorca, Philip invited a further seven towns— Barcelona, Cervera, Gerona, Lérida, Tarragona, Tortosa, and Palma de Majorca—in those territories to send representatives, bringing the total to thirty-seven. All thirty-seven were invited to send representatives to the

Cortes which recognised Ferdinand as heir in 1724 (above). This was not the creation of a national representation, given the limited number of towns concerned, the fruitless efforts of Asturias under Philip V to secure (or recover) a vote in the Cortes, and the exclusion of those territories, namely, Vizcaya and Navarra, which retained their own representative institutions, which continued to meet (see chapter 5). But, clearly, king and ministers recognised the need to consult the Cortes on specific issues. In 1725 the treaty of Vienna included a commitment by Philip V to have the Cortes, referred to as the *juntas públicas del Reino*—sanction as a perpetual or fundamental law of succession never to have a Spanish prince or princess marry into the French royal house.[37]

Consent was crucial respecting taxation. In 1713 the voting towns were consulted on Count Bergeyck's single tax proposal, which the majority rejected, effectively killing this radical reform. Consultation was also advisable to obtain approval for extraordinary impositions. In June 1715 Philip V ordered the Council of Castile to secure the consent of the voting towns to the continuation for another two years of the surcharge on salt which had been levied during the succession conflict and which was due to expire in 1716. The Cámara, whose responsibilities included summoning the Cortes, sent out the appropriate letters, requesting consent to and justifying the continuation of the levy. By early September 1715 replies had been received from all of the voting towns except Toledo, Jaén, and Salamanca. Although Jaén's regidores overwhelmingly rejected prorogation, prompting the Cámara to assert the king's regalian right to vary the price of salt, the Cámara declared the measure agreed. This process was repeated in 1717–18 against the background of war in Italy, the king's letter to the voting towns of November 1717 justifying the continuation of the surcharge by referring to the need of fleets to defend trade and of armies to defend the realm. Typically, the regidores of Valladolid took longer to agree on this occasion than in 1715 but did consent in late December 1717, after some chivvying by the corregidor. The imposition was continued on this occasion for three years. Prorogation was agreed again in 1721. The abolition of the levy in 1724 rendered unnecessary further consultation. Philip did not seek approval when reintroducing the levy in wartime in 1741.[38]

Regular consultation and consent throughout this and subsequent reigns were crucial to the continued receipt of the vital millones revenues (see chapter 3), which were granted by the Cortes for six years at a time. Monarch and ministers secured the necessary approval. Prorogation was agreed in 1716, 1722, 1728, 1733, 1739, and 1745. However, just as before 1700 and just as with the salt surcharge, the consent of the voting towns could not be taken for granted, unanimity might be out of the question, and securing consent might take time. In 1722 the process took very little time; by late March, within about ten weeks of the start of the consultation, the majority of towns, eighteen, had agreed, although Valladolid, Galicia, and Jaén had still not given their consent, pointing towards some reluctance to agree on their part. Sometimes, king and ministers needed to work to win consent.[39]

The Council of Castile and corregidores played a part in this. The process began with a circular letter from the king to the voting towns explaining and justifying the need for prorogation. The letters frequently referred to the expense of the African garrisons; that of October 1733 and that of September 1739, for example, both referred to the costs of defence of those presidios, described as the bulwarks, or *antemurales,* of Christianity, and to Philip's reluctance to burden his subjects with new taxes. These arguments, also deployed in the reign of Charles II, imply the persistence of a powerful religious, that is, Christian, mentalité which Philip and his ministers could exploit, as during the Spanish succession struggle. In the spring of 1741, after the outbreak of war against Britain in the Caribbean but before intervention in Italy, an anti-English, anti-Protestant rhetoric was deployed to justify the 10 percent levy on incomes and thus preserve the Indies. Perhaps signalling the fact that Spanish intervention in Italy was not so easily justified and less popular, it was not referred to when the king sought the consent of the voting towns to the prorogation of the millones in September 1745, at a time when other demands of the king were fuelling tension. But other factors also weighed with the regidores in the voting towns. A very different argument frequently deployed by Philip V's ministers was that prorogation of the millones would enable the king to pay the annuities due on *juros,* in which many of the Castilian elites and a great array of ecclesiastical and other institutions had a vested interest in that those annuities were often paid out of those revenues. In fact, that interest was rarely paid in full (see chapter 3); nevertheless, that the argument was used hints that it had some sway.[40]

Most voting towns made no difficulty about renewal. In 1745 the regidores of Burgos received the king's letter seeking prorogation of the millones on 2 October and agreed on 9 October. Management of the sessions in which the office-owning regidores who determined each voting city's vote discussed and generally complied with the royal requests was the responsibility of the corregidor, who, as before 1700, sometimes had to cajole and sometimes to bargain and who, again as before 1700, intimated to the Council of Castile which regidores should be rewarded for their cooperation. Regidores expected to be rewarded, mercedes being another crucial element in securing the consent of the voting towns. In 1745 the regidores of Murcia, having agreed the prorogation of the millones, promptly prepared a list of mercedes they might request from the king in return for their consent. For their part in managing the regidores, the corregidores of voting towns themselves expected to be and were also rewarded, some receiving, for instance, pensions payable out of episcopal revenues.[41]

The Council and Cámara of Castile liaised with the towns on these and other issues. In consequence they were very aware of the concerns of those towns and, as noted earlier, acted as what might be called, in the absence of the Cortes, the voice of the realm, reminding the king, for example, of the formal conditions attached by earlier Cortes to their millones grants, in the so-called *escrituras de millones*, a collection of which was reprinted in 1734 and updated in 1742. Historians, primarily interested in the legislative role of the council, have often neglected this constitutional role, which was revealed, to take one case, in the tussle over royal grants of Castilian *naturaleza*, with all they implied in terms of the recipient's eligibility for mercedes of all sorts. According to earlier millones grants, the king was not supposed to grant naturaleza without the consent of the Cortes. However, the pressure on Philip V to make such grants grew as exiles and their families flocked to Spain from what had been Spanish Flanders and Spanish Italy in the War of the Spanish Succession. Between 1705 and 1715 Philip made twenty-three grants of naturaleza, more than two a year on average. This caused some worry. In August 1715 various voting towns, having refused to renew the millones on these grounds, Philip V confirmed that in future all grants of naturalisation intended to enable the recipient to enjoy ecclesiastical office or revenues must obtain the consent of those towns. But the Cámara raised the issue again the following month after receiving further representations from the city of Salamanca. In February 1716 the Diputación (above) circularised the voting towns to remind them that the grant of naturaleza contravened the terms of the grant of the millones and continued to make representations to the king on the subject.[42]

These complaints may have had some effect, as the number of such grants fell off after 1715. In 1727 the petition of the duke of Solferino for naturaleza for his brother D. Almérico Gonzaga was refused, as was that in 1728 of the duke of Castropignano for his brother D. Nicolás de Eboli. Philip continued to grant naturalisation but made sure he secured the approval of the voting towns. Those towns concurred, but still had misgivings. In 1733 the regidores of Valladolid approved the naturalisation of D. Miguel Zapata de Cárdenas of Siracusa (Sicily), on condition that no precedent was set thereby. The following year D. Ignacio Reggio e Gravina, the son of the Sicilian prince of Campoflorido, was granted naturaleza in order to enjoy ecclesiastical revenues although resident abroad; on this occasion the regidores of Valladolid approved the grant, although one thought the beneficiary should reside in Spain. In 1739 the Cámara advised that the king could grant the naturaleza requested by the duke of Mirandola for his cousin but that he should consult the voting towns. Philip thus got his way but could not ignore the constitutional norms and practices inherited from the Habsburgs.[43]

The Cortes-voting towns, the Council of Castile, and the Cámara did not limit themselves to insisting that Philip V respect the terms of earlier millones grants. In 1723 the council, in a lengthy representation to the king, called for taxes to be reduced since the succession conflict was over, 1724 seeing the abolition of most of the extraordinary charges imposed during that struggle. The council also protected the subject in other ways. In 1733, reacting to a request by the duque de Montellano for a four-year moratorium on his debts to enable him to pay the dowry of his daughter, the governor of the council, acting to protect the interests of creditors, noted the inconvenience of allowing the request but said the king could grant it on condition that Montellano continued to satisfy obligations to various religious foundations. That same year, addressing a request to the king from the corregidor of Ecija that, in view of the scandal caused by local offenders, the king send them to Oran, the governor declared this was a matter which must be determined by the proper judicial authorities.[44]

The mobilisation of men and money in wartime offered the council further opportunities to intervene to protect the king's subjects. In 1741 it added its voice to the widespread criticism of the 10 percent income levy; that year the governor of the council effectively vetoed a *quinta* levy of troops proposed by Secretary of War Montemar, counselling instead that the king invite individuals to raise units at their own expense. Such interventions were not always entirely disinterested: during the War of the Austrian Succession the council protested at the way its authority and tutelary role regarding the finances of local communities were undermined by agents of the secretary of state for finance. It also expressed opposition to the resumption and sale of *baldíos,* one of the most serious sources of complaint of the reign (below).[45]

Philip V did not always appreciate the role assumed by the Council of Castile and the Cámara as constitutional watchdog and protector of his subjects, especially in wartime. In 1719 the Cámara demurred at a request to burden an entail in order to fund recruiting of men for the king, seeking to protect the rights of the heirs. Philip, while acknowledging that objective, insisted that his need of troops must take priority (see chapter 1). Nor was Philip always inclined to heed the contractual constitutional arguments of the Cortes or its representatives as he sought to improve the finances after the costly overseas operations of the 1730s. In November 1738 the Diputación made representations in the name of the reino against the recently established Junta de Baldíos, which was to oversee the resumption and sale of commons and wastes (see chapter 3) and which the Diputación claimed breached the terms of the millones grants. The Diputación complained as well about a recent plethora of extraordinary revenue-raising devices, including quotas and extraordinary appropriations, or *valimientos.* In large part the Diputación was acting on complaints received from the Cortes-voting towns. In June 1738 the city of Burgos argued that the appointment of a *juez de comisión* to investigate and sell off baldíos to the advantage of the royal treasury was contrary to both the laws of the realm and the conditions of grants of the millones, The resumption and sale of baldíos prompted complaints from other privileged corporations as well, including, for example, the national organisation of carters, the Hermandad de Carreteros de la Cabaña Real. On this occasion the governor of the Council of Castile defended the king, maintaining not only—referring to the seventeenth-century *arbitrista* Caxa de Leruela's *Restauración de la abundancia de España*, originally published in 1631 and reprinted in 1713 and 1732, hence remaining relevant to political debate in Spain—that the measure would stimulate Spain's agriculture but also that there was no question the monarch was the rightful owner of the *tierras baldías*. But the urban elites had not given up the struggle. In 1739 the regidores of Valladolid took the opportunity to remind Philip of earlier legislation on the baldíos, but, not least because the status of those lands was contentious, with little immediate effect.[46]

The regidores did not convince the king to change tack on this occasion and do not seem to have exploited the renewal of the millones in 1745, in wartime, to attack the policy anew. However, monarch and ministers did sometimes recognise the need to be more flexible, to negotiate, even to reverse policy. In 1741, as we have seen (see chapter 3), the radical demand for a 10 percent income tax was fundamentally recast in view of the reaction of the Castilian urban elites. More telling perhaps, some years later, in December 1747, following further representations from the Diputación and a consulta by the Council of Castile, Ferdinand VI halted the sale of baldíos. It has been suggested that this episode demonstrated that the early Bourbons did not have an agrarian policy.[47] What it really exhibits is that agrarian policy was trumped or determined by their political and military and associated fiscal priorities and the extent to which an individual monarch, Philip V if not Ferdinand, was prepared to face down criticism from a broad swathe of opinion.

Spanish Political Life: 2. Opinion

The opportunities for formal opposition or even just discussion of contemporary issues may have been more limited than in earlier times, when the Cortes had assembled, but monarchs and ministers could not entirely ignore the existence of a critical public opinion of sorts. It would be extravagant to claim for opinion in the Spain of the first Bourbon the status of a public sphere of the sort evident in eighteenth-century Britain and France and in Spain itself in the reign of Charles III. However, a critical opinion unmistakably existed in late Habsburg Spain, something which the struggle for hearts and minds during the War of the Spanish Succession had built on and further stimulated.[48]

Nonetheless, the subject is not an easy one to pursue in view of the difficulties in discovering just whose views public opinion in fact represented—how widely held and popular its manifestations were and what its concerns were. There exists for Spain nothing like the police reports used by historians of opinion in early modern Venice and eighteenth-century Paris, although those of the *alcaldes de casa y Corte*, the magistrates answerable to the Council of Castile responsible for the policing of Madrid, might be useful in this respect. Similarly, the reports reaching many of the councils, notably that of Castile, and the secretary of state for war relating to the success or failure of recruiting and extent of desertion might be very revealing about attitudes and opinion. In the spring of 1747 Ensenada acknowledged a general truculence regarding the war in Italy, noting that deserters claimed the war, which was going badly at this stage, was being fought not in the interests of the Spanish crown but to establish one who did not deserve it, an allusion to the Infante Felipe. Preambles to royal orders can reveal opinion, by addressing it, responding to it, effectively constituting one-half of a dialogue with the king's subjects. Useful, too, are the reports of foreign diplomats, who were keen to appreciate both the resources of Philip ahead of any potential conflict and the attitudes of his subjects, although they rarely got much beyond Madrid. Those diplomats frequently referred to the public mood at critical moments. In September 1728, for example, during one of Philip's bouts of depression, the Savoyard representative reported the widespread and unrestrained expression by the population of Madrid of a desire for the crown to pass to the prince of Asturias, the future Ferdinand VI, and of an expectation, wishful thinking, really, that this might happen on his forthcoming fifteenth birthday. The minister was sceptical, however, in view of the likely opposition of Isabel. Unfortunately, foreign ministers rarely identified precisely who voiced the opinions they reported, often referring simply to an anonymous public. They also sometimes contradicted each other, as they did in reporting reactions to the peace of Vienna in 1725. The Venetian representative, Daniele Bragadin, did not share the British minister Stanhope's assessment of the perceived popular antagonism towards that settlement, although the French representatives, too, reported revulsion once the details were known. These conflicting reports might be a sign of real differences of opinion among the public, uncertainty on its part about just what to make of developments, and the way opinion was something in constant flux. Nevertheless, Spain's revival after 1713 without doubt stimulated the growth of what we might call a nascent public sphere.[49]

Opinion might be articulated and discovered through the developing periodical press. This included the quasi-official *Gaceta de Madrid*, produced under privilege by the Goyeneche family from 1697 until 1762; the short-lived *Diario de los Literarios* (1737–42); the *Mercurio Histórico Político*, from 1738; and various local gazettes and, most popular of all perhaps, almanacs. Most of these publications enjoyed official approval and were unlikely to voice criticism of royal policy. But the same could not always be said of another type of publication, the pamphlet. Philip's resumption of the crown in 1724 triggered a wave of publications of this type as well as of that other phenomenon, the satire or pasquinade, whose essential characteristic was its critical, sometimes offensive quality. As early as 1718 satires directed against Alberoni were on the streets of Madrid; the accession of Luis I stimulated a surge of such productions in 1724; and in the summer of 1725, after an initially favourable reaction to the recently concluded treaty of Vienna, the subsequent shift of opinion found expression in the appearance of satirical epigrams mocking Orendáin's new title of marqués de la Paz, the peace.[50]

The most celebrated and notorious publication designed to lampoon was the manuscript newsletter *Duende Crítico* (Critical spirit), which briefly flourished between December 1735 and June 1736 and was produced by the Portuguese Carmelite fray Manuel Freyre de Silva. This work focused its attacks on Patiño's supposed ministerial despotism, on Isabel, on foreign policy, and on the fiscal burden associated with Spain's participation in the War of the Polish Succession. These criticisms were connected with an escalating confrontation with Portugal at that moment, the arrest of one of the servants of the Portuguese ambassador in Madrid being followed by tit-for-tat diplomatic expulsions and a war scare in the spring and summer of 1735. But the attacks also resonated with the broader jealousies of some among the nobility and with those of the "Spanish party" (below). The *Duende Crítico* made great play with the peace preliminaries agreed by the French and imperial courts in 1735 and then imposed upon Louis XV's allies, and which so abruptly terminated the Spanish monarchs' dream of expelling the Austrian Habsburgs from Italy to their own advantage. The *Duende Crítico* was not unique, a great deal of critical manuscript material no doubt still awaiting discovery by historians. In focusing on print, we should not ignore the continued significance of the circulation of manuscript compositions, including private correspondence, which might also be critical. Manuscript or printed, such materials provided a persistent, if ephemeral, critical commentary on the resurgent Spain of Philip V and, later, of Ferdinand VI.[51]

Just how popular, how widely read, these satires were is difficult to gauge. The same is true of that other manifestation of opinion, rumour. Nevertheless, neither could be wholly ignored. In 1726 Philip ordered an investigation into rumours of another abdication, murmurs which may have been deliberately circulated by the disaffected. King and ministers sought to control opinion and the press in two very distinct ways. On the one hand, they aimed to prevent broader discussion of affairs of state. Thus, after the Cape Passaro fiasco in 1718, Alberoni sought to ban public discussion of the disaster. In the summer of 1725 the authorities seized a pamphlet published and distributed in Madrid which was hostile to the treaty of Vienna and which it was feared might reduce confidence in Philip's commitment to it at the Austrian court. Ripperda, too, sought to keep matters from the public. In 1742, following the publication by the dean and chapter of Toledo cathedral of a memorial questioning the legality of the papal brief granting Philip V a levy of 8 percent on ecclesiastical incomes to help pay for the war with Britain, Philip banished those responsible.[52]

To help them restrict such discussion, ministers censored the press. In 1744 the authorities were said to have suppressed publication of Admiral Navarro's account of the recent naval engagement off Toulon because it "reflected too much on their [the French] behaviour" at a time when Spanish opinion was already strongly Francophobe following that action. The year after, subsequent to the publication by D. Josef de Arenas of *Oráculo de la Europa*, Philip V decreed that the Council of Castile, which oversaw censorship in Castile and Aragon, should not allow publication of any book or paper which discussed matters of state, including foreign policy. In part, this order was simply enforcing the privilege granted in 1741 to Miguel José de Aoiz to publish and sell the *Mercurio Político y Económico*. But there may have been more to this than just safeguarding a privilege. Arenas's book, translated from the French, comprised a series of *consultas* in which various European sovereigns outlined their policy and conduct since the start of the War of the Austrian Succession, each of which was followed by a commentary or reply by the *oráculo*. The subject of Consulta XIII was the king of Spain. The reply to Philip V's supposed defence of his position in the current conflict declared that in a defensive war, which was always just, there would be divine aid. It claimed this had been the case in America, where the British assault had ultimately failed, a reference to the abortive attack on Cartagena de Indias in 1741. But, Arenas continued, an aggressive war was another matter. One implication of the commentary was that Philip's war in Europe, in Italy, was not a just one. Philip could not allow such discussion, although the attitude may have been more widely held. Carvajal's *Testamento* discussed the just war and might also be construed as a critique of the war in Italy, while the duque de Huéscar, in private correspondence with Carvajal in 1748, after Philip's death, was more directly disparaging of that conflict, a view which now had the support of the reigning monarch.[53]

In focusing on the circulation of print and manuscript publications we should not ignore private correspondence, which might also contain and fuel criticism. Thus Carvajal's letters from his elder brother, Nicolás, who was serving in Italy, gave an unvarnished account of the precarious situation of the Spanish forces there in the spring of 1746. The authorities might seek to control the flow of such communication, as when in 1732 letters from Oran were detained. Nevertheless, such measures could not be wholly effective, and letters continued to convey unwelcome intelligence, for example, in the War of the Austrian Succession, having to do with the precarious situation of the Spanish army in Italy in the spring of 1746. At the end of 1746 reports from Galicia told of a government crackdown on criticism and opposition, of the detention of those who spoke out or wrote critically, and of orders being sent to the post offices to open private letters in order to discover critics.[54]

It proved impossible, however, to prevent widespread knowledge of, discussion, and speculation about royal policy inside and outside the capital. In the autumn of 1726 the British minister in Madrid reported the astonishment of Spaniards at the daily publication of accounts of sums to be paid to various German princes (as Philip V contributed to the expansion of the Vienna alliance) at a time when Spain itself was hard-pressed and Philip unable to meet his domestic obligations without remittances from the Indies. In the spring of 1730 the British consul at Coruña reported the impressment of seamen and the recruiting of regiments to serve in Italy, remarking that it was generally believed war with the emperor was unavoidable; four weeks later the consul reported that all talk at Coruña was of the expedition to Italy, although in fact no such expedition took place. Similarly, in 1732 the consul at Málaga observed that a Spanish expedition was "much talked of," although opinion differed as to its object, some saying, correctly as it turned out, that its destination was Oran, others Italy. In distant Galicia, too, at Coruña, despite efforts to keep it a secret the same expedition stimulated discussion and varying opinions as to its destination.[55]

It was impossible to prevent discussion and speculation. The authorities therefore sought to influence and shape opinion and to put a positive gloss or spin on government policy. In 1741, for example, Campillo wanted to explain to the *public* the circumstances surrounding the 10 percent income levy. Royal orders invariably carried an explanatory, justificatory preamble in answer to or in anticipation of criticisms to which they might refer. In December 1746, for instance, the order for the levy of twenty-five thousand men began by referring to the problem of desertion, the lack of volunteers and the fact that the king's enemies obliged him to continue the war despite his wish for peace, thus explaining both his need for so many men and his finding them in this way.[56]

Ministers also sought to manage opinion through the press. In the summer of 1741, great efforts were made in the secretary of state's office preparing for the press the news of the defeat of the British at Cartagena de Indias. In wartime the *Gaceta de Madrid* frequently carried upbeat reports on the achievements of Spanish arms or sought to gloss over setbacks, as did one published account of the disaster at Cape Passaro; the *Gaceta*, in reporting that defeat, also described Spanish successes on land in Sicily. During the War of the Austrian Succession the *Gaceta* carried frequent reports of successful engagements with the enemy at sea: in 1745 one issue included an account of a heroic encounter off Finisterre between the frigate *La Flecha* and an English ship. The paper also reported captures made by Spanish privateers, giving details of their rich cargoes. In January 1743, for example, the *Gaceta* related that the corsair the *Marte Vizcaino* had captured an English ship carrying a load worth twenty-one thousand pesos.[57]

Besides the reports in the official *Gaceta* separate accounts of battles were published. In 1744, following news of the success of Don Carlos in halting the Austrian invasion of Naples at Velletri, the *Gaceta* declared, "As soon as [a] relation arrives it will be given to the public so that it knows all the circumstances of the action which brings such honour and fame to the king and the arms he commands." The next year saw the publication of separate accounts of other Spanish successes in Italy. The existence of such material implies there was some demand or market for this type of publication. This might also offer opportunities to those who had been on an expedition: D. Pedro de la Cueva, the auditor general on the Oran expedition, published his own account of that adventure. Some commentators were sceptical of the positive spin these publications put on events: in 1733 the British minister, Keene, dismissed the "pompous" narratives circulating of the conquest of Oran. Nevertheless, such reports may have had a positive impact on opinion, no doubt one of the reasons they were issued.[58]

Philip and his ministers did not limit themselves to printed propaganda. Like his Habsburg predecessors and his contemporaries elsewhere in Europe, the Catholic King resorted to another conspicuous medium, that of public, primarily religious, ceremony, including the Te Deum Mass, in which thanks were given for divine aid in specific successes, which might certainly seem credible in victories over the Moors. Such Masses, often accompanied by more secular celebrations like days of illuminations, palace balls, and bullfights in various towns were ordered to celebrate triumph over the emperor's troops in Sicily in 1719 and the raising of the siege of Ceuta in 1720. Manifestations of this sort continued to advertise victory abroad thereafter and were ordered on the conclusion of the peace of

Vienna in May 1725, the start of a succession of related celebrations which lasted until September 1725, when the treaty was published; on the departure of Don Carlos for Italy in 1731; and in 1732 after the capture of Oran. The War of the Polish Succession triggered a further round of such celebrations. Te Deum Masses were ordered in June 1734 after Don Carlos's proclamation as king of Naples and following his landing in Sicily. The first years of the War of the Austrian Succession offered further opportunities to proclaim Spanish military successes in this manner, a Te Deum Mass being ordered after the encounter at Campo Santo in 1743. The string of ceremonies of this sort and accompanying celebrations in that annus mirabilis of 1745 would have impressed upon at least some of the king's subjects the achievements of Spanish arms in Italy: Philip ordered a Te Deum after the surrender of Tortona, Piacenza, Parma, Pavia, Alessandria, Valenza, Asti, and Casale and after the Infante's entry into Milan in December 1745. It was not only the successes of Philip's forces which were celebrated: so, too, were those of his allies, in what was probably an attempt to hearten the king's subjects. In the War of the Austrian Succession the Catholic King ordered Te Deum Masses following French successes in Flanders in 1744, 1745, and 1746 and in the Dutch Republic in 1747.[59]

Opinion in general might be difficult to pin down and also the impact, if any, of government efforts to control and shape it. But certain themes and issues emerge as matters of concern. There was widespread hostility to both the treaty of Vienna (1725) and the treaty of Seville (1729): both were thought to sacrifice Spanish interests in the Americas, the first to secure the emperor's alliance, the second that of Britain and France in order to establish Don Carlos in Italy, although opinion was more critical of Isabel than of Philip V. A few years later, the nation was said to have reacted badly to the cession of Naples and Sicily to Don Carlos in 1734—reconquered at great cost to Spain in men and money only to be again dismembered from the body of the Monarchy. There was also a widely held, enduring sense that in successive alliances to secure those Italian objectives the French court had humiliated Spain, fuelling a powerful Francophobia.[60]

Historians of eighteenth-century Spain have identified on the back of this opinion a specific opposition, one very relevant to Philip V's

Mediterranean adventures. This was the so-called Spanish party, defined by hostility to both the advent of a French dynasty and, after 1713, the sacrifice of Spanish interests, exemplified by concessions in the Indies and Gibraltar, in the pursuit of Italian ambitions. We must be careful not to be too rigid in identifying parties and their adherents. After all, Philip himself wanted to reverse the settlement of 1713 insofar as it related to Gibraltar and the Indies. Nevertheless, his apparent readiness to subordinate this to achieving his goals in Italy antagonised the Spanish party, which briefly triumphed under Luis I and which subsequently resented the sacrifice of Spanish interests in the treaty of Vienna (1725), the treaty of Seville and the (second) treaty of Vienna (1731). Regarding the first of these agreements, the Spanish party favoured alliance with the emperor, but clearly the price paid appalled even some Austrophiles: thus, in 1745 Carvajal, while endorsing alliance with Austria, remained hostile to the treaty of 1725, which he thought very damaging to Spain. As for the treaties of 1729 and 1731, as the Savoyard representative observed, English trading privileges were so prejudicial to Spain that "veritables bons sujets nationaux qui voudroient le bien solide de l'Etat" (the truly devoted national subjects who wished for the solid good of the State) did not enjoy the sight of the establishment of the Infante (Don Carlos) in Italy, which they believed could succeed only by surrendering the wealth of the Indies to England. Opposition focused on the Italian policy, not that in Africa, suggesting that the centuries-old struggle against the Moors was more popular, not least because it represented a practical defensive need and reflected religious values which Philip had exploited to very good effect during the succession struggle. But the members of the Spanish party also resented their exclusion from power and influence and the monopoly of these by Italian favourites.[61]

The Spanish party was not a party in any recognisably modern sense, that is, a well-organised body with a large membership distributed across the country, being more a faction, even an attitude, than an organisation. Members included Miraval (above) and his confessor, while the most obvious head of any opposition of this sort, particularly after Philip V's resumption of the throne in 1724, was the future Ferdinand VI, whose rights had been set aside on that occasion. In 1728 the prince's undergovernor told the envoy of Ferdinand's uncle, the king of Sardinia, that his arrival

had delighted the prince's party. Ferdinand enjoyed great popularity because of his birth in Spain and the fact that the popular affection for his
mother, Philip's first wife, grew with hostility towards Isabel and the policies associated with her. In 1735, during the War of the Polish Succession,
with Spain denuded of troops (see chapter 1) and in the wake of Philip's
gift of Naples and Sicily to Don Carlos, Ferdinand's father-in-law, the
king of Portugal, claimed that the prince need only issue a manifesto
against the supposed tyranny of Isabel and the incapacity of Philip to incite general insurrection in Spain. A few years later, in 1738, when Don
Carlos's marriage prompted official celebrations in Madrid, the people—
no more precise description was given—were said to have shown no satis-
faction because no such festivities had occurred on Ferdinand's marriage
in 1729. However, the king of Portugal exaggerated both the degree of
disaffection within Spain and, more important, the extent to which any
opposition was prepared to act. Above all, the malcontents expected too
much of Ferdinand. He plainly resented his stepmother and the prefer-
ence accorded her sons, his half brothers, which depleted his inheritance,
and he would not cooperate with Isabel in 1733 during another of Philip's
illnesses, wanting power for himself. However, he was reluctant to play the
role of leader of the opposition, a position sometimes assumed by heirs to
the throne in early modern monarchies.[62]

Ferdinand's passivity was matched by that of the aristocracy. Among
the most striking features, politically, of Philip V's reign is the extent to
which the upper nobility, the grandees and títulos, did not play the role
they had under Charles II. Indeed, Philip's reign represented a real contrast with that of his immediate predecessor in this regard. The collapse
of the political, though not the economic or social, power of the titled
nobles and grandees was the gain of a new cadre of titled (and untitled)
nobles of less distinguished ancestry who owed everything to the king and
constituted in effect a new nobility of service. The supposed taming of
the grandees had begun in the War of the Spanish Succession, when
some of those who had been most prominent in the previous reign, including the *almirante* of Castile, the conde de Oropesa, the duque de
Medinaceli, and the marqués de Leganes, embraced the wrong side in
the succession struggle, some following the putative "Charles III" into
exile, some suffering confiscation of property, some remaining in Spain

but withdrawing from public life. The duque de Infantado decided, after being tried and acquitted of disloyalty in the War of the Spanish Succession, to abandon the court, breaking with the seventeenth-century tradition of his family; he preferred to live on and cultivate his estates rather than to dabble in public life, with all its risks. Generally speaking, the upper, or titled, nobility was less prominent and visible in Spanish political life after 1713. Other nobles, often of slightly lesser standing, *hidalgos* and *caballeros*, benefitted from this situation, responding to the new opportunities offered by Philip V in army, navy, and administration. In some respects, this development was the culmination of the emergence in the reign of Charles II of new noble cadres, whose attitude was crucial to the outcome of the succession struggle, a conflict which entrenched them as a nobility of service. Their role in Spain's revival after 1713 would consolidate their position.[63]

However, while individual títulos and grandees and individual families suffered in the succession struggle, it would be a gross error to see this as the end of the Castilian grandees. For one thing, most grandees and títulos, about two-thirds of the total, were loyal to Philip V during that conflict. As for those whose loyalty was suspect or who declared openly for "Charles III," Philip inclined to punish individuals rather than whole families such that properties were not necessarily confiscated for good. Individual exiles were, on petition, pardoned and allowed to return to Spain, especially after 1713, while the peace of Vienna of 1725 provided for not only a general amnesty and return to Spain but also the recovery of confiscated property. Taking advantage of those provisions was not always easy, not least because of the opposition of those who would have to restore property. Nevertheless, the settlement prompted the return of many exiles and led to some recovery of property. The son of the duque de Uceda, who had died in exile in Vienna in 1718, recovered some of his father's property in 1725, while most of the almirante's inheritance was secured by his nephew. Philip V also confirmed some of the titles granted by "Charles III": in 1730, for example, he confirmed the status of grandee (2nd class), or *grandeza*, originally bestowed by Charles on Bartolomé Debrián y Alagón, conde de Fuenclara, for the latter's nephew, the conde de Fuenclara who married Patiño's niece and served Philip as ambassador in various European capitals and who in 1740 was promoted by

Philip to grandee (1st class). In this way what had constituted since the succession conflict two parallel, rival Spanish nobilities was knitted together.[64]

In fact, grandees and títulos were not completely ousted from public life and deprived of a share in power. They continued to occupy the most prestigious posts in the army (see chapter 1), at court, and in diplomacy. The 6th duque de Osuna, who had fought for Philip V throughout the war of succession, headed his negotiating team at the congress of Utrecht. He died in 1716, however, without male issue and was succeeded by his brother, who himself died in 1733, to be succeeded by his five-year-old son, demonstrating that some of the families prominent before 1700 were temporarily prevented from playing an active, public role by factors which had little to do with the policies of individual monarchs. The new administrative structures also meant that the older and some more recently ennobled families participated more indirectly in power, through relations and office-holding clients. They were happy to adapt in this way not least because there was no need to intervene in politics, as Spain was ruled by a capable, adult male. Philip's occasional lapses offered opportunities to act against a detested queen or favourite, of the sort which were seized on before 1700, but these were not taken advantage of. On the whole, grandees and títulos were content with or at least resigned to their position under the first Bourbon, who in any case continued to employ them and who also created new ties of fidelity between himself and them by means, for example, of new institutions like the royal guards.[65]

In addition, as the succession conflict had revealed, the great families preferred stability as less harmful to their interests, and serving the king served those interests—the 6th duque de Osuna (above) securing royal support when, during his absence at Utrecht, anti-seigneurial riots disturbed Osuna. For all of these reasons and the fact that some of the individuals who had contended for power under Charles II had died, some in exile, their families were less pushy in this reign. For his part, particularly after 1713, Philip V was by no means hostile to the titled nobility and grandees in principle or as a bloc, although he was not sympathetic to those with elevated views of the position of the upper ranks of the nobility vis-à-vis the crown. The conde de Aguilar, who had backed Philip in the succession struggle, may have been disgraced (1711–25) for views of this sort. As he did some of those who served in senior positions in the army and fleet, Philip rewarded certain of his ministers with noble titles (if they did not already have them), for example, Grimaldo in 1714 and Orendáin in 1725, awarding more than three hundred titles in the course of his reign; in 1736 he rewarded Patiño with grandeza (1st class) as a sort of lifetime award following the conquest of Naples and Sicily. Philip handled the grandees and títulos firmly but carefully: his incorporation in 1729 of the Puerto de Santa María into the crown was preceded by negotiation with and accompanied by compensation for the duque de Medinaceli. Philip thus ensured that he benefitted from the lustre the greater nobility could add to his court and regime. In consequence, títulos and grandees continued to enjoy great wealth and influence, as they had before 1700. This continuity, which both reflected and underpinned a more fundamental stability in Spain's political and social structure, played its part in the Monarchy's reemergence as a significant power between 1713 and 1748.[66]

Perhaps the most serious opposition, because more effective, given the new administrative and political arrangements, was that associated with the clash of views within government (see above). The rapprochement with Vienna (1725) was clearly divisive (above). In the spring of 1731 the Savoyard minister to the Spanish court was told that Philip's ministers were divided over the treaty of Seville, in view of Philip's concessions to Britain to secure the installation of Don Carlos in Italy. Some also had doubts about the forward policy in Africa. In the autumn of 1732 the determination of the king to defend the recent conquest of Oran was said to make some ministers unhappy at wasting so much—money, men—to save the honour of the king and the gloire of the Spanish monarchy; they preferred to abandon the place. Accumulating salary and other arrears in the royal household by 1732 resulted in a reform of the financial management of the latter which triggered some criticism of Philip's Italian projects. The dissenters were not successful in this phase of the ongoing debate about policy and strategy. Nevertheless, Philip's revanchism and the political, diplomatic, military, and financial measures to pursue it continued to spark rumblings of discontent from within the administration: in 1737 the Junta de Medios, echoing broader debates about policy and strategy, while accepting the need to fund the fleet thought the army and particularly the recent increase in the number of senior officers should be cut. In 1741 widespread opposition both from within the Councils of Finance and Castile and from corregidores and intendentes contributed to the climbdown over the 10 percent income levy of that year. By the mid- to late 1740s, if Carvajal's *Testamento Político* and the private correspondence of some ministers are anything to go by, various ministers had real doubts about the value to Spain of Philip V's Italian policy: the duque de Huéscar, for one, articulated the view in the summer of 1747 that the Catholic King was more powerful without Flanders or Italy.[67]

Just how this court-based dissent connected with opinion across Spain is unclear, but it is suggestive that in October 1747 Ferdinand VI expressed concern about the lack of secrecy surrounding discussions in the Council of Castile. But that a more general unease of some sort existed, for example, in Galicia and elsewhere, is evident in the War of the Austrian Succession, provoked above all by the demands of war in Italy. Galicia's complaints, conveyed to the king by deputies sent to Madrid, had some impact in 1742 and again in the summer of 1743, when Philip made concessions as to how the men he demanded from local communities were to be found. The population at large was aware of developments in Italy, especially because Spanish losses in the battle at Campo Santo meant the king was likely to demand more men. In December 1744 Galicia again sent deputies to Madrid, to make representations against the quinta after having given so many men already and about the level of taxation, Philip conceding that men could be taken from the militia. In the summer of 1745 Galicia's representations on the king's use of the militia again delayed matters, although ministers pressed ahead to secure the men needed to strengthen the army in Italy.[68]

There was little if any overt, violent resistance in Galicia or elsewhere in Spain. Efforts to revise tax obligations upwards provoked rioting in the reino of Granada in 1746 (see chapter 3). But, as in the previous century, when Castile remained relatively quiescent when Catalonia and Portugal rebelled, Castile's resentments did not find expression in sustained, outright revolt. In 1734–35, when foreign commentators reported resentment among Philip's subjects at the Spanish resources pumped into a war which appeared to benefit only Don Carlos, they thought that no formal opposition could be expected; and in 1738 one foreign commentator observed that despite widespread ill will toward Isabel, "the nation is abject and low spirited enough to suffer even more than they do." Some commentators pointed to the fact that Philip V had troops quartered throughout the realm, forces who might enforce his will on truculent subjects if need be. But important, too, was the extent to which ancien régime Spain was a polity in which the inclination was to obey, not oppose, the legitimate monarch, as had been demonstrated during the Spanish succession struggle.[69]

But we also need to acknowledge the existence of positive support in Spain for Philip's and Isabel's Italian policy. Unfortunately, the makeup of this backing remains shadowy, such that it has been too easy to think of the Italian policy in particular as that merely of the court, when in fact there existed what might be called an Italian lobby as well as a broader body of favourable opinion: according to the Venetian ambassador in Madrid (1725), the recovery of Italy was desired not only by the king but also by the whole Spanish nation. One potential body of support was to be found among the titled nobles and grandees, who had largely monopolised the lucrative Italian viceroyalties before 1707. Successive duques de Osuna all held one or more captaincy general or viceroyalty in Italy between circa 1580 and 1700. The American viceroyalties were generally held by members of less illustrious, but still noble, families in the eighteenth century. These Spanish champions of revanchism were supplemented by the many more Spaniards who had built up family and other connections in Italy over the past two hundred years (see chapter 5). To these must be added the many exiles from former Spanish Italy and Flanders, men like Jacinto de Pozobueno, marqués de Pozobueno (1721), born in Spanish Flanders (1659), governor of Trapani in Sicily (1699-), either wishing to return home or dependent in Spain on the king's favour or both, who were also generally supportive of royal policy.[70]

However, that broader base of support may well have declined after 1725 as the cost and who was to benefit became clearer. Bragadin's Spanish nation was arguably disenchanted by the cession of Naples and Sicily and thereafter less supportive of a forward policy in Italy, which manifestly had so little to do with Spain and which in the 1740s demanded the mobilisation of money and men on a scale exceeding that of the 1730s and not seen since the Spanish succession conflict. This development contributed to what we might call a process of Hispanicisation in Spain, which was in full flow by 1746, and in consequence to a growing resentment of the demands made of Philip's Spanish subjects in order to secure states in Italy for Isabel's sons that would ultimately be independent of Spain. Ferdinand VI's accession offered an opportunity to respond to this hostile Spanish opinion. The dedication of volume 3 of Benito Jerónimo Feijo's *Cartas Eruditas* (Erudite Letters) (Madrid, 1750) to Ferdinand "the Just" praises him on precisely these grounds and might be considered an implicit criticism of the last years of Philip V. Ministers, some at least, were certainly aware of that hostility: in 1747 Ensenada remarked on the widespread unpopularity of the war in Italy, noting that a belief that it was not being pursued in furtherance of Spanish interests was being asserted by deserters from the army (see above). Ensenada himself and his correspondent, the duque de Huéscar—and no doubt many more, high and low—had come to share these views and to believe that Spain's resources should benefit Spain and the Spaniards.[71]

The revival of Spain after 1713 had important implications for its government and politics. Philip V's success in the Spanish succession conflict had secured his throne, but his ambitions—and they were his at least as much as his wife's—in Italy and African complicated that achievement. The need to mobilise Spain's resources for war was one pressure for administrative reform and helped reform embed itself, although the infrastructure and the individuals inherited by Philip also contributed to success. Those adventures made some ministerial careers. To some foreign commentators, Philip was absolute, even despotic, and in some respects their assessment was justified: Philip was more determined and more successful in imposing his will than his predecessor. However, war undermined absolutism, not least because of a growing resentment on the part of Philip's subjects, not least in relation to the disposal of the reconquered Italian territories. There existed in Spain an Italian lobby, one hardly acknowledged by historians hitherto, which did not simply date from the arrival of Isabel in 1714 but which included exiles fleeing Italy after the Spanish collapse there and which supported intervention in Italy. However, Philip's gift of Naples and Sicily to Don Carlos disappointed many Spaniards and triggered the return home of Neapolitan and Sicilian exiles in Spain, thereby weakening the lobby. But far more important was the War of the Austrian Succession, as the king's demands on his subjects—men for his army and navy, money for both—provoked resistance of one sort or another. It did not go as far as challenging or threatening the outcome of the earlier struggle for the Spanish crown, partly because Castile's traditions were otherwise, partly because monarch and ministers recognised the need to make some concessions, however belated in the case of the baldíos. Nevertheless, war in and for Italy in the 1740s may have soured relations between subjects and sovereign, not least because the monarch, Philip V, had felt impelled to state in a more assertive manner his absolute authority as monarch. In this respect, too, Spain's resurgence had shaped Philip V's reign and that of Ferdinand VI.

CHAPTER FIVE

FORAL SPAIN

By appointing as officers of the militia those most loyal to His Majesty,
we can ensure that the nobility [of Valencia] serve His Majesty, which
they are little inclined to.

—*Marqués de Campoflorido, August* 1726

The Spanish Habsburg Monarchy had been a composite polity, one in
which the sovereign ruled a collection of territories, inside and outside
Spain, which owed him obedience as ruler (king, duke, count, and so on)
of that individual territory rather than as sovereign of a monolithic empire. Each territory had its own distinctive administrative, fiscal, legal,
and other institutions, and the ruler was expected to respect these. This
did not prevent the prince, resident as he was in Madrid, from drawing
on the resources of those territories in pursuit of Monarchy-wide objectives. Nevertheless, it has been suggested that the failure to develop a
coherent theory or justification of empire before 1700 helped ensure that
few of Philip V's subjects in Spanish Italy mourned the end of Spanish
dominion in 1713. The most striking example of this quasi-contractual
relationship was in the Crown of Aragon—comprising, in peninsular
Spain, the realms of Aragon and Valencia and the principality of
Catalonia—where the authority of the monarch was much weaker than

in Castile. Failure to respect the laws and practices of those territories, the so-called *fueros*, might bring serious political consequences, as the Catalan revolt of 1640–52, which almost destroyed the Monarchy, shows.[1]

The polity which emerged from the War of the Spanish Succession was very different from that which Philip V inherited. Besides the territorial reconfiguration implied by the loss of Flanders and most of Italy and that of Menorca and Gibraltar in Spain itself, the Crown of Aragon lost its quasi-autonomy. For many subsequent commentators, this meant that Spain was emerging as a modern, nation-state, what Ricardo García Carcel has termed a vertical as opposed to a horizontal Spain. Indeed, the hostility of some historians to Philip's Italian ambitions in part reflects a view that he was deviating from the path of modernisation, although that is to apply to the eighteenth century the concerns and criteria of a later age. A proper appreciation of what Philip and his ministers attempted and achieved has also been bedevilled by the fact that the reign and particularly its impact on the Aragonese territories remain a political battleground in a Spain in which regional autonomy and national identity are still matters of fierce debate.[2]

Philip V's Mediterranean ambitions and the survival of foral regimes in Spain (Navarre, the Basque country) suggest he was not trying to create a modern, national realm, preferring instead to resurrect the old, supranational Habsburg Monarchy. However, his revanchism did not embrace all parts of that polity equally. It certainly included, for example, Spanish Flanders, itself a composite territory, into which considerable resources had been poured in the previous two centuries. An abortive project to establish there the princesse des Ursins in the peacemaking in 1713–14 implied maintaining a Spanish foothold. The scheme was abandoned after the arrival in Spain of Isabel Farnese and the disgrace of the princess, but Philip continued to list Flanders among his titles, and in 1725 he hoped to secure the territory as part of his peace with the emperor. Later, in 1733, anticipating the collapse of the Austrian Habsburgs in the War of the Polish Succession, Philip and Isabel hoped to secure Flanders for their son Luis. Thereafter, following the death of Charles VI, Philip appears to have aspired to recover the entire Spanish Habsburg inheritance, including Flanders. In accord with these ambitions, the Spanish court sought to retain links with the Flemish elites through the Walloon Guards (see chapter 1) and appointments at court. Among the many Flemish army officers in Philip's service was the comte de Gages, one of the ablest commanders of his forces in Italy in the War of the Austrian Succession. However, the recovery of Flanders was far less of a priority to Philip than that of Spanish Italy. This may be explained by the fact that he had visited Naples, the Tuscan presidios, and Milan at the start of his reign; that Italy was more accessible from Spain and among the most vulnerable parts of the Austrian Habsburg polity; that there was a residue of pro-Spanish sentiment in what had been Spanish Italy; and, last but by no means least, that Spanish Italy was the home or refuge of numerous exiles who had embraced the cause of the Habsburg pretender in the succession struggle and been obliged in consequence to abandon Spain. Seen in that light, the experience of the Aragonese realms and Spanish Italy is difficult to disentangle and is therefore discussed in conjunction in this and the next chapter, which should be regarded very much as complementary, companion pieces.[3]

Philip's bid to restore Spain's position in Italy after 1713 was closely bound up with his recovery of the Crown of Aragon and the curtailment of its fueros. On the one hand, the recovery of Levantine Spain was a crucial prelude to that of Italy: to attempt the reconquest of Italy from the ports of non-Aragonese Spain was not impossible but would have been more difficult. On the other hand, Philip's ambitions in Italy risked what had been achieved in the Crown of Aragon, as his European rivals exploited lingering pro-Habsburg feeling there, particularly in Catalonia, against him, just as Philip himself exploited Jacobitism against the Hanoverian regime in Britain. At the same time, however, as we shall see, the role of Catalan contractors in supplying Philip's war effort may have aided the integration of that territory into the Bourbon state.

In some respects the drive to restore Spanish Italy represented an attempt to rebuild what had been, in origin, an Aragonese rather than a Castilian empire. The Balearic Islands, Sardinia, Sicily, and Naples (but not Milan) had essentially constituted an Aragonese contribution to the early modern Spanish Monarchy. Sicily had been governed by the ruling house of Aragon since 1283, and Sardinia from soon thereafter, while Naples had been conquered by Alfonso the Magnanimous in 1442 and again by Gonzalo Fernández de Córdoba in 1503; Milan (1541) was a late addition by Charles V. These territories had themselves enjoyed a largely foral relationship with Madrid. In this chapter and the next I consider the experience of these Aragonese territories inside and outside Spain in relation to the Spanish resurgence in the Mediterranean, and clarify how the newly recovered Italian territories were fitted into Philip V's polity. This merits discussion because Spain's relations with the new Neapolitan state created in 1734 have implications for the way we should understand that state, given the importance attached by historians of Italy in recent decades to the establishment of an independent Naples in setting into motion a wide-ranging process of reform and revival in Italy as a whole. I also explore here identities and perceptions of identity, a subject which has attracted much attention in recent years. Modern historians who have any interest in the development of state, society, and national identity in eighteenth-century Spain are too inclined to apply concepts of identity which are more appropriate to the nineteenth century and the twentieth. In consequence, those historians miss the persistence of older identities, which meant that in the decades after 1713 more people in Spain supported, initially at least, the Spanish Risorgimento in Italy than merely the king, his consort, and a few Italian courtiers. The omission seems especially noteworthy in view of recent emphasis on the fact that the Spanish Monarchy depended in part upon an international or transnational alliance or network of elites for whom the events of 1705–13 were a traumatic caesura at least as much as for the ruling dynasty. In that sense, too, this was a period of transition, at the end of which—and because of the efforts put into war in and for Italy—there was a reaction against Spain's Italian inheritance such that it was from 1748, rather than from 1700 or 1713, that Spain and its government were at last Hispanicised or on the way to being so.[4]

The Crown of Aragon

Philip V had visited Aragon and Barcelona, but not Valencia, at his accession and sworn to respect the fueros of Aragon and Catalonia as well as those of Majorca and Sardinia. However, following the Catalan revolt and its defeat, relations between Aragon and Madrid were very different. The Crown of Aragon was itself a composite territory and felt

Philip's authority in diverse ways, reflecting both the various times at which the three component territories in peninsular Spain, Aragon, Catalonia, and Valencia, were subjected to that authority from 1707 and the fact that the king and his ministers were not implementing a predetermined programme. The kingdoms of Aragon and Valencia were promptly reoccupied by the Bourbon forces from May 1707 onwards, following their victory at Almansa. The next month Philip decreed, in a remarkable expression of his wish for uniformity, that in consequence of their supposed rebellion and his subsequent reconquest both kingdoms had forfeited their fueros; henceforth they were to be governed by the laws of Castile. Many Aragonese, Catalans, and Valencians petitioned Philip, citing their loyalty and consequent victimisation, prompting him to modify, but not revoke, his earlier decree in July 1707. The military recovery of Catalonia, culminating in the fall of Barcelona in September 1714, was followed by similar measures, notably the *nueva planta*, or new plan of government, of 1716; so, too, was the subjection by force of arms of Majorca in 1715.[5]

The defeat of "Charles III" was followed by the punishment of those who had supported him, which was most pronounced and severe in Catalonia, the most determinedly anti-Bourbon of the Aragonese territories. About four thousand so-called Austrians fell into Philip's hands and were variously condemned. Between twenty-five and thirty thousand people had followed Charles into exile and found refuge in the Austrian Habsburg territories, many of them in Spanish Italy. This ensured that Philip V's interventions in Italy between 1717 and 1735 to some extent represented a continuation there of the succession struggle which in the peninsula itself had ended in 1714, in effect, a continuing Spanish civil war. The properties of the exiles in Spain were confiscated, the value of confiscated Catalan property totalling more than one million reales; this was less than half the value of confiscated property in Castile but double that in Aragon and Valencia combined. Like others who had backed Charles, whether in exile or not, some secured within a few years a pardon and recovery of their property on petition. However, a blanket pardon and recovery had to await the peace of Vienna (1725) and the amnesty included in that settlement.[6]

The Bourbon reconquest of Aragon, continually asserted by the crown from 1707 onwards, was the prelude to a major overhaul of the institutions of the reconquered territories, each of which received (above) its own unique nueva planta. Therefore, although the decree abolishing the fueros of Aragon and Valencia (1707) expressed a wish for uniformity according to the laws of Castile, Philip V did not create a unitary state, while the imposed regimes may have been progressively less drastic. Whereas hitherto each of the component territories of the Crown of Aragon had been ruled, as had Sardinia, Sicily, and Naples, by a viceroy representing the king, henceforth Madrid would appoint only a captain general or *comandante general*. This was among the most notable examples of the militarisation of government in Spain in this era, which was most obvious in the Aragonese territories. Philip also abolished, in 1707, the Madrid-based Council of Aragon, which had effectively overseen the affairs of the kingdom since circa 1494 but whose function now passed to the Council of Castile. The distinctive representative assembly, or Cortes, of each of the Aragonese realms was also abolished, Philip granting representation in the Castilian Cortes to a limited number of Aragonese, Catalan, and Valencian towns (see chapter 4). Municipal government, too, was overhauled and royal authority increased. Nevertheless, within this more absolutist framework some foral elements did survive throughout the Crown of Aragon.[7]

The Aragonese territories were also incorporated more obviously into the monarchy's military (see chapter 1), naval (see chapter 2), and fiscal structures, the various impositions in the Crown of Aragon adding up to more than 26 million reales, or 15 percent of all revenues in 1722 and across the reign as a whole about 10 percent (see chapter 3). Integration was not complete, however. Many of the military reforms of the reign, for example, that of the militia in 1734, were confined to Castile, not least for fear of arming a population whose loyalty remained suspect and that had been subject to a process of disarming after the succession conflict. Nevertheless, Aragon, Catalonia, and Valencia were expected to draft men. In 1730 the Crown of Aragon was asked for almost 20 percent of the 4,086 men to be levied by *quinta* that year, Aragon being expected to supply 289, Valencia 355, and Majorca 140. It continued to be assigned quotas, Catalonia, which had been exempted from the quinta levies of 1719 and 1730, being expected to contribute just over 10 percent of the levy of almost 8,000 men ordered in December 1741 for 1742 (see chapter 1). The Crown of Aragon was contributing to the Spanish resurgence in Italy with men as well as with money. In addition, while those who had been loyal in the Spanish succession struggle were rewarded in new royal units, by allowing natives of the Crown of Aragon to raise new regiments at their own cost, monarchs and ministers hoped to stimulate loyalty and thus to ensure the further integration of Aragon, Catalonia, and Valencia into the Bourbon monarchy. Those territories also constituted a major military centre, in that large numbers of troops were concentrated there throughout this period (see chapter 1). Aragon, Catalonia, and Valencia were integrated into the developing naval structure as well. The coastal communities of Catalonia and Valencia were expected to participate in the refurbished register of seamen, the *matrícula de mar*, while Barcelona was the seat of a naval intendant within the department of Cartagena (see chapter 2).[8]

The extensive deployment of troops in Catalonia was intended at least in part to cow the population, which may explain why those were the best—or most regularly—paid of Philip's troops. Indeed, Philip V's authority in the Aragonese territories was, initially at least, founded upon this large military presence, made necessary by malcontents who remained loyal to Charles III and whose resistance to the Bourbon regime underpinned a persistent banditry in the Crown of Aragon after 1713, above all in Catalonia. This in turn offered Philip's opponents an opportunity to reignite civil war. Thus Spanish intervention in Sardinia and Sicily from 1717 and the resulting confrontation with the emperor and the Quadruple Alliance resulted in renewed disturbances in Catalonia in 1719. British ministers urged the French to seize the opportunity to invade Catalonia and to proclaim the restoration of the fueros, while Spanish exiles in Vienna were invited to the French court. For his part, Charles VI had not entirely abandoned his Spanish ambitions. He not only maintained a Spanish administration in exile in Vienna and supported numerous Spanish exiles in his dominions, including in Italy, but also continued to seek to protect his erstwhile Spanish subjects by diplomatic means. Only in 1725 did Charles, as part of that astonishing volte-face by both courts, the peace of Vienna, abandon those claims, while also making a final, fruitless effort in the negotiations to have Philip agree to the restoration of the fueros. In fact, the conclusion of that peace triggered celebrations in Valencia, in expectation of the restoration of the fueros. However, the nueva planta remained in place, although its continuation was still closely bound up with Philip's and Isabel's Italian ambitions. It was reported in 1728 that in the previous year Isabel, anticipating Philip's demise—and with Don Carlos still not established in Italy—had the king add a remarkable codicil to his will bequeathing the Crown of Aragon to Don Carlos and stipulating that the Infante's succession would be accompanied by the reinstatement of some of the fueros.[9]

For their part, Philip's enemies continued to see opportunities in Catalonia. In 1734, during the War of the Polish Succession, Spanish diplomats in Italy reported that exiles in Vienna were plotting to send agents to Catalonia to incite civil war, building on the support the emperor still had there. Such moments were clearly propitious for the articulation of a persistent Austrianism, one which was supposedly characterised by an alternative model to the absolutist one imposed on the Aragonese territories since 1707. The international situation frustrated any hopes of realising this alternative vision during the Polish succession conflict, but the threat continued to exercise Philip V's ministers. In 1740, following the outbreak of war with Britain, the captain general of Catalonia, the Fleming conde de Glimes, dismissed suggestions that the British fleet might foment rebellion in Catalonia but admitted there was cause for alarm if imperial troops were to appear in Catalonia, in view of lingering loyalty there to the emperor.[10]

The concentration of troops in the Aragonese territories also reflected the fact that they were among the most obvious launchpads for any expedition to Italy. Preparations were ongoing at Barcelona and Alicante, but also throughout Andalusia, for the Sardinia expedition in 1717 and again at Barcelona for the invasion of Sicily in 1718. In 1729, as war in Italy loomed, Isabel considered moving the court to Catalonia to oversee the embarkation of troops, while Barcelona and Alicante were the main ports from which men and matériel were shipped to Italy during the War of the Polish Succession. But many other settlements along the Catalan and Valencian coasts felt the impact too; most of the new regiments raised in 1734 and 1735 were given assembly points in the Crown of Aragon, above all in Catalonia, for precisely this reason. Catalonia was also the route whereby Philip's troops reached Italy when going by land rather than sea, and in 1746, too, when they were sent to Provence to counter an allied invasion of the territory of Philip's ally, Louis XV of France.[11]

This military and naval presence—and the end of the foral regimes— was not a wholly negative experience for the territories of the Crown of Aragon, as it reduced banditry, in some parts at least. In addition, the expeditions to Italy may have contributed to the economic growth of Catalonia in the early eighteenth century. The development of the Catalan economy in the wake of the imposition of the nueva planta is a matter of debate, although the focus of most investigation is on the later eighteenth century; the role of the state in earlier decades is rather ne-glected, while Pierre Vilar tends to play down the role of the state. But just as Catalan contractors and financiers had profited from the wars against France under Charles II, so the concentration in the principality in peace and wartime of large numbers of troops and the military expe-ditions to Africa and Italy may have stimulated the Catalan economy in the reign of Philip V. The presence there of so many of Philip's troops also meant the expenditure of considerable sums, as was revealed by the papers prepared for the Junta de Medios in 1737. While some of that expenditure was of money raised in the new *catastro* tax, the royal, or fiscal-military, state was also directing into Catalonia resources extracted from Castile and elsewhere, Catalonia absorbing just over 25 percent of the monthly cost of more than two million reales for the provisioning of the troops.[12]

Barcelona was already emerging as an industrial centre. Not surpris-ingly, given that manufacturing capacity, officials often looked to Barcelona when seeking supplies for a major military operation. Thus the preparations for the Oran expedition of 1732 involved the placing of or-ders in Barcelona for the manufacture of hundreds of tents and of six thousand pairs of shoes. At the same time, great quantities of arms, sad-dles, and boots were being produced at Barcelona and in Madrid, while the king's commissary there had contracted for four hundred thousand sea rations, later increased to one million. In the autumn of 1732 Catalan contractors agreed to supply two thousand draught animals for the artillery train. The next year large numbers of mules were again hired in Catalonia for the expedition to Italy. In addition, there was great activity reported at Barcelona with the casting of cannon, the making of carriages, and the preparation of a great quantity of clothing for the troops.[13]

Catalan and Majorcan shipowners and others benefitted from the need for transports in 1718 to carry men to Sicily and in the War of the Austrian Succession to transport men, munitions, and supplies to Italy. This was not always a positive experience, many ships being effectively seized, but it did mean employment and profit. Mediterranean operations offered opportunities to the Catalan marine in the form of privateering as well. In addition, local firms secured lucrative naval supply contracts.[14]

These economic possibilities and those associated with Philip's Africa adventures may have contributed to a greater integration of Catalonia's mercantile community by the 1730s, encapsulated in the experience of one Barcelona merchant family, the Durán. They were champions of "Charles III" in the succession conflict but suppliers of the Bourbon army in Catalonia from 1717. A more general enthusiasm for the new dynasty in the principality is suggested by the reception of Don Carlos as he passed through it in 1731 en route to Italy.[15]

A preoccupation with the experience of the Aragonese territories obscures the fact that the early Bourbon Spanish state remained a foral polity, in which Philip V ruled territories in diverse ways. Where those territories had shown loyalty during the succession struggle, Philip did not need or wish to assert his authority, as he had in the Crown of Aragon, Thus the kingdom of Navarre retained a distinctive identity and institutions, including its own Cortes, to which appeal could be made against measures ordered by the royal councils in Madrid as *contrafueros*, or breaches of the fueros. There were occasional tensions, but on the whole the system worked as it had before 1700. In 1692 the crown had agreed that all contrafuero petitions should be heard before the Cortes would discuss a grant, or *donativo*, to the monarch. The Cortes met in Philip V's reign in 1701–2, 1705, 1709, 1716–17, 1724–26, and 1743–44. The last of these received fifty-four such petitions, the second highest for the century as a whole. In addition, the *servicio* offered on that occasion, during the War of the Austrian Succession was initially rejected as insufficient. However, one was agreed, and most of that servicio of 1744 was remitted to Italy. That the system continued to work owed something to the fact that networks of Navarrese enjoyed great opportunities by and made great profits from collaborating with the early Bourbon state at this moment, helping it to meet, as contractors and financiers, the challenges of its revanchist policy.[16]

In the Basque territories, too, where in 1704 Philip V confirmed the recent compilation (1696) of the fueros of Guipuzcoa, loyalty in the succession conflict ensured the survival of a distinctive status within the early Bourbon state. Here also there were occasional confrontations, set off by the crown's war-related demands. The most celebrated of these occurred after the removal of the customs posts from the internal frontier between Castile and the Basque territory to the coast in 1717–18, at the height of Philip's first major bid to recover Spanish Italy. The move was a clear attempt to increase royal revenues by capturing the illegal trade which profited from the internal customs barrier. The measure provoked serious opposition in Vizcaya and had subsequently to be repealed. Demonstrating the close connection between Philip's ambitions in Italy and developments in Spain itself, in September 1718 the captain general of Vizcaya, the Sicilian prince of Campoflorido, reported that the news of the defeat of the Spanish fleet at Cape Passaro had encouraged those opposed to the new measure since they believed that only *turbulencias* of this sort would save them from these innovations. Sensitivity about the fueros persisted thereafter. In 1725, in a decree regulating the passage of royal troops through Guipuzcoa and following complaints about disorders committed there by troops in transit in 1718 and 1719, Philip explicitly declared his commitment to its fueros. In 1734 during the War of the Polish Succession when the Junta General, the representative assembly of the territory, was summoned, Patiño's order to send wood to the arms manufactory at Placencia for rifle casing was referred to the king as a possible contrafuero. Some years later, following the outbreak of the War of the Austrian Succession, there was resistance in 1741 to the introduction of the jurisdiction of the Almirantazgo, while in 1747 San Sebastián sought to evade the levy of twenty-five thousand men (see chapter 1). It did so by pointing out its earlier services to the king, by claiming that the demand contravened the fueros, by arguing that its *naturales* were not apt for foreign service, and, equally pragmatically, by offering the king in lieu a servicio of 240,000 reales. Confrontation should not be exaggerated, or the absence of common interests: in 1719, after the disturbances of the previous year—but also faced with French invasion—the Basques offered Philip V five hundred men, subsequently increasing that number to seven hundred. Vizcaya's integration into Philip's state, like that of neighbouring Navarre, was facilitated by the many Basques employed in the central administration (see chapter 4). It has been proposed that 1718, or, rather, the fiscal agreements subsequently concluded with Patiño in 1727, represented a turning point in Vizcaya's relationship with the government in Madrid. Nevertheless, whatever the explanation, here was another part of the state which remained largely foral.[17]

The principality of Asturias was not foral in so marked a manner as the Aragonese territories, the Basque provinces, and Navarre. Nonetheless, the territory insisted that certain foral aspects of its relation with the crown be respected. These concerns were most to the fore during the succession conflict but did not completely disappear thereafter. In 1726 the principality's governing elite expressed a preoccupation that the levy of that year, with war looming in the wake of the treaty of Vienna, was both a breach of the principality's fueros and, more practically, too great a burden for its small population. Indeed, its relative poverty may have saved the principality and its fueros from being burdened by greater royal demands.[18]

Spain was not completely united under Philip V, not least because Castile itself remained a diverse territory, one composed of a number of realms—Castilla, León, Andalusia, and so on—in each of which a variety of jurisdictions, ecclesiastical, feudal (seigneurial), and royal, coexisted.[19]

Nevertheless, the reconquest of the Aragonese territories by 1715 was an important stage in the greater integration of Philip V's Spanish territories, a process which was not only administrative or political but also cultural and social and a crucial accompaniment of and contribution towards the Spanish resurgence in the Mediterranean and Italy. It afforded additional resources in men, money, and shipping with which to intervene overseas, even as Castile remained the crucial resource base; it also offered strategic advantages. The reconquest of Majorca meant the recovery of what had been an important staging post between Spain and Italy under the Habsburgs and was so again between 1715 and 1748, the British occupation of Menorca enhancing Majorca's role in this respect. Finally, participation also implied greater integration in the new regime than might otherwise have been the case; this implies, despite a persistent Austrianism in the Aragonese territories, that we should not think of relations between those territories, and above all Catalonia, and Castile as only and essentially confrontational.[20]

CHAPTER SIX

ITALY AND IDENTITY

—❧—

We will always be guided by the orders that come from Spain.
—*Bartolomeo Corsini, in Naples, October* 1735

Between 1707 and 1713 Spanish Italy was largely dismembered.[1] However, Aragonese, Castilians, and natives of the other Iberian territories of the Spanish Monarchy had been present in Italy since well before 1500, and in consequence enduring links of all sorts—cultural, economic, religious, political—had been established. Many of these survived the formal end of Spanish dominion. So, too, did the monuments to that Spanish presence. These included educational institutions like the *colegios mayores* at Bologna of San Clemente and of Santa Catalina de los Españoles, where a Te Deum Mass in 1743 celebrated Spanish success at the battle of Camposanto, and numerous religious foundations. In 1744 Philip V ordered that a canonry in one of Spain's cathedrals be reserved for the senior member of those institutions. In addition, a large number of Spaniards stayed in Italy in the former Spanish territories, many remaining in Sicily, for example, when the island was evacuated in 1713, but also elsewhere. For their part, many Italians, and not only the inhabitants of what had been Spanish Italy, had important cultural, economic, familial, and other interests in Spain. The Spanish court had long attracted the elite families of non-Spanish Italy and continued to

do so. In 1734 a scion of the Genoese Balbi, a family which had had extensive financial dealings with the Spanish crown, acquiring fiefs in Spain and
Milan, served as a volunteer with the Spanish forces in Italy. Another scion
of one of Genoa's patrician families in Philip V's service was the marchese
Stefano de Mari, who had a distinguished career in the Spanish fleet (see
chapter 2). Non-Genoese who served Philip included among the princely
families the prince of Masserano. He entered the Spanish service in the War
of the Spanish Succession, rose to captain general in 1734, was appointed
captain of a company of the royal bodyguard in 1737, and twice represented
Philip in Turin, in 1730–31 and 1741–42; his rewards were the Golden
Fleece, granted to him in 1709, *grandeza,* and the (Neapolitan) Order of San
Gennaro.[2]

Despite the supposed hostility to Spain which is the leitmotiv of
Risorgimento-influenced approaches to this topic, following the elaboration of a Black Legend of Spain and its impact on Italy, which apparently
developed in the first decades of the eighteenth century, many Italians
appeared to retain a deep attachment to Spain.[3]

Sardinia and Sicily (1717–20)

The island of Sardinia was perhaps the least significant of the Spanish
Monarchy's Italian territories but had not been neglected in the decades
before 1700. In 1701 Charles II's last viceroy, D. Ferdinando de Moncada,
duque de San Juan, took possession of the realm on Philip V's behalf,
receiving the usual oath from the three estates, clergy, nobility, and commons. The island remained loyal to Philip, and in 1707, on the
suppression of the Council of Aragon, it and the Balearic Islands were
rewarded for their fidelity by being put under the jurisdiction not of the
Council of Castile, as the mainland Aragonese territories were, but of the
Council of Italy. In August 1708, however, a British force conquered
Sardinia for Philip's Habsburg rival. Nevertheless, a Philipist party survived
among the island's elite, along with an enduring Hispanic identity. In 1717
Lede's expeditionary force conquered Sardinia in just two months. This
rapid success owed something to Habsburg weakness in Italy, largely because of the ongoing war against the Ottomans in the Balkans, and to
the strength of Spanish arms, but it also rested upon local support or at

least sympathy. The flight of Charles VI's viceroy, the marqués de Rubí, a Catalan exile and Charles's viceroy of Majorca until its surrender in 1715, was followed by a popular rising in Sassari in favour of Philip, although the large-scale adherence of the local population came after Spanish military success. In a striking demonstration of the way developments in the Iberian peninsula might have implications for the Catholic King's policy in former Spanish Italy and of the extent to which Philip's Italian expeditions must be seen as a continuation of the struggle within the peninsula, Rubí sought to mobilise resistance to the invaders by claiming that the Spanish troops came to treat them like Catalans, a clear reference to the *nueva planta* of 1716. Lede countered by declaring that he came instead to restore the privileges, or *fueros,* of the realm.[4]

In fact, the Spanish regime imposed in Sardinia between 1717 and 1720 was far less indulgent of local privilege than Lede had promised, the Sardinian planta of November 1717 resembling that of Catalonia as Rubí had predicted. As in the Aragonese territories, a captain general was appointed rather than the traditional viceroy. So, too, echoing another recent innovation in Spain, was an intendant, whose financial and other demands, among them imposition of the tobacco monopoly, unknown in pre-Bourbon Sardinia, provoked widespread resentment and complaints to Madrid. In fact, Philip was obliged to subsidise the government of Sardinia and a military establishment, that is, his invasion force, which this small, poor island could not support unaided. The Sardinian Cortes was not summoned during the almost three years of Spanish occupation.[5]

Military occupation, the billeting of troops on the civilian population, especially before the invasion of Sicily in 1718, and Philip V's appointment of Spaniards to local offices alienated some of his advocates among the Sardinian elite. The discontent was fanned by those loyal to Charles VI. As early as the summer of 1718, with Sardinia largely denuded of troops despatched to neighbouring Sicily, rioters in the city of Alghero destroyed the royal arms of Philip V that hung over the door of the tobacco monopoly office. The city of Cagliari, which was especially hard-pressed, sent an agent to Madrid to protest the demands made of it. It was only when the Spaniards were obliged by the Quadruple Alliance to abandon the island that, before departing, they eased the fiscal and other burdens in what may have been a deliberate attempt to ensure that

Sardinia's population retained more positive memories of this short-lived reimposition of Spanish dominion. Philip had also loaded the episcopal revenues of Sardinia (and Sicily) with pensions for his followers.[6]

Despite its less attractive aspects, the brief Spanish occupation had arguably confirmed the Spanish or, rather, Aragonese identity established there over the previous centuries. This legacy shaped the initial approach to the government of Sardinia of the Savoyard regime which succeeded the Spaniards. Any inclination to innovate or to implement radical reform during the first decades of Savoyard rule in Sardinia was restrained by the restrictions imposed by Philip V's act of cession of 1720 and the fact that Philip had a reversionary interest in the island; by an awareness that Victor Amadeus II had ruled Sicily with too heavy a hand, alienating its population, with disastrous consequences (below); by fears in Turin of another Spanish invasion of Sardinia; by the fact that some at least of the magnates of Sardinia were Spanish subjects, resident in Spain; and by a sense that the island was just too poor to merit the effort. For all these reasons Sardinia was largely neglected by the court of Turin before 1748. Indeed, in 1720 Victor Amadeus instructed his first viceroy to govern according to the traditional, that is, Spanish, laws and practices of the realm. Later that year the viceroy swore, in Castilian, to obey those laws, Victor Amadeus only gradually introducing the use of Italian on the island; his second viceroy had formerly represented Victor Amadeus in Madrid. Finally, rather than eradicating the opposing pro-Austrian and pro-Spanish factions among the elite, Victor Amadeus sought to exploit their rivalry to his advantage.[7]

As for Sicily, that island, unlike most of the rest of Spanish Italy, was not conquered by Philip V's enemies but was ceded by him in 1713 as the price of peace, an act he thought had been extorted improperly and was not therefore binding. His act of cession was carefully prepared by the Sicilian regent in the Council of Italy and had important implications. For one thing, the realm remained foral in the sense that its new sovereign, Victor Amadeus II of Savoy, was expected to respect the traditional laws. In addition, Philip retained a foothold in Sicily: the defection to "Charles III" of the almirante of Castile in the succession conflict and the consequent sequestration of his properties throughout the Spanish Monarchy left Philip with the largest feudal territory in Sicily, the county of Modica, which he retained after 1713. To manage this and other confiscated properties, about 10 percent of the island, Philip had his own administration in Sicily, which in some respects constituted a state within a state and which fomented opposition to the Savoyard regime. Finally, Philip's reversionary interest in the island, written into the act of cession, should the house of Savoy lack direct male heirs ensured that he took a great interest in and sometimes complained in Turin about Savoyard innovations there.[8]

Victor Amadeus's reforms, his failure to settle his court and seat of government in Palermo after his coronation there in December 1713, together with a residual loyalty to Spain had serious consequences in 1718, when Spanish forces invaded the island. As in Sardinia, conquest was eased by the fact that the Spaniards were welcomed by a population which felt Victor Amadeus had breached the traditional framework of laws and which was encouraged and aided by the administrators of Modica. Some among the local elites even raised troops for Philip. As in the case of Sardinia, there was no thought of subjecting Sicily to a revived Council of Italy in Madrid. As in Sardinia, too, when the occupying force left in 1720, to be replaced by the Austrian Habsburgs, it left behind, in some circles at least, an enduring commitment to the Spanish Monarchy which may have aided the reconquest of the island in 1735. This was due in part to the fact that Philip's officials deliberately sought to encourage loyalty to the Spanish king by distributing offices and titles and promising to return. Certainly in the negotiations to end the occupation Philip sought to keep in post in Sicily and in Sardinia those who had bolstered him and to safeguard the privileges of the Sicilians. This helps explain why, after 1720, and although many of those who had collaborated with the occupying force went into exile in Spain, the Spanish court enjoyed the services of various agents and informants on the island. Following the conclusion of the peace of Vienna of 1725, many of those Philip had appointed to office in Sicily between 1718 and 1720 but ousted thereafter sought reinstatement. That same peace facilitated renewed contacts between the Spanish court and its supporters on the island.[9]

Parma, Piacenza, and Tuscany (1731–38)

Sardinia and Sicily had both been part of Spanish Italy, but this was not true of the duchies of Parma, Piacenza, and Tuscany, which, Isabel

Farnese claimed, were assigned to her eldest son, Don Carlos, by the Quadruple Alliance, and in which he was installed between 1731 and 1735 / 38. Don Carlos's possession of these territories was relatively brief but long enough to offer some insight into how the relationship between the Spanish court and its new Italian satellite was conceived in Madrid. Even before 1732 the Spanish court sought to defend the territorial integrity of the Tuscan state, in anticipation of Don Carlos's succession. In 1725, for example, it obstructed the sale of fiefs to Genoa and the establishment of a free port at La Spezia for fear of its impact upon the prosperity of Livorno. In the summer of 1731 agreement had been reached between Philip V and the last Medici grand duke of Tuscany, Giangastone, the duke accepting the succession of the Infante in his states should he die without direct male heirs; the Catholic King promised in return to respect the constitution of the grand duchy and the privileges of its capital, Florence, which would be the residence of Don Carlos, and that Carlos would honour the Tuscan debt and maintain the military Order of San Stefano.[10]

This agreement implied that the new state(s) was to be formally independent of Madrid. In fact, however, the young prince maintained a regular correspondence with his parents, for whom this offered a means of informal control, not least because, as the Florentine legist and longtime collaborator of Don Carlos, Bernardo Tanucci, commented, Carlos, who was only fifteen in 1731, was an obedient son. In addition, instructions were prepared in Spain to guide the prince in his new states. Besides receiving regular parental advice Don Carlos was accompanied by his Spanish entourage, headed by his former tutor José Manuel Benavides y Aragón, conde de Santisteban. It was not only counsel that Don Carlos received from Spain. He was protected by the more than six thousand troops who had accompanied him to Italy and in addition received financial aid. His presence encouraged an influx of young Spanish nobles to the renowned noble academies of central Italy: the future chief minister the count of Aranda, for example, entered the Jesuit college at Parma.[11]

Following the conquest of Naples and Sicily, in November 1735 Don Carlos established a Giunta di Sicilia to oversee the affairs of Sicily, Parma, and Piacenza in his absence. However, Philip V having failed to convince the other powers that the new Neapolitan state was too poor to survive without the additional resources of Tuscany and that it needed a protective barrier in central Italy against the Habsburgs in northern Italy, the Spanish forces evacuated the duchies in 1736 and Tuscany in 1737, concluding this phase of the attempt to establish Spanish dominion there. Thereafter a Spanish party persisted in Tuscany, heartened by doubts about the ability of the house of Lorraine to retain the grand duchy in the face of Bourbon success in the War of the Austrian Succession. However, the installation in Parma and Piacenza of the Infante Felipe had to wait until the conclusion of that conflict in 1748.[12]

Kingdom of Naples and Sicily (1734–48)

The most striking achievement of the Spanish resurgence in Italy in the reign of Philip V was undoubtedly the conquest (or reconquest) in 1734–35 of Naples and Sicily. Naples had been the jewel in the crown of Spanish Italy before 1707, subsidising the other parts of that collection of territories, and was described in 1675, with pardonable hyperbole, as Spain's "richest and most dependable Peru."[13]

Philip had visited Naples in 1702, the first Spanish monarch to do so since Charles V in 1536. In this way he reestablished the link with the kingdom's elite, reinforcing the Spanish connection following the abortive anti-Bourbon Macchia conspiracy of 1701 and forging a personal link between himself and the realm. Indeed, Philip went further, securing from Pope Clement XI the proclamation in 1702 of St. Januarius as copatron of Spain, in what may have been a bid to bind his Neapolitan subjects more closely to Spain. He continued to observe the Neapolitan saint's day long after 1707. Philip was clearly reluctant to lose Naples, hoping, before and immediately after his victory at Almansa in 1707, that troops could be sent to Naples and Sicily from Spain to prevent an Austrian conquest and maybe take advantage of an anti-Austrian revolution. Philip continued to hope to recover Naples thereafter, prioritising its recovery when instructing his plenipotentiaries to the looming Utrecht peace congress at the end of 1711.[14]

The conquests of 1734–35 recalled the exploits of Gonzalo Fernández de Córdoba, the Gran Capitán, in Italy under the Catholic Kings more than two centuries earlier. They also established Don Carlos in a much larger state than Parma, Piacenza, or Tuscany with the more prestigious rank of king and with the resources to cut a European figure: in 1747 his viceroy of Sicily offered that the king of Naples could play the role in Italy that the king of Prussia did in Germany. As in Sardinia and Sicily in 1717–18, the Spanish conquest of Naples and Sicily was remarkably speedy in 1734–35. Once again this owed much to the weak resistance put up by the Austrian Habsburgs, whose main military effort was being made elsewhere. But there was more to it than that. It is unlikely that Don Carlos could have secured Naples (and Sicily) so quickly without broad support among the population at large. He was enthusiastically welcomed in both realms. One Spanish diplomat, commenting on the recovery of Naples in April 1734, referred to a persistent loyalty of the Neapolitans to Philip V, and there was undoubtedly some enduring Hispanophile sentiment in the kingdom. Philip had lost Naples in 1707 amid signs of hostility towards the distant Spanish regime and a prefer-ence for rule by an Austrian archduke who would reside in Naples (above). The growing disenchantment with Spanish rule owed something to resentment of the exploitation of Naples (and Sicily) by absent Spanish rulers, an attitude later articulated by the celebrated Neapolitan jurist and historian Pietro Giannone in his *Istoria civile* (1723). Yet growing disil-lusion with an Austrian regime which also ruled at a distance and with a heavy fiscal hand fed a renewed affection for Spanish rule in Sicily and Naples, from where approaches were made to the Spanish court to put Don Carlos on the throne well before 1734. The Spanish reconquest was helped too by the fact that many Neapolitan nobles loyal to Philip and Spain and who had lived in retirement since 1707 declared for the Infante in 1734.[15]

The Spanish invaders exploited local grievances to maximum advan-tage. Soon after Don Carlos's departure from Parma, Philip V sent him a letter—for publication, obviously with propagandistic intent—declaring that the Spanish forces had originally been sent to the north of Italy in 1733 in pursuit of the Infante's rightful claims but that, moved by the clamour of the populations of Naples and Sicily to be free of the Austrian Habsburg yoke, Philip had diverted his forces south. He in-structed his son to pardon all who had breached the oath of loyalty they had taken to Philip when he visited Naples in 1702 and to promise both the confirmation of privileges—the restored Spanish regime would thus be foral—and the removal of the hated Habsburg impositions. Don Carlos issued a decree along these lines on 14 March 1734 before entering the kingdom of Naples ten days later. On 10 May 1734 the Infante made his formal entry into the capital as commander of the forces of the king of Spain, the apparently miraculous liquefaction of San Gennaro's blood that same day auguring well for the new regime. Five days later a courier arrived from Spain with Philip V's formal cession of Naples to the Infante. This was a remarkable development: as Giannone, for one, observed, it represented the alienation, without the consent of the parliaments or Cortes of Spain, of a part of the inheritance of the future Ferdinand VI and of the old Spanish Monarchy. It was variously interpreted. Tiberio Carafa, prince of Chiusano, a Habsburg loyalist and the author of an account of the Bourbon conquest, attributed the cession to Isabel; he believed it was the only way to ensure Neapolitan loyalty and the retention of the realm. For his part, Philip explained the cession to Louis XV in terms of the opposition of the other powers to Spain's retaining Naples and upsetting the balance of power. Whatever the truth of the matter, Philip's cession implied that Don Carlos's possession of Naples derived by gift of the Catholic King following a conquest by Spanish troops. Sicily, where Charles VI's viceroy was the Catalan exile the marqués de Rubi, again seeking (as earlier in Majorca and Sardinia) to fend off Philip V, also proved a relatively easy conquest, the Spanish forces again being welcomed by a population alienated by Austrian Habsburg rule. In September 1734 in Messina the Spanish commander, the count of Montemar, swore on behalf of Don Carlos to uphold the constitutions of the realm and the privileges of that city. The following summer Don Carlos was crowned king of the Two Sicilies in Palermo cathedral, the coronation taking place in Sicily rather than in Naples because of a dispute with Rome regarding the investiture of the king with a realm, Naples, which was a fief of the church.[16]

These were developments of real importance, reversing the peace settlement of 1713–14 and creating a new sovereign state in southern Italy. Their significance, however, has been a subject of some debate. An older strand of Italian historical writing, influenced by the nineteenth-century Italian Risorgimento, could interpret the advent of Don Carlos, or Carlo di Borbone, only within a framework of a malign Spain. Thus in Michelangelo Schipa's *Il Regno di Napoli al tempo di Carlo di Borbone* (The Kingdom of Naples in the time of Carlo di Borbone) (Naples, 1904) Philip's grant of Naples to Don Carlos was an act of expiation for two hundred years of Spanish misgovernment. The late Franco Venturi, however, took a much more positive view. To Venturi, the installation of Don Carlos in Naples ended more than two centuries of foreign rule, the creation of an independent Neapolitan state with its own king and court, and the launching of a great wave of reform throughout Italy, the Settecento Riformatore, or seventeenth-century reformation. Rafaello Ajello, too, has interpreted the new regime more constructively. Upbeat views were certainly articulated at the time by some Neapolitans, who anticipated a brave new world of independence, as opposed to subordinate provincial status; they included that leading light of the Neapolitan reform movement Antonio Genovesi. Some saw Don Carlos as a potential king of Italy. These expectations, some at least, were understandable and some were, in part at least, realised. The peace which concluded the War of the Polish Succession, insisting on the independence of the new realm, ruled out any union of Spain and Naples and thus the recreation of a formal Spanish empire in Italy, and Naples now had a resident king, although Sicily was still governed by a viceroy, appointed from Naples.[17]

Don Carlos's propaganda, while refuting the legitimacy of the former regime, asserted that of his own, among other things by linking it with the much earlier, independent Norman kingdom. But the young king and his ministers and later historians have surely exaggerated the autonomy of the resurrected realm of the Two Sicilies, at least in the first decade and a half of its existence, when the Infante continued to depend enormously on Spain. Until the War of the Polish Succession ended and other states recognised Don Carlos as king, Philip V left in Naples about half of the force which had conquered the Two Sicilies. In what represented a reversal of the pre-1700 relationship between Spain and Naples, the Spanish court also funded the new monarch in these crucial early years and paid him a subsidy in the War of the Austrian Succession (see chapter 3).[18]

The new state needed and developed its own diplomatic network, but initially the new king depended on that of his parents. Spanish diplomats notified other sovereigns of Don Carlos's accession, securing their recognition of him, and also negotiated his marriage to María Amalia of Saxony. Once it was up and running, Carlos's own diplomatic system was hardly independent of Spain. In 1735 the young king despatched the duke of Sora as ambassador to Madrid with instructions which amounted to a manifesto of the guiding principles of Neapolitan policy: the new monarch, they stated, wished only to demonstrate his affection, obedience, and gratitude towards his parents. Indicative of the way Neapolitan policy followed that of Madrid was the fact that when the prince of Torella was sent as Neapolitan ambassador to the French court in 1735, his instructions were first sent to Madrid for approval and that he was expected to be guided by the Spanish minister at Louis XV's court. Similarly, as soon as news of the death of Charles VI reached Naples in November 1740 Don Carlos sent to Madrid for guidance, the subsequent military preparations in the realm being attributed to direction from there. Nor was the influence of the Catholic King limited to Neapolitan relations with Christian powers: negotiations with the Ottoman sultan, from 1739, proceeded only once Philip V had agreed.[19]

The establishment of the new state was accompanied by the overhaul of existing institutions and the creation of new ones, a process in which the directing influence of Madrid was again evident. Spanish ministers sought to remodel the government of Naples and Sicily along Spanish lines. Thus, between 1734 and 1738 Secretariats of State were introduced, in imitation of those established in Spain after 1713 (see chapter 4). In 1734, in the meantime, and at the suggestion of Patiño, a Superintendency of those revenues had been created, headed by the Sicilian exile Giovanni Brancaccio, with instructions from Patiño to reform the Neapolitan finances and increase their yield. Brancaccio, in a clear acknowledgment of the continued influence of the Spanish court, corresponded with Patiño until the Spaniard's death, in 1735 informing him of those who had served the Austrian Habsburgs and been purged. In 1737 Brancaccio was appointed secretary of state for finance in Naples. Perhaps inevitably Brancaccio's reforming initiatives clashed with the Camara della Sommaría, the supreme financial agency of the realm, which was understandably jealous of its role and powers. Unfortunately for the reformers Brancaccio obtained little support from the conde de Santisteban, the de facto chief minister in Naples, as he had been in Parma, or, after Patiño's death, from Santisteban's patron in Spain, Isabel Farnese. Among the casualties of the stalled reform process was an attempt to eradicate venality.[20]

Many of the reforms implemented in Naples from 1734 reflected a distinctive conception of government, one which drew on attitudes and practices that Don Carlos brought with him from Spain but also on a native, Neapolitan strand of French-inspired approaches associated above all with the lawyer elite. This new conception did not always go down well with those who had expected Carlos's arrival to mean greater freedom. In January 1739 the young king informed his parents that his new subjects were too accustomed to the liberties associated with viceregal government. More than two decades later, Tanucci, who had been appointed secretary of state in Naples in 1734, lamenting what he saw as the selfish factionalism of some among the Neapolitan nobility, compared the conduct of some of that elite with that encountered by the incoming regime in 1734, but which Santisteban, backed by Patiño in Madrid, had apparently eradicated. On the other hand, the administration of Sicily, particularly during Santisteban's primacy, was much more foral, as befitted a realm where the Parliament continued to function and to grant funds to the king and where government in general was more reminiscent of what it had been before the earlier cession of the island to Victor Amadeus of Savoy.[21]

The making of a new state involved as well some remodelling of the Neapolitan elite, Spanish influence again being to the fore. There were two key elements to this. The first was the establishment of a new hierarchy of grandees, or magnates. In this as in so much else Don Carlos consulted his father, who approved the initiative but insisted that the recipients should be worthy of the dignity. The names of those identified as possible beneficiaries, numbering thirty-eight, were therefore sent to Madrid: they included the conde de Santisteban, the duque de Montemar, Manuel d'Orleans Comte de Charny, all subjects or in the service of Philip who had participated in the Spanish conquest. The second strand in this refashioning of the elite was the creation of a new chivalric order, in what was often an integral part of the process of state creation in early modern Europe. Don Carlos's intention to establish the new order was communicated to Philip V almost immediately after the conquest of Naples, in July

1734. Philip approved the initiative but wanted to see the constitution of the body before this was made public. Accordingly, the draft rules were sent to Madrid in August 1735 and agreed by Philip. The Infante, who also consulting his father on the timing of the announcement of the creation, allowed Philip to nominate to nine places in the order. Philip, who invested the Spanish recipients with the insignia at his own court, subsequently claimed a right to fill the vacancies created by the death of his nominees, such that the new body was at least in part a Spanish as much as a Neapolitan institution.[22]

The presence of Spaniards within the new Order of San Gennaro ex-emplified the extent to which Philip V's Spanish and non-Spanish subjects secured rewards of all sorts in Naples from 1734 onwards. Some Spaniards gained social promotion in the new state. In 1737, for example, Montemar was promoted grandee and duke of Bitonto in recognition of his victory there; D. Pedro de Castro Figueroa y Salazar, another of the Spanish generals who conquered Naples, was rewarded by Don Carlos with the ducal title "of the Conquest"; and D. Francisco Ovando, a ship's captain who had captured Brindisi, was rewarded with the title of mar-quis of Brindisi. Among the administrators, D. Zenón de Somodevilla received a Neapolitan title, as marqués de Ensenada, as did Casimiro Uztáriz, a senior official in the Secretariat for War. Some other Spaniards achieved real power in the Neapolitan state. They included the conde de Santisteban, the de facto chief minister between 1734 and 1738, when, in part owing to the machinations of Don Carlos's queen, he was ousted and returned to Spain, and Santisteban's rival and successor, José Joaquín Montealegre, the marqués de Salas and duque de Montealegre, chief minister from 1738 to 1746.[23]

But many more of Philip V's subjects inserted themselves into the Neapolitan civilian and military administration, the use of Spanish possi-bly becoming more common in consequence. Spanish officers were ap-pointed to key governorships, while a number of officers in the Spanish army obtained Philip's permission to serve in the newly created army of Naples, in which opportunities for promotion were no doubt greater. Much the same was true of the nascent Neapolitan fleet, which Miguel Reggio Branciforte, a Sicilian in exile in Spain since 1713, was appointed to com-mand. The many non-Spaniards in Philip V's service who transferred to that of Naples included the Irishman Count Mahony, who was appointed vicar general of the Two Calabrias. Some Spanish ministers in Naples received pensions from Spain, as did Montealegre. This restructuring of the Neapolitan elite was often at the expense of those Spaniards who had joined the archduke Charles during the succession struggle and who in exile received pensions, posts, and property in Naples and Sicily forfeited by the supporters there of Philip V. In that sense, as has been noted (above), the reconquest of Naples and Sicily represented a continuation of sorts of the Spanish succession struggle.[24]

Some of those who served Don Carlos in Naples were subsequently rewarded in Spain, so that service in the kingdom of the Two Sicilies could be an integral part of a career spanning the recreated Spanish Mediterranean. D. Jaime Tedeschi, marqués de Casaleto, went to Sicily in 1734 on Philip V's orders to serve Don Carlos and, after being appointed *comisario general* at Catania, returned to Spain and the service of the Catholic King. For his part, In 1745 D. Roque Agustín de Vallejo, an official in the secretary of state's office in the kingdom of the Two Sicilies, was granted an *hábito* of the Spanish Military Order of Calatrava by Philip. In addition, the construction, or reconstruction, of a Spanish–Neapolitan elite involved the granting of Spanish honours and titles to Neapolitans. Thus the coveted Order of the Golden Fleece, sovereignty of which was fiercely contested by the courts of Madrid and Vienna long after 1713, was bestowed by Philip on four Neapolitan nobles who had distinguished themselves in the reconquest of the realm. Other Neapolitan nobles were promoted within the Spanish noble hierarchy. On his return to Naples from his embassy to the French court in 1739, the prince of Torella was promoted Spanish grandee 1st class, and in December 1742 the prince of Melfi Doria, whose family had enjoyed Spanish *grandeza* since the reign of Charles V, was able to enjoy that rank at Don Carlos's court after it was confirmed by Philip V.[25]

The recreation of an integrated Spanish–Neapolitan elite and the fact that Don Carlos, only eighteen years old in 1734, was still largely dominated by parents with whom he continued to correspond regularly long after that year gave the Spanish court considerable influence in Naples. In 1736, typically, orders arrived from Madrid for the appointment of Bartolomeo Corsini as viceroy of Sicily, while in December 1738 Don

Carlos sent to the Spanish court for approval the arrangements for the household of his queen. Madrid was kept abreast of the developing reform programme in Naples. In 1739, following the establishment of the Supremo Magistrato del Commercio, one of the most innovative but also contentious reforms, not least by creating a new and rival jurisdiction to those already operating in the realm, and Don Carlos's grant of permission to Jews to settle in his realms, a list of those who took advantage of this measure was sent to Spain. In clear recognition of the fact that the real decisions were made in Spain, many of those hoping for office and honours in the kingdom of the Two Sicilies applied to Philip V, Isabel, and their ministers. Montealegre was able to best Santisteban in the struggle for power in Naples because he enjoyed the favour of the Catholic Kings and of the Spanish secretary of state, de la Cuadra, with whom he corresponded. Later, in 1742, it was said that Montealegre himself was out of favour with Don Carlos and his queen and supported only by the marqués Scotti and, through him, by Isabel Farnese, without whose backing he would have been disgraced long before. In such circumstances, it was hardly surprising that those competing for influence in Naples needed agents or supporters in Madrid, in a manner reminiscent of practice before 1707.[26]

The political culture of the new kingdom reflected the Spanish origins of its monarch and much of its ruling elite and the fact that Spanish customs and practices had become so entrenched before 1707 that they had survived the Austrian interlude. Hence what we might think of as Spanish issues preoccupied some Neapolitan intellectuals: in 1743, for example, Carlantonio Broggia's treatise on taxation, *Trattato de' tributi,* was not only dedicated to Montealegre but also lavished extravagant praise on Farnese and Philip V for having restored Spain. As for public celebrations, these included the feast day of Santiago, protector of Spain, a festival long celebrated in Naples. Court life was punctuated by festivities in honour of the birthdays, name days, marriages, and so on of members of the Spanish royal family. In June of each year, on the feast of San Fernando, the Castilian monarch who had been a hero of the medieval Reconquista and whose cult was especially popular in Spain as well as in Naples, the Neapolitan court celebrated both that Spanish saint and the name day of Don Carlos's half brother, the future Ferdinand VI; in

October the birthday and in November the name day of Don Carlos's mother, Isabel; and in December the birthdays of Philip V and the prince of Asturias. For its part, the Spanish court honoured important dates connected with the Neapolitan royal family. January saw the celebration there of Don Carlos's birthday and November that of his name day. Not surprisingly, the birth of a Neapolitan Infanta in May 1743 was another occasion for festivity at the Spanish court, as was the birth in Naples in 1747 of a son, declared an Infante of Spain by Ferdinand VI.[27]

Some Spaniards were shocked by Philip's cession of Naples and Sicily because they continued to consider these as effectively Spanish provinces. Montemar, the conqueror of Naples, certainly thought so, although this was in part because it justified his claims to authority in his power struggle with Santisteban. Many foreign observers saw the new court and state as a Spanish satellite: in one of the most arresting comments of this sort, in 1736 the British consul at Naples observed, "The first motion of all important Transactions [came] from the Court of Madrid almost equally as if this was still a Vice Royalty." Six years later, in his *relazione*, or end-of-mission report, the Sardinian minister at the court of Naples, the conte di Monasterolo, observed that Farnese controlled Don Carlos from Madrid, although he thought that the king of the Two Sicilies began to find his mother's domination irksome. Indeed, a growing restlessness regarding control from Spain may explain Don Carlos's growing appreciation of Tanucci, who had resented the continual references to the realm as having been ceded by the king of Spain in the negotiations with Rome. Naples also reverted to its role as a granary of Spain, as before 1700. In 1737, despite a poor harvest, 150,000 *tomole* of grain were exported from Naples, most of it to Spain, where harvests were also bad. Another indicator of the close integration of the new realm into the Spanish world was the plan, devised in 1745–46, to allow Melchor de Macanaz, Philip's former minister, now being rehabilitated after a long exile but still condemned by the Inquisition in Spain, to find refuge in Naples along with his papers.[28]

Spanish influence shaped Don Carlos's reign in Naples in many respects. It is surely no coincidence that the great reform period of his reign occurred between 1734 and 1741–42, that is, before Spain got bogged down in war in Italy. Neapolitan reform stalled thereafter as the king of the Two Sicilies was dragged into the War of the Austrian Succession, reflecting the fact that his realm was part of what can be called an informal Spanish Monarchy in Italy. Don Carlos was expected by his parents to support further Spanish adventures in Italy in favour of his younger brother, the Infante Felipe, although it would surely have been difficult for Don Carlos to avoid participation in the war on his own account. Historians have placed great emphasis on Mara Theresa's determination to recover Silesia after its seizure by Frederick the Great of Prussia, but they have paid insufficient attention to her resolve to recover the territories in southern Italy, the Two Sicilies, only recently torn from her father's possession by the Spanish Bourbons. Whatever the reason for Don Carlos's taking a role in the conflict, Naples and Sicily did supplement the Spanish war effort further north, fourteen thousand men leaving Naples to join Philip's forces at the end of 1741. Indeed, the initial contribution was such that when, in early 1742, Montemar asked Don Carlos for another five thousand troops the Infante claimed their departure would leave his realm exposed. But while Naples and Sicily may not have been able to meet all of the court of Madrid's demands, they were participating in the defence (or further rebuilding) of Spanish Italy in a way reminiscent of their role in the Spanish system there before 1707. Indeed, the Spanish intervention in Italy from 1741 onwards was predicated upon it playing that former role.[29]

Not all Neapolitans had welcomed the return of the Spaniards, even in the guise of an independent Don Carlos, while the reforms implemented from 1734 generated criticism, not least of the implicit absolutism of the Bourbon regime. The Genoese writer Paolo Mattia Doria, long resident in Naples, attacked what might be termed the administrative monarchy of the *afrancesados*, those inspired by Bourbon models and practices. He saw it as being in sharp contrast with an older tradition which emphasised the role of the monarch as dispenser of justice. But such disquiet, a lingering *antispagnolismo*, was of little moment before participation in the War of the Austrian Succession necessitated making substantial demands of Don Carlos's subjects. These impositions provoked domestic difficulties which fed on a certain disappointment with the new regime after the exaggerated hopes of 1734 and which escalated into a crisis of the Bourbon Neapolitan state in 1743–44. In the summer of 1742 a British threat to bombard Don Carlos's capital from the sea had obliged the king to promise to give no further military aid to Spain, which weakened the position of Montealegre, who was accused of neglecting the realm's defences. The king's parents in Madrid found this reasoning difficult to appreciate. Some thought the realm ready to revolt against Don Carlos on this occasion, if the British fleet cooperated. The opportunity to topple the Spanish Bourbon regime was not seized on this occasion. However, in 1743–44 Maria Theresa sought to exploit the disaffection in Naples and Sicily and the survival there of a supposed Austrian party by ordering an invasion of Naples. To gain Neapolitan support, she issued a manifesto in April 1744 which echoed that of the Spaniards in 1734 but which also implied that, as many had feared, the Naples of Don Carlos was little more than a Spanish province. The manifesto accused the Spaniards of tyranny and promised that posts in the realm would be reserved to Neapolitans, plainly seeking to exploit resentment of the influx of Spaniards since 1734. Some believed that the mere entry into the realm of the Austrian forces would trigger an anti-Bourbon uprising.[30]

Austrian fortunes and support in the kingdom certainly appeared to revive. Don Carlos abandoned his capital, while the arrest of those suspected of favouring Maria Theresa was ordered. The Bourbon monarchy in Naples was saved by what became known as the miracle of Velletri, an engagement which won Don Carlos widespread praise for his behaviour in action against the enemy and which, more important, halted the invasion: the Austrian forces were obliged to retreat, abandoning their attempted reconquest of Naples. However, Don Carlos's need to buy support at home for his regime and the war effort was at the expense of key elements of his reform programme, allowing the opponents of change to reassert themselves. In 1744, for example, the decree of 1738 which had sought to limit feudal jurisdictions, the abuse of which was widely regarded as one of the most urgent reforms, was effectively revoked, the feudal barons offering Carlos in return in 1746 a badly needed donativo of three hundred thousand ducats. Carlos could therefore, despite the promise of neutrality in the war between Britain and Spain given in 1742, continue to support the Spanish war effort against Austria and the king of Sardinia in Italy. Throughout 1745 great quantities of supplies reached the Genoese Riviera by sea from Naples for the

Neapolitan and Spanish forces in north Italy, while in August 1745 six thousand Neapolitan troops were preparing to cross Tuscany to join Gages's army. The exceptional success of Spanish arms in Italy in 1745 would not have been possible without this Neapolitan input. Neapolitan seaborne supply, for example, made up for the lack of supply from Spain when the Spanish fleet was penned up in Cádiz and Cartagena from 1744 onwards.[31]

The death of Philip V was followed by the fall in Naples of Montealegre, vilified in Madrid and Naples for his poor management of the war, and by his replacement as first secretary of state and de facto chief minister by the Piacentine noble Marchese Giovanni Fogliani Sforza d'Aragona, a protégé of the Spanish minister in Rome, Cardinal Acquaviva. Fogliani had followed Isabel to Madrid in 1714 and had accompanied Don Carlos to Italy in 1731. Despite Fogliani's Spanish connections, the events of the summer of 1746 brought to a close a decade in which Spaniards had effectively directed Neapolitan affairs and in some respects reflected a growing determination that Naples would no longer play the subordinate role it had done. Montealegre's fall also reflected something more meaningful, a growing awareness by the later stages of the War of the Austrian Succession there of a divergence of both aims and strategy developing between the courts of Naples and Madrid, where Philip had been succeeded by Ferdinand VI and Isabel Farnese was no longer all-powerful. In late 1747 the 30,000-ducats monthly subsidy Don Carlos received from Madrid as Infante of Spain was suspended. Nevertheless, despite this supposed liberation of Naples and its king from Spanish control, the links between the two courts and realms remained close and were in some respects confirmed when, in 1759, Carlos succeeded his half brother as Charles III.[32]

Milan (1745–46)

The duchy of Milan had been the hub of Spanish Italy since the middle of the sixteenth century and the location of a fighting force second only to the Army of Flanders. Philip had visited the duchy in 1702, but it had been lost following the defeat of the Bourbon forces outside Turin in 1706 and the subsequent Bourbon withdrawal from north Italy. Philip resented the loss of this component of Spanish Italy, although—witness the instructions for Philip's negotiators at Utrecht—the recovery of the Milanese was not as high a priority as that of Naples, with all the resources Naples offered. However, as in other territories which had been part of the Spanish Monarchy, there were enduring links between the Milanese and Spain after the passage of Milan to the Austrian Habsburgs. In 1718 Count Giacomo Brivio and his brother Francesco were convicted of collaboration with Philip V and was later one of those hoping to be rehabilitated after the peace of Vienna of 1725. Milanese, like Neapolitans, found favour and opportunities in Spain after 1707, Count Mariani being appointed in 1732 the first inspector general of artillery in Spain.[33]

The War of the Polish Succession offered Madrid an opportunity to exploit these connections. Indeed, in 1733 the Spanish court briefly hoped to detach the provinces of Cremona and Lodi from the Milanese for Don Carlos and was reluctant to see Milan pass to its ally King Charles Emanuel III of Sardinia. Spanish prospects benefitted from the way members of the Lombard elite reacted to the fortunes of the war. In January 1734, following the conquest of the Milanese by the king of Sardinia, and his publication of an edict summoning home all Milanese vassals, Prince Antonio Tolomeo Gallio Trivulzio, scion of one of the duchy's greatest families, passed through Venice en route to Milan. The prince informed Philip's minister in Venice, José Carpintero, that only his desire to live under "our [Spanish] *clementissimos amos* [most happy sovereigns]" had led him to abandon a senior military command in the Austrian Habsburg emperor's service. Clearly hoping for some equally prestigious office in Philip's service, he asked to be remembered to Patiño, recalling his friendship for the Spanish chief minister and his family. Another member of one of Milan's great families, Prince Francesco Saverio Melzi, also appeared in Venice. Having been deprived of his offices in Milan by the king of Sardinia, Melzi hoped Patiño would speak on his behalf with the Savoyard representative in Madrid. Carpintero pressed Melzi's case to his superior in Madrid on the grounds that the prince was very able, that he might be useful to Philip V because of his family connections, which included most of the great nobility of Milan, and that his reputation and influence elsewhere in Italy stood him well. Spanish ambitions in Lombardy may have been stimulated by the Polish succession conflict and the patent hostility there to

Savoyard rule. Certainly Philip V and Isabel Farnese hoped to install the Infante Felipe in Milan, but the war ended with Philip's forces having failed to restore Spanish dominion there.[34]

In the next conflict, however, Milan was a serious Spanish objective. Indeed, as soon as the death of Charles VI was known in December 1740 Philip V again aimed at securing Milan for the Infante Felipe. In March 1742 Philip declared his intention to reconquer the Milanese but also re-nounced it in favour of Isabel's second son, recalling his cession of Naples in 1734. Three years later Spanish forces occupied the duchy, the Infante entering the city of Milan in December 1745. The Bourbon suc-cess in what remained of the duchy of Milan and in those parts of it which had been acquired in and after 1713 by the duke of Savoy no doubt encouraged Spanish sympathisers to show themselves. In the spring of 1743 contessa Clelia Borromeo, born into the Genoese Grillo family, which had enduring links with Spain and maintained them with the court of Philip V, and married to a scion of one of Milan's oldest, most distin-guished families, had contacted Ensenada to say how much she had suf-fered for her pro-Spanish attitudes and hoping to be rewarded with appointment to the household of the Infante when the Spaniards eventu-ally took Milan; and in 1744 the Venetian representative in Milan had re-ported a pro-Bourbon conspiracy there. Significantly, too, few of the Lombard elite went into political exile during the occupation. As for Alessandria, which had been dismembered from the Milanese and given to Victor Amadeus II at the peace of Utrecht, many of the elite families there continued to look to the Spanish court and in 1745–46 appear to have willingly collaborated with the Spanish occupation. A deputation from Alessandria expressed its joy at being restored to "su legítimo Dueño" (its legitimate owner), and when the Infante visited the city in October 1745 among those receiving him were magistrates wearing the very traditional collar associated with Spain's conciliar elite, the *golilla*, and which Philip V himself sported in one of his earliest portraits as king of Spain painted by Hyacinthe Rigaud.[35]

But the occupation was short-lived. The Infante was obliged to abandon Milan, never to return, early in 1746 as the forces of Maria Theresa suc-cessfully counterattacked in north Italy. The Austrian recovery of Milan was followed by the punishment of some of the leading exponents of the

Spanish party there. These included the financier Conte Giulio Biancani, who was executed, Prince Francesco Saverio Melzi, who was condemned to banishment and confiscation, and Contessa Clelia Borromeo, who was also penalised by temporary banishment and loss of some of her property. As for Alessandria, the withdrawal of the Spanish forces in 1746 triggered not only retribution for many individual collaborators but also a reform of the administration at the expense of the traditional elite. The departure of the Infante's forces largely, but not completely, cut the links between the Lombard elites and Spain.[36]

Identity

Philip V's ambitions in Italy have frequently been condemned, above all by Spanish historians, as being against the national interest. This raises the question of the extent to which, as is often asserted, the first Bourbon, while not pursuing national goals, presided over the creation of a new, national Spanish state, culture, and identity.[37]

No common, single identity had been either assumed by or grafted onto the subjects of the diverse territories of the Spanish Monarchy before 1700. This is not to deny that individuals and families established their own connections and ties, that families and individuals moved from one territory to another and intermarried, that ministers considered allowing those born in one part of the Monarchy to acquire naturaleza in other parts or that there was some sense of community. Indeed, in the closing decades of the sixteenth century and the opening decades of the seventeenth the notion of a Spanish "monarchy" had, with some success, been deliberately crafted in ruling circles in Madrid as a means of drawing the various territories of the Spanish empire into a common defence. To some extent this project supplied that want of an integrating imperial ideology noted earlier. Philip V clearly sought to exploit that same ideology in Spain itself, when, for example, he appealed to the Cortes voting towns to consent to new impositions to defend existing or recover lost territories (see chapter 4). Philip's success in retaining and regaining the territories he had inherited from Charles II owed something to the force of those appeals. These, in turn, were clearly related to a heightened sense of "Spain" and of Spain's place in a larger "Monarchy" which was already evident in Spain in the later seventeenth century, and one element of that was a decline of a narrower Castilian rather than Spanish "national" loyalty. These developments represented a central precondition for the Bourbon Hispanicisation of the polity Philip had inherited. A sense of a common bond did not rule out tensions and hostility between Spaniards and Italians (and other groups). There had been conflict between them before 1700, and there would be after that year. A Spanish national feeling was unmistakably a factor both in a perceptible popular hostility towards the Italian presence in Spain in these decades and in a growing disenchantment with intervention in Italy. In 1731 in Seville, apparently, families of sailors pressed to serve on the fleet carrying six thousand Spanish troops to Italy invoked Saint Ferdinand, the medieval king who had delivered Seville from the Moors and who they now hoped would save them from the Italians. The African expeditions, in marked contrast, seem to have attracted little or no criticism (see chapter 4), not least because the Moors were a traditional enemy who continued to represent a real threat to the coastal populations of Spain. They were also infidels. In that sense, awareness of a shared interest and identity in Spain rested upon powerful religious foundations.[38]

There had always been Italians—Milanese, Neapolitans, Sicilians, and Sardinians as well as subjects of the other sovereigns in Italy—Genoese, Venetians, and so on—whether short-term visitors or long-term residents in Spain. It would thus be completely wrong to assume that an Italian presence was something new and alien which arrived with Isabel Farnese in 1714. Like the monarch's Spanish subjects, in earlier reigns his Italian ones also hoped for and sometimes secured *mercedes* of all sorts. In the preceding century, about 10 percent of Philip IV's grants of hábitos in the Military Orders, for example, had been made to his Italian subjects. Competitors in the struggle for royal favour, Italian subjects enjoyed success in this respect that had already contributed to the development of anti-Italian feeling well before 1700.[39]

But the numbers of Italians and of others, for example. Flemings, swelled as Spanish Italy and Spanish Flanders and Oran collapsed between 1706 and 1713 and after the Spanish evacuation of occupied Sardinia and in Sicily in 1720: prominent among those in Sicily was Giovanni Brancaccio, who was to return to Naples as finance minister in 1734 (above). Many of those who chose or who were forced to leave Italy, among them administrators, soldiers, ecclesiastics, and their families, headed for Spain, asserting their loyalty to Philip and what it had cost them and expecting succour in return. Their petitions for relief reveal the trauma the collapse of Spanish Italy meant for countless individuals and families in those years. They included Doña Leonor Bernet, the widow of Colonel D. Carlos Boet (or Voet). According to her petition, her husband had served the king, that is, Charles II and Philip V, for twenty-five years and had levied troops at his own cost for the defence of Milan until its fall, after which he had passed with his troops to Spain, abandoning his estate in Milan. Philip had appointed him governor of Porto Ercole, one of the Tuscan presidios, where he had died, leaving his widow in desperate straits; she claimed to have lost all, including her dowry, and that she had three children to support. She hoped the king would grant her son an ecclesiastical pension and order that her two daughters be received into the Real Colegio de San Isabel.[40]

Many of the exiles from Spanish Italy did obtain help of one sort or another. Some were rewarded with, or relieved out of, the forfeited property of those in Spain who had backed "Charles III": indeed, of the property confiscated in Valencia a large proportion was given to those dispossessed for their loyalty to Philip in Italy. In 1715 Marcos Antonio Barla petitioned for remuneration for his services and compensation for property seized and destroyed in Italy and was granted a pension out of the confiscations in Catalonia. Some were granted pensions paid from episcopal revenues, although to enjoy these an individual born outside the realm needed to be granted naturalisation and to have that grant approved by the Cortes-voting towns (see chapter 4). Some others were appointed to official posts, carving out successful careers in Spain, not least as administrators in the Aragonese territories. Some achieved high office, like D. Juan de Herrera, the last chancellor of Spanish Milan (to 1707), who was rewarded by Philip for his loyalty with the see of Sigüenza and who was appointed president of the Council of Castile in 1724. Just how many of these Italian exiles there were in Spain is unclear, but their presence and the identity of many of them are revealed both by the list of pensions paid by the king, which was prepared for the Junta de Medios in 1737, and by the petitions many of them submitted to the junta, which was seeking to cut costs of all sorts (see chapter 3). In Spain these exiles and their families constituted a sort of lobby with enduring links in what had been Spanish Italy; they hoped to recover the lost territories and perhaps their own forfeited property. Having backed Philip's Italian irredentism, many returned to Italy in the 1730s and 1740s, subsequent to the reconquest of Naples and Sicily. These included, besides Brancaccio (above), Francesco Eboli, duke of Castropignano, who accompanied Don Carlos to Italy in 1731, serving as captain general and supreme commander of the Neapolitan army from 1740, and the prince of Campoflorido, who returned to Sicily in 1747.[41]

Just how far those exiles were foreigners in Philip V's Spain is a moot point because identities were not so clear-cut. Most of those from Milan, Naples, Sardinia, and Sicily regarded themselves as, above all, subjects of Philip V, of the Spanish Monarchy, and expected (above) the king to recognise his obligation towards them by rewarding them, in Spain, for a loyalty which cost them dearly. Some of those who left Italy for exile in Spain during and after the War of Succession were in fact of Spanish ancestry, so many are best thought of as Spanish Italians, who must be distinguished from those arriving from Parma in and after 1714. Caution is therefore needed in speaking both of an Italian party and of a generalised hostility to Italians. The family of Baltasar Patiño, secretary of state for war, and his brother José had originated in Galicia before moving to Milan, where both men were born and where both started their careers in the Spanish administration. Monteleón, too, was of a Galician family, based in Milan (and related to the Patiño family), where his father sat in the Senate and where he got his first post. José Carpintero, who, like his patron Monteleón, served Philip V in a diplomatic capacity, was an official in the Army of Lombardy before 1707. Admiral José Navarro was born in 1687 in Messina, Sicily, of Spanish ancestry, his grandfather (d. 1679), natural of Xativa in Valencia, having served in Catalonia before passing with his family to serve in Sicily, where he took part in the suppression of the revolt of Messina (1674–78); the future admiral's father fought in the Army of Lombardy from 1691 onwards, and so did his son before removing to Spain in 1707 following the evacuation of Milan. Navarro's Spanish ancestry meant he did not need legal naturalisation to enjoy office or mercedes in Spain. These individuals represented just a small sample of the many "Italian" Spaniards in Spanish service after 1713, some but not all of whose members reached high office, some but not all returning to Italy after an often penurious exile. At the same time, numerous Spanish families, that is, those long resident within Spain, had experience of and links with Spanish Italy, many having fought to preserve it in the recent succession conflict.[42]

The reality was that Italy and Spain did not exist in their modern guise, and modern identifying labels like Italian and Spanish were not yet appropriate; individuals certainly did not apply these to themselves. Instead, they would think of themselves very largely as subjects of and personally bound to a monarch and dynasty, even to that seventeenth-century notion of the Monarchy, and the king, Philip V, would think the same. In that sense the dynastic and patrimonial Bourbon state was as much one created from below, by Philip's subjects, as imposed from above by Philip and his ministers.

Nonetheless, it is possible that Philip's Italian revanchism did contribute to the emergence of a narrower Spanish identity. The cost of his wars did suggest that Spanish Italy was, on balance, a burden and not an aid, despite the support given by the Two Sicilies in the War of the Austrian Succession. In addition, the transfer of the Two Sicilies to Don Carlos in 1734–35 meant that the fragmentation of the Monarchy effected between 1707 and 1713 was confirmed rather than concluded. The early seventeenth-century concept of Monarchy, at least one which embraced what had been Spanish Italy, could not persist. For the articulation of a narrow Spanish consciousness in elite circles we need only consider Ensenada's reaction at the end of 1747 to the Infante Felipe's response to a request to make economies in his household. Don Felipe proposed to dismiss some of his Spanish officials, provoking Ensenada to expostulate that the Spaniards were sacrificing their lives and wealth for the Infante, himself Spanish, in a war in which the Monarchy had no interest at stake, an attitude by no means confined to Ensenada (see chapter 4). A nascent Spanish nationalism, if such it was, may not alone explain why Charles III's Neapolitan ministers were resented in Spain in the 1760s but may have contributed to the hostility they inspired.[43]

The Spanish resurgence in Italy after 1713 had implications for more than just the territories which had been part of the old Spanish Habsburg Monarchy, Philip V's Spain continuing to offer opportunities to Italians from all parts of that peninsula. Resurgence did not depend upon, but was facilitated by, the recovery of the territories of the Crown of Aragon in the Iberian peninsula; without them, intervention in Italy might have been much more problematic. It probably helped, too, that royal authority was enhanced in those territories, although we need to be wary of overstating the extent to which Philip V pushed centralising absolutism in his Monarchy. The Basque territories and Navarre as well as Spanish America, loyal during the succession conflict, were largely exempt from any such process, although the presence of Basques in government (see chapter 4) and of Navarrese in finance (see chapter 3) also made for integration. In addition, participation in the reconstruction of Spanish Italy may have eased the process of insertion into the new Bourbon state in Aragon, Catalonia, and Valencia. As for Spanish Italy, where the presence of exiles from Bourbon Spain ensured that Philip's military interventions represented in part a continuation of the struggle in the peninsula which had ended in 1714, hostility to the successor regimes— Savoyard and Austrian Habsburg—and a lingering sympathy for and identification with Spain after centuries of Spanish dominion may have facilitated reconquest. What is clear is that identities were as yet not so narrowly defined in national terms as some historians seem to suggest. Many Italians, some of them in exile in Spain, continued to define themselves as subjects of a supranational Spanish Monarchy and its ruling dynasty. The same may also be true of many Spaniards, such that we cannot simply assume or conclude that Spaniards willingly abandoned the burden of empire in Europe in 1713. On the other hand, it is possible that the long-term impact of the cession of Naples and Sicily in 1734 and the burden (men, money) of the struggle to rebuild Spanish Italy, above all during the War of the Austrian Succession, may have done far more to erode such attitudes and stimulated the development by midcentury of a more narrowly Spain-centred national identity.[44] However, from 1759, with Don Carlos on the throne of Spain as Charles III and governing, indirectly, the kingdom of the Two Sicilies from there, and with Neapolitan ministers, notably Leopolde de Gregorio, marqués de Esquilache, in power in Madrid, contemporaries might have been justified in thinking that informally at least the old Monarchy had risen from the ashes.

CHAPTER SEVEN

SPAIN'S RESURGENCE, 1713–1748

———————————————————

The state of affairs is still uncertain, and the only undoubtable thing is
that Spain, happy in all its enterprises, furnished with abundant means,
and armed on land and sea, making itself respected by all, and feared . . .
pursues its own goals without being distracted by other objects.
—*Papal nuncio in Madrid, August* 1734

According to Pierre Vilar, in 1713 Philip V renounced Flanders and
Italy, preferring instead to rule over a more compact, Spanish state and
empire. Thus the Spanish Monarchy of the Habsburgs became the
Spanish kingdom of the Bourbons. The reality was very different.
Between 1713 and 1748 Philip sought to reassert Spanish power in the
Mediterranean and to recover dominion and authority which had been
forfeited in the recent succession struggle in north Africa but above all in
Italy. Philip did not always succeed, a sign of Spain's fundamental lack of
essential resources. But he came much closer to complete triumph—in
the War of the Polish Succession and above all in the War of the
Austrian Succession (in 1745–46)—than historians who focus on the abortive efforts to recover Sardinia and Sicily between 1717 and 1720 have
been willing to acknowledge. Indeed, Philip's interventions in Italy ensured that the Utrecht settlement was substantially overturned there and

the old Spanish Monarchy partially restored in the Mediterranean. Equally important was the fact that Spain's known ambitions, apparently erratic diplomacy, and near-constant preparations for war kept Europe on edge for a generation. In fact, Philip's Spain posed the single greatest threat to peace in Europe in the decades after 1713. Taking a longer perspective, Philip's revanchism, which was by no means confined to the Mediterranean, should be seen as a remarkable transformation of the fortunes and performance of Spain. In the generation preceding the War of the Spanish Succession, Spain preoccupied policy makers elsewhere because of its supposed weakness and the king's want of heirs; in the generation which followed the end of that conflict it preoccupied them because of its aggression and strength and determination to raise royal cadets to thrones in Italy. More broadly, Philip V's success contributed to what might be thought of as an impressive Indian summer of Spanish power in the late eighteenth century before the dramatic collapse of the opening decades of the nineteenth.[1]

In seeking to explain Philip V's Mediterranean adventures and broader revanchism, it can no longer be maintained that they were little more than an expression of excessive maternal ambition on the part of Philip's second wife, Isabel Farnese, or of the king's slavish obedience to the dictates of his second consort. Isabel undoubtedly enjoyed great influence, and after 1746 and even before, it was suggested that personal or dynastic ambitions in Italy had been pursued at the expense of real Spanish interests across the Atlantic. But this simplistic black legend of the reign cannot go unchallenged. Philip's Italian concerns, focused on the territories which had constituted Spanish Italy and only briefly and incidentally on Isabel's interests in Parma, Piacenza, and Tuscany, predated his second marriage, as did his ambitions in north Africa, which hardly interested Isabel at all. Spanish policy in the Mediterranean was the king's policy.

Philip V's achievements abroad owed a great deal not only to the weakness of his opponents, notably the Austrian Habsburgs, but also to his ability to secure allies, above all Bourbon France in the 1730s and 1740s, following the collapse of the unusual Anglo–French entente of the years after 1714. To that extent, Philip's achievement is explained by international developments which he could only seek to take advantage of but could not himself dominate or control. But Philip's ability to find allies was in part the consequence of his domestic achievement, such that Spain was re-garded as a power worth allying with, one which could contribute with its army and navy and funds to the success of any coalition in wartime. Within Spain, the demands of war, in terms of the need to mobilise scarce resources for the army and the fleet, explain some of the most important developments in these decades, most notably the reestablishment on completely new foundations of the militia in 1734 and that of the naval registration scheme, the *matrícula*, in 1737. At the same time, mounting these operations was a major challenge for and arguably the achievement of the new administrative arrangements introduced after the succession conflict had ended. They were also extremely costly. The way Philip's Spain rose to the multifaceted challenge justifies branding it a fiscal-military state, al-though since it was also dependent enormously upon the private sector it remained emphatically also a contractor state. Participation in these adven-tures was the springboard and possibly the crucial stage in their careers for a number of very successful ministerial careers, notably those of Patiño, Campillo, and Ensenada.

To many historians, Philip's reign and his success were due very largely to the fact that his rule witnessed a noteworthy phase of *afrancesamiento*, anticipating that of the Napoleonic era by a century. Certainly Philip was French, brought many French with him, and long hankered after the French throne. More important, his overhaul of Spain's institutions like the army and navy and the introduction of secretarial or ministerial, as opposed to conciliar, government seemed to be modelled on French prac-tice. Other aspects of policy seemed equally French, some elements of economic policy pointing towards a Spanish Colbertism. However, we need to be cautious. Some of the changes introduced by Philip were anticipated in the previous reign, that of Charles II, or simply adapted or overhauled older Spanish institutions or both. As for the factors influ-encing change, the years subsequent to the conclusion of the War of the Spanish Succession, a conflict which had seriously strained the capacities of most of the participants, were ones in which reform was in the air in many parts of Europe and in which there were many more influences and models available than just that offered by Bourbon France. Spain did experience some Frenchification in this period, but we should not exaggerate one single, French source of reforming ideas.[2]

Among the many changes wrought by Philip's regime in Spain, some historians have identified a degree of militarisation. As was true of Frenchification, there are some indications that this was indeed happening, above all in the Aragonese territories. However, it was largely limited to soldiers and former soldiers being appointed to civilian offices and to civilian authority losing out to that of the military. Some were worried at the time. Yet there was little militarisation in this sense in Castile or other parts of Spain, while despite the imposition of greater military burdens on the male population, Spanish society was not put into a military straitjacket, certainly not in the way we would recognise today, nor did Philip's subjects seem to have acquired a distinctive military mentality. Further, although many nobles continued to identity themselves in terms of their fighting role, the Spanish people as a whole did not perceive themselves primarily in terms of a military function.

Just what Philip V's Spanish subjects made of his Mediterranean ambitions and efforts is not always clear. There was, however, contrary to the black legend of the reign, a domestic constituency within Spain backing Philip's Mediterranean revanchism or some elements of it. The inhabitants of the coastal provinces could see much merit in a forward policy in Africa. There were, too, supporters of Philip's efforts to rebuild what had been Spanish Italy, certainly more than just a small coterie accompanying Isabel Farnese from Parma in 1714 and surrounding her at Philip's court. In fact, there existed a lobby in Spain, comprising Italians, Spaniards, and others, who defy simple national categorisation of a sort influenced by nineteenth- and twentieth-century ideas of nationhood. Many of these individuals and their families had fled Spanish Italy upon its collapse in the War of the Spanish Succession and gone into exile in Spain. Having no obvious connection to Farnese, they stood to gain from Philip's recovery of Spanish Italy. In Italy as well there were ready collaborators with the returning Spaniards who contributed to the reconquest, for example, of Naples and Sicily in 1734–35.

Historians have perhaps been too ready to take at face value the international agreements separating Spain from its newly refurbished Italian empire; they have also perhaps been too quick to see a prototype of the modern Spanish state in that ruled by the first Bourbon. In fact, the Bourbon states created in Italy between 1731 and 1748 were in many respects

Spanish dependencies. Philip in effect created what we might call a neo–Spanish Monarchy in its evocation of that of his Habsburg predecessors, one in which supranational identities focused on the ruling dynasty continued to resonate and to powerfully underpin loyalty. In that sense, while recognising a degree of Hispanicisation in the course of Philip V's reign, we need to treat with caution the idea that it also witnessed the emergence of a new national space.[3]

At the same time, the pursuit of Philip V's revanchist aspirations in the Mediterranean necessitated the imposition of great burdens on his Spanish subjects. This added up to a remarkable Hispanicisation of the Monarchy, since Philip could not spread the burden as his Habsburg predecessors had done or tried to do. The weight of these charges was most marked during the War of Jenkins' Ear or, rather, the War of the Austrian Succession, which soon largely eclipsed that conflict, and above all in 1745 and 1746. This fact has not been properly appreciated by historians, who too often ignore Philip's so-called second reign (1724–46), although crucial measures regarding, for instance, vagabonds and gypsies, were introduced during and triggered by war, by the later conflict in particular. Philip's wars, especially that last war, shaped Spain—something that a new and closer reading of the postwar *catastro* of Ensenada should reveal—but the demands made during the War of the Austrian Succession also created some unease, even resentment, among Philip's subjects as well as widespread efforts to evade them. They may even have fomented a rejection of any lingering sense of identity with the Italian territories, which in turn contributed more than has been recognised to an emerging sense of Spanish identity.[4]

Finally, while pursuit of Philip's objectives had involved the elaboration of new institutions (above) which further complicated the mosaic of privilege that was Spanish society, rather than see the advent of the Bourbon dynasty in 1700 as the beginning of a new, progressive, modernising phase in Spanish history, Philip V's preoccupation with the recovery or retention of the Habsburg Monarchy in Italy and the western Mediterranean suggests an essentially conservative impulse. This harking back to the past cannot be separated from the fact that many of those who served Philip V—Grimaldo, Macanaz, Montemar, Navarro, Patiño and many more—had been born and reached maturity in the last decades of Habsburg

Spain. These individuals and many other men and women may have carried over from the old dynasty into the new attitudes and practices whose influence should not be underestimated. The Spanish Monarchy bequeathed to Philip by Charles II had an even more profound resilience than even recent apologists of late Habsburg Spain have themselves realised.

This raises a final question, one related to Henry Kamen's observation half a century ago about the neglect of Spain's history in the years between 1665 and 1746. The neglect implies a link between the reigns of Philip V and of his Habsburg predecessor. But what does Philip's achievement say about Charles II and his Spain? On the one hand, Philip was an adult, with sons, and thus many of the issues which triggered instability in the previous reign simply didn't dog Spanish political life under Philip. In addition, Philip was, most of the time, lucid and able to lead in a way Charles had not been. To some extent, then, it was a question of leadership. The new king was able to harness the talents of the men described above and to get more out of Spain in pursuit of his Mediterranean revanchism. But he would not have been able to do this if the resources were not there to be exploited and if there had not been the men to collaborate with him, men who had grown up with and were committed to the Monarchy. The two reigns which spanned the years between 1665 and 1746 are linked not just historiographically but also, in some respects, in terms of real historical experience.

NOTE ON SOURCES

The source materials for an exploration of Spain's remarkable resurgence after 1713 are extensive, inside and outside Spain. In Spain the key sources are those generated by the new central administrative agencies which emerged in this period. Some of the materials generated by the Secretariats of War, Navy, and Indies and Finance perished in the fire which consumed the old Habsburg royal palace, or *alcázar*, in Madrid in 1734.[1] Nevertheless, abundant documentation survives relating to the army, the navy, and the finances in the Archivo General at Simancas (AGS) and in the Archivo Histórico Nacional (AHN) in Madrid.[2] In some respects, the material for the eighteenth century is better organised in Simancas than it is for the Habsburg era, at least insofar as the researcher is concerned, because it is catalogued by specific theme or topic. Thus *legajos*, or files, 2041–2201 of the Secretaría de Guerra series relate to operations in Italy between 1731 and 1749, while legajos 543–46 relate to the supply of arms and uniforms between 1714 and 1751. In addition, the Supplementary legajos 234–38 in that same series contain material specific to the invasion of Sicily between 1718 and 1720, 480–81 with the expedition to Ceuta (1720) and 482–88 with that to Oran (1732). The

Secretaría de Marina is less ample and diverse, but it, too, is helpfully organised, legajos 251–302, for example, containing material relating to the *matrícula*. Both the AGS and the AHN have excellent holdings relevant to Spanish diplomacy in this period (not separately discussed by me) in the Estado series. The AHN is also the place to find the records of all the councils, including the all-important Council of Castile and its adjunct Cámara.

Official publications—above all, the *Gaceta de Madrid*—are also useful, not least for plotting army, navy, and other careers and for tracing the public record of the overseas operations mounted by Spain under Philip V and Ferdinand VI to 1748. The scholar hoping to use these in Scotland can draw on the selection available in the National Library in Scotland, in the so-called Astorga collection of early modern Spanish and Portuguese books held by that library and purchased by Sir Walter Scott's son-in-law for the Advocates Library at the start of the nineteenth century. That collection also includes invaluable printed Spanish books published in the reigns of Philip V and Ferdinand VI which relate to the topics at the heart of my book.

But the public or state records are by no means the sole source one can draw on. Also invaluable are the records of the municipal authorities who were expected to supply men and money for Philip V's Mediterranean adventures in response to requests from, for example, the secretary of state for war. Some of the records of the sessions and decisions of those authorities—the *libros de actas* or *de acuerdos*—are fuller than others, facilitating a more complete exploration of the attitudes of municipal elites. I have used those of Burgos, Murcia, and Valladolid, the last now very usefully digitised and available online. The records of some others are described in published catalogues, including, for instance, Astorga, but many others merit and need further, fuller investigation.[3]

Furthermore, within Spain there are the papers of noble and other families and private correspondence, although these are the most problematic, not least because they are scarce or difficult to access or both. Fortunately, many, though by no means all—the Alba archives remain in the family archive in the Palacio de Liria in Madrid—of the archives of noble families are now housed in a distinct archive, a branch of the AHN, the Sección de Nobleza, located in Toledo. Much of this material is now also digitised. So far the material has been largely used for studies of individual families or houses—Infantado and Osuna, for example— and for investigation of economic and social issues, but those archives will surely throw more, and less state-oriented, light on the aspects of Philip V's Spain which are the concern of this book.

Last but by no means least, there is the correspondence in non-Spanish archives of the many foreign diplomats in Madrid and Seville, whither the court relocated between 1729 and 1733. The Spanish court had long been one of Europe's great diplomatic centres under the Habsburgs and remained so under the Bourbons. Among the countless functions of the many foreign diplomats sent to Madrid and Seville were those of discovering and reporting on Spanish policy and resources to sovereigns who were frequently alarmed by Spain's warlike preparations and aggression; as well, they worked to secure advantageous grants, for example, regarding commercial access to Spanish America. Excellent use was made of the French diplomatic correspondence by Alfred Baudrillart, but less use has been made hitherto of the reports of successive representatives of a number of other contemporary sovereigns, including, for example, the dukes of Savoy, later kings of Sicily (1713–20) and Sardinia (from 1720), Victor Amadeus II (d. 1730), and Charles Emanuel III. Not only was the court of Turin among the most obvious victims of Spanish revanchism in the Mediterranean, but Victor Amadeus was the grandfather (and Charles Emanuel the uncle) of the future Ferdinand VI, while the house of Savoy had a reversionary interest in the Spanish succession should Philip V's line die out, a claim enshrined in the Utrecht settlement. Savoyard diplomats therefore took a very close interest in developments in Spain in these decades, as did the representatives of most other sovereigns. Their correspondence is found in the series Lettere Ministri, Spagna, in the Archivio di Stato, Turin, while papers relevant to specific negotiations are contained in the series Negoziazioni, Spagna, in the same archive. While diplomatic history of a certain type has largely fallen out of fashion, either being neglected altogether or reemerging as New Diplomatic History, the reports of foreign representatives contain a myriad of interesting, relevant, important detail and comment on developments in the courts to which they were sent—in this case Spain—which is not always easily found in the Spanish records, public or private.

NOTES

Abbreviations Used in the Notes

AMB:	Archivo Municipal Burgos
AMM:	Archivo Municipal Murcia
AMV:	Archivo Municipal Valladolid
Add:	Additional Manuscripts
AGS:	Archivo General, Simancas
AHPC:	Archivo Historico de la Provincia de Cantabria,
AST:	Archivio di Stato, Turin
ASV:	Archivio Segreto Vaticano
BL:	British Library
BN:	Biblioteca Nacional, Madrid
CEIII:	Charles Emanuel III of Sardinia
DGT:	Dirección General del Tesoro
GJ:	Gracia y Justicia
LA:	Libros de Actas
LM:	Lettere Ministri
NA:	National Archives, London (Kew)
NLS:	National Library of Scotland
SG:	Secretaría de Guerra
SP:	State Papers

SS: Segretaria di Stato

SSH: Superintendencia de Hacienda

TMC: Tribunal Mayor de Cuentas

Note on Money

1. G. de Uztáriz, *Theory and Practice of Commerce and Maritime Affairs . . . translated . . . by John Kippax* (London, 1751), 1:88

2. Anna Mur i Raurell, ed., *Diplomacia Secreta y Paz: La correspondencia de los embajadores españoles en Viena Juan Guillermo Ripperda y Luis Ripperda (1724–1727) / Geheimdiplomatie und Friede: Die Korrespondenz der spanischen Botschafter in Wien Johan Willem Ripperda und Ludolf Ripperda (1724–1727)*, 2 vols. (Madrid: Ministerio de Asuntos Exteriores y de Cooperación, 2011), 2:333

3. Arvillars to CEIII, 14 March 1732, AST, LM Spagna/64.

4. Revenus Annuels du Roy d'Espagne [1737], sent with Trevor to [?], 18 March 1738, NA, SP/94/130.b.

Introduction

Epigraph: Bolingbroke to Earl of Marchmont, [23] September 1743, in *A Selection from the Papers of the Earls of Marchmont . . . from 1685 to 1750 in the possession of Sir George Henry Rose*, 3 vols. (London: John Murray, 1831), 2:317.

1. Since I refer to the first Bourbon as Philip, rather than Felipe, I call the last Habsburg Charles rather than Carlos, both for consistency and to reduce the likelihood of confusing the last Habsburg with Philip's and Isabel's son, the Infante Don Carlos.

2. Henry Kamen, *The War of Succession in Spain 1700–15* (London: Weidenfeld, 1969), xi; Louis XIV feared a Moorish invasion of Spain if Oran was lost, Louis XIV to Amelot, Fontainebleau, 3 October 1707, *Correspondance de Louis XIV avec M. Amelot, son ambassadeur en Espagne*, ed. baron de Girardot, 2 vols. (Nantes: Merson, 1864), 1:239–41. There is a vast literature on Spain's supposed seventeenth-century decline. To Stanley J. Stein and Barbara H. Stein, *Silver, Trade, and War: Spain and America in the Making of Early Modern Europe* (Baltimore: Johns Hopkins University Press, 2000) 91, 101, and passim, late seventeenth-century Spain was effectively subject to British, Dutch, and French "informal (economic) empire."

3. There is a vast bibliography on the experience of the Aragonese territories in the succession struggle: see Joaquim Albareda, *Felipe V y el triunfo del absolutismo: Cataluña en un conflicto europeo (1700–1714)* (Barcelona: Generalitat de Catalunya, 2002). Philip abdicated in favour of his son Luis in early 1724 and resumed the throne later that year on Luis's death, leading some historians to speak of Philip's two reigns: Henry Kamen, *Philip V: The King Who Reigned Twice* (New Haven: Yale University Press, 2000); Kamen, *War*, xi; Francisco A. Eissa-Barroso and Ainara Vázquez Varela, "Introduction," in *Early Bourbon Spanish America: Politics and Society in a Forgotten Era (1700–1759)*, ed. Francisco A. Eissa-

Barroso and Ainara Vázquez Varela (Leiden: Brill, 2013), 1–8, echoes the point but also reflects historians' renewed interest in the period.

4. Paolo Preto, "Daniele Bragadin," *Dizionario Biografico degli Italiani, 81* vols. to date (Rome: Istituto dell'Enciclopedia Italiana, 1960-), available online at http://www.treccani. it/enciclopedia/daniele-bragadin. The Utrecht settlement had further included Philip's renunciation of his claim to the French crown, which he also resented, periodically hoping to realise that claim. This is the theme of Alfred Baudrillart, *Philippe V et la Cour de France,* 5 vols. (Paris: Firmin-Didot, 1890–1901); for the Spanish Atlantic, Enriqueta Vila Vilar, *Hispanismo e Hispanización: El Atlántico como nuevo Mare Nostrum* (Madrid: Real Academia de la Historia, 2012); H. M. Scott, *The Birth of a Great Power System 1740–1815* (London: Pearson, 2006), 73 (the end of the *asiento*).

5. See Faruk Tabak, *The Waning of the Mediterranean, 1550–1870: A Geohistorical Approach* (Baltimore: Johns Hopkins University Press, 2008). Anson's expedition to the Pacific (1740–44) captured the Manila galleon with its fabulous cargo of bullion but did not trigger the collapse of Spanish authority in Chile and Peru as initially envisaged in London, Gwyn Williams, *The Prize of All the Oceans* (London: Harper Collins, 1999), 13–14 and passim; Steve Pincus, "Absolutism, Ideology and English Foreign Policy: The Ideological Context of Robert Molesworth's *Account of Denmark,*" in *Ideology and Foreign Policy in Early Modern Europe (1650–1750),* ed. David Onnekink and Gijs Rommelke (Farnham: Ashgate, 2011), 29–54 (at 54).

6. Frans Van Kalken, *La fin du regime espagnol aux Pays-Bas: Etude historique politique, economique et sociale* (Brussels: Lebegue, 1907); Miguel Angel Echevarría Bacigalupe, "La Guerra de Sucesión en los Paises Bajos Meridionales," in *Hispania-Austria III: Der Spanische Erbfolgekrieg / La Guerra de Sucesión española,* ed. Friedrich Edelmayer, Virginia León Sanz, and José Ignacio Ruiz Rodríguez (Vienna: Verlag fur Geschichte und Politik and Munich: Oldenbourg Wissenschaftsverlag, 2008), 193–210; Grimaldi to Signori, 26 September 1741, in *Istruzioni e Relazioni degli Ambasciatori Genovesi,* vol. 6: *(1721–1745),* ed. Raffaele Ciasca (Rome: Istituto Storico Italiano per l'Eta Moderna e Contemporanea, 1967), 265–67; Baudrillart, *Philippe V,* 4:477; Edward Armstrong, "The Bourbon Governments in France and Spain: I," in *The Cambridge Modern History,* vol. 6: *The Eighteenth Century,* ed. A. W. Ward, G. W. Prothero, and Stanley Leathes (Cambridge: Cambridge University Press, 1909), 122; Guido Quazza, *Il problema italiano e l'equilibrio europeo, 1720–1738* (Turin: Diputazione Subalpina di Storia Patria, 1965), 61–71; G. H. Jones, *Great Britain and the Tuscan Succession Question, 1710–1737* (New York: Vantage, 1998), 1–8. Philip had—and was aware of—his (own) claims on Tuscany before his second marriage

7. See Christopher Storrs, "The Role of Religion in Spanish Policy in the Reign of Carlos II, 1665–1700," in *War and Religion after Westphalia, 1648–1713,* ed. David Onnekink (Farnham: Ashgate, 2009), 25–46; Julio Muñoz Rodríguez, *La Séptima Corona: El Reino de Murcia y la construcción de la lealtad castellana en la guerra de sucesión (1680–1725)* (Murcia: Universidad de Murcia, 2014), passim; David Martín Marcos, *El Papado y la Guerra de Sucesión española* (Madrid: Marcial Pons, 2011); Antonio Bethencourt Massieu, *Relaciones de*

España bajo Felipe V: Del Tratado de Sevilla a la Guerra con Inglaterra (1729–1739) (Alicante: AEHM, 1998), 47; David González Cruz, *Propaganda e Información en Tiempos de Guerra: España y América (1700–1714)* (Madrid: Silex, 2009), 19; Angel Benito y Durán, "Don Luis Belluga y Moncada, cardenal de la Santa Iglesia y obispo de Cartagena, consejero de Felipe V," in *Estudios sobre el cardenal Belluga,* ed. Carmen María Cremades Griñan (Murcia: Academia Alfonso X El Sabio, 1985), 137–210.

8. For Spanish grain imports from Africa, see Eloy Martín Corrales, "El comercio de la bahía de Cádiz con el norte de Africa (1492–1767)," in *El Sistema Comercial Español en la Economía Mundial (siglos XVII–XVIII),* ed. Isabel Lobato and José María Oliva (Huelva: Universidad de Huelva, 2013), 257–81; William Coxe, *Memoirs of the Kings of Spain of the House of Bourbon,* 5 vols. (London: Longman, 1818), 2:270ff.

9. Antonio Miguel Bernal, *España, proyecto inacabado: Los costes / beneficios del Imperio* (Madrid: Marcial Pons, 2005), 54–55; on the construction of Spanish Africa, c. 1500, see J. H. Elliott, *Imperial Spain, 1469–1716* (London: Arnold, 1963), 53–56, and Manuel Rivero Rodríguez, "Monarquía Católica o Hispánica? Africa o Levante: La encrucijada de la política mediterránea entre Lepanto (1571) y la anexión de Larache (1618)," in *La Monarquía Hispánica en Tiempos del Quijote,* ed. Porfirio Sanz Camañes (Madrid: Silex, 2005), 593–613. During the War of the Austrian Succession, this foothold on the African coast enabled Spanish ships to reach Italy, evading British countermeasures, Bartolini to (Venetian) Senate, 26 June 1742, in *Corrispondenze diplomatiche veneziane da Napoli: Dispacci,* ed. Eurigio Tonetti (Venice: Istituto Poligrafico e Zecca dello Stato, 1994), 17:352; Burnett to Craggs, 15 September 1720, National Archives [NA], Kew (London), State Papers [SP] 89/28 f. 118; Arvillars to King Charles Emmanuel III of Sardinia [CEIII], 8 February 1732, Archivio di Stato, Turin [AST], Lettere Ministri [LM] Spagna, mazzo 64; Bethencourt, *Relaciones de España,* 142; Leila Maziane, "Los cautivos europeos en Marruecos (siglos XVII–XVIII)," in *Circulación de Personas e Intercambios Comerciales en el Mediterráneo y en el Atlántico (siglos XVI, XVII, XVIII),* ed. José Antonio Martínez Torres (Madrid: CSIC, 2008), 66.

10. José María Blanco Núñez, "La Real Armada," in Hugo O'Donnell y Duque de Estrada, *Historia Militar de España,* tomo 3: *Edad Moderna,* vol. 3: *Los Borbones,* ed. Carmen Iglesias (Madrid: Ministerio de Defensa, 2014), 303–24 (at 305); Miguel Angel Alonso Aguilera, *La Conquista y el Dominio Español de Cerdeña (1717–1720)* (Valladolid: Universidad de Valladolid, 1977), 61–63, 74–76, and passim. Alonso Aguilera notes the difficulty of reconciling the figures regarding the number and types of ships involved given by the contemporary accounts—notably those of V. Bacallar y Sanna, *Comentarios de la guerra de España e historia de su rey Felipe V, el Anomoso,* ed. Charles Seco Serrano (Madrid: Atlas, 1957), Jesus Belando, *Historia civil de España, sucesos de la guerra y tratados de paz,* 3 vols. (Madrid, 1740–43), and Jaime Miguel de Guzmán Dávalos Spinola, marqués de la Mina, *Memorias sobre la Guerra de Cerdeña y Sicilia en los años de 1717 a 1720,* ed. Antonio Cánovas del Castillo, 2 vols. (Madrid, 1898)—an observation applicable to all the other expeditions under consideration and to the number of troops involved in them. Tim Blanning, *The Pursuit of Glory:*

Europe, 1648–1815 (London: Penguin, 2007), 563, claims, mistakenly, that this was the largest Spanish armada since Lepanto; César Fernández Duro, *La Armada Española, desde la Unión de los Reinos de Castilla y de Aragón,* 9 vols. (Madrid, 1895–1903), 6:140; Carlos Martínez Shaw and Marina Alfonso Mola, *Felipe V* (Madrid: Arlanza Ediciones, 2001), 260; A. de Bethencourt, "Las aventuras italianas de Felipe V," in *España y el mar en siglo de Charles III,* ed. V. Palacio Atard (Madrid: Marinvest, 1989), 324–25; H. Kamen, *Spain's Road to Empire: The Making of a World Power 1492–1763* (London: Allen Lane, 2002), 453–55; Derek McKay, "Bolingbroke, Oxford and the Defence of the Utrecht Settlement in Southern Europe," *English Historical Review* 86 (1971): 264–84; Coxe, *Memoirs of Kings,* 3:3–4; printed *Relacion* [1720], National Library of Scotland, Edinburgh [NLS], Astorga Collection, G.25.e.2 (117–19).

11. Juan Sanz Sampelayo, "Un informe anónimo sobre las operaciones militares Africanas de 1720–1721," *Baética* 8 (1985): 417–22; Coxe, *Memoirs of Kings,* 3:5–6; Lede to Tolosa, Ceuta, 10 and 23 November and 17 December 1720, Archivo General de Simancas [AGS], Secretaría de Guerra [SG], Suplemento, *legajo* 481; Derek McKay and H. M. Scott, *The Rise of the Great Powers, 1648–1815* (London: Longman, 1983), 126–34; Fernández Duro, *Armada Española,* 6:198. Since there was some uncertainty about the grand duke of Tuscany's reception of this force, the expedition carried artillery for the siege of Livorno if necessary, Arvillars to CEIII, 7 September 1731, AST, LM Spagna/63. In June 1732 Don Charles received the homage of the Florentine Senate as Gian Gastone's heir, in September he took possession of the duchy of Parma, and in October he made his formal entry into the duchy of Piacenza, Roberto Fernández, *Charles III* (Madrid: Arlanza Ediciones, 2001), 57–67, and María Angeles Pérez Samper, *Isabel de Farnesio* (Barcelona: Plaza y Janes, 2003), 263–64.

12. Arvillars to CEIII, 29 June 1731, AST, LM Spagna/63. Apparently the prince also offered Tetuan, and the following year his supporters promised to help the Oran expedition, Arvillars to CEIII, 8 February 1732, AST, LM Spagna/64. According to Coxe, *Memoirs of Kings,* 3:249–50, Isabel Farnese, hoping to revive Philip's spirits, reminded him of a vow to recover Oran; Fernández Duro, *Armada,* 6:200–203; Bethencourt, "Aventuras," 331; Edward Armstrong, *Elisabeth Farnese, the "Termagant of Spain"* (London: Longmans, Green, 1892), 272–76; Kamen, *Spain's Road,* 455–56. W. N. Hargreaves-Mawdsley, *Spain under the Bourbons, 1700–1833: A Collection of Documents* (London and Basingstoke: Macmillan, 1973), 91–97, reproduces the account in Belando, *Historia civil.* The printed account, *Segundo papel y mas copioso de la Armada que ha salido para la conquista de Oran* (Madrid, 1732), gives an incorrect total of the forces: it lists 36,796, the correct total being 26,796. Anon., *The Spanish Conquest: or, a journal of their late expedition . . . Oran . . . Mazaquivir* (London, 1732).

13. [?] to [?], Madrid, 18 May 1740, AGS, SSH/396; Armstrong, *Elisabeth,* 287; Fernández Duro, *Armada,* 6:205; Bethencourt, "Aventuras," 331; Bagshaw to Newcastle, 12 December 1733, 18 May and 7 October 1734, and 12 and 19 February 1735, NA, SP 79/17; Borré to CEIII, 16 October 1733, AST, LM Spagna/65, and enclosed list of troops des-

tined for Italy, totalling 35,900 men (including 3,500 for the Tuscan garrisons), and same to same, 18 January 1734, AST, LM Spagna/66. By the start of 1734, the army in Italy totalled about 40,000 men, Johann Hellwege, *Die spanischen Provinzialmilizen im 18. Jahrhundert* (Boppard am Rhein: Harald Boldt Verlag, 1969), 34. Rafael Torres Sánchez, "'Las Prioridades de un Monarca Ilustrado' o las limitaciones del Estado Fiscal-Militar de Charles III," *Hispania* 68 (2008): 407–36, omits this conflict in discussing Spain's eighteenth-century wars. Bethencourt, *Relaciones de España*, 260–63; Skinner to Walpole, 21 January 1735, British Library, London [BL], Additional Manuscripts [Add], 73,987. J. del Campo-Raso, *Memorias . . . continuación a los "Comentarios de San Felipe . . ."* (Madrid, 1957), 4, 140–; Diario del Rexto de cavalleria de Malta . . ., 200–201. Intervention abroad left Spain exposed: in 1735 the king of Portugal proposed to the British government an offensive alliance against an apparently defenceless Spain, William Coxe, *Memoirs of the Life and Administration of Sir Robert Walpole*, 3 vols. (London: Cadell and Davies, 1798), 1:457–60. In 1735–36 the walls of Tuy (Galicia) were repaired for fear of attack, Ofelia Rey Castelao, *Tuy 1753, Según las Respuestas Generales del Catastro de Ensenada* (Madrid: Tabapress, 1990), 31. Relacion de la conquista de . . . Nápoles y Sicilia, BL, Add. 22,722; María Dolores Gómez Molleda, "El pensamiento de Carvajal y la política internacional española del siglo XVIII," *Hispania* 15 (1955): 22; Rafael Escobedo, "La Expansión Geográfica de la Renta del Tabaco," *Estudis* 33 (2007): 206–7. Contemporaries, like later historians, were not always sure of the composition of the Tuscan *presidios* complex, see count Tallard to Louis XIV, 6 June 1698, in *Letters of William III and Louis XIV,* ed. Paul Grimblot, 2 vols. (London, 1848), 2:23–24; Pérez Samper, *Isabel*, 280.

14. Coxe, *Memoirs of Walpole*, 1:461, 471; Quazza, *Problema*, 235–50, 271–82; Arthur M. Wilson, *French Foreign Policy during the Administration of Cardinal Fleury* (Cambridge: Harvard University Press, 1936), 240–89. The Spanish court was suspected, nevertheless, of hoping to exploit the emperor's war against the Turks to seize Tuscany, see the end-of-mission report of the Venetian resident in Madrid, Cappello, *Relazione* (1738), 16; Cristina Borreguero Beltrán, "The Spanish Army in Italy, 1734," *War in History* 5 (1998): 126; McKay and Scott, *Rise of the Great Powers*, 150–51. This alleged French betrayal was recalled ten years later after revelations of secret French wartime peace discussions with the king of Sardinia, Huéscar to Ensenada, 29 January 1747, in Didier Ozanam and Diego Téllez Alarcia, eds., *Misión en Paris* (Logroño: Instituto de Estudios Riojanos, 2010), 189–90.

15. Spanish participation in this conflict, above all in Italy, is thinly dealt with in M. S. Anderson, *The War of the Austrian Succession 1740–1748* (London: Longman, 1995). José A. Ferrer Benimeli, "El Conde de Aranda y las Campañas de Italia a Favor de los Hijos de Felipe V," in *Felipe V y su tiempo: Congreso Internacional*, 2 vols., ed. Eliseo Serrano (Zaragoza: Institución Fernando el Cátolico, 2004), 725–45, is a general account of the war from a Spanish perspective. María del Carmen Melendreras Giménez, *Las Campañas de Italia durante los años 1743–1748* (Murcia: Universidad de Murcia, 1987), omits the early years of the conflict. Spenser Wilkinson, *The Defence of Piedmont, 1742–1748: A Prelude to the Study*

of Napoleon (Oxford: Oxford University Press, 1927), 37–38, 44–45, 56–57; Birtles to Newcastle, 11 and 15 November 1741, 24 January 1742, 28 February and 7 March 1742, NA/SP 79/19. For rather different figures, see Valguarnera to CEIII, 13 November 1741 and 22 January 1742, AST, LM Spagna/70. The first convoy (November 1741) comprised 3 warships, 4 galleys, and 240 transports, the second (January 1742) about 100 transports escorted by 40 (French and Spanish) men-of-war. Wilkinson, *Defence*, 224; Michael Hochedlinger, *Austria's Wars of Emergence, 1683–1797* (London: Longman, 2003), 256; Pérez Samper, *Isabel*, 298; Edouard Revel, "La Savoie et la domination espagnole: Guerre de Succession d'Autriche (1742–1749)," *Mémoires et Documents publiés par la Société Savoisienne d'Histoire et d'Archéologie* 62 (1925): 103–245; Ensenada to Campillo, 1 January 1743, AGS/SG/2117. This contributed to a remarkable improvement in Savoyard–Genevan relations: Dino Carpanetto, *Divisi alla fede: Frontiere religiose, modelli politici, identita storiche nelle relazioni tra Torino e Ginevra (XVII–XVIII secolo)* (Turin: UTET, 2009); Estado del exercito . . ., [1745] AGS/SG/2158. See also Estado del ejercito . . ., in Rodríguez Villa, *Ensenada*, 474–75, and Didier Ozanam, "La política exterior de España en tiempos de Felipe V y Fernando VI," in *Historia de España Menéndez Pidal*, vol. 29 / 1: *La época de los primeros Borbones,* ed. Vicente Palacio Atard (1985; repr. Madrid: Espasa Calpe, 1996), 520.

16. Hochedlinger, *Austria's Wars*, 256; Martínez Shaw and Alfonso Mola, *Felipe*, 162.

17. Anderson, *War of Austrian Succession*, 136–37, 203; instructions for Melchor de Macanaz for the Breda peace conference (1746), Antonio Dominguez Ortiz, *Sociedad y Estado en el siglo XVIII español* (Barcelona: Ariel, 1976), 280–81; Scott, *Birth*, 65. Like most accounts of the peace, those of Anderson and Scott omits the important guarantee of Don Charles's hold on Naples. Didier Ozanam, *La Diplomacia de Fernando VI: Correspondencia entre Carvajal y Huéscar, 1746–1749* (Madrid: CSIC, 1975), 426; Scott, *Birth*, 73–74. Don Charles reproached his half brother respecting some of its provisions, see María Victoria López Cordón, "Carvajal y la política exterior de la Monarquía española," in *Ministros de Fernando VI,* ed. José M. Delgado Barrado and José L. Gómez Urdáñez (Córdoba: Universidad de Córdoba, 2002), 41, and José L. Gómez Urdáñez, "Carvajal–Ensenada: Un Binomio Político," in ibid., 89.

18. William invaded in 1688 with more than twenty-one thousand men, aboard four hundred or so transports escorted by fifty-three assorted warships, Jonathan I. Israel, *The Dutch Republic: Its Rise, Greatness, and Fall, 1477–1806* (Oxford: Oxford University Press, 1995), 841–43, while the expedition of 1741 comprised more than thirty ships of the line and a few lesser vessels, convoying one hundred transports carrying more than eleven thousand troops, J. C. M. Ogelsby, "Spain's Havana Squadron and the Preservation of the Balance of Power in the Caribbean, 1740–1748," *Hispanic American Historical Review* 49 (1969): 473–88 (at 478–79). In 1720 the British minister in Madrid sought to reassure ministers in London that the preparations for the relief of Ceuta were not intended against Britain or Gibraltar, Stanhope to Craggs, 5 August 1720. NA SP 94/90. For anxieties in Turin, see Christopher Storrs, "Ormea as Foreign Minister, 1732–45: The Savoyard State between England and Spain," in *Nobiltà e Stato in Piemonte: I Ferrero d'Ormea,* ed. Andrea

Merlotti (Turin: Silvio Zamorani, 2003), 231–48. Blanning, *Pursuit*, 564, is dismissive of the diplomacy of the period; his account of the War of the Polish Succession, 566, ignores the Spanish conquest of Naples and Sicily, and his exiguous narrative of developments in Italy in the War of the Austrian Succession, 573, omits the Spanish success up to 1746. These omissions make the peace settlements which ended both wars less intelligible. John Lynch, *Bourbon Spain, 1700–1808* (Oxford: Blackwell, 1988), 375; Equipo Madrid, *Charles III, Madrid y la Ilustración* (Madrid: Siglo XXI, 1988), passim; and Francisco Sánchez-Blanco, *El Absolutismo y las Luces en el reinado de Charles III* (Madrid: Marcial Pons, 2002), passim.

19. These aspects of the supposed significance of Philip V's reign have generated a substantial bibliography. Among Spanish language works, see Xavier Gil Pujol, "Un rey, una fe, muchas naciones: Patria y nación en la España de los siglos XVI–XVII," in *La Monarquía de las naciones: Patria, nación y naturaleza en la Monarquía de España*, ed. Antonio Álvarez-Ossorio Alvariño and Bernardo J. García García (Madrid: Fundación Charles de Amberes, 2004), 69, José Manuel de Bernardo Ares, "La sucesión de la monarquía católica: Del Imperio hispánico al Estado español (1665–1713)," in Sanz Camañes, *Monarquía Hispánica*, 665–84, and, most recently, Rafael Torres Sánchez, "Prólogo," in *Volver a la "hora navarra": La contribución navarra a la construcción de la monarquía española en el siglo XVIII*, ed. Rafael Torres Sánchez (Pamplona: Ediciones Universidad de Navarra, 2010), 17, and Antonio Calvo Maturana, *Cuando manden los que obedecen: La clase política e intelectual de la España preliberal (1780–1808)* (Madrid: Marcial Pons, 2013), 81. As for Anglophone historians, according to Lynch, *Bourbon Spain*, xiii, "The Bourbons helped to make Spain a nation state." To Francisco Comín Comín and Bartolomé Yun Casallila, "Spain, from Composite Monarchy to Nation-State, 1492–1914: An Exceptional Case?," in *The Rise of Fiscal States: A Global History, 1500–1914*, ed. Bartolomé Yun Casalilla and Patrick K. O'Brien, with Francisco Comín Comín (Cambridge: Cambridge University Press, 2012), 248–53, Bourbon Spain was a "proto-nation state." Pablo Fernández Albaladejo, "Dinastía y comunidad política: El momento de la patria," in *Los Borbones: Dinastía y memoria de nación en la España del siglo XVIII*, ed. Pablo Fernández Albaladejo (Madrid: Marcial Pons, 2001), 485–532. Armstrong, *Elisabeth*, vii. Typical of the prevailing view of Isabel is Lynch, *Bourbon Spain*, 74–76; Bethencourt, *Relaciones de España*, 302. In 1733 the British minister in Turin concluded, after a conversation with Philip's minister, the duke of Liria, that the Spaniards aspired to regain all of Italy, earl of Essex to Newcastle, 18 November 1733, NA SP 92/35; Richard Lodge, *Studies in Eighteenth-Century Diplomacy, 1740–1748* (London: John Murray 1930), 344–45, and Anderson, *War of Austrian Succession*, 204. One source of dissatisfaction for Don Charles and others was the insistence of the other powers that the territories in Italy which comprised this reconstructed Spanish empire be legally separated from Spain; Lynch, *Bourbon Spain*, 336–54. Ricardo García Cárcel, *Felipe V y los españoles: Una visión periférica del problema de España* (Barcelona: Plaza y Janes, 2002), is an excellent introduction to many of these issues.

20. Philip's successes in Africa contrast with Charles III's abortive Algerian expedition in 1775, Lynch, *Bourbon Spain*, 311–12; Bethencourt, *Relaciones de España*, 170, 351; Pérez Samper, *Isabel*, 115. Carvajal was ready to offer Oran and Mazalquivir (and money) for Gibraltar, López Cordón, "Carvajal," 40.

21. Many of those making policy after 1713 had experienced the war directly (Stanhope) as serving army officers or indirectly (Walpole) as ministers. In France, Cardinal Fleury's diocese had suffered during the allied expedition to Toulon in 1707. The War of the Spanish Succession can be compared to the First World War in its broader impact on the following generation. It is arguable that between the Jacobite rebellions of 1715 and 1745–46 Spain, not France, was the leading European supporter of the exiled Stuarts, Daniel Szechi, *The Jacobites: Britain and Europe, 1688–1788* (Manchester: Manchester University Press, 1994). Bethencourt, *Relaciones de España*, 301

22. J. L. Sutton, *The King's Honour and the King's Cardinal: The War of the Polish Succession* (Lexington: University Press of Kentucky, 1980), largely omits the Spanish aspects of the struggle, ignoring the battle of Bitonto, which, to Jeremy Black, *The Rise of the European Powers, 1679–1793* (London: Arnold, 1990), 86–87, was among the most important battles of the century; Brendan Simms, *Three Victories and a Defeat: The Rise and Fall of the First British Empire* (London: Penguin, 2008), 135–41, for British concerns in the Mediterranean; Villarias to Bena, 19 May 1745, AHN, E/3383; Juan Carlos Lavandeira Hermoso, "Proyecto Español para nombrar a Felipe V Emperador de Alemania: Instrucciones al Conde de Montijo 1741," in *El equilibrio de los Imperios: De Utrecht a Trafalgar*, 2 vols., ed. Agustín Guimera Ravina and Víctor Peralta Ruiz (Madrid: Fundación Española de Historia Moderna, 2005), 2:179–90.

23. In late 1732, with the Oran expedition over, Philip threatened to redeploy his troops to Italy, Bethencourt, *Relaciones de España*, 176; John Brewer, *The Sinews of Power: War, Money and the English State, 1688–1783* (London: Arnold, 1988), Jan Glete, *War and the State in Early Modern Europe: Spain, the Dutch Republic and Sweden as Fiscal-Military States, 1500–1660* (London: Routledge, 2002), and Glete, "War, Entrepreneurship, the Fiscal-Military State," in *European Warfare 1350–1750*, ed. Frank Tallett and David Trim (Cambridge: Cambridge University Press, 2010), 316, 320; and Christopher Storrs, "Introduction: The Fiscal-Military State in the 'Long Eighteenth Century,'" in *The Fiscal-Military State in Eighteenth-Century Europe*, ed. Christopher Storrs (Farnham: Ashgate, 2009), 1–22; Francisco Andújar Castillo, review of Rafael Torres Sánchez, *War, State and Development: Fiscal-Military States in the Eighteenth Century* (Pamplona: Ediciones Universidad de Navarra, 2007), *Hispania* 69 (2009): 870.

24. Juan Luis Castellano, *Gobierno y Poder en la España del Siglo XVIII* (Granada: Universidad de Granada, 2006), 84, 99; Martínez Shaw and Alfonso Mola, *Felipe*, 238; Antonio García-Baquero González, "El Comercio Colonial en la Epoca de Felipe V: El Reformismo Continuista," in Serrano, *Felipe V*, 1:75–102, and Pedro Peréz Herrero, *La América Colonial (1492–1763): Política y sociedad* (Madrid: Editorial Síntesis, 2002), 318. According to José Álvarez-Junco, *Spanish Identity in the Age of Nations* (Manchester:

Manchester University Press, 2011), 71, Philip's reforms "enjoyed the support of modernising elites." For the debate about origins, see Henry Kamen, "Melchor de Macanaz and the Foundations of Bourbon Power in Spain," *English Historical Review* 80 (1965): 699–700, 715–16, Allan J. Kuethe and Lowell Blaisdell, "French Influence and the Origin of Bourbon Colonial Reorganisation," *Hispanic American Historical Review* 71 (1991): 579–607, and J. H. Elliott, *Empires of the Atlantic World: Britain and Spain in America, 1492–1830* (New Haven: Yale University Press, 2006), 232. For a view that Philip's innovations had no single French or Spanish origin but reflected a more general reforming atmosphere in Europe c. 1713, see Anne Dubet and Jean-Philippe Luis, "Introduction," in *Les financiers et la construction de l'Etat France, Espagne (XVIIe–XIXe siècle)*, ed. Anne Dubet and Jean-Philippe Luis (Rennes: Presses Universitaires de Rennes, 2011), 24–26, and Muñoz Rodríguez, *Séptima Corona*, 222.

25. Reflexiones sobre las deudas del Rey . . ., [post 1746], BNM, MSS/13814 f. 1ff. To Kamen, *War*, 200, the Spanish monarchy relieved itself in 1713 of the burden of Italy and Flanders, a view echoed by Bubb to Stanhope, Madrid, 19 February 1716, NA, SP 94/85. Belluga's letter to Philip (1715, above) urging advance in Africa suggests some of Spain's elite may have agreed; Bethencourt, *Relaciones de España*, 105, 136–75, 352. For plans to link Trieste and Livorno with the Atlantic via Cádiz, see José M. Delgado Barrado, "Ordenación territorial y puertos privilegiados: El proyecto de Juan Amor de Soria (1741)," in *Monarquías, Imperios y Pueblos en la Edad Moderna*, ed. Antonio Mestre, Pablo Fernández Albaladejo, and Enrique Giménez López (Alicante, 1997), 189–200; Bethencourt, "Las aventuras," 323–35; Borreguero Beltrán, "Spanish Army," 105. For a later, positive image of Patiño, see A. Valladares de Sotomayor, *Fragmentos históricos para la vida del excellentíssimo Señor D. Josef Patiño* (Madrid, 1790). Javier María Donézar Díez de Ulzurrun, "De las naciones-patrias a la nación-patria: Del antiguo al nuevo régimen," in Álvarez-Ossorio Alvariño and García García, *Monarquía de las naciones*, 93–118 (at 104). Álvarez-Junco, *Spanish Identity*, focuses on the later eighteenth century onwards and makes no specific reference to Philip V.

26. See Nicholas Rogers, *Mayhem: Post-War Crime and Violence in Britain, 1748–1753* (New Haven: Yale University Press, 2013)

27. Christopher Clark, "After 1848: The European Revolution in Government," *Transactions of the Royal Historical Society*, 6th ser., 22 (2012): 171–97, for the French Revolutionary and Napoleonic era and 1848 as turning points; Muñoz Rodríguez, *Séptima Corona*, 319, sees an acceleration under Philip V of processes already under way under Charles II; Antonio Luis Cortés Peña, "La Iglesia y el Cambio Dinástico," in Serrano, *Felipe V*, 1:991–1012; Martínez Shaw and Alfonso Mola, *Felipe*, 226; Pablo Fernández Albaladejo, "La Monarquía de los Borbónes," in ibid., *Fragmentos de Monarquía* (Madrid: Alianza, 1992), 353–454; Carla R. Phillips, *The Treasure of the San José* (Baltimore: Johns Hopkins University Press, 2007), 3. The transformation thesis respecting Spanish America is questioned by John R. Fisher, *Bourbon Peru, 1750–1824* (Liverpool: Liverpool University Press, 2003), 4, 22. Evaristo C. Martínez-Radío Garrido, *La Guerra de Sucesión y Asturias* (Oviedo: KRK, 2009),

86. For the context of reform, José M. Delgado Barrado, *Aquiles y Teseos: Bosquejos del reform-ismo borbónico (1701–1759)* (Granada: Universidad de Granada, 2007).

28. Armstrong, *Elisabeth,* 322; José M. Delgado Barrado, "La transmisión de las obras de Carvajal: Del 'Testamento Político' a 'Mis pensamientos' (1745–1753)," in Delgado Barrado and Gómez Urdáñez, *Ministros,* 45–64 (at 59); Bustanzo to Genoa, 1 January 1735, Ciasca, *Istruzioni,* 6:200–203.

29. Calvo Maturana, *Cuando manden,* 79–86.

Chapter One. The Army

Epigraph: Papal nuncio to secretary of state, 14 June 1734, ASV, SS, Spagna/244, f. 61

1. Kamen, *War,* 57; Francisco Andújar Castillo, *El sonido del dinero: Monarquía, ejército y venalidad en la España del siglo XVIII* (Madrid: Marcial Pons, 2004), 41. However, these accounts paint too negative a picture of the military establishment inherited by Philip V, see C. Storrs, *The Resilience of the Spanish Monarchy, 1665–1700* (Oxford: Oxford University Press, 2006), 17–62; Geoffrey Parker, *The Army of Flanders and the Spanish Road, 1567–1659* (Cambridge: Cambridge University Press, 1972); Davide Maffi, *La Cittadella in Armi: Esercito, società e finanza nella Lombardia di Carlo II, 1660–1700* (Milan: Franco Angeli, 2010). In 1703 Philip's troops in Spain itself were said to total just over 18,000 men, Kamen, *War,* 59. *Ibid.,* passim. Muñoz Rodríguez, *Séptima Corona,* 20–21, suggests that French support was not the only factor in Philip's success.

2. Hochedlinger, *Austria's Wars,* 208–18. The king of Sardinia was an ally in the earlier conflict, the king of Naples and republic of Genoa in the later one. In 1745 Philip V contributed 53,000 men to an allied army in Italy of almost 96,000, Biblioteca Menéndez Pidal, Santander, MS 342, f. 114ff, and in 1746 over 56,000 men to one of 100,000, Antonio Rodríguez Villa, *Don Cenon de Somodevilla, marqués de la Ensenada: Ensayo biográfico, formado con documentos* (Madrid: Librería Murillo, 1878), 474–75. Ozanam, "Política," 441–699; Francisco Andújar Castillo, "El ejército de Felipe V: Estrategias y problemas de una re-forma," in Serrano, *Felipe V,* 1:661–82; Pere Molas Ribalta, "The Early Bourbons and the Military," in *Armed Forces and Society in Spain Past and Present,* ed. Thomas M. Barker and Rafael Bañon Martínez, (New York: Columbia University Press, 1988), 51–80 (at 71); Muñoz Rodríguez, *Séptima Corona,* 213–45. In 1728 a wide-ranging military regulation, the first since 1633, codified many of these changes and was superseded only in 1768, Juan Carlos Domínguez Nafria, "Recopilación y codificación del derecho militar en el siglo XVIIII: La colección general de ordenanzas militares de Jose Antonio Portugués," in *El Ejército y la Armada en el Noroeste de America: Nootka y su tiempo,* ed. Leandro Martinez Peñas and Manuela Fernández Rodríguez (Madrid: Universidad Rey Juan Carlos, 2011), 211–50, and Francisco Andújar Castillo, *Los militares en la España del siglo XVIII: Un estudio social* (Granada: Universidad de Granada, 1991), 33–34.

3. Eric Robson, "Armed Forces and the Art of War," in *The New Cambridge Modern History,* vol. 7: *The Old Regime, 1713–63,* ed. Jean O. Lindsay (Cambridge: Cambridge University Press, 1957), 163–90, completely ignores the Spanish army, which is also largely

absent from M. S. Anderson, *War and Society in Europe of the Old Regime 1618–1789* (London: Fontana, 1988), from Peter Wilson, "Warfare in the Old Regime, 1648–1789," in *European Warfare 1453–1815,* ed. Jeremy Black (Basingstoke: Macmillan, 1999), 69–95, and from Olaf van Nimwegen, "The Transformation of Army Organisation in Early-Modern Western Europe," in Tallett and Trim, *European Warfare,* 159–80. See the excellent Martine Galland Seguela, *Les ingenieurs militaires espagnols de 1710 a 1803: Etude prosopographique et sociale d'un corps d'élite* (Madrid: Casa de Velázquez, 2008). In the summer of 1718, against the background of the invasion of Sicily, and in 1743, following renewed intervention in Italy, Philip V issued landmark orders regarding the type of firearms and artillery to be produced for and used by his forces, Carlos J. Medina Avila, "Industria militar y armamento," in Iglesias, *Historia Militar,* 181–208. Jaime Contreras Gay, "Las milicias en el antiguo régimen: Modelos, características generales y significado histórico," *Chronica Nova* 20 (1992): 75–103; Andújar Castillo, "Ejército," 661–82, and *Militares;* Cristina Borreguero Beltrán, *El Reclutamiento Militar por Quintas en la España del Siglo XVIII: Orígenes del Servicio Militar Obligatorio* (Valladolid: Universidad de Valladolid, 1989). Exceptions are Borreguero Beltrán, "Spanish Army," 101–26, and Melendreras Giménez, *Campañas de Italia.*

4. Angel de la Plaza Bores, *Archivo General de Simancas: Guía del Investigador,* 2d ed. (Madrid: Ministerio de Cultura, 1980), 183–207. For the militarisation debate, see Molas Ribalta, "Early Bourbons," 56–60; Pablo Fernández Albaladejo, " 'Soldados del Rey, soldados de Dios': Ethos militar y militarismo en la España del siglo XVIII," in *La Espada y la Pluma: Il mondo militare nella Lombardia spagnola cinquecentescha. Atti del Convegno Internazionale di Pavia 16, 17, 18 ottobre 1997* (Lucca: Mauro Baroni, 2000), 83–101; and Víctor Peralta Ruiz, *Patrones, clientes y amigos: El poder burocrático indiano en la España del siglo XVIII* (Madrid: CSIC, 2006), 115.

5. At the end of 1744 the Spanish infantry in Piedmont was more than six thousand men short of an establishment of almost twenty-four thousand men, more than 25 percent, Estado, Demont, 11 November 1744, AGS, SG/2131. For estimates of the size of the force Don Charles led from Tuscany in 1734 to Naples ranging from under twenty thousand to over thirty-eight thousand, see Mirella Mafrici, *Il re delle speranze: Carlo di Borbone da Madrid a Napoli* (Naples: Edizioni Scientifiche Italiane, 1998), 89–90.

6. Lyle N. McAlister, "The Reorganisation of the Army of New Spain, 1763–1766," *Hispanic American Historical Review* 33 (1953): 1–32; Juan Marchena Fernández, "Italianos al servicio del rey de España en el ejército de América 1740–1815," in *Italiani al servizio straniero in eta moderna,* vol. 1 of *Annali di storia militare europea,* ed. Paola Bianchi, Davide Maffi, and Enrico Stumpo (Milan: Franco Angeli, 2008), 135–75 (at 149–50). Baudrillart, *Philippe,* 3:243. According to Valguarnera to CEIII, 27 November 1741, AST, LM Spagna/70, six thousand men had been sent to the Indies in recent years. The more than ten thousand troops sent in 1815 to quell the independence movement was the largest ever sent to the Indies, John Lynch, *The Spanish American Revolutions, 1808–1826,* 2d ed. (New York: Norton, 1986), 209, and was smaller than almost all of Philip V's Mediterranean expeditions.

7. See Jaime Contreras Gay, *Las milicias provinciales en el siglo XVIII: Estudios sobre los regimientos de Andalucía* (Almería: Instituto de Estudios Almerienses, 1993), 72–73; Philip's order, July 1717, to increase troop numbers, J. A. Portugués, *Colección general de las Ordenanzas Militares*, 10 vols. (Madrid: Antonio Martin, 1764–65), 2:213–26; Keene to Newcastle, 26 May 1738, NA, SP 94/130.

8. Josep Juan Vidal, "El reino de Mallorca del filipismo al austracismo, 1700–1715," in Serrano, *Felipe V,* 2:151–210 (at 207). Papers of Junta de Hacienda, AGS, Segretaria y Superintendencia de Hacienda [SSH], *legajo* 458; Reglamento y Ordenanza . . . Melilla, Penon . . ., 1 April 1717, BN, Sección de Manuscritos, 12,050, f. 683ff. Ceuta could accommodate seven thousand men, Burnett to Craggs, 10 March 1720, SP 89/27 f. 159. See also Antonio José Rodríguez Hernández, *La ciudad y guarnición de Ceuta (1640–1700): Ejército, fidelidad e integración de una ciudad portuguesa en la Monarquía Hispánica* (Ceuta: Instituto de Estudios Ceutíes, 2013). In 1746–47 ministers considered sending the troops there to Genoa against the Austrians, Carvajal to Huéscar, 2 January 1747, Ozanam, *La Diplomacia de Fernando VI,* 115.

9. *Reglamento* of February 1715, Portugués, *Colección,* 2:30–74; Francisco Andújar Castillo, "Entre la corte y la guerra: Militares italianos al servicio de España en el siglo XVIII," in Bianchi, Maffi, and Stumpo, *Italiani al servizio,* 126, and Andújar, *Sonido,* 75–77, 114, 141–43, 169–70, 446–47 (annexe 3). According to a *Mapa General* of July 1720, NA, SP 94/90, between February 1718 and July 1720, 18 new infantry regiments, or 31 battalions, were raised to give a total of 158 battalions, and 8 new cavalry and 40 dragoon squadrons, for a total of 178 cavalry and dragoon squadrons. Andújar, *Sonido,* 85, 87, 98, "Ejército," 674, and "La privatización del reclutamiento en el siglo XVIII: El sistema de asientos," *Studia Historica, Historia Moderna* 25 (2003): 123–47; Portugués, *Colección,* 2:592–93, 606; Borré to CEIII, 15 February 1734, AST, LM Spagna/66; Andújar, "Privatización," 123–25, 132. In 1744 a company formerly in the service of the king of Sardinia was taken on by the Infante, [?] to [?], Embrun, 1 July 1744, AGS, SG/2138; Francisco Andújar Castillo, "La 'reforma' militar del marqués de La Ensenada," in Guimerá and Peralta, *Equilibrio de los imperios,* 519–36.

10. Storrs, *Resilience,* 25–26.

11. Stanhope to Craggs, 21 and 28 October 1720, NA, SP 94/90; Baudrillart, *Philippe,* 5:98–99; Bartolini to Senate, 31 March 1744, in Tonetti, *Corrispondenze,* 17:518–21; Montemar to Patiño, 13 March 1734, AGS, SG/2190; royal order, 14 June 1716, Portugués, *Colección,* 2:179.

12. Francisco de Oya y Ozores, *Tratado de las Leyes Penales de la Milicia Española* (Madrid: Antonio Marin, 1732), 126–27; S. M. de Sotto, conde de Clonard, *Historia orgánica de las armas de infantería y caballería españolas desde la creación del ejército permanente hasta el día,* 16 vols. (Madrid, 1851–62), 5:228; Wilkinson, *Defence,* 189–90; *Gaceta de Madrid,* 1 December 1744; Portugués, *Coleccion,* 2:213–26; order, November 1745, see NLS, Astorga, G.31.c.1 f. 208; Tineo to Ensenada, 19 October 1745, AGS, SG/2131. The Infante Philip had amnestied deserters from his army in 1744, *Gaceta,* 21 April 1744.

13. Wilkinson, *Defence*, 80, 253; Ferrer Benimeli, "El Conde de Aranda," 737; Relacion de . . . muertos y heridos . . ., NA, SP 89/43 f. 170. About 750 wounded officers and men entered the field hospitals in Bologna, Rebollar to Campillo, 13 February 1743, AGS, SG/2011; list of officers, soldiers. . . ., BL, Add. 20,440 f. 107.

14. Alonso Aguilera, *Conquista*, 99–100; Estado . . . [Demont], 11 November 1744, AGS, SG/2131; Meléndez to Siruela, 8 May 1747, AGS, SG/5051/1; Valguarnera to CEIII, 25 December 1741 and 15 January and 19 March 1742, AST, LM Spagna, 69; Birtles to Newcastle, 10 January 1742, NA, SP/79/19; D. Antonio de Alos y Rius, *Carta, instrucciones y relación de servicios que el Excmo D. Antonio Alos y Rius, marqués de Alos . . . escrivió a sus hijos.* . . . (Barcelona: Imprenta Manuel Texero, 1800), 86. See Wilkinson, *Defence*, 88–93, 253–78.

15. Ozanam, "Política," 521, 530. For 1717 see Portugués, *Colección*, 2:213–26, and for 1724, Hellwege, *Provinzialmilizen*, 36; Arvillars to CEIII, 22 June 1731, AST, LM Spagna/63; Estado del exercito . . ., AGS, SG/2158; Andújar Castillo, "Privatización," 135, Mina to Ensenada, 12 March 1747, in Rodríguez Villa, *Ensenada*, 495–96.

16. The *vecindario* of Campoflorido (1712–17), which probably gives too low a figure, the *catastro* of Ensenada (1749–), and another survey of 1768 are not easily comparable, Alberto Marcos Martín, *España en los Siglos XVI, XVII y XVIII: Economía y sociedad* (Barcelona: Crítica, 2000), 554; José Manuel Pérez García, "La demografía española en la primera mitad del siglo XVIII," in Serrano, *Felipe V,* 1:15–48; Martínez Shaw and Alfonso Mola, *Felipe*, 271–73; José Miguel López García, "'Sobrevivir en la Corte': Las condiciones de vida del pueblo llano en el Madrid de Felipe V," in Serrano, *Felipe V,* 1:161. For Murcia, see Muñoz Rodríguez, *Séptima Corona*, 51–60. See Admiral José Navarro, quoted in Josef de Vargas y Ponce, *Vida de D. Juan Josef Navarro, primer Marqués de la Victoria* (Madrid: Imprenta Real, 1808), 113–14, and Count Konigsegg's "Relation d'Espagne" (c. 1726), Mur i Raurell, *Diplomacia Secreta y Paz*, 2:355–71. Andújar, *Sonido*, 446–47; Enrique García Hernán, "Regimientos extranjeros: Continuidad y ruptura de una elite privilegiada," in Iglesias, *Historia Militar*, 277–302, with an invaluable appendix of all foreign units raised; Ensenada's Representation (1751), Rodríguez Villa, *Ensenada*, 120–22; Storrs, *Resilience*, 46–49 (for Habsburg practice before 1700).

17. Andújar, *Militares*, 313–25; Kamen, *War*, 120–21; Lede to Tolosa, 19 December 1720 and 10 February 1721, AGS, SG/Sup/481; Worsley to Craggs, 11 September 1719, NA, SP/89/27 f. 159; Oscar Recio Morales, *Ireland and the Spanish Empire, 1600–1825* (Dublin: Four Courts Press, 2010); Andújar Castillo, *Sonido*, 48; Diego Téllez Alarcia, "La Misión Secreta de D. Ricardo Wall en Londres (1747–1748)," *Brocar* 24 (2000): 49–71.

18. Thomas Glesener, "Nación flamenca o elite de poder? Los militares 'flamencos' en la España de los Borbones," in Álvarez-Ossorio Alvariño and García García, *Monarquía de las naciones*, 701–22; Alonso Aguilera, *Conquista*, 63; Borré to CEIII, 6 March 1733, AST, LM Spagna/65; Relacion de los Officiales . . . 1743, NA, SP 89/43 f. 170. For Juan Wanmarck, who served on all of Philip V's Mediterranean expeditions during a very distinguished career, Francisco Andújar Castillo, *Consejo y Consejeros de Guerra en el Siglo*

XVIII (Granada: Universidad de Granada, 1996), 286–87; Andújar Castillo, "Entre la corte," passim; Bartolini to Senate, 20 March 1742, Tonetti, *Corrispondenze,* 17:324–25.

19. Sobre la Justicia . . . de los . . . Suizos [no date], AGS, SG/5239. In 1733 two battalions of Besler's regiment went to Oran, Borré to CEIII, 9 January 1733, AST, LM Spagna/65; Cayley to Newcastle, 14 June 1735, BL, Add. 28,146 f. 174; copy of prorogation, 1 March 1737, AGS, SG/5239; capitulations, 10 August, 29 September and 24 October 1742, AGS, SG/5239; Tercer socorro de tropas . . . año 1743 . . ., in Biblioteca Menéndez Pidal, MS 342 f. 22; Vanmarck to Ensenada, 25 June 1745, AGS, SG/5239; Estado del ejército . . . a fines de Julio de 1746, Rodríguez Villa, *Ensenada,* 474–75; Mina to Ensenada, 24 August 1746, AGS, SG/2161. Besides seeking Swiss troops for himself, Philip sought to prevent his enemies from securing them: see Ensenada to Jover, 28 March 1743, AHN, E/4594, urging Jover to use the religious argument with the Catholic cantons, and Jover to Ensenada, 13 April 1743, AHN, E/4594, acknowledging receipt of two thousand doblones for distribution as gratifications among the elites of those cantons.

20. Alonso Aguilera, *Conquista,* 113–14; Andújar Castillo, *Sonido,* 100; order, 20 July 1717, Portugués, *Colección,* 2:213–26; Portugués, *Colección,* 5:128–29; order, 27 February 1717, Portugués, *Colección,* 2:202–3; Estados . . ., Barcelona, 7 and 15 March 1745, AGS, SG/2158; Andújar, *Sonido,* 139. See Mina, Dictamen del marqués de la Mina, Niza, 2 June 1748, in *Semanario Erudito,* ed. Antonio Valladares de Sotomayor, 34 vols. (Madrid, 1787–), 12:222–44, and Jaime Miguel de Guzmán [marqués de la Mina], *Máximas para la Guerra* (Tolosa: Pedro Robert, 1767[?]), 373–408. These maxims are in part a sort of memoir with useful material on the many Italian operations on which Mina served.

21. Muñoz Rodríguez, *Séptima Corona,* 21, 27–29; AGS, Segreteria de Marina, *legajo* 767 f. 121.

22. Storrs, *Resilience,* 32–33; Rosa M. Pérez Estévez and Rosa M. González Martínez, *Pretendientes y Pícaros Españoles en Roma* (Valladolid: Universidad de Valladolid, 1992), 10, 21–22. To John Campbell, *The Spanish Empire in America* (London: Cooper, 1747), 305, remittances home by foreign troops in Spanish service were a means whereby the wealth of the Indies left Spain.

23. Storrs, *Resilience,* 33–34; Clonard, *Historia,* 5:125; Concepción de Castro, *La Revolución Liberal y los municipios españoles* (Madrid: Alianza, 1979), 25–26; Henry Kamen, "El establecimiento de los intendentes en la administración española," *Hispania* 24 (1964): 368–95; Fabrice Abbad and Didier Ozanam, *Les intendants espagnols du XVIIIe siècle* (Madrid: Casa de Velázquez, 1992), 6–31, 192–220; Juan Pro and Manuel Rivero, *Breve Atlas de Historia de España* (Madrid: Alianza, 1999), 91.

24. Concepción de Castro, *A la sombra de Felipe V: José de Grimaldo, ministro responsable (1703–1726)* (Madrid: Marcial Pons, 2004), 343; order, 19 September 1717, Portugués, *Colección,* 2:243–48; Ensenada to bishop of Oviedo, 22 January 1748, AGS, SG/2195. For the certificate, which included details of the man's age, place of origin, and distinguishing marks, see order, 20 November 1721, Portugués, *Colección,* 2:564–78; Martínez Shaw and Alfonso Mola, *Felipe,* 249. For "passports" for the Numancia and Francia

dragoon regiments to recruit volunteers in Burgos, 25 February 1747, see AMB, LA/1747, ff. 66–68.

25. Martínez-Radío Garrido, *Guerra de Sucesión*, 336–37, 348–49; Carmen M. Cremades Griñan, *Economía y hacienda local del Consejo de Murcia en el Siglo XVIII (1701–1759)* (Murcia: Academia Alfonso X el Sabio, 1986), 120. However, these sums did not attract sufficient recruits. See Portugués, *Colección*, 2:213–26, for official enlistment rates. José Miguel López García, El *Impacto de la Corte en Castilla: Madrid y su territorio en la época moderna* (Madrid: Siglo XXI, 1998), 269–77. In 1707 the soldier's pay was fixed at twenty-one reales a month, Francisco. Andújar Castillo, "La Situación Salarial de los Militares en el Siglo XVIII," in *Ejército, Ciencia y Sociedad en la España del Antiguo Régimen*, ed. Emilio Balaguer and Enrique Giménez (Alicante: Instituto de Cultura Juan Gil-Albert, 1995), 94. Concepción de Castro, *El pan de Madrid: El abasto de las ciudades españoles del Antiguo Régimen* (Madrid: Alianza, 1987), 109–10; Pérez Moreda, *Las crisis,* 107–12. See Francisco Andújar Castillo, "El Fuero Militar en el Siglo XVIII: Un Estatuto de Privilegio," *Chronica Nova* 23 (1996): 11–31. For a snapshot of volunteers that reveals their age and what they received on enlisting and that demonstrates the importance of Madrid as both a magnet attracting men from all parts of Spain and hence as a recruiting area, see the list of men recruited there by D. Juan Antonio Alvarado, a captain in the Lombardy infantry regiment, March 1726, AGS, SG/Sup/543: most were eighteen or nineteen years old. For the age, parentage, origins, height, and general physical description of fifty-one volunteers in the Cuatro Villas (Cantabria) in 1748, see AHPC, Corregimiento de Laredo, *legajo* 217–1, doc. 50.

26. See David Parrott, "From Military Enterprise to Standing Armies: War, State, and Society in Western Europe, 1600–1700," in Tallett and Trim, *European Warfare,* 74–95; Storrs, *Resilience,* 36–37; Andújar Castillo, *Sonido,* passim; Francisco Andújar Castillo, *Necesidad y venalidad: España e Indias, 1704–1711* (Madrid: Centro de Estudios Políticos y Constitucionales, 2008), passim; Francisco Andújar Castillo, "Milicia, venalidad y movilidad social: Un análisis a partir de familias granadinas del siglo XVIII," in *La movilidad social en la España del Antiguo Régimen,* ed. Ines Gómez González and M. L. López Guadalupe Muñoz (Granada: Universidad de Granada, 2007), 223–47; *consulta* of Cámara de Castilla, 13 February 1719, AHN, Consejos, 4481/1719/7.

27. Andújar Castillo, *Sonido,* 85–88; Condiciones . . ., Palermo, 24 December 1718, and Lede's response, Melazzo, 1 January 1719, AGS, SG/Sup/234. San Blas was asked for more men; Caylus to de los Reyes, 8 May 1748, AGS, SG/Sup/295; Andújar Castillo, *Sonido,* 128. In 1743 the inspector of infantry dismissed more than a third of 655 men raised by the Catalan noble Menna Sentmenat on various grounds, including age, fitness, and religion, and subsequently suspended him from his command, Andújar Castillo, *Sonido,* 161, 168.

28. Andújar Castillo, "Privatización," passim; Andújar Castillo, *Sonido,* 42, 75–77, 87, 98–99, 106, 111, 141–42. Many of the new regiments were reformed once the conflict was over.

29. Contreras Gay, *Milicias,* 142; José-Miguel Palop Ramos, "La condena a presidio en Melilla: Aproximación a la criminalidad en Valencia del Setecientos," *Estudis* 15 (1989):

271–72; Ruth Pike, *Penal Servitude in Early Modern Spain* (Madison: University of Wisconsin Press, 1983), 49–65, 111–33; Rafael Escobedo Romero, *El tabaco del rey: La organización de un monopolio fiscal durante el Antiguo Régimen* (Pamplona: Ediciones Universidad de Navarra, 2007), 242, Domínguez Ortiz, *Sociedad y Estado,* 137; Glimes to Villarias, 8 July 1741, AHN, E/541; Cabello to Ensenada, 20 May 1748, AGS, SG/Sup/295; López García, *Impacto,* 473, for the destination of the 4,000 or so men condemned to garrisons and the galleys between 1701 and 1750. Of the 689 men in one newly raised battalion in 1744, 15 percent were convicted criminals, Andújar Castillo, *Sonido,* 167. For one Catalan smuggler, see Mina to Campillo, Barcelona, 11 November 1742, AGS, SG/2090.

30. Order of 21 July 1717, Portugués, *Colección,* 2:114; order, 4 July 1718, AHN, Consejos, *libro* 1477, f. 186. In 1732 an English ship left Barcelona for Oran carrying twenty-nine *muchachos vagamundos* destined to serve in the presidio, [Patiño?] to Santa Cruz, 23 October 1732, AGS, SG/Sup/485. Order, 19 December 1733, NLS, Astorga G. 31, c. 1, f. 111, and AHN, Consejos, libro 1477, f. 186. Such means yielded enough men to complete not only the Oran garrison but also the regiments in Italy, Borré to CEIII, 15 March and 12 April 1734, AST, LM Spagna/66; Cremades Griñan, *Economía y hacienda local,* 122; *Gaceta,* 11 May 1745. The decree of April 1745 represented a milestone in defining *vagos,* Pérez Estévez and González Martínez, *Pretendientes,* 33.

31. For a contemporary (1747) articulation of the distinction between the different types of levy made by the corregidor of Burgos, AMB, LA/1747 f. 19–20; Borreguero Beltrán, *Reclutamiento,* 9–10, 101, 151–79; Arvillars to CEIII, 4 February, 13 June and 5 September 1732, AST, LM Spagna/64; Contreras Gay, *Milicias,* 207. Oya y Ozores's treatise was republished in 1744, along with his treatise on military justice. His discussion included invaluable references to specific cases and their outcome; an appendix included the text of the levy ordered at the end of 1732 and models of relevant documents; Andújar Castillo, *Sonido,* 179; Portugués, *Colección,* 7:434–49; NLS, Astorga, G.31.c.1 ff. 388–92; Valguarnera to CEIII, 22 January 1742, AST, LM Spagna/69; Copia de los capítulos . . . para la leva de los 25,000 hombres . . .; Relacion de las Partidas . . . [1746/47]; Parages y Cuerpos . . . los 12,000 hombres . . . [1746/47]; Oficiales nombrados a reconocer y recibir la Gente . . . [1746/7], AGS, SG/5051; certification by D. Joseph Alonso de Huydobro, contador, 8 January 1747, AHPC, Corregimiento de Laredo, legajo 271–1/2. As in 1732–33, the resort to such forcible means was justified by the lack of volunteers: Aviles to Ensenada, 21 December 1746; Regent of Audiencia of Asturias to same, 21 December 1746, AGS, SG/5051.

32. AMB, LA/1733 f. 25–26; Campillo to corregidor of Burgos, 16 December 1741, AMB, LA/1741, f. 406ff.; Aviles to Ensenada, 21 December 1746, AGS, SG/5051/1; Campillo to corregidor of Burgos, 16 December 1741, AMB, LA/1741, f. 406ff.; Argain to Ensenada, 15 June 1748, and Contamine, to Ensenada, 7 September 1748, AGS, SG/Sup/ 295.

33. Borré to CEIII, 30 January 1733, AST, LM Spagna/65; Contreras Gay, *Milicias,* 96. For Asturian concerns that the levy breached the principality's *fueros* (and weighed too heavily on its population), see Martínez-Radío Garrido, *Guerra,* 368–69; consulta of [?],

24 December 1732, AHN, Consejos, libro 877 f. 53–54; Patiño to Flon, 4 April 1733, AHN, Consejos, libro 8013 f. 89. See Rafael Escobedo Romero, "Los Empleados de la Renta del Tabaco durante los siglos XVII y XVIII: El imán del privilegio," *Hispania* 67 (2007): 1025–40. Oya y Ozores, *Tratado de Levas*, discusses various cases of this sort; royal order, 6 November 1736, granting various privileges to D. Joseph Solornan and the new paper manufactory at Oruzco (Alcala), Eugenio Larruga, *Memorias políticas y económicas sobre los frutos, fábricas, comercio y minas de España*, 45 vols. (Madrid, 1785–1800), 9:259–70.

34. Valdes y Quiros to Campillo, 13 December 1741 and 11 April 1742, and Salamanca y Cordova, corregidor of Logroño to [?], 5 January 1742, AGS, SG/5018; Extracto de la Sumaria ..., Madrid, 2 November 1735. See Baudrillart, *Philippe*, 4:544–45, and the charges laid against the corregidor of Ponferrada relating to the *quinta* of 1733–34, Borreguero Beltrán, *Reclutamiento*, 254–55; Borré to CEIII, 6 March 1733, AST, LM Spagna/65.

35. Valdes y Quiros to Campillo, 9 February and 11 April 1742, AGS, SG/5018. In 1746 Philip decreed that those destined for the army or fleet who took refuge in convents and other sacred places would be seized, Ensenada to Barrero, 12 February 1746, AGS, Marina/767 f. 120; sessions of *ayuntamiento* of Murcia, 5 and 7 July 1744, and Extracto de los setenta y ocho hombres ..., AMM, LA/1744, f. 128ff. See Ofelia Rey Castelao, "Mutaciones Sociales en una Sociedad Inmutable: El Reino de Galicia en el Reinado de Felipe V," in Serrano, *Felipe V,* 1:355–73; D. Joseph Alberto Bonet to Campillo, 24 January and 14 February 1742, AGS, SG/5018. Burgos's quota (400 men) was finally met in August, Cuellar to Campillo, 6 August 1742, AGS, SG/5018. By late March 1747 Córdoba had to find just 41 men to fulfil its quota of 546, see Estados. ... Cordova, 2 March and 20 April 1747, AGS, SG/5051/1; Urdainz to Ensenada, 20 January 1748, AGS, SG/Sup/295; *relación de méritos* of D. Martin Collado y Contreras, *alcalde mayor* (and interim corregidor) of Ecija, BN, Mss 12316 f. 130.

36. The best study remains Hellwege, *Provinzialmilizen*. See also Contreras Gay, *Milicias;* David Parrott, *The Business of War: Military Enterprise and Military Revolution in Early Modern Europe* (Cambridge: Cambridge University Press, 2012), 96–100. Parrott is critical of militias but focuses largely on the sixteenth and seventeenth centuries. For Philip V's efforts to re-form and use the militia in the succession struggle, Castro, *A la sombra*, 86–87, Muñoz Rodríguez, *Séptima Corona*, 171–89. Militias were deployed to Melilla (1719) and Ceuta (1721).

37. Hellwege, *Provinzialmilizen*, 34–42. Contreras Gay, *Milicias*, 96, 98. The militia was not extended to Aragon until 1754, Jesús Pradells Nadal, "Reorganización militar de Valencia durante el reinado de Felipe V," in Serrano, *Felipe V,* 2:293–320 (at 313). Typically, the coastal community of the Cuatro Villas (Santander, Laredo, San Vicente de la Barquera, and Castro Urdiales) was expected to raise a regiment, Hellwege, *Provinzialmilizen*, 59–61, Portugués, *Colección*, 7:140–41. For the refashioning of the militia in the Savoyard state from 1713, see Christopher Storrs, *War, Diplomacy, and the Rise of Savoy 1690–1720* (Cambridge: Cambridge University Press, 1999), 71. Clonard, *Historia*, 5:226–30. The original decree was modified in February 1736 and April 1745 in view of

the demands of war in Italy. The city of Murcia was to provide 142 of that realm's 700 men, AMM, AC/1734 f. 118ff. The first inspector general (1734–42) was D. Joseph Tineo, Contreras Gay, *Milicias*, 103–4. During the War of the Austrian Succession the key role was played by D. Francisco Martinez Gallego, who had served in the militia regiments of Murcia and Málaga before being appointed subinspector of militias in 1743, Contreras Gay, *Milicias*, 104–7. For the office of inspector general, McAlister, "Reorganisation," 9. See also Ozanam, *Diplomacia*, 123, note.

38. Borré to CEIII, 18 January 1734, AST, LM Spagna/66; Hellwege, *Provinzialmilizen*, 271–302; for Galicia, see Rey Castelao, "Mutaciones," 355–73. For Burgos, see council minutes, 15 April, 7 June, and 3 July 1734, AMB, LA/1734, f. 106, 130–31, 148. In 1743 the militia of Murcia was sent to garrison Barcelona, AMM, AC/1744, f. 138ff.; Hellwege, *Provinzialmilizen*, 375–79; Tercer Socorro de Tropas . . . en el año 1743 . . ., in Biblioteca Menéndez Pidal, ms 342, f. 22. Philip had ordered the establishment of units of grenadiers, the shock troops of the eighteenth century, in the militia regiments as early as 1735, possibly hinting at their offensive deployment, Portugués, *Colección*, 7:74–76; Contreras Gay, *Milicias*, 110.

39. Miscellaneous other units were also raised in Spain, including, in 1734, a regiment of so-called *Cuantiosos* of Andalusia and of Estremadura, reviving an older practice of expecting the wealthy to serve, Andújar Castillo, *Sonido*, 93, 115–16. The *hidalgos* of the Cuatro Villas, where the majority of the population were of noble, or hidalgo, status, sought exemption from the *sorteo* for the militia on the grounds of their obligation to be ready to serve the king, a request initially granted by the king (October 1737) until a review exposed their complete unpreparedness; the king therefore ordered (October 1738) that they must serve in the militia but reserved their other noble privileges, Portugués, *Colección*, 7:131–32, 140–41; Hellwege, *Provinzialmilizen*, 145–74, 222–23. This might be thought of as part of a longer term erosion of the status of the hidalgo population of northern Spain, one of whose most dramatic consequences was to halve the number of those regarded as noble by 1800; Contreras Gay, *Milicias*, 82–83, 92–93, 103–5, 146. At the end of 1743 the subinspector was ordered to Andalusia to find almost three thousand volunteers from among the militia regiments there, to serve at Barcelona, which he did without apparent difficulty, *Gaceta*, 24 November 1744. For desertion in the War of the Austrian Succession, see Hellwege, *Provinzialmilizen*, 378. Grimaldi to Signori, 2 April 1743, Ciasca, *Istruzioni*, 6:293–95. Contreras Gay, *Milicias*, 112, 120; Portugués, *Colección*, 7:218–49. (cl. 9).

40. Portugués, *Colección*, 7:218–49; Contreras Gay, *Milicias*, 201. At the same time, militia recruiting districts were restructured in 1745 to prevent the sort of resistance which had obstructed earlier efforts to impose militia quotas: Contreras Gay, *Milicias*, 59–61.

41. Many mobilised patrons in the hope of securing exemption, prompting countermeasures by the authorities: see subinspector of militias to colonels, 1 June 1745, Portugués, *Colección*, 7:250–54; Ofelia Rey Castelao, "Hombres y ejército en Galicia: La leva de 1762," *Espacio, Tiempo y Forma*, ser. 4, *Historia Moderna* 7 (1994): 199–224; Burnaby Parker to Newcastle, 28 August and 4 December 1746, NA SP 89/45. In January 1746

the *junta of the reino* of Galicia, having agreed to the prorogation of the *millones*, called for the suppression of the militia, Manuel María de Artaza, *Rey, Reino y Representación: La Junta General del Reino de Galicia (1599–1834)* (Madrid: CSIC, 1998), 400. Parker was clear that these problems were not peculiar to Galicia.

42. For new appointments and promotions prior to the despatch of expeditionary force(s) to Africa and Italy, see *Gaceta*, 1732, 1733–34, 1741–42, passim. For the new hierarchy, see Andújar Castillo, *Militares*, 105–19; Andújar, *Militares*, 35; Contreras Gay, *Milicias*, 80, 101; Kamen, *War*, 83–117.

43. Jean-Pierre Dedieu, "Dinastía y Elites de Poder en el Reinado de Felipe V," in Fernández Albaladejo, *Los Borbones*, 381–99; Kamen, *War*, 92; Portugués, *Colección*, 5:1–2, and decrees of 5 February 1716 and 9 June 1720, ibid., 64–70, 81–84; Enrique Martínez Ruiz, "La Guardia Real: Antecedentes y desarrollo," in Iglesias, *Historia Militar*, 253–76; Francisco Andújar Castillo, "Las Elites de Poder Militar en la España Borbónica: Introducción a su estudio prosopográfico," in *Sociedad, Administración y Poder en la España del Antiguo Régimen*, ed. Juan Luis Castellano (Granada: Universidad de Granada, 1996), 207–35; itinerary circulated in 1732 by Patiño regarding the lodging of the royal bodyguard, Portugués, *Colección*, 5:107–10. For another distinctive—privileged—corps, see Francisco Andújar Castillo, "Nobleza catalana al servicio de Felipe V: La Compañía de Granaderos Reales," *Pedralbes* 27 (2007): 293–313.

44. Order of 1722, Portugués, *Colección*, 2:582–84; Andújar, *Militares*, 102–3. Jean Pierre Dedieu, "L'apparition du concept de noblesse dans la Castille moderne: La mise en place des marqueurs de considération sociale (XVIe–XVIIIe siècles)," in *A la recherche de la considération sociale*, ed. Josette Pontet (Pessac: Maison des Sciences de l'Homme d'Aquitaine, 1999), 11–26.

45. For earlier grants, see L. P. Wright, "The Military Orders in Sixteenth- and Seventeenth-Century Spanish Society," *Past and Present* 43 (1969): 34–70, and Elena Postigo Castellanos, *Honor y Privilegio en la Corona de Castilla: El Consejo de las Ordenes y los caballeros de hábito en el siglo XVII* (Valladolid: Junta de Castilla y León, 1987). Unfortunately, Domingo Marcos Giménez Carrillo, "Las Ordenes Militares Castellanas en el Siglo XVIII" (PhD diss., Universidad de Almería, 2014), covers only the period 1701–24; Francisco Eissa Barroso, "Politics, Political Culture and Policy Making: The Reform of Viceregal Rule in the Spanish World under Philip V (1700–1746)" (PhD diss., University of Warwick, 2010), 295. In 1745 Nicolás de Carvajal was rewarded for the capture of Alessandria with the *encomienda* of Valdepeñas (Santiago), *Gaceta*, 9 November 1745; Hellwege, *Provinzialmilizen*, 303–8; Contreras Gay, *Milicias*, 74, 143; Rafael de Fantoni y Benedi, "La milicia, fuente de nobleza: Títulos y grandezas concedidos al estamento militar por Felipe V y Fernando VI," *Emblemata: Revista aragonesa de emblemática* 12 (2006): 143–55.

46. Martínez Ruiz, "Guardia," 267; Andújar, *Sonido*, 119–20; María de los Angeles Pérez Samper, "La Familia Alós: Una Dinastía Catalana al Servicio del Estado (Siglo XVIII)," *Cuadernos de Investigación Histórica* 6 (1982): 195–239; Alos y de Rius, *Carta*, 91–92. These memoirs were completed around 1767.

47. Order, 10 February 1718, renaming all regiments, Portugués, *Colección*, 2:347–60; Andújar, *Militares*, 313–25. Seventy-three percent of Spain's military engineers were born abroad or outside Spain in 1721 but only 47 percent in 1750, Galland Seguela, *Ingenieurs militaires*. For a larger presence of non-Spaniards among the high command, see Fernando Sánchez Marcos, "Los Oficiales Generales de Felipe V," *Cuadernos de Investigación Histórica* 6 (1982): 241–46. Unfortunately, Muñoz Rodríguez, *Séptima Corona*, 401–15, lists those Murcians who held civilian posts in the eighteenth century but not army officers; José Vicente Gómez Pellero, "La nobleza militar en la Monarquía Borbónica: Cursus honorum del conde de Ricla," in Serrano, *Felipe V*, 1:429–37, and, more broadly, Christopher Storrs and H. M. Scott, "The Military Revolution and the European Nobility, c. 1600–1800," *War in History* 3 (1996): 1–41; Guy Rowlands, *The Dynastic State and the Army under Louis XIV: Royal Service and Private Interest, 1661–1701* (Cambridge: Cambridge University Press, 2002), passim; Alos y de Rius, *Carta*, 91–92.

48. Andújar, *Sonido*, passim, is the best treatment of this topic. Five years' service was supposed to be completed before a man could hope for promotion to captain, but this was not always respected, ibid., 51, and ibid., *Militares*, 206, for the promotion in 1747 of a cadet distinguished by the merits of his relations. For Campillo's criticisms, Andújar Castillo, *Militares*, 179. In his earlier *Discurso sobre la Expedición de Italia*, Campillo said much the same thing about the high command on the Italian expeditionary force of 1733, which he accompanied as army *intendente;* Mina to Ensenada, 13 September 1746, AGS, SG/2161.

49. Wilkinson, *Defence*, 257–58; in 1741 Philip issued a new order of regimental precedence in his expanding army, Clonard, *Historia*, 5:233–40; Borré to CEIII, 15 March 1734, AST, LM Spagna/66; Anne Dubet, "Los intendentes y la tentativa de reorganización del control financiero en España, 1718–1720," in *Más Estado y más mercado: Absolutismo y Economía en la España del Siglo XVIII*, ed. Guillermo Pérez Sarrión (Madrid: Silex, 2011), 126; Andújar, *Militares*, 84–97; Portugués, *Colección*, 2:644.

50. Andújar Castillo, *Sonido*, 82, for a captain who was thought incapable by Montemar and who was suspended, and 93, 98, the fact that few (venal) commanders were promoted; [?] to Siruela, 21 November 1733, AGS, SG/Sup/228; in 1732 a captain whose carelessness was blamed for losses in an ambush outside Oran faced a court-martial, Arvillars to CEIII, 25 July 1732, AST, LM Spagna/ 64; Santa Cruz to Patiño, 21 October 1732, AGS, SG/Sup/485. In 1748 the marquis de Lior d'Eglegatte, a brigadier in the Walloon Guards, having spent three years in Flanders when he had permission to be absent for only six months, was dismissed, Ensenada to Huéscar, 24 January 1748, *Misión*, 376; Juan Carrillo de Albornoz, "Los ingenieros: Fortificación en España y Ultramar," in Iglesias, *Historia Militar*, 209–33 (at 216). Monitoring of officers was facilitated by the introduction after 1713 of the *hojas de servicio*, in which individual officers' service, abilities, and zeal were recorded, Andújar, *Militares*, 21 and passim; Andújar, *Militares*, 226–27; Andújar Castillo, *Sonido*, 124–25; Borré to CE III, 10 August 1733, AST, LM Spagna/65. For contemporary criticism of a preoccupation with seniority, see Andújar, *Militares*, 235–37.

51. Wilkinson, *Defence,* 53, 63, and Charles Emanuel III to his son, 10, 12, 17, and 24 December 1742, in *Carlo Emanuele III nella Guerra di Succesione Austriaca (1742–1743),* ed. R. M. Borsarelli and A. Corbelli, 83–90 (Rome: Edizioni Roma, Anno XIV/1935). The king's son thought the Spanish queen "change de generaux comme de chemise" (changes generals the way she changes blouses), ibid., 96. See also Campo-Raso, *Memorias,* 4, 194–200; Manuel-Reyes García Hurtado, "Los militares y las letras," in Iglesias, *Historia Militar,* 443–56; Antonio Morales Moya, "Milicia y nobleza en el siglo XVIII," *Cuadernos de Historia Moderna* 9 (1988): 121–38 (at 130). Martine Galland-Seguela, "Las condiciones materiales de la vida privada de los ingenieros militares de España durante el siglo XVIII," *Scripta Nova, Revista Electrónica de Geografía y Ciencias Sociales* 8 (2004): http://www.ub.es/geocrit/sn/sn-146(007).htm identifies relevant texts and their ownership, but the engineers was arguably a more technical, bookish arm and her data relate mainly to the period after 1746. For an example of the translation of French technical works, see Raimondo Sanz, *Diccionario militar, o recolección alfabética de todos los términos propios al Arte de Guerra . . .* (Barcelona: Juan Piferrer, 1749).

52. Philip's officers could be very critical of other armies, particularly that of Louis XV, Huéscar to Carvajal, 16 September 1747, Ozanam, *Diplomacia,* 227–28; Andújar Castillo, *Consejo,* 176–77 (Juan Francisco de Bete y Croy, marqués de Lede, born 1668), 186–87 (José Francisco, conde y duque de Montemar, born 1671), 197–98 (Isidro de la Cueva Benavides, marqués de Bedmar, born 1652).

53. Andújar Castillo, *Consejo,* 176–77, omits to mention Lede's role at Ceuta (1720); *Gaceta,* 12 March and 9 April 1743, 11 February, 31 March, 14 April, 19 May, 9 June, 29 September, and 17 November 1744; and 15 April, 25 May, 24 August, 7 September, and 16 November 1745; María del Mar Felices de la Fuente, *La nueva nobleza titulada de España y América en el siglo XVIII (1701–1746): Entre el mérito y la venalidad* (Almería: Editorial Universidad de Almería, 2012), 458. The following year Gages's manoeuvring enabled Castelar to fight his way out of Parma after the debacle at Piacenza, Armstrong, *Elisabeth,* 370–71, 387. To Armstrong, "Bourbon Governments . . . II," 165, Gages was the best of many very able generals in the Spanish service. Huéscar praised Castelar's skillful withdrawal of his troops from Parma: Huéscar to Ensenada, 3 June 1746, Ozanam and Téllez Alarcia, *Misión,* 109–10

54. There is a a useful, brief general discussion of this issue in Wilson, "Warfare," 76–77. Helpful, too, in defining militarism and militarisation in this period is Anderson, *War and Society,* 170–80. See also Enrique Giménez López, "El debate civilismo–militarismo y el régimen de Nueva Planta en la España del siglo XVIII," *Cuadernos de Historia Moderna* 15 (1994): 41–75; ibid., *Los servidores del rey en la Valencia del siglo XVIII* (Zaragoza, 2006), 21–50, and ibid., "Marte y Astrea en la Corona de Aragón: La preeminencia de los Capitanes Generales sobre los togados en los primeros años de la Nueva Planta," *Revista de Historia Moderna* 22 (2004): 251–70. In the militia regulations of April 1745 Philip ordered that all requests for *facultades* for *arbitrios* (see chapter 3) for militias must be vetted by the inspector of militia before passing to the Council of Castile, Portugués, *Colección,*

7:218–49. (at clauses 67, 68). For the government of Asturias, see Martínez-Radío Garrido, *Guerra*, 217–27. For the use of the army to discipline recalcitrant communities, see consultas of Council of Orders, 23 June 1734, AGS, SG/5459, and of Council of Finance, 6 July 1744, AGS, SSH/98; and Francisco Andújar Castillo, "Capitanes generales y capitanías generales en el siglo XVIII," *Revista de Historia Moderna* 22 (2004): 291–320 (at 314), for Antequera, 1734, and Granada, 1748. Militiamen needed permission to marry, Contreras Gay, *Milicias*, 142–43, 145

55. For the militarisation of Murcia between 1700 and 1713, see Muñoz Rodríguez, *Séptima Corona*, 171–89, 314. The construction of barracks had been ordered in 1718, thus solving the problem (evident before 1700) of civilian resentment at the billetting of troops in transit, but it was some decades before it was put into full effect, José Omar Moncada, "El cuartel como vivienda colectiva en España y sus posesiones durante el siglo XVIII," *Scripta Nova, Revista Electrónica de Geografía y Ciencias Sociales* 146 (2003): http://www.ub.es/geocrit/sn/sn-146(007).htm.; Peter H. Wilson, "Prussia as a Fiscal-Military State, 1640–1806," in Storrs, *Fiscal-Military State*, 98 f. Philip Williams, review of Álvarez-Junco, *Spanish Identity, Reviews in History* (May 2012): http://www.history.ac.uk/reviews/review/1260.

56. I. A. A. Thompson, "Almansa y la Guerra en torno a 1700: Cambios y permanencias," in *La Guerra de Sucesión en España y la Batalla de Almansa: Europa en la encrucijada*, ed. Francisco García González (Madrid: Silex, 2009), 31–49, and Ensenada to Huéscar, 27 March 1747, Ozanam and Téllez Alarcia, *Misión*, 219–20; Borré to CEIII, 26 December 1732 and 1 February 1734, AST, LM Spagna/64, 66; Carmen Sanz Ayán, "Arrendamientos de rentas por suministros: El mantenimiento de presidios en el estrecho durante la segunda mitad del siglo XVII," in ibid., *Estado, monarquía y finanzas*, (Madrid: Centro de Estudios Políticos y Constitucionales, 2004), 65–77; Lede to Tolosa, 5 November 1720, AGS, SG/Sup/481. In 1730 D. Lucas Spinola, conde de Siruela, opposed an invasion of Sicily (to establish Don Carlos in Italy) given the logistical difficulties, Bethencourt Massieu, *Relaciones de España*, 75. Spinola had fought in Sicily between 1718 and 1720; Valguarnera to CEIII, 20 November 1741, AST, LM Spagna/69; Huéscar to Carvajal, 26 July 1746, Ozanam, *Diplomacia*, 95–96

57. Francisco José Corpas Rojo, "Financiación de la guerra," in Iglesias, *Historia Militar*, 47–66, and Medina Avila, "Industria," passim; Instructions for the intendente with the Oran expedition, 1732, AGS/SG/Sup/484, cl. 12; Proyecto o estado . . ., [1720], AGS, SG/1480. In December Philip ordered the despatch from Cádiz of 4,000 *fusiles*, Tolosa to Lede, 19 December 1720, AGS, SG/Sup/481; Segundo Papel . . . Oran; Belando, *Historia Civil*, 4, 539; Ferrand to Skinner, 14 May 1732, NA, SP 98/34; the Sicilian expedition (1718) embarked 5,000 horses, many of which were abandoned when the Spaniards evacuated the island in 1720, Alos y Rius, *Instrucción Militar*, 59. In 1732 orders were given for 20,000 horseshoes, Arvillars to CEIII, 29 February 1732, AST, LM Spagna/64; Alonso Aguilera, *Conquista*, 63–64, 113. For the Sicilian expedition, see Worsley to Craggs, 5 July 1718, NA, SP 89/26 f. 43ff. The Oran expedition embarked at least 50 guns and 30 mortars, Segundo Papel . . . Oran; [Ferrand?] to Skinner, Barcelona, 13 April and 14 May 1732,

NA, SP 98/34. In 1745 the Spanish and Neapolitan forces in north Italy had more than 100 siege guns besides field guns and mortars, *Gaceta*, 24 August 1745. The artillery was a distinct arm, Ozanam, "Política," 542–50; Estado de las Raciones . . ., [1732], Contamine to Patiño, Oran, 25 July 1732; Noticia de los sacos . . ., Oran, 23 July 1732. See also Supuesto de las Raziones . . ., Oran, 25 July 1732, AGS, SG/Sup/484. According to Belando, *Historia Civil*, 4, 539, the expedition was accompanied by 81 campaign ovens. The expedition to Sardinia in 1717 was equipped with 650 tents, Alonso Aguilera, *Conquista*, 64. In 1741, 1,800 tents were being prepared for the expedition to Italy, Valguarnera to CEIII, 16 January 1741, AST, LM Spagna/70.

58. Parrott, "War," 94. In 1738 Montemar, as secretary of war, issued two new types of inventory of artillery in both garrisons and in the field, thereby ensuring greater uniformity and clarity, Ramón de Salas y Cortes, *Memorial histórico de la artillería española* (Madrid: Garcia, 1826), 142. For the director of artillery, see Agustín González Enciso, "Empresarios navarros en la industria de municiones para la artillería," in Torres Sánchez, *Volver*, 191. Andújar Castillo, *Militares*, 43; Muñoz Rodríguez, *Séptima Corona*, 231–33; Eduardo Garrigós Picó, "Organización territorial a fines del Antiguo Régimen," in *La Economía española al final del Antiguo Régimen*, vol. 4: *Instituciones*, ed. Miguel Artola, 3–105 (at 32 and appendices) (Madrid: Alianza, 1982); Artaza, *Rey*, 399.

59. Alonso Aguilera, *Conquista*, 116; Abbad and Ozanam, *Intendants*, 157–58; Instructions, AGS, SG/Sup/484; for Contamine, see Abbad and Ozanam, *Intendants*, 79.

60. For D. Alexandro de Huarte, "thesorero de el exercto de la expedición de Africa," who prepared the final accounts, see Relacion distinta . . ., Alicante, 10 September 1732, AGS, GM/Sup/484.

61. Kamen, *War*, 62–68; José Calvo Poyato, "La industria militar española durante la Guerra de Sucesión," *Revista de Historia Militar* 66 (1989): 51–72; María Concepción Hernández Escayola, *Negocio y servicio: Finanzas públicas y hombres de negocios en Navarra en la primera mitad del siglo XVIII* (Pamplona: Ediciones Universidad de Navarra, 2004), 247–63; González Enciso, "Empresarios," passim (for Eugui); Martínez Shaw and Alfonso Mola, *Felipe*, 250; Coxe, *Memoirs of Kings*, 2:379–80; Proyecto o estado . . ., [1720], AGS/ SG/1480. For an order to manufacture 3,840 fusiles with bayonets and 1,500 pistols, see Los tres mil . . ., [nd], AGS, SG/Sup/228; Uztáriz, *Theory*, 1:174.

62. Martínez Shaw and Alfonso Mola, *Felipe*, 250; Arvillars to CEIII, 15 February 1732, AST, LM Spagna/64. For orders for more heavy guns, see same to same, 10 October 1732, AST, LM Spagna/64, and Borré to CEIII, 9 January and 6 February 1733, AST, LM Spagna/65; Borré to CEIII, 20 February 1733, AST, LM Spagna/65; González Enciso, "Empresarios," 208–11; Medina Avila, "Industria," 190–94; Grimaldi to Signori, 18 January 1746, Ciasca, *Istruzioni*, 7:39–46.

63. Alonso Aguilera, *Conquista*, 64, 79; *Gaceta*, 9 March, 15 and 27 April 1745; Noticias que es conveniente tener presentes . . . (1748), Rodríguez Villa, *Ensenada*, 506–12.

64. Andújar Castillo, *Sonido*, 119–20; Portugués, *Colección*, 2:345–46, 647–67; C. Espejo de Hinojosa, "Enumeración y atribuciones de algunas juntas de la administración

española desde el siglo XVI hasta el año 1800," *Revista de la Biblioteca, Archivo y Museo de Madrid* 32 (1931): 325–62 (at 353). See also Ensenada's Representación . . . (18 June 1747), Rodríguez Villa, *Ensenada*, 43–65 (at 61–62); according to Tucker to Newcastle, 25 June 1732, SP 94/216, 100 horses were thrown overboard in contrary winds. For the collection of eight hundred horses for Italy, see Borré to CEIII, 1 March 1734, AST, LM, Spagna/66. Later that year almost two thousand horses disembarked at Naples, Keene to Newcastle, 14 June 1734, NA, SP 94/119; *Gaceta*, 11 May 1745.

65. Proyecto o estado . . ., [1720], AGS, SG/1480; Fusiles que ay en Cadiz inclusos los . . . remitidos a aquella plaza [1720], AGS, SG/Sup/481; Armstrong, *Elisabeth*, 118.

66. Christopher Storrs, "Health, Sickness and Medical Services in Spain's Armed Forces c. 1665–1700," *Medical History* 50 (2006): 325–50. For that at Ceuta, see Carmona Portillo, "Los extranjeros," passim; Ozanam, "Política," 556–57. For the medical staff on the expeditionary force sent to Italy at the end of 1733, see consulta of Junta de Medios, June 1738, AHN, Estado, libro 776; Proyecto o estado . . ., [1720], AGS, SG/1480. In December there were thirteen hundred men in the two hospitals, Lede to Tolosa, 20 December 1720, AGS, SG/Sup/481; Sartine to Patiño, 12 February 1732, AGS, SG/Sup 483. The English consul thought the hospital would accommodate two thousand men, Ferrand to Skinner, 10 February 1732, NA, SP 98/34. Regulations were issued in May 1732 detailing the duties of the staff and the diet of those treated in the field hospital, Contamine to [?], 21 May 1732, AGS, SG/Sup/483; Rubalcava to Patiño, 4 June 1732, AGS, SG/Sup/483; Segundo Papel . . . Oran; AGS, SG/Sup/484, cl. 11. The instructions gave hospital spending high priority. According to Belando, *Historia Civil*, 4, the expedition was accompanied by forty-eight surgeons.

67. Ozanam, "Política," 556–57. See Resumen del haver de Empleados en Hospitales, produced in 1737 for the Junta de Medios, AGS, SSH/408. Of more than 5 million reales' expenditure under this head each year, well over half was absorbed by 11 hospitals in Catalonia; Revel, "La Savoie et la domination espagnole," 167. Ferrer Benimeli, "El Conde de Aranda," 736; *Gaceta*, 4 Mar. 1720; Rebollar to Campillo, 13 February 1743, AGS, SG/2011; *Gaceta*, 16 May 1744 and 30 March 1745. Recruits who were too ill to embark for Italy were expected, once they recovered, to join another unit heading there, Wanmarck to Ensenada, 27 April 1748, AGS, SG/Sup/295.

68. I. A. A.Thompson, *War and Government in Habsburg Spain, 1560–1620* (London: Athlone Press, 1976), passim; the contract is in Clonard, *Historia*, 5:206–14; royal order on pay, etc., 1 January 1718, Portugués, *Colección*, 2:257–345; BL, Rare Books, 1322.l.22/1–52 (32). In 1736 D. Matheo López de Sedano contracted to supply the uniforms of all militia regiments, royal order, 28 February 1736, Portugués, *Colección*, 7:84–123 (at 117, cl. 89). The contract was renewed in 1744 after renegotiation of the price, Hellwege, *Provinzialmilizen*, 252; Instructions for intendente, AGS, GM/Sup/484, cl. 21, 30; Windsor to Newcastle, 25 October 1732, NA, SP 94/216. See contract with Antonio Vallesca and Co. of Barcelona for draught animals for the artillery train for Italy [November 1733], AGS, SG/Sup/228.

69. González to Lede, and Lede to Tolosa, 13 December 1720, AGS, SG/Sup/481; Borré to CEIII, 27 February 1733, AST, LM Spagna/65; Thompson, *War*, passim. In 1720 troops at Ceuta fell ill after eating rotten meat supplied by the contractor, Santos Madrazo, *Estado débil y ladrones poderosos en la España del siglo XVIII: Historia de un peculado en el reinado de Felipe V* (Madrid: Catarata, 2000), 69. The scandal led to the arrest of the minister of war, the navy and the Indies, the marqués de Tolosa, the brother-in-law of the contractor. More than two hundred thousand reales were owed in 1737 to Antonio Ballesca, on his contract to supply the artillery train in Italy, AGS, SSH/1040. The settling of accounts could take time and was complicated in this case by the deduction of the cost of barley supplied to Ballesca for his animals from royal magazines.

70. Rafael Torres Sánchez, "Cuando las reglas de juego cambian: Mercados y privilegio en el abastecimiento del ejército español en el siglo XVIII," *Revista de Historia Moderna, Anales de la Universidad de Alicante* 20 (2002): 1–66, and "Los navarros en la provisión de víveres a la armada española durante el siglo XVIII," in ibid., *Volver*, 244–45 (the cost of army rations rocketed between 1743 and 1748, 251); Hernández Escoyala, *Negocio*, 233–41; M. Díaz Ordóñez, *Amarrados al Negocio: Reformismo Borbónico y suministro de jarcia para la Armada Real (1675–1751)* (Madrid: Ministerio de Defensa, 2009), 642; order, June 1739, for clothing the Royal Carabineers, Portugués, *Colección*, 5:599–600; Ensenada to Campillo, 6 February 1743, AGS, SG/2117; Rebollar to Gordillo, 12 July 1743, AGS, TMC/4464; Tineo to Ensenada, [?], 28 April 1745, AGS, SG/2157.

71. Uztáriz, *Theory*, 1:246–50. For the impact on the royal cloth factory at Guadalajara, see Larruga, *Memorias políticas y económicas*, 14:109ff., and 15:1ff. According to Ripperda, almost half of the cloth sold by the factory between its establishment in 1722 and September 1724 went for army uniforms, the cost representing half of total sales of 2,634,832 reales. In 1730 the contract for the supply of 300,000 rations to Porto Longone provided that the foodstuffs must be obtained in Philip's dominions, AGS, SSH/1040. In 1736 the provincial militias were directed to purchase arms from Spanish factories, Portugués, *Colección*, 7:84–123. Cf J. Clayburn La Force, "Royal Textile Factories in Spain, 1700–1800," *Journal of Economic History* 29 (1964): 337–63.

72. Discurso sobre la expedición; Alonso Aguilera, *Conquista*, 130; Antonello Mattone, "La cessione del Regno di Sardegna dal Trattato di Utrecht alla presa di possesso sabaudo (1713–20)," *Rivista Storica Italiana* 102 (1990): 5–89 (at 75–76). For the War of the Austrian Succession, cf. Noticia de los géneros . . ., [January 1743], AGS, SG/2117. Most of the artillery lost in 1746 was recovered at the peace, Ozanam, *Diplomacia*, 414; Wilkinson, *Defence*, 181; Piatti to Senate, 8 June 1745 and 4 and 25 October 1746, Tonetti, *Corrispondenze*, 17:628–30, 713–14, 716–17; contracts for the provision of the Spanish forces in Naples and the Tuscan presidios, Aversa, 2 May 1734, and the expedition to Sicily, Naples, 22 August 1734, negotiated by Campillo, AGS, SG/2050.

73. Arvillars to CEIII, 16 May, 25 July and 31 October 1732, AST, LM Spagna/64; Armstrong, *Elisabeth*, 275. These difficulties may explain Philip's supposed hostility towards Patiño; González Enciso, "Empresarios," 208–11; *Gaceta*, 30 June 1744. That

summer the retreat of the Spanish and Neapolitan army in Italy was attributed in part to lack of supply, the Spanish commander blaming the contractor, Beretta, who in turn blamed the lack of transport, for which he was not responsible, Bartolini to Senate, 2 June 1744, Tonetti, *Corrispondenze*, 17:541–43. In 1747, however, echoing developments in the fiscal sphere, powder manufacture, which hitherto been contracted out, was taken over by the royal administration, Medina Avila, "Industria," 189, Hernández Escayola, *Negocio*, 256.

Chapter Two. The Fleet

Epigraph: G. de Uztáriz, *Theory and Practice of Commerce . . . translated . . . by John Kippax*, 2 vols. (London: Rivingtons, 1751), 1:352.

1. Molesworth to Carteret, 28 March, 22 May and 27 July 1722, NA, SP 92/31, and Allen to Newcastle, 22 March 1732, NA, SP 92/33 f. 699 (anxieties in Turin); Jeremy Black, "Anglo-Spanish Naval Relations in the Eighteenth Century," *Mariner's Mirror* 77 (1991): 235–58 (at 236–37), for anxieties in Britain and, paradoxically, references to 1588; José María Blanco Núñez, "Táctica y acciones navales," in Iglesias, *Historia Militar*, 355–88, omits (table of operations) the interventions in Italy in 1733–34 and 1741–42; Fernández Duro, *Armada*, 6:297; Herbert W. Richmond, *The Navy in the War of 1739–1748*, 3 vols. (Cambridge: Cambridge University Press, 1920), 2:50, 235–36, 244, 3:155, 157, 165, 173–74; Lynch, *Bourbon Spain*, 166.

2. Armstrong, *Elisabeth*, 362–63; Richmond, *Navy*, 1:171–73. France and Britain were not yet at war, France not declaring war against Britain until 1744; Josef de Vargas y Ponce, *Vida de Navarro* (Madrid: Imprenta Real, 1808), 213–18; José L. Gómez Urdáñez, "La Estrategia político-militar en la España discreta: El Ensenadismo," in Pérez Sarrión, *Más Estado y más mercado*, 137–53 (at 147). For the earlier period, see Storrs, *Resilience*, 63–105.

3. Hugo O'Donnell y Duque de Estrada, "Nacimiento y desarrollo de la armada naval," in Serrano, *Felipe V*, 1:683–700; Carlos Pérez Fernández-Turégano, *Patiño y las Reformas de la Administración en el Reinado de Felipe V* (Madrid: Ministerio de Defensa, 2004), 87–134. Black, "Anglo-Spanish"; Jaap R. Bruijn, "States and Their Navies from the Late Sixteenth to the End of the Eighteenth Centuries," in *War and Competition between States*, ed. Philippe Contamine (Oxford: Oxford University Press, 2000), 69–98 (at 94–96); Rolf Muhlmann, *Die reorganisation der spanischen Kriegsmarine im 18 Jahrhundert* (Cologne: Bohlau Verlag, 1975); Ozanam, "Política," 457–80; José Patricio Merino Navarro, *La armada española en el siglo XVIII* (Madrid: Fundación Universitaria Española, 1981), focuses mainly on the period after 1748; Richard Harding, "Naval Warfare 1453–1815," in Black, *European Warfare 1453–1815*, 96–117; Patrick O'Brien, *Fiscal and Financial Preconditions for the Rise of British Naval Hegemony, 1485–1815*, London School of Economics Working Papers in Economic History, 91/05 (2005); Díaz Ordóñez, *Amarrados,*, 21–26; Pike, *Penal Servitude*, 25–26; Harding, "Naval Warfare," 111. Geoffrey Walker, *Spanish Politics and Imperial Trade, 1700–1789* (London: Macmillan, 1979), 99, states incorrectly that Patiño phased out the galleys. Francisco Javier Guillamón Álvarez and Jesús Pérez Hervas, "Los Forzados de

Galeras en Cartagena durante el primer tercio del Siglo XVIII," *Revista de Historia Naval* 19 (1987): 63–76 (at 67); Louis Sicking, "Naval Warfare in Europe, c. 1330–c. 1680," in Tallet and Trim, *European Warfare 1350–1750*, 236–63 (at 238). Unfortunately, the Tallett and Trim collection omits naval warfare between c. 1680 and 1750.

4. Nicholas A. M. Rodger, "Introduction: Navies and State Formation," in *Navies and State Formation: The Schumpeter Hypothesis Revisited and Reflected*, ed. Jurgen G. Backhaus (Berlin: Lit Verlag, 2012), 9–20; I. A. A. Thompson, "Navies and State Formation: The Case of Spain (1500–1800)", in Backhaus, *Navies*, 347–51.

5. Bolingbroke to Shrewsbury, Whitehall, 25 January 1712 (OS) and Shrewsbury to Bolingbroke, Paris, 16 February 1713, in *Letters and Correspondence . . . of . . . Viscount Bolingbroke*, 4 vols., ed. Gilbert Parke (London: Robinson, 1798), 3:335–40, 404–6; Kamen, *War*, 379–80; Armstrong, *Elisabeth*, 102; Uztáriz, *Theory*, 1:342ff., 355, 358, 399, 404 (the president of the Council of Castile took the same view, Baudrillart, *Philippe*, 3:119); Vargas Ponce, *Vida de Navarro*, 114; Kamen, *Philip V*, 171; José M. Delgado Barrado, *José de Carvajal y Lancaster: Testamento político o idea de un gobierno católico (1745)* (Córdoba: Universidad de Córdoba, 1999), 30–31; Carvajal to Huéscar, 25 December 1748, Huéscar to Carvajal, 20 January 1749, in Ozanam, *Diplomacia*, 421–22, 432–33.

6. Angel Guirao de Vierna, "Organización de la Armada durante el reinado de Felipe V: Diferencias y Semejanzas con la Británica," *Revista de Historia Naval* 18 (1987): 73–86, O'Donnell y Duque de Estrada, "Nacimiento," 683–700, Kamen, *War*, 379–80, and Muhlmann, *Reorganisation*, passim; José María Blanco Núñez, "La Real Armada," in Iglesias, *Historia Militar*, 303–24; Gloria Angeles Franco Rubio, "Reformismo institucional y elites administrativas en la España del siglo XVIII: Nuevos oficios, nueva burocracia, La Secretaría de Estado y del Despacho de Marina (1721–1808)," in *La pluma, la mitra y la espada: Estudios de historia institucional en la Edad Moderna*, ed. Juan Luis Castellano, Jean Pierre Dedieu, and María Victoria López Cordon (Madrid: Marcial Pons, 2000), 95–130; Cesar Fernández Duro, *Disquisiciones Nauticas*, 6 vols. (Madrid: Impresores de Cámara de SM, 1876), 5:167; Pérez Fernández-Turégano, *Patiño*, 87–90; Fernández Duro, *Armada*, 6:211–12, 221–23.

7. Martínez Shaw and Alfonso Mola, *Felipe*, 251–52; Fernández Duro, *Disquisiciones*, 1:271–72. See also Ivan Valdez-Bubnov, "War, Trade and Technology: The Politics of Shipbuilding Legislation, 1607–1728," *International Journal of Maritime History* 21 (2009): 86–87. In 1715–16 a plan of naval reconstruction funded from the Cruzada suggested a fourth naval base at Tortosa in Catalonia, Progetto di 24 Navi da Guerra da mantenersi a spese della Crociata, ASV, Fondo Albani/104, 182ff., the justification for having more than one naval base being Spain's lack of the resources and facilities necessary for a fleet of any size; Muhlmann, *Reorganisation*, 40; Fernández Duro, *Disquisiciones*, 1:266, 270, 3:262–64. In December 1741 ships from Cádiz convoyed troops to Italy, Valguarnera to CEIII, 11 December 1741, AST, LM Spagna/70

8. Muhlmann, *Reorganisation*, 305; David Matamoros Aparicio, "Administración y Jurisdicción de Marina en Cataluña (1714–1777)," in *El Derecho y el Mar en la España*

Moderna, ed. Carlos Martínez Shaw (Granada: Universidad de Granada, 1995), 273–97; Rodríguez Villa, *Ensenada*, passim.

9. Patrick Williams, "The Spanish Council of War Under Charles II: Professionalism— and Decline?," in *Redes de nación y espacios de poder: La comunidad irlandesa en España y la América española, 1600–1825 / Power Strategies: Spain and Ireland, 1600–1825*, ed. Oscar Recio Morales (Madrid: Albatros Ediciones, 2012), 137–53.

10. María Luz González Mezquita, *Oposición y disidencia en la Guerra de Sucesión española: El Almirante de Castilla* (Valladolid: Junta de Castilla y León, 2007), 63, 492; Lynch, *Bourbon Spain*, 127; Angel Guirao de Vierna, "Notas para un estudio del Almirantazgo de 1737," *Revista de Historia Naval*, año 2, número 4 (1984): 83–100. In the winter of 1740–41 the board met frequently prior to intervention in Italy, Valguarnera to CEIII, 6 February and 17 April 1741, AST, LM Spagna/70; Guirao de Vierna, "Organización," 79–80; Vargas Ponce, *Importancia de la historia de la Marina española* (Madrid: Imprenta Real, 1807), 74, 83; patent of appointment of D. Nicolás Espluga as galley captain (1738), F. Pavia, *Galería biográfica de los generales de marina . . . desde 1700 a 1868* (Madrid: Imprenta J. Lopez, 1873–74), 1:538; Castellano, *Gobierno y Poder*, 115–16; O'Donnell y Duque de Estrada, "Nacimiento," 699; Carlos Pérez Fernández-Turégano, "El Almirantazgo del Infante Don Felipe (1737–1748): Conflictos competenciales con la Secretaría de Estado y del Despacho de Marina," *Anuario de Historia del Derecho Espanol* 74 (2004): 409–76. All funds hitherto channelled to the Almirantazgo were to revert to the royal treasury, R. Antúnez y Acevedo, *Memorias históricas sobre la legislación y gobierno del comercio de los españoles en sus colonias en las Indias occidentales* (Madrid: Imprenta de Sancha, 1797), appendix, doc. XII, and were to be applied to the public debt, Ozanam and Téllez Alarcia, *Misión*, 522.

11. Muhlmann, *Reorganisation*, 307–10; Olivares to Patiño, 22 March 1732, AGS, SG/Sup/486.

12. For numbers, see José Alcalá Zamora, "Evolución del tonelaje de la flota de vela española durante los siglos modernos," *Estudios* 1 (1975): 177–224, and Thompson, "Navies," 329, 347–48; José Alcalá-Zamora, "Aportación a la historia de la siderurgia española," in ibid., *Altos hornos y poder naval en la España de la Edad Moderna* (Madrid: Real Academia de la Historia, 1999), 19–55 (at 40); Bruijn, "States and Their Navies," 73. Bruijn's figures obscure how new the Spanish fleet was, but see Daniel Panzac, "Armed Peace in the Mediterranean, 1736–1739: A Comparative Survey of the Navies," *Mariner's Mirror* 84 (1997): 41–55; Díaz Ordóñez, *Amarrados*, 604–5.

13. Panzac, "Armed Peace," 49–50; Ensenada to Huéscar, 9 November 1747, in Ozanam and Téllez Alarcia, *Misión*, 336; Ogelsby, "Havana Squadron," 474; Kuethe and Blaisdell, "French Influence," 583; María Baudot Monroy, *La defensa del Imperio: Julián de Arriaga en la Armada (1700–1754)* (Madrid: Ministerio de Defensa, 2013), 78, 104.

14. Muhlmann, *Reorganisation*, 339; Valguarnera to CEIII, 24 October and 14 and 28 November 1740, AST, LM Spagna/69; Ogelsby, "Havana Squadron," 476, Williams, *Prize*, 28.

15. Sessions of the city council of Murcia, 14 and 18 January 1744, AMM, AC/1744, f. 8; for Galician waters, [?] to [?], Coruna, 11 July 1729, SP 94/100; Informazione sopra il Sussidio, ed Escusado, che si domanda dal Re di Spagna nelle Indie [1716], ASV, Fondo Albani/104, f. 182. See also Ellen G. Friedman, *Spanish Captives in North Africa in the Early Modern Age* (Madison: University of Wisconsin Press, 1983), 3–32; Thompson, "Navies," 341–42; Holloway to Newcastle, 11 and 25 May, 1728, NA, SP 94/215.

16. The Armada of 1588 comprised 130 fighting ships plus numerous other vessels and carried 2,431 guns and 22,000 mariners and soldiers, J. H. Elliott, *Europe Divided 1559–1598,* 2d ed. (Oxford: Blackwell, 2000), 222; that of 1639 comprised 100 ships totalling 36,000 tons, carrying 2,000 guns and 23,000 men (soldiers and mariners), David Goodman, *Spanish Naval Power, 1589–1665: Reconstruction and Defeat* (Cambridge: Cambridge University Press, 1997), 25.

17. Storrs, *Resilience,* 75–81. Arvillars to CEIII, 3 August 1731, AST, LM Spagna/63, Charles Emanuel III to cavaliere Tigrini, 10 October 1732, Turin, AST, Lettere SAR/17, f. 64.

18. Juan Carlos Galende Díaz, "Reglamento para la Formación de los Batallones de Marina en 1717," *Revista de Historia Naval,* año 3, número 10 (1985): 85–88. Ozanam, "Política," 473; Fernández Duro, *Armada,* 6:147–50; C. T. Atkinson, "British Regiments Afloat: Cape Passaro and Other Incidents," *Journal of the Society for Army Historical Research* 23 (1945): 46–53;, Grimaldi to Signori, 10 March 1744, Ciasca, *Istruzioni,* 6:333–38, Fernández Duro, *Armada,* 6:304–5.

19. Fernández Duro, *Disquisiciones,* 3:262–64; Montealegre to Patiño, 14 June 1735, AGS, E/7732.

20. Alonso Aguilera, *Conquista,* 67, 96–97. Arpe to Patiño, 26 January and 23 May 1734, AGS, E/5511; Felices de la Fuente, *Nueva nobleza,* 448; Pavia, *Galería,* 1:297–303; Borré to CEIII, 30 August and 6 September 1734, AST, LM Spagna/66. *Gazeta,* 29 August 1719;

21. Uztáriz, *Theory,* 1:407, 415–16; Fernández Duro, *Armada,* 6:137; Worsley to Craggs, 23 April and 5 July 1718, NA, SP 89/26 f. 27, 41; Estado de las Embarcaciones . . ., June 1718, NA, SP 89/26 f. 49; Bethencourt, "Aventuras," 326, 327; Francisco Javier Salas, *Historia de la matrícula de Mar . . .* (Madrid: Fortanet, 1870), 148; Arpe to Patiño, 9 February and 9 March 1734, AGS, E/5511, Patiño to Campillo, 26 February 1734, and Campillo to Patiño, 6 March and 14 December 1734, AGS, SG/2050; Santisteban to de la Quadra, 16 July 1737, AGS, E/5810; *Gaceta,* 9 July and 24 September 1743; Le Roy Deville to Ensenada, 28 April 1744, and Castro to Ensenada, 8 September 1744, AGS, SG/Sup/2131; *Gaceta,* 22 December 1744; Argain to Ensenada, 26 January 1745, AGS, SG/2158. When the British squadron blockading the Ligurian coast was weakened in the spring of 1745, a reinforcement of three thousand men left Barcelona for Nice, Richmond, *Navy,* 2:242; *Gaceta,* 27 April and 18 May 1745.

22. For what follows, see Richmond, *Navy,* 3:152–56.

23. For Philip's shipbuilding programme from 1713, see Kamen, *War,* 379, and H. O'Donnell y Duque de Estrada, " "La construcción naval dieciochesca," in Iglesias, *Historia*

Militar, 328–30; Fernández Duro, *Armada,* 6:162; Bethencourt, "Aventuras," 325; Pérez Samper, *Isabel,* 126, 131–32; O'Donnell y Duque de Estrada, "Nacimiento," 696; Fernández Duro, *Armada,* 6:39; Ogelsby, "Havana Squadron," 479–80. For the life expectancy of ships, see Ozanam, "Política," 497. For individual ships, see website "Listado de los Navíos."

24. Goodman, *Spanish Naval Power,* 137; Walker, *Spanish Politics,* 95; Kamen, *War,* 379–80; Muhlmann, *Reorganisation,* 60–61; Walker, *Spanish Politics,* 96; Black, "Anglo-Spanish," 237; Fernández Duro, *Armada,* 6:473. Davies, "George Camocke," *Oxford Dictionary of National Biography;* Stanhope to Townshend, 11 February 1726, in Coxe, *Memoirs of Walpole,* 2:586; Baudrillart, *Philippe,* 3:57; Armstrong, *Elisabeth,* 205, and Black, "Anglo-Spanish," 243–44. Blanco Núñez, "Táctica y acciones navales," 377–78. According to Valguarnera to CEIII, 30 January 1741, AST, LM Spagna, m. 70, the Spanish court was then hoping to buy ships in Denmark.

25. Carlos Martínez Valverde, "La Campaña de Don Juan José Navarro en el Mediterráneo y la Batalla de Cabo Sicie (1742–1744)," *Revista de Historia Naval,* año 1, número 2 (1983): 5–28. See, earlier, Burnett to Craggs, 10 March 1720, NA, SP 89/28 f. 41

26. Cf. Ozanam, "Política," 485 (and graph of output of different yards); O'Donnell y Duque de Estrada, "La construcción," 325–54, Pansac, "Armed Peace," 48–49. See also John Robert McNeill, *Atlantic Empires of France and Spain* (Chapel Hill: University of North Carolina Press, 1985), 132–33, 173–77; Blanco Núñez, "Táctica," 377–78.

27. Walker, *Spanish Politics,* 94–97; Kamen, *War,* 379–80; Alcalá-Zamora, "Aportación," 40; Panzac, "Armed Peace," 43, 54; Díaz Ordóñez, *Amarrados,* 604–18; Fernández Duro, *Disquisiciones,* 5:234, 253; M. Lourdes Odriozola Oyarbide, "La industria naval guipuzcoana (1650–1730): Crisis o auge del sector?," in *Economía y empresa en el norte de España,* ed. María Montserrat Garate Ojanguren and Pablo Martín Acena (Bilbao: Universidad del País Vasco, 1994), 19–58; José Martínez Cardós, "Don José del Campillo y Cossio," *Revista de Indias* 119–22 (1970): 503–42; Ramón Maruri Villanueva, "Ensenada y el Real Astillero de Guarnizo," *Brocar* 25 (2001): 123–36; Martínez Cardós, "José del Campillo," 515–17; Muhlmann, *Reorganisation,* 88–90, Manuel Ibáñez Molina, "D. José del Campillo ante los Problemas Fiscales a Principios de 1741," *Cuadernos de Investigación Histórica* 15 (1984): 47–68 (at 58). Estado de los navíos . . ., 8 February 1727, BL, Rare Books 1322.l.22/MS 8; Juan M. Castanedo Galán, "Un asiento singular de Juan Fernández de Isla: La fábrica de ocho navíos y la reforma de un astillero," in Martínez Shaw, *Derecho,* 457–75 (at 459). Arvillars to CEIII, 10 August 1731, AST, LM Spagna/63. Ensenada to Bustamante, 10 December 1745, AGS, SM/767 f. 118; Ozanam, "Política," 490–91; Ensenada to Navarro, 27 August 1743, same to Comisario General de Cruzada, 26 October 1743, and Barrero to Ensenada, 10 June 1744, AGS, SM/436 (for galleys constructed at Barcelona). For shipbuilding before 1700, see Goodman, *Spanish Naval Power,* 109–37, and Storrs, *Resilience,* 81–89.

28. Díaz Ordóñez, *Amarrados,* 409; Muhlmann, *Reorganisation,* 89; Thompson, *War and Government,* 256–73; Storrs, *Resilience,* 81–89; María Mestre Prat de Padua, "La construcción naval de guerra en la España del siglo XVIII: El marco legal de los procesos de

financiación," in Martínez Shaw, *Derecho*, 299–332, and Marcelino Manuel Sobrón Iruretagoiena, "Algunos aspectos del estudio de costes y otras consideraciones en los asientos del Guarnizo," in Martínez Shaw, *Derecho*, 477–88, for the different methods; Worsley to Craggs, 5 July 1718, NA, SP 89/26 f. 41; Ozanam, "Política," 498–99; McNeill, *Atlantic Empires*, 133.

29. Ofelia Rey Castelao, *Montes y Política Forestal en la Galicia del Antiguo Régimen* (Santiago de Compostela: Universidade de Santiago de Compostela, 1995), and "Mutaciones Sociales," 343–73; Goodman, *Spanish Naval Power*, 68–108; Muhlmann, *Reorganisation*, 87–88; John T. Wing, "Spanish Forest Reconnaissance and the Search for Shipbuilding Timber in an Era of Naval Resurgrence, 1737–1739," *Journal of Early Modern History* 18 (2014): 357–82; Carla R. Phillips and William D. Phillips, *Spain's Golden Fleece: Wool Production and the Wool Trade from the Middle Ages to the Nineteenth Century* (Baltimore: Johns Hopkins University Press, 1997), 76 (for competitors for the resources of the *montes*). Holloway to Newcastle, [May] 1728, NA, SP 94/215; Fernández Duro, *Armada*, 6:483 (order to *subdelegados*, 1739); for the response of the city of Murcia to an order of the naval intendant of Cartagena, see council session of 13 March 1745, AMM, AC/1744, f. 61–64; Mestre Prat de Padua, "Construcción," 308; Matamoros Aparicio, "Administración," 277; Bartolomé Yun Casalilla, "La manzana de la discordia: Montes, señores, vassalos y gestión señorial en Castilla a fines del Antiguo Régimen," in ibid, *La gestión del poder* (Madrid: Akal, 2002), 221–45. Julio Valdeón Baruque, *Olmedo 1753, Según las Respuestas Generales del Catastro de Ensenada* (Madrid: Tabapress, 1991), 33; Ensenada to Huéscar, 13 December 1748, Ozanam and Téllez Alarcia, *Misión*, 546–47.

30. Carla R. Phillips, *The Treasure of the San José: Death at Sea in the War of the Spanish Succession* (Baltimore; Johns Hopkins University Press, 2007), 6–34; Goodman, *Spanish Naval Power*, 114–37; Fernández Duro, *Disquisiciones*, 5:168, and Phillips, *Treasure*, 6–34, for the principles on which ships were built in Spain c. 1700 and the career of Gaztañeta; Fernández Duro, *Disquisiciones*, 5:395–98, for relevant orders. The manual prepared by Jerónimo de Aizpurua, who worked at Guarnizo between 1723 and 1750, *Observaciones que se practican para la delineación de navíos en las costas de Cantabria* (c. 1731), is available online: http://aquariums.com/es/prensa/notas_prensa/2004/manuscrito_071004_cas.htm. Estado de las Tripulaciones . . ., Alicante 14 September 1733, AGS, SM/430/1. See Fernández Duro, *Armada*, 6:315–16; and Phillips, *Treasure*, 13 (for the problems associated with the nomenclature and classification of Spanish warships), 140, 234, 235. Alcalá-Zamora, "Evolución," largely ignores the reign of Philip V.

31. Muhlmann, *Reorganisation*, 120–27, 332; Díaz Ordóñez, *Amarrados*, 603. For the seventeenth century, see Goodman, *Spanish Naval Power*, 145–51, and C. R. Phillips, *Six Galleons for the King of Spain: Imperial Defense in the Early Seventeenth Century* (Baltimore: Johns Hopkins University Press, 1986) 91–93. Fernández Duro, *Armada*, 6:161, 198–99, 382. Uztáriz, *Theory*, 1:376–77, lists 27 ships (plus two fire ships and three bomb vessels), carrying 1,188 guns. Liste des navires . . ., December 1728, in Poyntz to [Newcastle], Paris, 27 February 1729, NA, SP 78/190. They included 31 warships, carrying between 54 and

(one vessel, the *Real*) 114 guns, 10 frigates, bearing between 16 and 46 guns, 4 corvettes, with between 6 and 10 guns, and 4 armed keels of between 60 and 80 guns. Campo-Raso, *Memorias*, 379–80 (but a total of 1,432). This figure omitted the lightly armed galleys: the seven which sailed to Italy in 1731 carried just 35 guns between them, Arvillars to CEIII, 24 August 1731, AST, LM Spagna/63, and enclosed Note. See also Estado de la Armada . . ., [August–September 1731], AGS, SM/429; Blanco Núñez, "Táctica," 377–78; Martínez Valverde, "Campaña," 12–13; Panzac, "Armed Peace," 42, 54.

32. Richmond, *Navy*, 3:173–74 (for small craft in Italian waters in the War of the Austrian Succession); Armando Alberola Romá, "En torno a la política revisionista de Felipe V: Los fletamentos de buques extranjeros en el Puerto de Alicante y su empleo en la expedición a Sicilia del año 1718," *Revista de Historia Militar* 10 (1991): 263–83 (at 266); Arvillars to CEIII, 13 March, 4 April, and 6 June 1732, AST, LM Spagna/64; Borré to CEIII, 7 September 1733, AST, LM Spagna/65; Relacion de las embarcaciones . . . Barcelona, 9 December 1733, AGS, SM/430/1. For the number of transports needed for Philip II's invasion of England in 1588, see Geoffrey Parker, *The Grand Strategy of Philip II* (New Haven: Yale University Press, 1998), 237–43.

33. Poyntz to Addison, 13 August 1717, NA SP 89/25 f. 148, for seizures in 1717; Worsley to Addison, 27 February 1718, NA SP 89/26 f. 13, and Estado de las Embarcaciones . . ., June 1718, NA SP 89/26 f. 49, for 1718, including fifty-eight English vessels, thirty-five Genoese, and eighteen Irish; Holloway to Newcastle, 6 and 30 April 1732, NA SP 94 216; Keene to Newcastle, 13 March 1734, NA SP 94/119; Winder to Castres, 2 February 1737; Keene to Newcastle, 4 February 1737, NA SP 94/127, Genoese, Dutch, and English vessels were all used to evacuate Philip's troops from Italy at the close of the War of the Polish Succession; Valguarnera to CEIII, 24 April, 8 May, 31 July, and 2 October 1741, 6 November and 11 December1741, AST, LM Spagna/70. Castro to Ensenada, 8 September 1744, AGS, SG/Sup/2131.

34. Martínez Shaw, and Alfonso Mola, *Felipe*, 255–56; Cayley to Newcastle, 14 June and 10 July 1735, BL, Add. 28,146 f. 174, 182; Black, "Anglo-Spanish," 244; Carla R. Phillips, "The Life Blood of the Navy: Recruiting Sailors in Eighteenth-Century Spain," *Mariner's Mirror* 87 (2001): 420–45, for an upbeat reassessment. For other states, see M. S. Anderson, *War and Society in Europe of the Old Regime, 1618–1789* (London: Fontana, 1988), 124–28, and Daniel Baugh, *British Naval Administration in the Age of Walpole* (Princeton: Princeton University Press, 1965), 147–240.

35. Uztáriz, *Theory*, 1:364; Muhlmann, *Reorganisation*, 103–266. Serrano to Patiño, 16 November 1732, AGS, SM/429.; Fernández Duro, *Armada*, 6:161, 198–99; Núñez Blanco, "Tactica," 377–78; Uztariz, *Theory*, 1:377, lists (1718) more ships but fewer men; Fernández Duro, *Armada*, 6:198–99; Campo-Raso, *Memorias*, 379–80 (a total of 10,010 in 1731). See Estado de la Armada . . ., [1731], AGS, SM/429, for crews totalling 12,050, the largest (750) aboard the two most heavily armed vessels, the *San Felipe* and the *Santa Isabel;* Martínez Valverde, "Campaña," 13. The smaller ships, carrying 60 guns, had 600 men, the largest and most heavily gunned *Real Felipe*, 1,250 men; Muhlmann, *Reorganisation*, 337–38. This

comprised 1,239 *artilleros,* 735 *marineros,* 390 *grumetes* (cabin boys) and 110 *pajes* (pages). *Plazas de marinería* comprised artilleros de mar, the largest category, marineros, grumetes, and pajes. For the previous century, see Goodman, *Spanish Naval Power,* 210.

36. Valguarnera to CEIII, 13 February, 6 and 27 March and 13 November 1741, AST, LM Spagna/70.

37. Fernández Duro, *Armada,* 6:304; Martínez Valverde, "Campaña," 25; Sartini to Patiño, 10 November 1731, AGS, SM/429; Keene to Newcastle, 3 April 1733, NA, SP 94/116; Arpe to Patiño, 2 February 1734, AGS, E/5511, for sickness aboard the fleet in Italy; Navarro to Campoflorido, 3 January 1744, AGS, SM/193; Relaz.on de la Gente del *Real. . . . Brill.te,* 4 November 1744, AGS, SM/257.

38. Freyre to Patiño, 12 May 1733, AGS, SM/251, Zenón de Somodevilla to Patiño, 26 August 1733, AGS, SM/430; Ozanam, "Política," 482–83; Mikel Astrain Gallart, "Profesionales de la Marina, Profesionales del Estado: La aportación del Cuerpo de Cirujanos de la Armada al proceso de profesionalización de la cirugía española del setecientos (1703–1791)," in Balaguer and Giménez, *Ejército, Ciencia,* 513–32; Rubalcava to Patiño, 4 June 1732, AGS, SG/Sup/483; Fernández Duro, *Armada,* 6:478, for the hospital contract of 1731; Sartine to Patiño, 10 November 1731, AGS, SG/429.

39. Adelaida Sagarra Gamazo and María Nieves Rupérez Almajano, "La Deserción en la Marina Española del Siglo XVIII," *Revista de Historia Naval,* año 9, número 35 (1991): 63–75; Arpe to Patiño, 13 November 1731, AGS, SM/429; [Campillo] to Quadros, 10 July 1742, AGS, SM/767 f. 92 [Campillo] to Quadros, 26 March 1743, AGS, SM/767 f. 94; Cardinal Molina to Ensenada, 5 September 1743, AGS, SM/256. For an example of a licence, see that issued to Alonso Gonzalez of Santoña (Galicia), 16 March 1742, AGS, SM/256.

40. Cayley to Norris, 2 July 1735, BL, Add. 28,146 f. 183. For the Basque country, see Basavilbasa [?] to [?], 31 October 1734, AGS, SM/251.

41. Phillips, "Life Blood," 420–55.

42. Ortega Sanz to Patiño, 3 March and 13 April 1733, AGS, SM/251 (Palma);[?] to Patiño, Valencia, 14 September 1733, AGS, SM/251 (Valencia and Murcia); Relación de la Jente de Mar . . . , *Paloma,* 3 November 1744, AGS, SM/257.

43. Relacion del importe . . ., AGS, SM/257; Navarro to Ensenada, 6 May 1744, AGS, SM/257, Martínez Valverde, "Campaña," 11. Carvajal urged better treatment of mariners, *Testamento,* 32; José Manuel Vázquez Lijó, "La Matrícula de Mar y sus repercusiones en la Galicia del siglo XVIII," *Obradoiro de Historia Moderna* 15 (2006): 289–322.

44. Ezpeleta to Patiño, 11 August 1733, AGS, SM/251.

45. For Habsburg Spain, see Goodman, *Spanish Naval Power,* 194–211, and Storrs, *Resilience,* 92–93; for eighteenth-century Britain, see Baugh, *British Naval Administration,* 147–62.

46. Arvillars to CEIII, 17 August 1731 and 26 April 1732, AST, LM, Spagna/64, 65; Borré to CEIII, 10, 17, and 24 April 1733, AST, LM Spagna, m. 65; Baudrillart, *Philippe,* 4:110–11. For Habsburg Spain, see Storrs, *Resilience,* 89–96, and for Hanoverian Britain, Baugh, *Naval Administration,* 147–240.

47. Cayley to Norris, 2 July and 11 August 1735, BL, Add. 28,146 f. 183, captain Smedley's Account, 12 July 1735, *Dreadnought*, Cadiz Bay, BL Add. 28,146 f. 184; Relación de la Jente de March . . ., *Paloma*, 3 November 1744, AGS/Marina/257. Most of the mariners who passed at the same time from the *Real* to the *Santa Isabel* had also been levied, Relacion de los Yndividuos . . . AGS, SM/257.

48. Freyre to Patiño, 28 April 1733, AGS, SM/251; [?] to Patiño, 14 September 1735, AGS, SM/251; Freyre to Patiño, 31 August 1733, AGS, SM/251; [?] to [?], Vizcaya, 31 October 1734, AGS, SM/251; Sangro to Patiño, 14 September 1735, AGS, SM/251. Cartagena and Lorca had both exceeded their quotas.

49. Ozanam, "Política," 475–77; Phillips, "Life Blood," 420–55; Olga López Miguel and Magda Mirabet Cucala, "La Institucionalización de la matrícula de mar: Textos normativos y consecuencias para la gente de mar y maestranza," in Martínez Shaw, *Derecho*, 217–40; and Matamoros Aparicio, "Administración," 273–97; Salas, *Historia de la matrícula*, 151–60; Sagarra and Rupérez, "Deserción," 65. For members of the guild of seamen being exempted from military service in Asturias in the succession conflict, see Martínez-Radío Garrido, *Guerra de Sucesión*, 367–68.

50. Eugene L. Asher, *Resistance to the Maritime Classes: The Survival of Feudalism in the France of Colbert* (Berkeley: University of California Press, 1960); Geoffrey Treasure, *Louis XIV* (London: Longman, 2001), 130–31; Goodman, *Spanish Naval Power*, 192–93; Vázquez Lijó, "Matrícula," 294.

51. Freyre to Patiño, 16 December 1732 and 31 August 1733, AGS, SM/251; Roberto Fernández Díaz and Carlos Martínez Shaw, "Las Revistas de Inspección de la Matrícula de Mar en el Siglo XVIII," in Martínez Shaw, *Derecho*, 241–71 (at 245–46).

52. In 1732 an attempt to carry out a *sorteo de matrícula* in Irun provoked a riot, Xavier Alberdi Lonbide and Alvaro Aragón Ruano, "La resistencia frente a la política de las autoridades de Marina en Guipuzcoa durante el período borbónico," in *Poder, Resistencia y Conflicto en las Provincias Vascas (Siglos XV–XVIII)*, ed. Rosario Porres Marijuán (Bilbao: Universidad del País Vasco, 2001), 367–94 (at 373, 382). Subsequently, it was declared sufficient for the mariners of these territories to be listed as members of their *cofradía*, Felipe de Urioste to the province, 12 January 1739, San Sebastián, in María Pilar de San Pío Aladrén and Carmen Zamorrón Moreno, *Catálogo de la colección de documentos de Vargas Ponce que posee el Museo Naval* (Madrid: Instituto Histórico de Marina, 1980), 18 (no. 215)

53. Josep Maria Delgado Ribas, "La organización de los servicios portuarios en un puerto preindustrial: Barcelona 1300–1820," in Martínez Shaw, *Derecho*," 107-45 (at 140); royal orders, 18 October 1737 and 14 January 1740, AHN, MH, libro 8014 f. 8ff.; Vázquez Lijó, "Matrícula," 300; Sagarra and Rupérez, "Deserción," 65–66; Rey Castelao, "Mutaciones," 355–73.

54. At the same time, the number of these registered in the Cartagena department rose (in contrast with those in Ferrol and Cádiz) to almost seventeen thousand, nearly half of the total, perhaps reflecting the greater activity in the Mediterranean after 1739; Vázquez Lijó, "Matrícula," 314, 317.

55. Iturralde to Quintana, 22 September 1739, AHN, MH, libro 8013 f. 428; [?] to Ensenada, 12 August 1744, Ensenada to [?], 23 August 1744, and [?] to Barrero, 18 September 1744, AGS, SM/257.

56. Relación de la Jente de Mar . . . , *La Paloma,* 3 November 1744, AGS, SM/257, Relaz.on de la Gente . . . 4 November 1744, AGS, SM/257; Victoria to Ensenada, 4 November 1744, AGS, SM/257. Ensenada ordered that better quality men be sent in future; for one resident of Luarca (Asturias) who registered to get the privileges, see Flores to Patiño, 13 June 1733, AGS, SM/251.

57. Progetto di 24 Navi, ASV, Fondo Albani/104, 203ff.; Espinosa to Patiño, 4 September 1731, AGS, SM/251, enclosing Noticia de lo número de [sixty-four] hombres . . ., who embarked in August 1731; Arpe to Patiño, 13 November 1731, AGS, SM/429; Relazión y quenta de los Marineros, 22 December 1734, AGS, SM/251; Skinner to Newcastle, 5 July 1733, NA SP 98/34. Black, "Anglo-Spanish," 238, 243–44; Lynch, *Bourbon Spain,* 129–30; Carvajal, *Testamento,* 32.

58. Morozzo to Victor Amadeus II, 17 April 1715, AST, LM Spagna/57. Tursi had been a protégé of the princess des Ursins; Villamayor to Gualterio, 22 June 1715, BL, Add. 20,574 f. 174; Fernández Duro, *Armada,* 6:211; Storrs, *Resilience,* 71.

59. Elisa Torres Santana, "Los marginados en tiempos de Felipe V," in Serrano, *Felipe V,* 1:323–42 (at 328); Juan José Laborda, *El Señorío de Vizcaya: Nobles y fueros (c. 1452–1727)* (Madrid: Marcial Pons, 2012), 552–53; Domínguez Ortiz, *Sociedad y Estado,* 137; Antonio Martínez Salazar, *Colección de memorias y noticias del gobierno* (Madrid: Antonio Sanz, 1764), 517; Pedro Ortego Gil, "Apercibimientos penales en la práctica criminal de la Real Audiencia de Galicia (siglos XVII y XVIII)," *Cuadernos de Historia del Derecho* 3 (1996): 11–42. Guillamón Álvarez and Pérez Hervas, "Forzados," 63–75, analyses offences and sentences of some of those condemned to the galleys between 1700 and 1730. For *forzados* of all types, see Manuel Martínez Martínez, *Los forzados de marina en la España del siglo XVIII (1700–1775)* (Almería: Editorial Universidad de Almería, 2011).

60. Ximénez de Cisneros to Patiño, 9 February 1732, AGS, SM/429; Meléndez to Ensenada, 24 October 1744, AGS, SM/436. According to Leyva to Ensenada, 24 October 1744, AGS, SM/436, there were still twenty-one of these *cumplidos* aboard the *San José.*

61. Guillamón Álvarez and Pérez Hervas, "Forzados," 67; Extracto de revista, 27 September 1744, AGS, SM/436. Fulbrook to Keene, 23 February 1734, NA, SP 94/119. Maximiliano Barrio Gozalo, "La esclavitud en el Mediterráneo Occidental en el Siglo XVIII: Los 'Esclavos del Rey' en España," *Crítica Storica* 17 (1980): 199–256, and "La mano de obra esclava en el arsenal de Cartagena a mediados del Setecientos," *Investigación Histórica* 17 (1997): 79–99; and Rafael Torres Sánchez, "La esclavitud en Cartagena en los siglos XVII y XVIII," *Contrastes: Revista de Historia Moderna* 2 (1986): 81–101; Wilkinson, *Defence,* 190; Indians captured in the Americas were often sent to Spain for galley service, Williams, *Prize,* 99.

62. Gómez Urdáñez, "Estrategia político-militar," 138; Patiño to Ensenada, 7 August 1734, Rodríguez Villa, *Ensenada,* 313–14. But a shortfall may have emerged by 1737;

Navarro to Court, 29 January 1744, Vargas Ponce, *Vida de Navarro*, 400–402; Fernández Duro, *Armada*, 6:299; Martínez Valverde, "Campaña," 10–15; Richmond, *Navy*, 3:165, 167; see Baugh, *British Naval Administration*, 147–48; Guipuzcoa to José de Carvajal and others, 11 June 1748, San Pío Aladrén and Zamorrón Moreno, *Catálogo*, 18 (no. 116), and Caroline Ménard, *La pesca gallega en Terranova siglos XVI–XVIII* (Madrid: CSIC, 2008), 231–35.

63. Díaz Ordóñez, *Amarrados*, 382, 614–15; for a British comparison, see Baugh, *British Naval Administration*, 52–61; for Habsburg Spain, Goodman, *Spanish Naval Power*, 151–60; Sartini [*sic*] to Patiño, 22 December 1731, AGS, SM/429; Valguarnera to CEIII, 26 February 1742, AST, LM Spagna/70; Birtles to Newcastle, 15 January 1742, NA, SP 79/19.

64. José Alcalá-Zamora, *Historia de una Empresa Siderúrgica Española: Los Altos Hornos de Liérganes y La Cavada, 1622–1834* (Santander: Institución Cultural de Cantabria, Centro de Estudios Montañeses, 1974), 27, 95, and "Aportación," 39–40; Fernández Duro, *Disquisiciones*, 5:246–47; Manuel Díaz Ordoñez, "La fabricación de jarcia en España: El Reglamento de Jorge Juan, 1750," in Martínez Shaw, *Derecho*, 395–426; Goodman, *Spanish Naval Power*, 140–44; Díaz Ordóñez, *Amarrados*, 388–89, 472, 490, 493, 497, 509–11, 515, 521, 581, 614.

65. Muhlmann, *Reorganisation*, largely omits this aspect of the fleet; Torres Sánchez, "Los navarros en la provisión," in ibid., ed., *Volver*, 213–62; Fernández Duro, *Disquisiciones*, 5:395–98, and *Armada*, 6:484, for contracts. The Catalan Buxos had long been involved in naval supply, Díaz Ordóñez, *Amarrados*, 307–16. Gerónimo Ruesga had bid successfully for this contract in 1742 and again in 1744 but had then lost out to Lasarte, Campillo to Gomez de Terán, 25 June 1742, AGS, SM/767 f. 78; king to marqués de Portago, 4 December 1744, AGS, SM/767; Cornejo to Villarias, 2 and 9 February 1744, AGS, E/5562.

66. Díaz Ordóñez, *Amarrados*, 408–18; accounts in AGS, DGT/Inv 25/15, and [?] to [?], 27 December 1741, AHN, Hacienda, libro 8014 f. 408. Fernández Duro, *Armada*, 6:478, 480; Hernández Escayola, *Negocio*, 235; Ibáñez Molina, "José del Campillo," 51; Santiago Aquerreta, "Reforma fiscal y continuidad en el sistema de arrendamientos: La renta de lanas en el reinado de Felipe V," in *El negocio de la lana en España (1650–1830)*, ed. Agustín González Enciso (Pamplona: Ediciones Universidad de Navarra, 2001), 109–33; and Torres Sánchez, "Los navarros," 213–62.

67. For the galleys, see king to Comisario della Cruzada, 14 September 1733, AGS, SM/767 f. 1; Díaz Ordóñez, *Amarrados*, 288–92, 329–30, 335–36, 348–74, 397, 421, 578–79, 619–45, 661; Diaz Ordóñez, "Fabricación," 403, 407–8, and passim; José Alcalá-Zamora, "Progresos tecnológicos y limitaciones productivas en la nueva siderurgia andaluza del siglo XVIII (avance de investigación)," in ibid., *Altos hornos y poder*, 229–75 (at 241–42, 272), and "Producción de hierro y altos hornos en la España anterior a 1850," in ibid., 277–413 (at 363–64). The purchase price, more than two million reales, was paid in *baldíos* and *despoblados* (see chapter 3).

68. Ozanam, "Política," 499; José Jurado Sánchez, *El gasto de la Hacienda Española: Cuantía y estructura de los pagos del Estado durante el siglo XVIII (1703–1800)* (Madrid: Instituto

de Estudios Fiscales, 2006), 50, 52, 78, 86–87, 161–62, 173–74; Didier Ozanam, "Notas para un estudio de los presupuestos de la Monarquía Española a mediados del siglo XVIII," in *Dinero y Crédito (siglos XVI al XIX): Actas del Primer Coloquio Internacional de Historia Económica*, ed. Alfonso Otazu (Madrid: Moneda y Crédito, 1978), 49–62; Kamen, *War*, 228–29, 380; Uztáriz, *Theory*, 1:407, and (for the costs of a "voyage"), 423; Muhlmann, *Reorganisation*, 25, for a budgeted figure for 1723 of over twenty-six million reales, 29–30, and 35, for arrears due to the fleet in the mid-1730s, and 346–54. See Panzac, "Armed Peace," 48, and Harding, "Naval Warfare," 117, for other states.

69. Muhlmann, *Reorganisation*, 267–80, and table, 318; María Baudot Monroy, "Orígenes familiares y carrera profesional de Julián de Arriaga, Secretario de Estado de Marina e Indias (1700–1776)," *Espacio, Tiempo y Forma*, ser. 4, *Historia Moderna* 17 (2004): 163–85; Andújar Castillo, *Consejo*, 194, Pavia, *Galería*, 1:377–95; Vargas y Ponce, *Vida de Navarro*, 28–30. The naval officer corps has not attracted the same interest as that of the army, but see Francisco Andújar Castillo, "Ejército y marina: Una historia social," in Iglesias, *Historia Militar*, 408–13.

70. "Varios puntos de Govierno . . .," 15 July 1747, Real Academia de la Historia, MS 9/2061, f. 72; O'Donnell y Duque de Estrada, "Nacimiento," 695. V. Bacallar y Sanna, marqués de San Felipe, *Comentarios de la guerra*, 284, was critical of the want of (fighting) experience of Gaztañeta, the commander at Cape Passaro. See also Bethencourt, "Aventuras," 325; Black, "Anglo-Spanish," 237, 244; Arvillars to CEIII, 10 August and 28 December 1731, AST, LM Spagna/63. To the chagrin of many Spaniards, Mari was subsequently appointed to the command of the naval department of Cádiz; Arvillars to CEIII, 5 December 1732, AST, LM Spagna/64; Vargas y Ponce, *Vida de Navarro*, 267. Navarro later dedicated a treatise on naval manouevres (1737) to Isabel Farnese, ibid., 99; Anderson, *War of Austrian Succession*, 138–39; Muhlmann, *Reorganisation*, 303–17; Armstrong, *Elisabeth*, 112–13; Cayley to Newcastle, 14 June 1735, BL Add. 28,146 f. 174; AGS, SM/794.

71. For D. Rodrigo de Torres, who fought at Cape Passaro, and D. Andrés Reggio, see Ogelsby, "Havana Squadron," 476, 483, and for Arriaga, Baudot Monroy, "Orígenes"; Kamen, *War*, 379, and Fernández Duro, *Armada*, 6:219–20; Wager to Walpole, 14 March 1726/7, Coxe, *Memoirs of Walpole*, 2:513; Vargas y Ponce, *Vida de Navarro*, passim; Hugo O'Donnell y Duque de Estrada, *El primer marqués de la Victoria, personaje silenciado en la reforma dieciochesca de la Armada* (Madrid: Real Academia de la Historia, 2004); Carlos Novi, "The Marqués de la Victoria and the Advancement of Naval Lexicography in Eighteenth-Century Spain," *Mariners Mirror* 83 (1997): 136–49; Martínez Valverde, "Campaña," 26–27.

72. Fernández Duro, *Armada*, 6:298; Pavia, *Galería*, 1:459 (Domas), Ensenada to Navarro, Aranjuez, 24 May 1743, AGS, SM/767 f. 98; Williams, *Prize*, 170 (and, for the career of the English admiral Commodore Anson, see Williams, *Prize*, 8–10).

73. Muhlmann, *Reorganisation*, 267–94, O'Donnell y Duque de Estrada, "Nacimiento," 693; Fernández Duro, *Armada*, 6:212; and Díaz Ordóñez, *Amarrados*, 137–41; Morales Moya, "Milicia y nobleza," 136. By 1721 two dancing masters and one fencing master—to

be found in any self-respecting noble academy at that time—had been recruited, but none to teach naval construction or manoeuvre, Alberto Lafuente Torralba and Manuel Sellés García, "El proceso de institucionalización de la Academia de Guardiamarinas de Cádiz (1717–1748)," in *Actas del III Congreso de la Sociedad de Historia de las Ciencias—San Sebastián 1984*, ed. Javier Echevarría Ezponda and Marisol de Mora Charles, 2 vols. (San Sebastian: Editorial Guipuzcoana, 1986), 2:153–76 (at 161, and 173, for the timetable devised by Patiño in 1717). Initially, however, the officer corps continued to recruit from the equally exclusive Knights of St. John of Malta. In 1728 Julián de Arriaga joined the fleet as *alférez de fragata*, avoiding the *academia*, after eleven years on the Order's galleys, Baudot Monroy, *Defensa*, 98–99.

74. AHN, Consejos, libro 1445 f. 62. In lauding the achievement of the book's dedicatee, Patiño, respecting the fleet, the author noted Patiño's role in the reconquest of Oran, Martín Fernández Navarrete, *Biblioteca Marítima Española*, 2 vols. (Madrid: Imprenta de la Viuda de Calero, 1851–52) 1:253; Manuel Sellés García, "Los instrumentos y su contexto: El caso de la Marina española en el siglo XVIII," *Endoxa: Series Filosóficas* 19 (2005): 139–40.

75. *Gaceta*, 12 May 1744. This was part of a general promotion of naval and civilian officers following that action: two ship's captains were promoted to squadron commander, nine officers (including the conde de Vega Florida, frigate captain) to ship's captain, and a further fifteen junior officers to frigate captain; Baudot Monroy, *Defensa*, 101; Felices de la Fuente, *Nueva nobleza*, 260, 458; Ogelsby, "Havana Squadron," 483. For Goodman, *Spanish Naval Power*, 241–53, the low status of the sea service hobbled the fleet in the seventeenth century, despite Olivares's efforts to enhance it.

76. Morales Moya, "Milicia," 136. Ignacio Atienza Hernández, *Aristocracia, poder y riqueza en la España moderna: La Casa de Osuna, siglos XV–XIX* (Madrid: Siglo XXI, 1987), 49, Pavia, *Galería*, 3:390; Andújar Castillo, *Consejo*, 194, Pavia, *Galería*, 1:377–95. For Clavijo (b. 1676), see Pavia, *Galería*, 1:421–24; Rosario Die Maculet and Armando Alberola Roma, "Una boda en la pequeña nobleza alicantina del Setecientos: Los Soler de Cornella y los Juan a través de su correspondencia," *Revista de Historia Moderna* 13/14 (1995): 255–311; Fernández Navarrete, *Biblioteca Marítima*, 1: 251; Javier Varela, *Jovellanos* (Madrid: Alianza, 1988), 17–18.

77. Bergeyck to Pontchartrain (1713), Kamen, *War*, 379–80; Gilbert Delage de Cueilly transferred to the Spanish from the French service, but after a public polemic with Navarro over their roles in the engagement off Toulon returned to the French service, Fernández Duro, *Armada*, 6:307–14; De Mari's maternal grandfather had been in Spanish service and led the resistance to the French bombardment of Genoa in 1684, and he himself entered Philip V's service as a contractor supplying vessels for the recovery of Barcelona (1714) and Majorca (1715): Giorgio Candiani, "Navi per la nuova marina della Spagna borbonica: L'asiento di Stefano De Mari, 1713–1716," *Mediterranea—Ricerche Storiche* (2015): 107–46; Antonio Álvarez-Ossorio Alvariño, "El final de la Sicilia Española? Fidelidad, familia, y venalidad bajo el virrey marqués de los Balbases (1707–1713)," in *La Pérdida de Europa: La Guerra de Sucesión por la monarquía de España*, ed. Antonio Álvarez-

Ossorio Alvariño, B. J. García García, and V. León (Madrid: Fundación Carlos de Amberes, 2007), 831–911. Navarro was born (1687) and raised in Sicily, though of Spanish ancestry, Vargas y Ponce, *Vida de Navarro*, 1–10. See the captains listed in Espedicion . . . [1731], AGS, SM/429, and Borré to CEIII, 31 August 1733, and enclosure, AST, LM Spagna/65.

78. *Gaceta*, 4 Mar. 1716; for collaboration against the Dutch between 1621 and 1648, see Jonathan I. Israel, "Conflict of Empires," *Past and Present* 76 (1977): 34–74 (at 44–49).

79. Kamen, *War*, 141–42; Fernández Duro, *Armada*, 6:331; Worsley to Craggs, 7 November 1718, NA, SP 89/26 f. 102; Stanhope to Newcastle, 11 April 1726, in Coxe, *Memoirs of Walpole*, 2:590–97; Ellen G. Friedman, *Spanish Captives in North Africa in the Early Modern Age* (Madison: University of Wisconsin Press, 1983), 30; Keene to Newcastle, 31 March 1738, NA, SP 94/130. The privateering ordinance of 1718 was modelled on a French original according to Bernard Pares, *Colonial Blockade and Neutral Rights 1739–1763* (Oxford: Oxford University Press, 1938), 153.

80. Parker to Newcastle, 18 July 1745, NA, SP 89/45 f. 41. Díaz Ordóñez, *Amarrados*, 415; Enrique Otero Lana, "La Relación de Presas de 1740 en la Biblioteca Nacional: Un Documento Propagandístico," *Revista de Historia Naval*, año 17, número 67 (1999): 63–75; *Gaceta*, 1745/16; *Gaceta*, 18 July 1719; *Gaceta*, 22 January 1743.

81. For the Austrian Succession conflict, see Otero Lana, "Relación"; Anderson, *War of Austrian Succession*, 18–19; D. Francisco Antonio Velez to Campillo, 6 February 1743, AGS, SM/256; Arvillars to CEIII, 17 October 1732, AST, LM Spagna/64. In 1741 Isabel blamed what might be a disastrous war with Britain on Basque officials, saying that all Basques wanted war because it meant prizes, Baudrillart, *Philippe*, 5:50; *Gaceta*, 31 December 1743; Carvajal, *Testamento*, 102; Geoffrey Symcox, *The Crisis of French Sea Power, 1688–97* (Hague: Martinus Nijhoff).

82. Agustín González Enciso, "La Industria en el Reinado de Felip V," in Serrano, *Felipe V*, 1:49–75; Torres Sánchez, "Los navarros," 237–38; Alcalá Zamora, "Producción," 319–20, 360–61.

Chapter Three. Finances

Epigraph: Charles Emanuel III [CEIII] to Ossorio, 26 September 1743, AST, LM Inghilterra/49.

1. Manuel Lobo Cabrera, "La coyuntura económica en tiempos de Felipe V," in Serrano, *Felipe V*, 1:225–40; Earl J. Hamilton, "Money and Economic Recovery in Spain under the First Bourbon, 1701–1746," *Journal of Modern History* 15 (1943): 192–206; Pablo Fernández Albaladejo, "El decreto de suspensión de pagos de 1739: Análisis e implicaciones," *Moneda y Crédito* 142 (1979): 51–85; Ramón Carande, *Carlos V y sus banqueros* (Barcelona: Criiica, 1977); Modesto Ulloa, *La Hacienda Real de Castilla en el reinado de Felipe II* (Madrid: Fundación Universitaria Española, 1977); Antonio Domínguez Ortiz, *Política y Hacienda de Felipe IV* (Madrid: Ediciones Pegaso, 1983); José Antonio Sánchez Belén, *La política fiscal en Castilla durante el reinado de Charles II* (Madrid: Siglo XXI, 1996); Carmen

Sanz Ayan, *Los Banqueros de Charles II* (Valladolid: Universidad de Valladolid, 1988); ibid., *Estado, monarquía y finanzas: Estudios de Historia financiera en tiempos de los Austrias* (Madrid: Centro de Estudios Políticos y Constitucionales, 2004); Renate Pieper, *Die spanischen Kronfinanzen in der zweiten Halfte ds 18. Jahrhunderts (1753–1788): Okonomische und soziale Auswirkungen* (Stuttgart: Franz Steiner Verlag Wiesbaden GMBH, 1988); Kamen, *War;* Jesús Marina Barba, "El Ayuntamiento de Ciudad Real y la presión fiscal durante la Guerra de Sucesión (1700–1715)," *Chronica Nova* 15 (1986–87): 235–87; Enrique Martínez Ruiz, "El cabildo municipal de Granada ante los impuestos estatales durante la guerra de sucesión, 1700–1713," *Chronica Nova* 11 (1980): 269–84.; Julio Caro Baroja, *La Hora Navarra del Siglo XVIII* (Pamplona: Institución Príncipe de Viana, 1969); Hernández Escayola, *Negocio;* Madrazo, *Estado débil.* Federico Mauro, "Moneda y finanzas de España vistas desde Londres (1670–1740)," in Otazu, *Dinero y Crédito,* 173–86, does not go beyond 1720; Comín Comín and Yun Casallila, "Spain, from Composite Monarchy to Nation-State," 233–66, effectively ignores Philip V's reign. Miguel Artola, *La Hacienda del Antiguo Régimen* (Madrid: Alianza, 1983), 224–321, is useful, as is Agustín González Enciso, "A Moderate and Rational Absolutism: Spanish Fiscal Policy in the First Half of the Eighteenth Century," in *War, State and Development: Fiscal-Military States in the Eighteenth Century,* ed. Rafael Torres Sánchez (Pamplona: Ediciones Universidad de Navarra, 2007), 109–32.

2. Ofelia Rey Castelao, "Los estudios sobre fiscalidad en la época moderna: Fenómeno historiográfico real o aparente?," *Obradoiro de Historia Moderna* 13 (2004): 215–52; Andújar Castillo, *Sonido,* 180, 195–97 (for proceeds of sales of military offices in the War of the Austrian Succession by-passing the Tesorería General); Fernández Albaladejo, "Decreto," 67; Jesús Marina Barba, "La Contribución Extraordinaria del Diez por Ciento de las Rentas de 1741," *Chronica Nova* 21 (1993–94): 279–355 (at 314); Ibáñez Molina, "D. José del Campillo ante los Problemas Fiscales," 49–50; Uztáriz, *Theory and Practice of Commerce,* 1:88 (for the difference between the gross value of the *rentas provinciales* of Castile in 1722, 2,624,268,839 maravedís, and their net value, 2,101,255,529); Miguel Angel Melón Jiménez, "Las fronteras de la Monarquía y las aduanas de Felipe V," in Serrano, *Felipe V,* 1:167–99 (appendix, figure 1), for the *rentas generales* for 1739; Orendain to Ezpeleta, 8 November 1725, in Mur i Raurell, *Diplomacia Secreta y Paz,* 1:73–74, for how the different units of account were combined in practice; Hamilton, "Money," 192–206; Javier de Santiago Fernández, *Política Monetaria en Castilla durante el Siglo XVII* (Valladolid: Junta de Castilla y León, 2000), 249–61. Melón Jiménez, "Fronteras," 184–86; S. Aquerreta, "Reforma fiscal," 127; María del Carmen Angulo Teja, *La Hacienda Española en el siglo XVIII: Las rentas provinciales* (Madrid: Centro de Estudios Políticos y Constitucionales, 2002), 203–11.

3. Mauricio Drelichman and Hans-Joachim Voth, *Lending to the Borrower from Hell: Debt, Taxes, and Default in the Age of Philip II* (Princeton: Princeton University Press, 2014), 17; Jurado Sánchez, *Gasto,* and "The Spanish National Budget in a Century of War: The Treasury Impact of Military Spending During the Eighteenth Century," in Torres, *War,*

State and Development, 201–30, use the records of the main accounting body, the Tribunal Mayor de Cuentas. Rosario Porres Marijuán, "Fueros y Sal: Controversias Fiscales entre la provincia de Alava y la Corona durante el período borbónico," *Cuadernos Dieciochescos* 1 (2000): 203–34 (at 239), sets changes in the administration of salt duties in 1740–41 in a context of reform aimed at increasing revenues and fighting fraud but omits to mention that Spain was at war, while Melón Jiménez, "Fronteras," 180, fails to set a radical change in the administration of the customs revenues in 1733–34 (below) in the context of costly military intervention in Italy.

4. Hernández Escayola, *Negocio*, 24; González Enciso, "La Industria,"Serrano, *Felipe V,* 1:55–57; Castro, *A la sombra*, 363; Uztáriz, *Theory and Practice*, 1:90; Madrazo, *Estado débil*, 105–7; R. Torres Sánchez, "Las Prioridades," and El p*recio de la guerra: El Estado fiscal-militar de Carlos III (1779–1783) (Madrid: Marcial Pons, 2013)*, 13–14, 414–19; Martínez Cardós, "Don José del Campillo," 529. For Alberoni's extraordinary measures between 1717 and 1719, see Coxe, *Memoirs of Kings*, 2:287–88; Anne Dubet, "Fernando Verdes Montenegro vs Nicolas de Hinojosa, ou la recherche du parfait Ministre des finances royales dans l'Espagne de Philippe V," in Dubet and Luis, *Les financiers*, 79.

5. Jurado Sánchez, 'Spanish National Budget," 205, and "Military Expenditure, Spending Capacity and Budget Constraint in Eighteenth-Century Spain and Britain," *Revista de Historia Economica / Journal of Iberian and Latin American Economic History* 27 (2009): 141–74; Kamen, *War,* 230; Fernández Albaladejo, "Decreto," 56; and Ozanam, "Notas para un estudio," 58.

6. Earl J. Hamilton, *War and Prices in Spain, 1650–1800* (Cambridge: Harvard University Press, 1943); Kamen, *War,* 371–75, and (for adjusted expenditure figures), Jurado Sánchez, *Gasto,* 37–43, 47–59; Carlos Gómez Centurión Jiménez and Juan Antonio Sánchez Belén, "La Hacienda de la Casa del Rey durante el Reinado de Felipe V," in *La herencia de Borgoña: La hacienda de las Casa Reales durante el reinado de Felipe V,* ed. Carlos Gómez Centurión Jiménez and Juan Antonio Sánchez Belén (Madrid: Centro de Estudios Políticos y Constitucionales, 1998), 11–155 (at 39–41, 61–68), where Don Carlos's expedition to Italy (1731) is included as a royal *jornada*, or expedition; Armstrong, *Elisabeth*, 161–62; Ignacio Vicent López, "Los Baldíos de Palacio," *Espacio, Tiempo y Forma*, ser. 4, *Historia Moderna* 11 (1998): 343–57.

7. Madrazo, *Estado débil*, 104–5, 108; AGS, SSH/ 408; Uztáriz, *Theory*, 1:407; Jurado Sánchez, "Spanish National Budget," 204, and "Military Expenditure," 141–74. Jurado Sánchez largely overlooks the period 1732–37, but his figures reveal it as another period of higher spending. See ibid., *Gasto,* 79, 127, 161–94.

8. D. Jaime Miguel de Guzmán Dávalos Spinola [marqués de la Mina], *Memorias sobre la Guerra de Cerdeña y Sicilia en los años de 1717 a 1720*, 2 vols., ed. Cánovas del Castillo (Madrid, 1898), 2:190. In January 1719 it was calculated that the army in Sicily had cost 305,661 escudos a month between July and October 1718, Estado de lo que Ymporta al mes la Paga . . ., [1719], AGS, SG/Sup/234. Caudal que se supone necesario . . ., [1720], AGS, SG/Sup/480. Relación distinta de los caudales . . ., Alicante, 10 September 1732,

AGS, SG/Sup/484. According to the instructions prepared for the intendant with the Oran expedition, the pay of the troops totalled 226,032 escudos a month, AGS, SG/Sup/484, cl. 6. It was calculated that the 26,212 daily rations of bread for the men and 5,426 rations of barley for the horses would amount to 757,354 reales a month, Estado de las Raciónes . . ., [1732], AGS, SG/Sup/484; Borreguero Beltrán, "Spanish Army," 117. See Campillo to Patiño, 6 March 1734, AGS, SG/2050; Keene to Newcastle, 21 November 1735, Coxe, *Memoirs of Kings,* 3:274; Memorial of junta, July 1737, José Canga Arguelles, *Diccionario de Hacienda,* 2 vols. (Madrid: Imprenta Don Marcelino Calero y Portocarrero, 1833), 2:130–31; Consulta of Junta de Medios, 3 May 1737, AGS, SSH/407. Campillo, Discurso sobre la expedición de Italia [January 1741], AGS, E/3149. This figure, which was well below that for the expeditionary force of 1733, may reflect Campillo's earlier experience in Italy (and his belief that he could on that basis be more thrifty) but also his wish to depict himself as both an efficient financial manager when money was scarce and one who could succeed in Italy. Fernández Albaladejo, "Decreto," 75. See, for the Army of the Infante, 1742–46, Relación Jurada y Cuenta de D. Francisco de la Rea, [1747/1750], AGS, TMC/4475.

9. Jurado Sánchez, "Spanish National Budget," 213, and *Gasto,* 86–90, 173; Muhlmann, *Reorganisation,* 25–31; Kamen, *War,* 229. Somodevilla to Patiño, 26 August 1733, and Noticia del Dinero que ha recivido y pagado . . . Alicante, 9 September 1733, AGS, SM/430/1. Transports, too, were expensive. In 1732 payments for those hired for the Oran expedition totalled more than 21/2 million reales, Contamine to Patiño, 22 August 1732, AGS, SG/Sup/484.

10. Alonso Aguilera, *Conquista,* 114, 119; Keene to Newcastle, 13 March 1734, NA, SP 94/119. For the remittance to Naples of 600,000 pesos for the expedition to Sicily, see Bustanzo to Signori, 14 August 1734, Ciasca, *Istruzioni,* 6:193–95. In October 1735 3 Spanish warships reached Naples carrying 1,800,000 pieces of eight for the new monarch, Fernández Duro, *Armada,* 6:206. In 1740 a British ship captured a Spanish vessel carrying a large sum for Naples, nuncio to cardinal Secretary of State, 31 July 1740, AHN, E/libro 1026.

11. Hochedlinger, *Austria's Wars,* 200; Coxe, *Memoirs of Kings,* 3: 152–53, 235–36, 274; Coxe, *Memoirs of Walpole,* 1:244, 251; Townshend to Newcastle 4 October 1725, ibid., 2:480–84; James F. Chance, *The Alliance of Hanover: A Study of British Foreign Policy in the Last Years of George I* (London: John Murray, 1923), 135, 319; Quenta y Distribución de la Cantidad de 130,000 Hungaros . . ., 1734, AGS, SSH/2/805; Philip also appears to have promised a subsidy to the elector of Bavaria at this time, Villarias to Verdes Montenegro, 25 November 1740, AGS, SSH/3/180, while money was subsequently also sent to Russia.

12. Borré to CEIII, 18 January and 14 and 19 April 1734, AST, LM Spagna/66; Villarias to Ensenada, 15 June 1744, AGS, SSH/4/59; Armstrong, *Elisabeth,* 327; Ensenada to Rebollar, 24 June 1744, in Accounts of Gordillo, AGS, TMC/4458, "Gastos Secretos." According to Ensenada's exposition of the state of the finances of 1748 and of possible reforms, Don Carlos's subsidy was paid to enable him to put 15,000 men in the field,

Rodríguez Villa, *Ensenada*, 91–94; AST, Negoziazioni Spagna/8/12. The elector was also promised an advance to be offset against 1 million écus promised in 1727 as compensation for his losses in the War of the Spanish Succession. His subsidy was later increased by 50 percent, to 12,000 livres a month, Baudrillart, *Philippe*, 5:56; Campoflorido to Villarias, 23 August 1746, AHN, E/3383; Grimaldi to Signori, 4 January 1746, Ciasca, *Istruzioni*, 7:36–39; Portago to Ensenada, 22 January 1746, AGS, SSH/4/384. In 1746 Philip agreed to pay the elector of Saxony a subsidy of 800,000 *libras* (or 3,200,000 reales), but a formal treaty was not concluded before Philip's death, Ozanam, *Diplomacia*, 142, 227; Clive Parry, The *Consolidated Treaty Series* (New York: Oxford University Press, 1969–), 32:353–56; Bustanzo to Signori, 8 March 1746, Ciasca, *Istruzioni*, 7:67–72; Instructions for Giovanni Battista De Mari, Genoa, 14 January 1747, and for Domenico Pallavicino, Genoa, 15 April 1747, Ciasca, *Istruzioni*, 7:119–24, 140–50; Ensenada to Huéscar, 31 July 1747, in Ozanam, *Diplomacia*, 216; Ozanam, *Diplomacia*, 230; Mina to Huéscar, 16 March and 7 April 1747, AHN, E/4103.

13. Antonio Domínguez Ortiz, *Política Fiscal y Cambio Social en la España del Siglo XVII* (Madrid: Instituto de Estudios Fiscales, 1984), 62; José Ignacio Andrés Ucendo and Ramón Lanza García, "Estructura y Evolución de los Ingresos de la Real Hacienda de Castilla en el Siglo XVII," *Studia Historica, Historia Moderna* 30 (2008): 147–90; Tomás García-Cuenca Ariati, "El Consejo de Hacienda (1476–1803): Los origenes, establecimiento y afianzamiento de la institución," in *La Economía española al final del Antiguo Régimen: Investigaciones*, vol. 4: *Instituciones*, ed. Miguel Artola (Madrid: Alianza, 1982), 405–502, and Jean Paul Dedieu and J. I. Ruíz, "Tres momentos en la historia de la Real Hacienda (1640–1800)," *Cuadernos de Historia Moderna* 15 (1994): 77–98; Madrazo, *Estado débil*, 38. From at least 1721, when Campoflorido was appointed secretary of state, that office was held with those of superintendente and governor of the council, Pérez Fernández-Turégano, *Patiño y las Reformas*, 187; Anne Dubet, "La nueva política crediticia de la Corona a principios del siglo XVIII: La creación del Tesorero Mayor de Guerra en España (1703–1706)," *Studia Historica, Historia Moderna* 30 (2008): 191–216; Rafael Torres Sánchez, *La llave de todos los tesoros: La Tesorería General de Charles III* (Madrid: Silex, 2012), 28–32 and passim for the rise of this agency and many other aspects of financial administration before the reign of Charles III. Madrazo, *Estado débil*, 32–33, outlines the functions and structure of the Treasury General in 1724; Hordenana to Ensenada, 3 November 1745, AGS, SG/436; Informazione sopra il Sussidio, ed Escusado, che si domanda dal Re di Spagna nelle Indie [no date but late 1716], ASV Fondo Albani/104, f. 182ff.; Hernández Escayola, *Negocio*, 189–209; Rosario Porres Marijuán, "Las contribuciones vascas a la hacienda real en la Edad Moderna: Algunos contrastes provinciales," *Obradoiro de Historia Moderna* 19 (2010): 87–124, for the Basque territories.

14. Kamen, *War*, 199–212, 223–35; Angulo Teja, *Hacienda*, 29–45; González Enciso, "Moderate," 111–13; Martínez-Radío Garrido, *Guerra de Sucesión y Asturias*, 248–66; Concepción Camarero Bullón, *El debate de la Unica Contribución: Catastrar las Castillas* (Madrid: Tabapress, 1993), 7–97; and Guillaume Hanotin, *Jean Orry, un homme des finances royales entre*

France et Espagne (1701–1705) (Córdoba: Universidad de Córdoba, 2009), 82–94; Melón Jiménez, "Fronteras" and "Hacienda," for the customs; Escobedo Romero, *Tabaco del rey;* Armstrong, *Elisabeth,* 272; Kamen, *Philip,* 129–30; Fernández Albaladejo, "Decreto," 53.

15. Jurado Sánchez, *Gasto,* 53–54; González Enciso, "Moderate," 127; Fernández Albaladejo, "Decreto," 54–56, 77–78; and Artola, *Hacienda,* 312. According to Jurado Sánchez, *Gasto,* 53, the yield of the royal revenues peaked at over 210 million reales in 1736 and 1737 (in the War of the Polish Succession), slightly more than the net figure in the table sent by the British minister in Madrid for 1737, and at more than 285 million in 1741. According to García-Lombardero, "Algunos problemas," 83, revenues (excluding those from the Indies and the clergy) rose from just under 196 million reales to just over 285 million in 1741; Etates des rentes . . ., Mur i Raurell, *Diplomacia Secreta y Paz,* 2:367; Revenus Annuels du Roy d'Espagne [1737], sent with Trevor to [?], 18 March 1738, NA, SP/94/130.b., Domínguez Ortiz, *Sociedad y Estado,* 73, and Delgado Barrado, *Aquiles y Teseos,* 97. According to the budget for 1724 (which omitted revenues from the Indies), gross revenues totalled just over 180 million reales, Madrazo, *Estado débil,* 104–5; Artola, *Hacienda,* 311, for ecclesiastical revenues yielding just over 18 million reales in 1737. The table referred to above also omits a total of just over 17 million reales in the list itself. Seville contributed 16 percent and Granada 11 percent of the net yield of the rentas provinciales between 1730 and 1742, Angulo Teja, *Hacienda,* chapter 5, figure 1, distribución porcentual del valor líquido de las rentas provinciales, 1730–1742 (CD-ROM). See also Alejandra Irigoin and Regina Grafe, "Bargaining for Absolutism: A Spanish Path to Nation-State and Empire Building," *Hispanic American Historical Review* 88 (2008): 180–81. Importe de los Fondos de la Corona en este año de 1737 . . ., AGS, SSH/407; Canga Arguelles, *Diccionario,* 2:120.

16. Patrick O'Brien, "Contentions of the Purse Between England and Its European Rivals from Henry V to George IV: A Conversation with Michael Mann," *Journal of Historical Sociology* 19 (2006): 341–63; Torres Sánchez, "Possibilities," 446; Dedieu and Ruiz, "Tres momentos," 97. Granada's rentas provinciales had been taken into administration in 1746, Artola, *Hacienda,* 260.

17. Thomson, *War and Government,* 67–100 and passim; Storrs, *Resilience,* 106–18; Angulo Teja, *Hacienda,* 44, 66; Kamen, *War,* 233–34; Artola, *Hacienda,* 254–55; Castro, *A la sombra,* 293–97; Carmen Sanz Ayan, *Estado, monarquía y finanzas. Estudios de Historia financiera en tiempos de los Austrias* (Madrid: Centro de Estudios Políticos y Constitucionales, 2004), 115–21 (for the farm of various revenues in 1700). García-Lombardero, "Algunos problemas," 60–62, lists all farmers of the rentas provinciales between 1714 and 1749.

18. Fernández Albaladejo, "Decreto," 51–52, 57, 64, and passim; Angulo Teja, *Hacienda,* 44; Artola, *Hacienda,* 310; González Enciso, "Moderate," 125–30; Escobedo Romero, *Tabaco del rey,* 21–22, 41; García-Lombardero, "Algunos problemas," 76–77, 82; Palmira Fonseca Cuevas, *Un Hacendista Asturiano: José Canga Arguelles* (Oviedo: Real Instituto de Estudios Asturianos, 1994–95), 404–5. In Seville yields rose the most, by 48 percent, in Córdoba the least, by 25 percent. For Toledo, see Angulo Teja, *Hacienda,* chapter 6,

figure 1 (CD-ROM) Valores por mayor de las rentas reales, los millones y las rentas provinciales en los distintos partidos del reino de Toledo, y porcentajes de los mismos respecto del total de rentas provinciales de este, 1742–1784; Delgado Barrado, *Aquiles y Teseos*, 118–35, for the debate about farming within the administration in the 1720s; Escobedo Romero, *Tabaco del rey*, 41; Aquerreta, "Reforma fiscal," 121–22.

19. Castro, *A la sombra*, 81; Uztáriz, *Theory*, 1:276; García-Lombardero, "Algunos problemas," 85–87. In 1746 the rentas provinciales of Palencia were farmed, as before 1741, Angulo Teja, *Hacienda*, 68. Avila, whose yield was among the lowest, was farmed throughout, the yield hardly varying between 1730 and 1742; the benefit to the royal finances of taking the province into administration after 1749 was just under 2 million maravedís (almost 600,000 reales). This suggests that in 1741 the crown assumed the administration in provinces whose yield it expected to be able to increase; Ibáñez Molina, "José del Campillo," 50. Between 1743 and 1748 the yield of the farm of the wool tax fell slightly, to 7,700,000 million reales a year. See also Phillips and Phillips, *Spain's Golden Fleece*, 264–67.

20. Borré to CEIII, 7 September 1733, AST, LM Spagna/65; Uztáriz, *Theory*, 1:276–75; Melón Jiménez, "Fronteras," 180, and "Hacienda," 47; Borré to CEIII, 15 February 1734, AST, LM Spagna/66; Artola, *Hacienda*, 258; Parker to Newcastle, 10 August 1745 and 15 January 1746, NA, SP 89/45 f. 43, 73.

21. Pérez Fernández-Turégano, *Patiño y las Reformas*, 190; for the reign of Charles II, see Storrs, *Resilience*, 119–20; Hernández Escayola, *Negocio*, 160; Melón Jiménez, "Hacienda," 43–45; Escobedo Romero, *Tabaco del rey*, 186–92 (table of cases) and 272–91; Keene to Newcastle, Madrid, 15 April 1737, NA, SP 94/127; Valguarnera to Ormea, 6 November 1741, AST, LM Spagna/ 70 (for Campillo's circularising foreign ministers in Madrid to combat tobacco fraud); Cremades Griñan, *Economía y hacienda local*, 134; Artola, *Hacienda*, 293–94 (in 1737 the stamped paper duty was said to yield 2,220,000 reales annually); Miguel Angel Melón Jiménez, "Carvajal y la Real Compañía de Comercio y Fábricas de Extremadura," in *Ministros de Fernando VI*, ed. José M. Delgado Barrado and José L. Gómez Urdáñez (Córdoba: Universidad de Córdoba, 2002), 233–50.

22. Ricardo Franch Benavent, "La nueva fiscalidad implantada en los territorios de la Corona de Aragón," *Norba* 16 (1996–2003): 525–42; Guillerrmo Pérez Sarrión, "El Nacimiento de la Contribución Directa en España: La Política de la Puesta en Marcha de la Real Contribución en Aragón," in Serrano, *Felipe V*, 2:405–47. See also Angulo Teja, *Hacienda*, 49, and Artola, *Hacienda*, 231–35; Angulo Teja, *Hacienda*, 48–50; Albareda Salvado, "Felipe," 102–5; Agustí Alcoberro i Pericay, "El cadastre de Catalunya (1715–1845) de la imposició a la fosilització," *Pedralbes* 25 (2005): 231–58; Winder to Castres, 2 February 1737, NA, SP/ 94/127; Arvillars to CEIII, 2 February 1731, AST, LM Spagna/63; Arvillars to CEIII, 3 October 1732, AST, LM Spagna/64; Keene to Newcastle, 19 May 1733, NA, SP/94, 116; Miguel Artola, *Antiguo Régimen y revolución liberal* (Barcelona: Ariel, 1978), 111–12; Fernández Albaladejo, "Decreto," 54–55; Uztáriz, *Theory and Practice*, 1:88–89; and for 1724, Madrazo, *Estado débil*, 104; González Enciso, "Moderate," 113–14.

23. For a recent restatement of the distinctiveness and significance of this royal resource, see Drelichman and Voth, *Lending to the Borrower*, 85–89; González Enciso, "Moderate," 128–30. In Peru the royal fifth averaged more than 500,000 pesos between 1726 and 1736, Adrian J. Pearce, "Huancavelica 1700–1759: Administrative Reform of the Mercury Industry in Early Bourbon Peru," *Hispanic American Historical Review* 79 (1999): 669–702 (at 674); Madrazo, *Estado débil*, 104–5; preamble to Philip V's order for an increase in the duty on cacao, 17 September 1720, AHN, Hacienda/libro 8011.

24. Peter Bakewell, *A History of Latin America* (Oxford: Blackwell, 1997), 257–58, Fisher, *Bourbon Peru*, 12–13, 21; Stein and Stein, *Silver, Trade, and War*, 189–90, 231–32; Pedro Pérez Herrero, "América colonial española (1698–1754)," in Delgado Barrado and Gómez Urdáñez, *Ministros de Fernando VI*, 297. Carlos Marichal and Matilde Souto Mantecón, "Silver and *Situados:* New Spain and the Financing of the Spanish Empire in the Caribbean in the Eighteenth Century," *Hispanic American Historical Review* 74 (1994): 587–613; Williams, *Prize*, xvii–xviii. Walker, *Spanish Politics*, 107–10, 228–29; Antonio García-Baquero González, "El Comercio Colonial en la Epoca de Felipe V: El Reformismo Continuista," in Serrano, *Felipe V*, 1:75–102; Allen J. Kuethe, "The Colonial Commercial Policy of Philip V and the Atlantic World," in *Latin America and the Atlantic World / El mundo atlántico y América Latina (1500–1850): Essays in Honour of Horst Pietschmann)*, ed. Renate Pieper and Peer Schmidt (Cologne: Bohlau, 2005), 319–33. A *flota* was prepared for 1739, but its departure was prevented by the outbreak of war.

25. In 1726 the galleons were said to be returning with cargoes worth 25 million dollars, half of which belonged to Philip or his subjects, while the flota was said to be carrying registered gold and silver and commodities worth more than 15 million dollars and another 1 million unregistered, Chance, *Alliance of Hanover*, 237. For the arrival at Cádiz of *azogues* carrying 2 million pesos for the king, Bustanzo to Signori, 10 September 1732, Ciasca, *Istruzioni*, 6:163–64; Arvillars to CEIII, 12 September 1732, AST, LM Spagna/64; Walker, *Spanish Politics*, 4–5; Stein and Stein, *Silver, Trade, and War*, 191–92. For the sale, for 500,000 pesos, of a licence for 5 register ships to go to Indies, see Valguarnera to CEIII, 6 March 1741, AST, LM Spagna/70; Lynch, *Bourbon Spain*, 155; Pearce, "Huancavelica," 696; Parker to Newcastle, 30 January 1745, encl. Account of the Registred Money.... NA, SP 89/45 f. 7. The total registered value of the cargo was almost 9 million dollars, but it was believed that the two Spanish ships, *Glorioso* and *Castilla*, which carried the king's share, and three French ships also carried between them more than 1 million unregistered dollars; Fernández Duro, *Armada*, 6:306; Parker to Newcastle, 22 January [?] 1746, NA, SP 89/45 f. 77; Carvajal to Huéscar, 27 March 1747, Ozanam, *Diplomacia*, 167–68.

26. In December 1720 Baltasar de Guevara reached Cádiz with a cargo valued at 12 million pesos, of which just 21/2 million represented Philip's share, *Gaceta*, 1720, number 51. In September 1732 ships arrived with 2 million piastres for the king and 1 million for private owners, Arvillars to CEIII, 12 September 1732, AST, LM Spagna/64. For the difficulties—by no means new—in distinguishing the two categories, Antonio Domínguez Ortiz, "Las remesas de metales preciosos de Indias, 1621–1665," in ibid., *Estudios americani-*

stas (Madrid: Real Academia de la Historia, 1998), 167–91 (at 169); Kuethe, "Colonial," 329; Coxe, *Memoirs of Kings*, 3:217; Baudrillart, *Philippe*, 3:532, 578–79; Bustanzo to Signori, 27 March 1734, Ciasca, *Istruzioni*, 6:188; Keene to Newcastle, 12 August, 2 September, and 11 November 1737, NA, SP 94/128. According to the last, Philip did this at the queen's insistence; Keene to Newcastle, 11 November 1737, NA, SP 94/128, and 13 January 1738, NA, SP/94/130. For efforts to extract more, see Pérez Fernández-Turégano, *Patiño y las Reformas*, 190; Keene to Newcastle, 3 February 1738, NA, SP 94/130.

27. Bustanzo to Signori, 15 August 1731, Ciasca, *Istruzioni*, 6:149–52; Borré to CEIII, 17 August 1733, AST, LM Spagna/65; Kuethe and Blaisdell, "French Influence," 585–88; Víctor Peralta Ruiz, *Patrones, clientes y amigos: El poder burocrático indiano en la España del siglo XVIII* (Madrid: CSIC, 2006), 58; Valguarnera to CEIII, 6 November 1741, AST, LM, Spagna/70; Encarnación Rodríguez Vicente, "Los Cargadores a Indias y su contribución a los gastos de la Monarquía, 1555–1750," *Anuario de Estudios Americanos* 34 (1977): 211–32. In the summer of 1745 Philip ordered the despatch to Madrid of what was received from America, for onward remittance to Italy, Parker to Newcastle, Porto, 10 August 1745, NA, SP 89/45 f. 43.

28. Lynch, *Bourbon Spain*, 58, 155, 357; González Enciso, "Moderate," 129; for fluctuating sums remitted from New Spain from 1720, Marichal and Souto Mantecón, "Silver," 590–91, 612; Domínguez Ortiz, "Remesas" 167–68; Arvillas to CEIII, 20 and 27 June 1732, AST, LM Spagna/64; Borré to CEIII, 21 September 1733, AST, LM Spagna/65; Borré to CEIII, 15 March 1734, AST, LM Spagna/66; Keene to Newcastle, 13 March 1734, NA, SP 94/119; Patiño to Campillo, 26 June and 16 and 22 July 1734, AGS, SG/2050; Noticia del caudal remitido de quenta de SM a D. Miguel Fermin de Granja Thesorero del Extto de Italia . . ., BN, MSS/12950/23; Ignacio González Casasnovas, *Las Dudas de la Corona: La política de repartimientos para la minería de Potosí (1680–1732)* (Madrid: CSIC, 2000), 429; Fisher, *Bourbon Peru*, 13–14, for the *nuevo impuesto* in Peru, imposed in 1739 and withdrawn in 1752.

29. Stanhope to Newcastle, 30 October 1726, NA, SP 94/95; Stanhope to Townshend, 27 December 1725, Coxe, *Memoirs of Walpole*, 2:547; same to Newcastle, 11 April 1726, ibid., 2:590–97. According to Coxe, *Memoirs of Walpole*, 2:228–29, Philip would have remitted to Vienna more money than he did if the galleons had arrived in time; Campillo y Cossio, *Nuevo sistema de gobierno económico para la América*, extracts from which are in *Early Modern Spain: A Documentary History*, ed. John Cowans (Philadelphia: University of Pennsylvania Press, 2003), 217–24. For the War of the Spanish Succession, see Stein and Stein, *Silver, Trade, and War*, 232–35, and for specific remittances to the army in Italy of sums received from the Indies, totalling almost 35 million reales, AGS, TMC/4475, Primer pliego/188, 189, 190, 193. For the crucial importance of the revenues of the Indies in framing cycles of royal finance and attitudes to credit under Charles III, see Torres Sánchez, *Precio de la guerra*, 412–19; Felices de la Fuente, *Nueva nobleza*, 260, 458; Gerald B. Hertz, "England and the Ostend Company," *English Historical Review* 22 (1907): 255–79. For (unsubstantiated) reports that, to fund operations in Italy in the War of the Austrian

Succession, a Genoese company had been formed to advance funds to the Spanish court in return for permission to trade with the Indies until it had recovered its loan, see Valguarnera to CEIII, 15 January 1742, AST, LM Spagna/70.

30. Jean Nicolas, *La Savoie au 18e siècle: Noblesse et Bourgeoisie*, 2 vols. (Paris: Maloine, 1978), 2:558–59; Revel, "La Savoie et la domination espagnole," 103–245; Primer pliego, AGS, TMC/4475, no. 34; Ensenada to Campillo, 2 February 1743, AGS, SG/2117; royal provision, 27 July 1734, AHN, Consejos, libro 1477 f. 220. See the appeal of D. Gregorio de Fuerte, 1735, in AHN, Consejos, libro 2789, f. 425. On embargoes, although it deals with an earlier era, see also Angel Alloza Aparicio, *Europa en el Mercado Espanol: Mercaderes, represalias y contrabando en el siglo XVII* (Valladolid: Junta de Castilla y León, 2006); Hamilton, "Money," 195.

31. Philip V's order, Pardo, 9 April 1737, AGS, SSH/407; Espejo de Hinojosa, "Enumeración y atribuciones," 336; Fernández Albaladejo, "Decreto," 655; Castellano, *Gobierno y poder*, 114; Delgado Barrado, *Aquiles y Teseos*, 90–99, for the papers of the junta, gathered by its secretary, Alejandro de la Vega, and 201–2; Keene to Newcastle, Madrid, 15 April 1737, NA, SP 94/127; Ibáñez Molina, "D. José del Campillo," 45; Andújar Castillo, *Sonido*, 175–77; Canga Arguelles, *Diccionario*, 2:20, 125–35. Andújar Castillo, *Sonido*, 176–77; Marina Barba, "Contribución," 281; Castellano, *Gobierno y poder*, 117.

32. In 1741 Moya Torres y Velasco oversaw the implementation of the equivalent of the 10 percent levy in the province of Avila, Marina Barba, "Contribución," 309; consulta of council of Castile, 21 January 1741, BN, MSS/10,684 f. 410ff.

33. Storrs, *Resilience*, 122–24, for venality under Charles II; for the War of the Spanish Succession, Francisco Andújar Castillo, *Necesidad y venalidad: España e Indias, 1704–1711* (Madrid: Centro de Estudios Políticos y Constitucionales, 2008); in 1732 Juan Crisóstomo Bonaria paid 120,000 reales for the office of *contador mayor de cuentas* in the Council of Finance, Castellano, *Gobierno y poder*, 121; Dedieu and Ruiz, "Tres momentos," 89; Andújar Castillo, *Sonido*, 175; Mark A. Burkholder and D. S. Chandler, "Creole Appointments and the Sale of Audiencia Positions in the Spanish Empire under the Early Bourbons, 1701–1750," *Journal of Latin American Studies* 4 (1972): 192–99; Félix Salgado Olmeda, "Tipología social de una oligarquía urbana: Los regidores de Guadalajara en el siglo XVIII, Elite nobiliaria o burguesía funcionaria?," *Hispania* 62 (2002): 703; consulta, 5 September 1738, AGS, SG/5459; Helen Nader, *Liberty in Absolutist Spain: The Habsburg Sale of Towns, 1516–1700* (Baltimore: Johns Hopkins University Press, 1990), largely ignores Bourbon policy, but the records of the Cámara de Castilla reveal numerous sales in this period, suggesting that Nader's list of Bourbon exemptions, 222, is incomplete, AHN, Consejos/4494 (1733), expedientes 4, 8, 21, 22, 29, 56 and AHN/Consejos/4497 (1736); expedientes 28, 55, 68, 70; and Consejos/4503 (1741), expediente 39; Chance, *Alliance of Hanover*, 458.

34. Atienza Hernández, *Aristocracia, poder y riqueza*, 38; Storrs, *Resilience*, 127; García-Cuenca Ariati, "Consejo," 452; Kamen, *War*, 217, 224, 383; Adolfo Carrasco, *El Poder de la Sangre: Los Duques del Infantado* (Madrid: Actas, 2009), 110, 431–32, for the implications for

one grandee family; Espejo de Hinojosa, "Enumeración y atribuciones," 345; Borré to CEIII, 26 December 1732, AST, LM Spagna/64; Ignacio M. Vicent López, "La Junta de Incorporación: Lealtad y propiedad en la monarquía borbónica," in *Antiguo Régimen y liberalismo. Homenaje a Miguel Artola,* 3 vols., ed. Pablo Fernández Albaladejo and M. Ortega López, 3:365–78 (Madrid: Alianza Editorial, 1995). According to the list of alienated percentage increases in the *alcabala* imposed from 1623 and prepared in 1740, in José López Juana Pinilla, *Biblioteca de Hacienda de España,* 6 vols. (Madrid: Aguado, 1840–48), 2:194–212, a handful had been alienated since 1700. For the duchess of Alba, see consulta of D. Pedro Díaz de Mendoza, 8 November 1746, AGS, SSH/98.

35. Storrs, *Resilience,* 121–22, for the pursuit of arrears under Charles II; Francisco Gallardo Fernández, *Origen . . . de las rentas de la corona de España, su gobierno y administración,* 6 vols. (Madrid: Imprenta Real, 1805–34), 1:89. This work and Juan de la Ripia, *Práctica de la Administración y Cobranza de las Rentas Reales,* 6 vols. (Madrid: D. Antonio Ulloa, 1796–1805), are invaluable compendia of orders regarding all revenues; Canga Arguelles, *Diccionario,* 2:19, 125 (among the first suggestions of the junta of 1737 was that Philip exact the arrears, almost 4 million escudos, of the *lanzas* tax paid by titled nobles on their succession); Cuenca-García Ariati "Consejo," 468; Angulo Teja, *Hacienda,* 378; Cremades Griñan, *Economía y hacienda local,* 341 (Murcia), Marina Barba, "Contribución," 289, 307 (Granada). On the *contribución de paja,* see Pio Pita Pizarro, *Examen económico, histórico-crítico de la hacienda y deuda del Estado* (Madrid: Imprenta de Narciso Sanchez, 1840), 208.

36. Cremades Griñan, *Economía y hacienda local,* 341. On arbitrios, see Carmen García García, *La Crisis de las Haciendas Locales: De la reforma administrativa a la reforma fiscal (1743–1845)* (Valladolid: Junta de Castilla y León, 1996), 33–34; session of ayuntamiento of Murcia, 30 April 1720, AMM, AC/1732, f. 51. The previous year Burgos, too, secured permission to apply the proceeds of an arbitrio to pay its quota (36,000 reales) of the *donativo,* AMB, LA/1719, ff. 158–60.

37. Royal order of 31 January 1734, Portugués, *Colección,* 7:25–48 (at 35–36), 84–123 (at 98–99); order to intendentes, corregidores, and superintendentes, July 1734, AHN, Consejos, libro 1477 f. 222; Cremades Griñan, *Economía y hacienda local,* 341. In some respects this echoed practice in the War of the Spanish Succession, Andújar, *Necesidad,* 26; council minutes, 23 December 1734, AMB, LA/1734 f. 245; sessions of ayuntamiento of Murcia, 17 and 19 May, 19 June and 10 July 1734, AMM, AC/1734, f. 125ff., 151, 170ff. In 1742 the city funded the formation of a body of militia from the yield of an arbitrio on wine sales, Cremades Griñan, *Economía y hacienda local,* 256; Artaza, *Rey,* 310–12; David Vassberg, *Land and Society in Golden Age Castile,* (Cambridge: Cambridge University Press, 1984), 21–6; Jesús Marina Barba, *Poder municipal y reforma en Granada durante el siglo XVIII* (Granada: Universidad de Granada, 1992), 207–10.

38. García García, *Crisis,* 131–35 (with a list of the total paid throughout Spain), 178. Angulo Teja, *Hacienda,* 39; Marina Barba, "Contribución," 281; Antonio Garcia-Baquero González, ed., *Cádiz 1753, Según las Respuestas Generales del Catastro de Ensenada* (Madrid: Tabapress, 1990), 83–84; Carmen García García, "Reformismo y Contrareformismo: El

Consejo de Castilla y la Administración de las Rentas Municipales (1740–1824)," in Fernández Albaladejo and Ortega López, *Antiguo Régimen y liberalismo*, 3: 121–42 (at 124–25); Marina Barba, *Poder municipal*, 219–35, 249–50. In February 1745 Philip had reformed the administration of these revenues in order to enhance their yield and his half share. Later that same year he exempted all arbitrios which were applied to military purposes from *valimientos*, Portugués, *Colección*, 7:256. Some exemptions were granted, but inevitably arrears accumulated.

39. Dominguez Ortiz, *Sociedad y Estado*, 73–75; Vassberg, *Land*, 172–76, Dominguez Ortiz, *Política Fiscal*, 213–15.; Andújar, *Necesidad*, 27; cardinal Molina [governor of Council of Castile] to [?], 27 September 1738, AHN, E/298.; D. Xavier Cubero to [?], [1738], encl. Relación de méritos/servicios, AHN, E/2981; Espejo de Hinojosa, "Enumeración," 325–62; García García, *Crisis*, 131, 179–80; Philip V's order of 8 October 1738, noted in the consulta of the Council of Castile, 18 September 1747, following a formal representation against the measure by the Diputación of the realm, AHN, Consejos, libro 1018. Artola, *Antiguo Régimen*, 129, mentions the policy but fails to set it in the context of the war.

40. Vicent López, "Baldíos," 343–57; Dominguez Ortiz, *Sociedad*, 74–75; Dominguez Ortiz, "Ventas de Tierras Baldías . . .," in *Política* (1984), 229–30; Laura Santolaya Heredero, "El Señorío Concejil de la Ciudad de Toledo a mediados del siglo XVIII," in Fernández Albaladejo and Ortega López, *Antiguo Régimen y liberalismo*, 339–49; José María Alcalde Jiménez, *El Poder del Señorío: Señorío y poderes locales en Soria entre el Antiguo Régimen y el Liberalismo* (Valladolid: Junta de Castilla y León, 1997), 224–34, and Emilio Pérez Romero, *Patrimonios Comunales, Ganadería Trashumante y Sociedad en la Tierra de Soria siglos XVIII–XIX* (Valladolid: Junta de Castilla y León, 1995), 275–77, for the junta's activity in the province of Soria, and García García, *Crisis*, 179–86, for Valladolid; consulta of the Council of Finance, 26 February 1744, AGS, SSH/98; Ensenada to Ventura Guella, August 1745, AGS, SG/2158; royal order, 18 October 1747, NLS, Astorga, G.31.c.1 f. 218–21; AMB/1749 f.; Atienza Hernández, *Aristocracia, poder y riqueza*, 139–44, for the impact on the dukes of Osuna (Andalusia). For Atienza Hernández the baldíos policy reflected a fundamental shift in crown policy whereas I see it as a temporary wartime expedient.

41. Mauro Hernández, "El desembarco de los nuevos mesteños en Extremadura: La venta de la dehesa de La Serena y las transformaciones de la trashumancia, 1744–1770," *Historia Agraria* 27 (2002): 65–100. To Angel García Sanz, *Desarrollo y crisis del Antiguo Régimen en Castilla la Vieja* (Madrid: Akal, 1986), 153, the reversal of policy on the sale of baldíos represented a successful counterattack by sheep owners.

42. García García, *Crisis*, 132. Marina Barba, "Contribución," 315–16, prints the decree; Artola, *Hacienda*, 252–53; Dominguez Ortiz, *Sociedad*, 75–76. The decree was accompanied by efforts at Rome to secure permission to impose it on ecclesiastical incomes, Grimaldi to Signori, 16 January 1741, Ciasca, *Istruzioni*, 6:256–58; Marina Barba, "Contribución," 285 and (table of original quotas) 332. The province of Burgos was assigned a quota of almost 23/4 million reales, and the city 7,241,347 maravedís (almost 213,000 reales), Campillo to corregidor of Burgos, 23 May 1741, Aranjuez, AMB, LA/1741

f. 329ff. Canga Arguelles, *Diccionario*, 2:20. For an abortive suggestion a century earlier to levy 5 percent on incomes, see Dominguez Ortiz, *Política Fiscal*, 90–93; Marina Barba, "Contribución," 286; Cremades Griñan, *Economía y hacienda local*, 343, 351. Jose Ruíz de Celada, *Estado de la bolsa de Madrid: Examen de sus tributos, cargas y medios de su extinción, de su gobierno y reforma* (Valladolid, 1775), ed. Bartolomé Yun Casalilla (Valladolid: Universidad de Valladolid, 1990), 166; García García, *Crisis*, 132; José A. Martín Fuertes, *Fondo Histórico del Archivo Municipal de Astorga: Catálogo* (León: Institución "Fray Bernardino de Sahagún," 1981), 109.

43. For the despatch of executors to press payment in Granada, see Marina Barba, "Contribución," 308–9.

44. For Granada, see Marina Barba, "Contribución," 282, 305.

45. Angulo Teja, *Hacienda*, 37–38; see the (unsuccessful) request of D. Juan Hispano for payment of a pension of less than 100 doblones a year, which went unpaid between 1718 and 1728, AGS, SSH/407; Storrs, *Resilience*, 129–34; Martínez Ruiz, "Cabildo municipal," 272–75; Castro, *A la sombra*, 286, 288; Dominguez Ortiz, *Sociedad y Estado*, 69; García García, *Crisis*, 118; Castro, *A la sombra*, 350; José Antonio Longo Marina, "El Real Donativo de 1719," *Boletín de Letras del Real Instituto de Estudios Asturianos* 62 (2008): 177–90. Donors often secured a *merced* in return, García García, *Crisis*, 39 (an annual fair); council meeting of 19 May 1719, AMB, LA/1719, f. 133ff. The royal facultad, of 20 June 1719, is at ibid., f. 159. In 1741 the Council of Castile proposed, among its alternatives to the 10 percent levy, demanding a donativo from all those who had, directly or indirectly, farmed the taxes since Philip's accession, Canga Arguelles, *Diccionario*, 2:20.

46. Kamen, *War*, 216; Marina Barba, "Ayuntamiento," 262; Uztáriz, *Theory and Practice*, 1:85; Carmen María Cremades Griñan, "Las Salinas como fuente de riqueza fiscal en el siglo XVIII," in VV.AA. (various authors), *Coloquio Internacional Charles III y su Siglo*, 2 vols. (Madrid: Universidad Complutense, 1990), 2:877–93. For the various prorogations, see Martínez-Radío Garrido, *Guerra*, 302–13; orders of 15 December 1740 and 15 December 1742, AHN, Mo Hacienda/libro 8014 f. 182, 526; Marina Barba, "Contribución," 281; Angulo Teja, *Hacienda*, 35; Royal order, 2 December 1749 (halving the increase), NLS, Astorga, G. 31. C. 1 f. 246; Marina Barba, "Contribución," 281; Order of 12 November 1743, AHN, Hacienda, libro 8015 f. 96; consulta of Cámara de Castilla, 12 January 1733, AHN, Consejos/4494/63; consulta of Junta de Medios, 22 April 1737, AGS, SSH/407. Individual petitions to be allowed to redeem the obligation provide invaluable data on property ownership and the size and condition of buildings in Madrid: see AHN, Consejos/4503 (1741), expediente 18.

47. Hernández Escayola, *Negocio*, 290–91; AGS, TMC/4475, Primer pliego/143; José Andrés-Gallego, El *Motín de Esquilache, América y Europa* (Madrid: CSIC, 2003), 160. Clearly, some bargaining went on, new privileges being granted, ibid., 174.

48. It is no coincidence that the summer of 1717 saw the settlement of a long-running quarrel with Rome, with the prorogation of the ordinary ecclesiastical revenues plus an additional subsidy from the clergy for five years, intended to fund the struggle against the

Moors, Maximiliano Barrio Gozalo, "El Cardenal Alberoni y España: Política Religiosa y Carrera Eclesiástica," *Hispania Sacra* 63 (2011): 205–34 (at 219); king to Comissary General of the Cruzada, 23 August 1721, AGS, Cruzada/521. For an earlier grant of this sort, to enable Charles II to expel Protestant Scots from the Indies, see Christopher Storrs, "Disaster at Darien (1698–1700)? The Persistence of Spanish Imperial Power on the Eve of the Demise of the Spanish Habsburgs," *European History Quarterly* 29 (1999): 5–38; Giuseppe Caridi, "Dall'investitura al Concordato: Contrasti giurisdizionali tra Napoli e Santa Sede nei primi anni del regno di Carlo di Borbone," *Mediterranea Ricerche Storiche* 23 (2011): 525–60 (at 551); Fernández Albaladejo, "Decreto," 69; consulta of Junta de Hacienda, 7 April 1740, AGS, SSH/397; Delgado Barrado, *Aquiles y Teseos,* 201, 204; Parker to Newcastle, 28 May 1746, NA, SP 89/45 f. 108; Real Instrucción, 24 October 1745.

49. Concepción de Castro, *El Pan de Madrid: El abasto de las ciudades españoles del Antiguo Régimen* (Madrid: Alianza 1987), 116–17, and J. Rodríguez Labandeira, "La política económica de los Borbones," in Artola, *Economía española,* 4:107–83 (at 146), for one example of tax remssion (1737); Marcos Martín, *España en los Siglos XVI, XVII y XVIII,* 552–706, and Lobo Cabrera, "Coyuntura"; Martínez Shaw and Alfonso Mola, *Felipe,* 242; García García, *Crisis,* 16, 116–17.

50. Kamen, *War,* 224. Pilar Toboso Sánchez, *La Deuda Pública Castellana durante el Antiguo Régimen (Juros)* (Madrid: Instituto de Estudios Fiscales, 1987), 291, and Artola, *Hacienda,* 313–14, give different figures; Carlos Álvarez-Nogal, "La Demanda de Juros en Castilla en Edad Moderna: Los Juros de Alcabalas en Murcia," *Studia Historica, Historia Moderna* 32 (2010): 47–82, and *Oferta y Demanda de Deuda Pública en Castilla: Juros de Alcabalas (1540–1740)* (Madrid, 2009), http://www.bde.es/f/webbde/SES/Secciones/Publicaciones/PublicacionesSeriadas/EstudiosHistoriaEconomica/Fic/roja55.pdf; and Torres Sánchez, *Precio de la guerra,* 285–93; Artola, *Hacienda,* 313; Toboso Sánchez, *Deuda,* 181, 221–24, 228–31; García-Cuenca Ariati, "Consejo," 458; Stein and Stein, *Silver, Trade, and War,* 51, 203; Madrazo, *Estado débil,* 110; González Enciso, "Moderate," 123; Artola, *Hacienda,* 314–15; Ana María Carabias Torres and Claudia Moller Recondo, "Denuncias, pesquisas y reformas municipales en Peñaranda de Bracamonte (1746), *Norba* 16 (1996–2003): 543–63 (at 560); Jurado Sánchez, *Gasto,* 91–94 (different figures but revealing a similar broad trend), 175; Carrasco, *Poder,* 460–61, for the juros of the dukes of Infantado.

51. Carmen Sanz Ayan, "La recuperación de rentas reales enajenadas en el reinado de Charles III," in *Coloquio Internacional Charles III y su Siglo,* 2:871–76; Order, 7 July 1742, AHN, Mo Hacienda, libro 8014 f. 448; *Colección legislativa de la Deuda pública de España,* (Madrid: Imprenta Nacional, 1863), 9:245–46, for a specific order for the application of the decree, regarding a contract for the supply of the African presidios in the 1680s, November 1743; González Enciso, "Moderate," 124; Toboso Sánchez, *Deuda,* 231–35, 262, and (for an agreement whereby one juro holder was bought out in 1749), 322–26; Artola, *Hacienda,* 316; Jurado Sánchez, *Gasto,* 91; Rey Castelao, *Tuy 1753,* 66. Political influences might determine whether to pay or not: in 1748 Ensenada thought the only means of putting pressure on the Genoese was to withhold their juro payments, Ensenada to Huéscar,

25 November 1748, Ozanam and Téllez Alarcia, *Misión*, 537–38. (As late as 1730, Genoese held almost 30 percent of the amount situated on the alcabalas of Murcia, Álvarez Nogal, "Demanda," 60, 79).

52. Chance, *Alliance of Hanover*, 319; Ibáñez Molina, "José del Campillo," 51; Larruga, *Memorias políticas y económicas*, 1:215–20;? to Villarias, 18–19 March 1741, AGS, SSH/3/241. In 1741 the Cinco Gremios also oversaw Madrid's contribution to the equivalent for the 10 percent levy, Marina Barba, "Contribución," 286, and in 1744 farmed Madrid's rentas provinciales, García Lombardero, "Algunos problemas," 70.

53. Torres Sánchez, *Precio de la guerra*, 293–305; González Enciso, "Moderate," 124; Jurado Sánchez, "Military Expenditure," 153. Despite Charles III's efforts, 91 million reales remained owing in 1794.

54. González Enciso, "Empresarios navarros," 185; Borreguero Beltrán, "Spanish Army," 119–20; Andújar Castillo, *Sonido*, 180; Andújar Castillo, "La Situación Salarial," 87–109; Muhlmann, *Reorganisation*, 25–28; Martínez Valverde, "Campaña," 11; consultas of Council of Castile, 26 April 1730, 18 February 1732, 27 September 1733, and 23 May 1736, AHN, Consejos, libro 1018, f. 312, 318, 322, 323. Dominguez Ortiz, *Sociedad*, 72, 75–76; Arvillars to CEIII, 28 January 1732, AST, LM Spagna/64; Keene to Newcastle, 13 January 1738, NA, SP 94/130; Gómez Centurión Jiménez and Sánchez Belén, " "Hacienda de la Casa," passim. For the appeals to and decisions of the Junta de Medios, see AGS, SSH/407–409.

55. Skinner to Newcastle, 3 April and January 1733, NA, SP 98/34; Monasterolo to CEIII, 19 January 1741 and 2 January 1742, AST, LM Napoli/8. During the War of the Polish Succession a Milanese banker in Madrid seeking repayment of sums he had advanced to the emperor on the strength of letters of change drawn on him by Madrid bankers was suspected of conducting secret negotiations between Vienna and the Spanish court, Borré to CEIII, 4 January 1734, AST, LM Spagna/66. By December 1744 Philip owed the elector of Bavaria (Charles VII) six quarterly payments of his subsidy, Baudrillart, *Philippe*, 5:263; Huéscar to Carvajal, 4 September 1747, Ozanam, *Diplomacia*, 226–27.

56. Kamen, *War*, 71; Torres Sánchez, "Los navarros," passim; Henry Kamen, *Spain in the Later Seventeenth Century, 1665–1700* (London: Longman, 1980), 369–72; Garcia Lombardero, "Algunos problemas," 86; Artola, *Hacienda*, 248; Jean-Pierre Dedieu, "Les groupes financiers et industriels au service dul roi—Espagne Fin XVIIe–debut XVIIIe siècle," in Dubet and Luis, *Les financiers*, 87–104; Aquerreta, "Reforma fiscal," 127; Teran, a *regidor* of Madrid, exemplified the way financiers penetrated the royal administration, Felices de la Fuente, *Nueva nobleza*, 226, 456; Castro, *A la sombra*, 87, 141; Ibáñez Molina, "José del Campillo," 50; Felices de la Fuente, *Nueva nobleza*, 453, which gives other examples.

57. Castro, *A la sombra*, 65; Carmen Sanz Ayán, "La evolución de los suspensos de pagos en el siglo XVII: Concepto y utilidad," in ibid., *Estado, monarquía y finanzas*, 39–64; Stanhope to Townshend, 25 March 1726, Coxe, *Memoirs of Walpole*, 2:588–90. Ripperda

claimed later that the bankruptcy of 1726 was intended to prevent the emperor from opening hostilities before the return of the flota from the Indies; Canga Arguelles, *Diccionario,* 2:19–20; Fernández Albaladejo, "Decreto," 51–56; Bustanzo to Signori, 4 April 1739, Ciasca, *Istruzione,* 6:244–46; consulta of Council of Finance, 7 March 1740, AHN, E, libro 798; consulta of Junta de Hacienda, 29 May 1740, AGS, SSH/397.

58. Jurado Sánchez, "Military Expenditure," 157, gives an annual average of 17.72 million reales, representing 8.56 percent for 1731–40; Fernández Albaladejo, "Decreto," 67, 75. For Philip's debt after 1748, see Rafael Torres Sánchez, "Las Prioridades," 432, and "Seguro de hombres y auxilio de reyes: El fondo vitalicio y la Real Hacienda en el reinado de Carlos III," *Obradoiro de Historia Moderna,* 15 (2006): 139–72 (at 148), and (for a donativo levied in 1764–65 to pay this and other obligations), Andrés-Gallego, *El Motín de Esquilache,* 159–60.

59. [Ensenada?] to Aviles, 25 January 1744, AGS, SG/2138; Arvillars to CEIII, 30 May 1732, AST, LM Spagna/64; Arpe to Patiño, 9 February 1734, AGS, E/5511; Patiño to Campillo, 26 February 1734, and Campillo to Patiño, 6 March 1734, AGS, SG/2050; Noticia del caudal remitido . . . . a D. Miguel Fermín de Granja Thesorero del Extto de Italia . . ., BN, MSS/12950/23; Valguarnera to CEIII, 15 January 1742, AST, LM Spagna/70; [Ensenada?] to Aviles, 25 January 1744, AGS, SG/2138. This included 240,000 escudos in the form of *plata doble* and 160,000 in gold. Specie amounting to perhaps a further 150,000 escudos was to be collected in Zaragoza and Barcelona en route.

60. John Sperling, "The International Payments Mechanism in the Seventeenth and Eighteenth Centuries," *Economic History Review* (1962): 446–68; Exercito de Sicilia, Caudales que se han remitido para su subsistencia . . ., AGS, SG/Sup/234. On leaving for Barcelona in May 1718, the treasurer, D. Esteban Joséph de Abaria, received 154,035 escudos in cash from the treasurer general; between June 1718 and January 1719 he received twenty-five letters, payable at Genoa, Livorno, Florence, and Rome, to a value of 335,000 doblones, or just over 2 million reales. See also Estado de lo q importa al mes . . . [October 1718], AGS, SG/Sup/234. Between January and July 1719 ten letters worth just over 22,000 doblones (or 1,320,000 reales) and payable at Genoa were sent to Porto Longone, Razón del Estado en que se halla el Presidio . . ., 21 July 1719, AGS, SG/Sup/234. In the autumn of 1733 the treasurer general, the marqués de Valbueno, remitted to the Treasury of the Army of Italy six letters of change, all dated 26 October, for a total of 40,000 doblones, or just over 3 million reales, Thesoreria del Ex.to de Italia. Resumen del cargo . . . y gastos . . ., Perugia, 1 March 1734, AGS, SG/2050; Birtles to Newcastle, 3 and 31 January 1742, NA, SP 79/19; AGS, TMC/4475, Primer pliego/170, 187, 216. In January 1746 nineteen letters were sent to Paris to pay Charles Edward Stuart's monthly subsidy (160,200 reales) for February, Portago to Ensenada, 22 January 1746, Ensenada to Villarias, 24 January 1746, AGS, SSH/4/384, 385.

61. Estado de las Letras que estan remitidas a D. Francisco de Varas . . ., [1720?], AGS, SG/Sup/480; Madrazo, *Estado débil,* 74–75, 136, 81–82; Artola, *Hacienda,* 317. The *asentista* was also allowed to export specie. During that same conflict, the intendant of the navy,

Ensenada, paid commissions of between 8 and 24 percent, Stein and Stein, *Silver, Trade, and War,* 248; Skinner to Walpole, 21 January 1735, BL, Add 73987 f. [?]; Ensenada to Treasurer General, 5 March 1744, AGS, SG/2131; De Mari to Signori, 14 February 1747, Ciasca, *Istruzioni,* 7:126–28.

62. Valladares de Sotomayor, *Semanario Erudito,* 27:123; Artola, *Hacienda,* 317–18; Fernández Albaladejo, "Decreto," 79; Cristina González Caizán, "El Primer Círculo de Hechuras Zenónicas," in Delgado Barrado and Gómez Urdáñez, *Ministros de Fernando VI,* 175–202 (at 194–95); Ildefonso Pulido Bueno, *El Real Giro de España: Primer proyecto de banco nacional* (Huelva: Universidad de Huelva, 1994); José L. Gómez Urdáñez, *El proyecto reformista de Ensenada* (Lleida: Editorial Milenio, 1996), 190–92; Torres Sánchez, *Llave,* 143–45; Guillermo Pérez Sarrión, "Intereses financieros y nacionalismo: La pugna entre banqueros españoles y franceses en Madrid, 1766–1796," *Cuadernos de Historia Moderna, Anejos* 7 (2008): 31–72 (at 39–41); Canga Arguelles, *Diccionario,* 1:572.

63. Ensenada to Huéscar, 12 February 1748, Ozanam and Téllez Alarcia, *Misión,* 381; Rodríguez Labandeira, "Política económica," 138; Castro, *A la sombra,* 109–10; Huéscar to Ensenada, 13 November 1747, Ozanam and Téllez Alarcia, *Misión,* 341, lauding Ensenada for funding the war without imposing new burdens on Fedinand VI's subjects; Jurado Sánchez, "Military Expenditure," 166–67; Torres Sánchez, *Precio de la guerra,* 13–20, 25–30, 131–39. Dedieu and Ruiz, "Tres momentos," 96–97, suggest important continuities after 1748, while Angulo Teja, *Hacienda,* 25, discusses the appropriateness of the term *system.*

Chapter Four. Government and Politics

Epigraph: Alberoni to count Rocca, 1 October 1714, in *Lettres intimes d'Alberoni addressées au comte J. Rocca,* ed. Emile Bourgeois (Paris: Masson, 1892), 342.

1. García Cárcel, *Felipe V,* 140–45; Giménez López, "Marte y Astrea en la Corona de Aragón," 2:67–89; Madrazo, *Estado débil,* 145; Arvillars to Victor Amadeus, Madrid, 30 August 1728, AST, LM Spagna/60, for earlier suggestions that Don Carlos might be appointed grand master of the four Military Orders (Alcantara, Calatrava, Montesa, and Santiago) with their revenues, even that he be given the Crown (and territories) of Aragon; Muñoz Rodríguez, *Séptima Corona,* passim, for the succession conflict as a turning point in the achievement of "absolutism," associated with a new "discourse" of loyalty and alliance between crown and local elites.

2. Joel Cornette, *Le Roi de Guerre: Essai sur la souveraineté dans la France du Grand Siècle* (Paris: Petite Bibliotheque Payot, 2000); García Cárcel, *Felipe V,* 135, for Philip as the "consort of his wife"; Baudrillart, *Philippe,* 4:460, for the instructions of the French ambassador in Madrid, 1738; Armstrong, *Elisabeth,* 390.

3. Baudrillart, *Philippe,* 1:passim; Baudrillart, *Philippe,* 2:554–56 (for Philip's conception of government, as revealed in his advice to his son Luis on his own abdication in 1724), 564–65; Baudrillart, Philippe, 3:179, 416; González Cruz, *Propaganda e información;* Muñoz Rodríguez, *Séptima Corona;* Baudrillart, *Philippe,* 3:40; Jean-Pierre Dedieu, "El aparato de

gobierno de la Monarquía española en el siglo XVIII," in Pérez Sarrión, *Más Estado y más mercado*, 53–73, L. Martinez Peñas, *El confesor del rey en el Antiguo Régimen* (Madrid, 2007); Castro, *A la sombra*, 303; Martínez Shaw and Alfonso Mola, *Felipe*, 102.

4. Nuncio to Secretary of State, Madrid, 5 June 1734, ASV, SS, Spagna/244, f. 56; consulta of Junta de Hacienda, 29 May 1740, Aranjuez, and Verdes Montenegro to [Villarias], Madrid, 17 June 1740, AGS/SSH/397.

5. Martínez Shaw and Alfonso Mola, *Felipe*, 103–10; Carlos Gómez Centurión Jiménez, "La Corte de Felipe V: El Ceremonial y las Casas Reales durante el Reinado del primer Borbón," in Serrano, *Felipe V,* 1:879–914; Castro, *A la sombra*, 378; Castellano, *Gobierno y Poder*, 107; Bethencourt Massieu, *Relaciones de España*, 147; Pérez Samper, *Isabel de Farnesio,* 111; Armstrong, *Elisabeth*, 259–60; Keene to Newcastle, 1 August 1733, in Coxe, *Memoirs of Kings*, 3:233–34; *Sevilla y Corte: Las Artes y el Lustro Real (1729–33)*, ed. Nicolás Morales and Fernando Quiles García (Madrid: Casa de Velázquez, 2010).

6. Stanhope to Townshend, 11 April 1726, Coxe, *Memoirs of Walpole*, 2:590–97 (at 592); the instructions prepared for successive Savoyard ministers to London, AST, Negoziazioni, Inghilterra/8; Niccolò Erizzo, *Relazione del n.u. Niccolò III Erizzo* (Venice: Alvisopoli, 1840), passim; Bartolini to Senate, 9 February 1745, Tonetti, *Corrispondenze*, 17:599–601; Miguel Martín, "The Secret Clause, Britain and Spanish Ambitions in Italy, 1712–1731," *European Studies Review* 7 (1976): 407–25, 413; Ilaria Zilli, *Carlo di Borbone e la rinascita del regno di Napoli: Le finanze pubbliche, 1734–1742* (Naples: Edizioni Scientifiche Italiane, 1990), 23; Baudrillart, *Philippe,* 4:28–29; ibid., 4:306–7; Peralta Ruiz, *Patrones, clientes y amigos,* 77; Jacques Soubeyroux, "Torres Villarroel entre Salamanca y Madrid: Acerca de las Relaciones de Don Diego de Torres con la Corte," in Delgado Barrado and Gómez Urdáñez, *Ministros de Fernando VI*, 206–7.

7. Ibáñez Molina, "D. José del Campillo ante los Problemas Fiscales," 47–68.

8. Charles C. Noel, "'Barbara succeeds Elisabeth ...': The Feminisation and Domestication of Politics in the Spanish Monarchy, 1701–59," in *Queenship in Europe, 1660–1815: The Role of the Consort*, ed. Clarissa Campbell Orr (Cambridge: Cambridge University Press, 2004), 155–85; Baudrillart, *Philippe*, 3:579. Surprisingly, Theresa Ann Smith, *The Emerging Female Citizen: Gender and Enlightenment in Spain* (Berkeley and Los Angeles: University of California Press, 2006), ignores the background presence of Isabel Farnese in discussing this period.

9. Baudrillart, *Philippe*, 2:398–99, for Alberoni's criticisms, among the most damning and most frequently repeated, made after his disgrace; Pablo Vázquez Gestal, *Una Nueva Majestad: Felipe V, Isabel de Farnesio y la identidad de la monarquía (1700–1729)* (Madrid: Marcial Pons, 2013), 179–85; treaty on the trade privileges of British subjects, December 1715, AHN, Consejos/12515 (for titles used by Philip after 1713–14); Martínez Shaw and Alfonso Mola, *Felipe,* 69–70; Reflexiones sobre el tratado que se han propuesto al Rey de España (1718), AHN, E/3381; Baudrillart, *Philippe,* 4:147; Martín, "Secret," 407–8. The opportunities offered by Isabel's Italian claims may have made her more attractive, Martínez Shaw and Alfonso Mola, *Felipe*, 96; Baudrillart, *Philippe*, 4:130–31, for the explanation of the

preparations for the Oran expedition given to the French ambassador by Isabel and Philip in 1732; Kamen, *Philip*, 111; Martínez Shaw and Alfonso Mola, *Felipe*, 147–48, 153.

10. Baudrillart, *Philippe*, 3:201–3; Stanhope to Townshend, Madrid, 25 March 1726, Coxe, *Memoirs of Walpole*, 2:588–90.

11. Baudrillart, *Philippe*, 2:214; Alberoni to count Rocca, in Bourgeois, *Lettres intimes d'Alberoni*, 585–88.

12. Antonio Álvarez-Ossorio Alvariño, "De la plenitud territorial a una prolongada agonia: El Consejo de Italia durante el reinado de Felipe V," in *Famiglie, nazioni e monarchia: Il sistema europeo durante la Guerra de Successione spagnola*, ed. Antonio Álvarez-Ossorio Alvariño (Rome: Bulzoni, 2003), 305–85 (at 305–8); Inmaculada Arias de Saavedra, "Los colegiales en la alta administración española (1701–1808)," in Castellano, *Sociedad, Administración y Poder*, 77–109 (at 84), for suppression of the Council of Flanders in 1702; Riol, Informe q hizo a Su Magestad, 16 June 1726, in Valladares de Sotomayor, *Semanario Erudito*, 13:153; Castellano, *Gobierno y Poder*, 76–77, 106, 129.

13. Castro, *A la sombra*, 11–25, Castellano, *Gobierno y Poder*, 17–34, 85–86; Baudrillart, *Philippe*, 1:566, 602.

14. Castro, *A la sombra*, 320; Gloria A. Franco Rubio, "La Secretaría de Estado y del Despacho de Guerra en la primera mitad del siglo XVIII," in Castellano, *Sociedad, Administración y Poder*, 131–56; BN, MSS/12950/26, for the working of the secretariat; king to [?], [June 1742], AGS/GM/767 f. 74, for the reform of the office of the secretary of state for war, largely to cut costs, against the background of war, Andújar Castillo, *Consejo*, 211–12, 277–78, for the careers of Uztáriz and Gordillo y Sánchez; Virginia León Sanz, "De Rey de España a Emperador de Austria: El archiduque Carlos y los austracistas españoles," in Serrano, *Felipe V*, 1:762; Espejo de Hinojosa, "Enumeración y atribuciones," 325–62; Delgado Barrado, *Aquiles y Teseos*, 90–105.

15. Anne Dubet, "La Importación de un modelo francés? Acerca de algunas reformas de la administración española a principios del siglo XVIII," *Revista de Historia Moderna* 25 (2007): 207–33; María del Mar Felices de la Fuente, "La Càmara de Castilla, el rey y la creación de títulos nobiliarios en la primera mitad del siglo XVIII," *Hispania* 70/236 (2010): 661–86; Delgado Barrado, *Testamento político*, 8; Baudrillart, *Philippe*, 5:67–68.

16. Gómez Centurión Jiménez, "La Corte de Felipe V," 879–914; Martínez Shaw and Alfonso Mola, *Felipe*, 105, 160; Glyn Redworth and Fernando Checa, "The Courts of the Spanish Habsburgs 1500–1700," in *The Princely Courts of Europe, 1500–1750*, ed. John Adamson (London: Seven Dials, 2000), 43–65; C. Désos, *Les Francais de Philippe V: Un modele nouveau pour gouverner l'Espagne (1700–1746)* (Strasbourg: Presses de l'Université de Strasbourg, 2009).

17. Stanhope to Townshend, Madrid, 27 December 1725, Coxe, *Memoirs of Walpole*, 2:547; Armstrong, *Elisabeth*, 170; Castro, *A la sombra*, 333, 347. Isabel Farnese apparently approved the move; Pere Molas Ribalta, "Carvajal y la administración española," in Delgado Barrado and Gómez Urdáñez, *Ministros de Fernando VI*, 8; Baudrillart, *Philippe*, 5:67–68, for the rather authoritarian Campillo trespassing on the spheres of his colleagues.

18. Francisco Tomás y Valiente, *Los Validos en la Monarquía Espanola del siglo XVII* (Madrid: Siglo XXI, 1982); Patrick Williams, *The Great Favourite: The Duke of Lerma and the Court and Government of Philip III of Spain, 1598–1621* (Manchester: Manchester University Press, 2006), 2–3, 265–68; Armstrong, *Elisabeth*, 45–46, 101, 107, 121, 135, 146, 294, 328, 333; Castellano, *Gobierno y Poder*, 90–91; Keene to Newcastle, Madrid, 29 August 1738, NA, SP 94/131; Pérez Samper, *Isabel*, 254–55. Arvillars to king Victor Amadeus I of Sardinia, Madrid, 16 August 1728, AST, LM Spagna/60; Baudrillart, *Philippe*, 4:146, 151, 160–61; Baudrillart, *Philippe*, 5:43–44,; *The World of the Favourite*, ed. J. H. Elliott and L. W. B. Brockliss (New Haven: Yale University Press, 1999); Borré to CEIII, 2 January 1733, AST, LM Spagna/65; Keene to Newcastle, 9 January 1733, NA, SP 94/116.

19. Castellano, *Gobierno y Poder*, 55, 85–91, 99, 101, 240–45; Andújar Castillo, *Sonido*, 188; María Victoria López Cordón Cortezo, "Cambio social y poder administrativo en la España del siglo XVIII: Las Secretarías de Estado y del Despacho," in *Sociedad, Administración y Poder*, ed. Castellano, 111–30; Juan Luis Castellano, "La carrera burocrática en la España del siglo XVIII," in *Sociedad, Administración y Poder*, ed. Castellano, 25–45; Castro, *A la sombra*, 316–17, 352–53, 356–58; Armstrong, *Elisabeth*, 36; Baudrillart, *Philippe*, 2:425–26 and 3:41–42, for the pen portraits given by St Simon and Tessé, and 5:67–68, for tensions between Uztáriz and Montemar that weakened the effectiveness of the secretariat; Martínez Shaw and Afonso Mola, *Felipe*, 224; Mur i Raurell, *Diplomacia Secreta y Paz*, 1:480, for a decree of January 1726 inviting all who felt aggrieved by any council to have recourse to Ripperda; Bethencourt, *Relaciones de España*, 135–36, 166, 224; Molas Ribalta, "Carvajal y la administración"; Keene to Newcastle, 1 April 1737, NA, SP 94/127, and 27 January 1738, NA, SP 94/130; Molas, "Carvajal y la administración," 10, for Carvajal's relationship with Villarias in 1746–47, and 14, for the expansion of the Junta de Comercio y Moneda at the expense of other bodies under Carvajal; Jacques A. Barbier, "The Culmination of the Bourbon Reforms, 1787–1792," *Hispanic American Historical Review* 57 (1977): 51–68 (at 55): Valguarnera to CEIII, 14 November 1740, AST, LM Spagna/69.

20. Ricardo Gómez-Rivero, "Consejeros de la Suprema de Felipe V," *Revista de la Inquisición* 4 (1995): 133–75; Andújar Castillo, *Consejo*; Carvajal, *Testamento*, 73–74; Elena Postigo Castellanos, "Monarca frente a *Maestre* o las órdenes militares en el proyecto político de la nueva dinastía: Los Decretos de 1714 y 1728," in Fernández Albaladejo and Ortega López, *Antiguo Régimen*, 3:309–18; Dedieu and Ruíz Rodríguez, "Tres momentos," 92; Gildas Bernard, *Le Secretariat d'Etat et le Conseil espagnol des Indes (1700–1808)* (Geneva: Droz, 1972); Martínez Shaw and Alfonso Mola, *Felipe*, 228–30; Portugués, *Colección*, 7:131–32; order for codification, April 1746, NLS, Astorga G. 31.c.1 f. 210; Juan Carlos Domínguez Nafría, "De la monarquía universal al centralismo borbónico," in *Spagna e Mezzogiorno d'Italia nell'età della transizióne: Stato, Fianze ed Economia (1650–1760)*, 2 vols., ed. Luigi De Rosa and Luis Miguel Enciso Recio (Naples: Edizioni Scientifiche Italiane, 1997), 1:361–82.

21. Janine Fayard, *Les Membres du Conseil de Castille a l'epoque moderne (1621–1746)* (Geneva: Droz, 1979), 1–30; María Isabel Cabrera Bosch, "El poder legislativo en la España del siglo XVIII (1716–1808)," in Artola, *Economía española*, 4:185–267.

22. Arvillars to CEIII, 13 June 1732, AST, LM Spagna/64; Patiño to [Comisario General of the Cruzada?], 18 June 1732, AGS, Cruzada/520; Campo-Raso, *Memorias*, 382–83; García García, *Crisis de las Haciendas Locales*, 124, 155, 168–70; Artola, *Hacienda en el Antiguo Régimen*, 263 (1745); Ruth Mackay, *The Limits of Royal Authority: Resistance and Obedience in Seventeenth-Century Castile* (Cambridge: Cambridge University Press, 1999); Juan Luis Castellano, *Las Cortes de Castilla y su Diputación (1621–1789): Entre Pactismo y Absolutismo* (Madrid: Centro de Estudios Constitucionales, 1990), 151–52; Bustanzo to Signori, Madrid, 11 September 1728, in Ciasca, *Istruzioni*, 6:130–32.

23. José Antonio Pujol Aguado, "España en Cerdeña (1717–1720)," *Studia Historica, Historia Moderna* 13 (1995): 191–214; AHN, E, libro 361 f. 101.

24. Fayard, *Membres*, 161–63, 159–61; Baudrillart, *Philippe*, 3:20–21, 30–31, 34, 43, 115; Baudrillart, *Philippe*, 4:149–50, 441; Keene to Newcastle, 15 April 1737, SP 94/127; Borré to CEIII, Seville, 6 July 1733, AST, LM Spagna/65.

25. Kamen, "Establecimiento de los intendentes," 368–95; Abbad and Ozanam, *Intendants*, 5–32, 62; and A. Dubet, "Los intendentes y la tentativa de reorganización del control financiero en España, 1718–1720," in Pérez Sarrión, *Más Estado y más mercado*, 103–36; Javier María Donézar Díez de Ulzurrun, *Riqueza y propiedad en la Castilla del Antiguo Régimen: La provincia de Toledo en el siglo XVIII* (Madrid: Instituto de Estudios Agrarios, Pesqueros y Alimentarios, 1984), 38; Benjamin González Alonso, *El Corregidor Castellano (1348–1808)* (Madrid: Instituto de Estudios Administrativos, 1970), remains the best broad study but is too general; Cremades Griñan, *Economía y hacienda local*, 33–40, for a local perspective; Martínez Shaw and Alfonso Mola, *Felipe*, 231; James Casey, *Family and Community in Early Modern Spain: The Citizens of Granada, 1570–1739* (Cambridge: Cambridge University Press, 2007), 25, 29–30; María López Díaz, "Reformismo borbónico y gobierno municipal (las regidurías compostelanas, siglo XVIII)," *Obradoiro de Historia Moderna* 15 (2006): 205–37; Castro, *A la sombra*, 106, 111–13.

26. AMB, LA/1741, f. 374; AMB, LA/1745, f.55; *Gaceta*, 14 January 1744; Abbad and Ozanam, *Intendants*, 108; *Gaceta*, 3 March 1744, for the appointment of a swathe of corregidores in 1744; Calvo Maturana, *Cuando manden*, 67–78, for ministerial concern to appoint able men as corregidor after 1749.

27. J. H. Parry, *The Spanish Seaborne Empire* (Harmondsworth: Penguin Books, 1966), 190–95; Tamar Herzog, *Upholding Justice: Society, State, and the Penal System in Quito (1650–1750)* (Ann Arbor: University of Michigan Press, 2004), 43–57; Fayard, *Membres*, 70–78; Storrs, *Resilience*, 183–84; Garrigós Picó, "Organización," 28.; AMV, LA/1734, f. 220; Marina Barba, "Contribución," 294–97.

28. Domenico Carutti, "Relazioni sulla Corte di Spagna dell'Abate Doria del Maro e del conte Lascaris di Castellar, ministro di Savoia," *Memorie della Reale Accademia delle Scienze di Torino*, ser. 2, 19 (1861): 139–40; Castellano, *Gobierno y Poder*, 104–6. Erizzo, *Relazione*, 43–45, the Venetian ambassador emphasising in his end- of-mission report (1730) the importance in Patiño's rise of his performance during the Sicilian expedition of 1718 on the Spanish court; Resumen de el Origen, Vida y Muerte. . . . Campillo, BN, MSS/8290 f. 298ff.; Martínez Cardós, "Don José del Campillo."

29. Peralta Ruiz, *Patrones, clientes y amigos*, 76; Murdo J. MacLeod, "Self-Promotion: The "Relaciones de méritos y servicios" and Their Historical and Political Interpretation," *Colonial Latin American Historical Review* 7 (1998): 25–42; petition, [post-1720], AGS, Gracia/804; consulta, on petition, [August 1746], AGS, SSH/98.

30. Carvajal to Huéscar, 14 January 1747, Ozanam, *Diplomacia*, 123–24; José Luis Gómez Urdáñez, *Fernando VI (Madrid: Arlanza Ediciones, 2001)*, 49; Rafael Guerrero Elecalde, "El partido vizcaino y los representantes del rey en el extranjero: Redes de poder, clientelismo y política exterior durante el reinado de Felipe V," in Agustín Guimerá Ravina and Victor Peralta Ruiz, eds., *El Equilibrio de los Imperios de Utrecht y Trafalgar* (Madrid: Fundación Española de Historia Moderna, 2005), 85–98; Pere Molas Ribalta, *Edad Moderna, 1474–1808* (Madrid: Espasa Calpe, 1989), 465; Peralta Ruiz, *Patrones, clientes y amigos*, 99; Pedro Luis Lorenzo Cadarso, "Los grupos cortesanos: Propuestas teóricas," in Delgado Barrado and Gómez Urdáñez, *Ministros de Fernando VI*, 141–55; Mur i Raurell, *Diplomacia Secreta y Paz*, 1:24–31. Andújar Castillo, *Sonido*, 121–22, Cornejo to Villarias, Genoa, 24 March 1743, AGS, E/5557 and 2 December 1743, AGS, E/5558; Rafael Valladares, *La Rebelión de Portugal 1640–1680: Guerra, conflicto y poderes en la monarquía hispánica* (Valladolid: Junta de Castilla y León, 1998), 298–99.

31. Pere Molas Ribalta, *Del Absolutismo a la Constitución: La adaptación de la clase política española al cambio de régimen* (Madrid: Silex, 2008); Marisa Linton, "Fatal Friendships: The Politics of Jacobin Friendship," *French Historical Studies* 31 (2008): 51–76; Martínez Cardós, "José del Campillo"; Martínez Shaw and Alfonso Mola, *Felipe*, 225; Abbad and Ozanam, *Intendants*, 175; Peralta Ruiz, *Patrones, clientes y amigos*, 115–17, 128; Cristina González Caizán, "El primer círculo de hechuras zenónicas," in Delgado Barrado and Gómez Urdáñez, *Ministros de Fernando VI*, 175–203. Ordeñana's son was *comisario* with the naval squadron at Toulon in 1744.

32. Castellano, *Gobierno y Poder*, 96, 98, 104; Armstrong, *Elisabeth*, 207–8; Ripperda to Philip, 31 July 1725, in Mur i Raurell, *Diplomacia Secreta y Paz*, 2:119.

33. Castellano, *Gobierno y Poder*, 96, 98, 104; Armstrong, *Elisabeth*, 207–8; Ripperda to Philip, 31 July 1725, in Mur i Raurell, *Diplomacia Secreta y Paz*, 2:119; Arvillars to CEIII, 18 May 1731, AST, LM Spagna/63; Valguarnera to CEIII, 16 October 1741, AST, LM Spagna/69; Baudrillart, *Philippe*, 5:30, 42–43, 67–68.

34. Campo-Raso, *Memorias*, 4, 168–70; Teófanes Egido López, *Opinión pública y oposición al poder en la España del siglo XVIII (1713–1759)*, 2d ed. (Valladolid: Universidad de Valladolid, 2002), 192–93, 300.

35. Storrs, *Resilience*, 175–82; Castellano, *Cortes de Castilla*, 184–88; Artaza, *Rey*, 310–12; Dedieu, "Dinastía," 381–99; Poyntz to [?], 26 October 1728, NA, SP 78/188/2 f. 330; MacKay, *Limits*, passim.

36. Castellano, *Cortes de Castilla*, 52–59, 85–112, 117–20, 141–68, 172–82, 184; Stanhope to Carteret, Madrid, 16 and 31 January 1724, in Historical Manuscripts Commission, Report on the Manuscripts of lord *Polwarth, 5 vols.* (London: HMSO, 1911–61), 4:1–2, 10. Since Castilian monarchs, neither Habsburg nor Bourbon, were not crowned, the crucial

act or ceremony on the accession of a new king—Philip V in 1700, Luis I in 1724, and Ferdinand VI in 1746—was the public proclamation, generally before the *ayuntamiento* in Madrid (and various provincial capitals), accompanied by the raising of the royal standard and followed by the acclamation of the new sovereign by the assembled crowd.

37. Castellano, *Cortes de Castilla*, 113–39, 178; Martínez-Radío Garrido, *Guerra de Sucesión*, 92–93; A. del Cantillo, *Tratados, Convenios y Declaraciones de Paz . . . desde el año de 1700 . . .* (Madrid: Alegría y Charlain, 1843), 233.

38. Kamen, *War*, 239–40; consultas of Cámara, 2 and 4 September 1715, AHN, Consejos/4478/57; AMV, LA/76, f. 91ff, 97ff.; consulta of Cámara, 31 March 1718, AHN, Consejos/4481/21. AMV, LA/76 ff. 513ff, 528ff.; consulta of Cámara, [1721], AHN, Consejos/4483/29; AMV, LA/78, f. 42ff, 47ff.

39. Consulta of Cámara, 7 January 1722, AHN, Consejos/4484/1; consulta of Junta de Asistentes de Cortes, 16 and 23 March 1722, AHN, Consejos/4484/22; royal order (*cédula*) of 24 March 1722, AGS, DGT/Inv. 24 (legajo 648), no. 81; Artaza, *Rey*, 359, for Galicia.

40. Royal cédula extending the millones, June 1716, in Pinilla, *Biblioteca de Hacienda*, 2:150–53; royal letter to city of Burgos, 1728, AMB, LA/1728 f. 107–10; royal cédula, 5 October 1733, AMB, LA/1733, f; Philip V to city of Valladolid, 29 September 1739, BNM, MSS/11,281 f. 397–8; AMB, LA/1741 f. 160; royal cédula, 21 September 1745, AMB, LA/1745, f. 206–8.

41. Burgos council session, 11 March 1728, AMB, LA/1728 f. 107ff., AMB, LA/1745 ff. 206ff; sessions of the ayuntamiento of Murcia, 17 and 19 October 1733, AMM, LA/1733, f. 294ff., and 9 October 1745, AMM, LA/1745, f. 294ff; AGS, GJ/608, 609.

42. Francisco Assensio, *Escrituras, Acuerdos . . . hasta el fin de 1733* (Madrid: Juan Muñoz, 1734); *Novísima Recopilación*, 1:109: book 1, title 13 (*naturaleza*), law VI; consulta of Cámara, 9 September 1715, enclosing letter from city of Salamanca, which included the declaration that the king had granted 23 naturalezas between 1705 and 1715; AHN, Consejos/4478/36; AMV, LA/76, f. 232, 309.

43. Consultas of Cámara, AHN, Consejos, legajo 4487/28 (1727) and 4488/49 (1728); king's letter on the grant of naturaleza to Zapata de Cárdenas, 11 August 1733, AMB, LA/1733, f. 163; king's letter of 9 November 1734 regarding the grant to the son of the prince of Campoflorido, AMB, LA/1734, f. 234; Cámara of Castile to city of Burgos on the naturalisation of D. Lorenzo Despuig y Cottoner of Mallorca, 22 November 1741, AMB, LA/1741, f. 401; AMV, LA/1733 f. 94, 101; AMV, LA/1734 f. 320, 322; consulta, AHN, E/3149/2/52.

44. Castro, *A la sombra*, 363, 368; consultas of the governor of the council, 11 November 1733, on enclosed representation from the corregidor of Ecija, and 12 November 1733, AGS, GJ/11

45. Marina Barba, "Contribución," 283; Andújar Castillo, *Sonido*, 179; García García, "Reformismo," 124; Domínguez Ortiz, *Sociedad y Estado*, 74.

46. Consulta of Cámara, 13 February 1719, AHN, Consejos/4481/1719/7; Representation of Diputación, 20 (18) November 1738, AHN, E/2981. 14 July 1739, AMB,

LA/?; Rodríguez Labandeira, "La política económica, 107–84 (at 141); Castellano, *Cortes de Castilla*, 192; consulta of Junta de Valdíos y Arbitros, Madrid, 7 February 1739, AHN, E/2981; Cardinal Molina to [?], 27 September 1738, AHN, E/2981; Miguel Caxa de Leruela, *Restauración de la Abundancia de España* (Madrid, 1732); session of Valladolid ayuntamiento, 23 October 1739, AMV, LA/84 f. 156; consulta on the province of Salamanca by D. Antonio García Batista, *juez de valdíos*, 15 April 1740, BN, MSS/12316 f. 200ff.

47. Consulta of Council of Castile, 18 September 1747, AHN, Consejos/libro 1018, f. 394–500; certification of D. Miguel Fernández Munilla, 18 October 1747, NLS Astorga G.31.c.1 f. 218–21; Martínez Salazar, *Colección de memorias*, 124–32; Rodríguez Labandeira, "Política económica," 141.

48. Storrs, *Resilience*, 166–74, for the earlier period; Ignacio M. Vicent López, "El discurso de la fidelidad durante la Guerra de Sucesión," *Espacio, Tiempo y Forma*, ser. 4, *Historia Moderna* 13 (2000); revised as "La Cultura Política Castellana durante la Guerra de Sucesión: El Discurso de la Fidelidad," in Fernández Albaladejo, *Los Borbones*, 217–43, and González Cruz, *Propaganda e información;* Jesús Astigarraga, "Esfera pública e instituciones ilustradas: El debate sobre las sociedades económicas en el último tercio del siglo en España," in Pérez Sarrión, *Más Estado y más mercado*, 235–60; Francisco Sánchez-Blanco, *El Absolutismo y las Luces en el reinado de Carlos III* (Madrid: Marcial Pons, 2002); the Spanish "public sphere" is absent from T. C. W. Blanning, *The Culture of Power and the Power of Culture: Old Regime Europe, 1660–1789* (Cambridge: Cambridge University Press, 2002) and James Van Horn Melton, *The Rise of the Public in Enlightenment Europe* (Cambridge: Cambridge University Press, 2001).

49. Karin Bowie, *Scottish Public Opinion and the Anglo-Scottish Union, 1699–1707* (London: Royal Historical Society, 2007), 1–10, Luis Miguel Enciso, "Opinión pública, Periodismo y Periodistas en la Epoca de Felipe V," in Serrano, *Felipe V,* 2:549–95, and Eva Velasco Moreno, "Proyectos y obstáculos para la formación de la opinión pública en la España de principios del siglo XVIII," in Serrano, *Felipe V,* 2:613–26, usefully seek to conceptualise opinion; Georges Desdevizes du Dezert, "La Chambre des Juges de l'Hotel de la Cour en 1745," *Revue Hispanique* 36 (1916): 1–51; Fayard, *Membres*, 21–24; Arvillars to Victor Amadeus II, 5 September 1728, AST, LM Spagna/60; Borré to CEIII, 20 February 1733, AST, LM Spagna/65; Keene to Newcastle, 8 July 1737, NA SP 94/128; Armstrong, *Elisabeth*, 183, Baudrillart, *Philippe*, 3:202; Ensenada to Huéscar, 19 April 1747, Ozanam and Téllez Alarcia, *Misión*, 230.

50. Enciso, "Opinión," 572–73, 587; María Dolores Sáiz, *Historia del periodismo en Espana*, vol. 1: *Los origenes: El siglo XVIII* (Madrid: Alianza, 1996), 54, 82; Gómez Pellejero, "La nobleza militar," in Serrano, *Felipe V,* 1:429–37; Giovanni Stiffoni, *Verità della storia e ragione del potere nella Spagna del primo '700* (Milan: Franco Angeli, 1989), 199, 207 (seeing the *Diario* as part of a larger "absolutist" project to "modernise" Spanish culture); Baudrillart, *Philippe*, 3:115, 202, 205; Storrs, *Resilience*, 167–69; Pérez Estevez and González Martínez, *Pretendientes*, 59; Coxe, *Memoirs of Kings*, 2:368–69; Martínez Shaw and Alfonso Mola, *Felipe*, 127, 129.

51. Rodríguez Villa, *Marqués de la Ensenada,* 102–3; Baudrillart, *Philippe,* 4:363–64; Teófanes Egido López, *Prensa Clandestina Española del Siglo XVIII: "El Duende Crítico,"* 2d ed. (Valladolid: Universidad de Valladolid, 2002), 92–93, 146, and passim; Enciso, "Opinión," 582–83; Gómez Urdáñez, "Carvajal–Ensenada," 72, 75; Delgado Barrado, *Aquiles y Teseos,* passim

52. Egido López, *Prensa,* passim; ibid., *Opinión,* passim; Enciso, "Opinión," 553; [? to [?], Faro, 19 September 1718, SP 89/26 f. 82; Baudrillart, *Philippe,* II, 318; Orendain to Ripperda, 28 August 1725, Mur i Raurell, *Diplomacia Secreta y Paz,* I, 430; Castellano, *Gobierno y Poder,* 99–100; Henry Kamen, *The Disinherited. The Exiles who created Spanish Culture* (London: Allen Lane, 2007), 148–9; king to governor of council of Castile, 29 March 1742, ASV, Archivo Nunziatura Madrid/180, f. 233.

53. Parker to Newcastle, 8 April 1744, NA, SP 89/43 f. 249; Sáiz, *Historia,* 92–93, 101; consulta of Council of Castile, 28 September 1744, AHN, Consejos, libro 1017 f. 356; Martínez Shaw and Alfonso Mola, *Felipe,* 288; Enciso, "Opinión," 572–5; Huéscar to Carvajal, 11 July and 12 October 1748, in Ozanam, *Diplomacia,* 25; Carvajal, *Testamento,* 26–27.

54. Arvillars to CEIII, 18 July 1732, AST, LM Spagna/64; Carvajal to Huéscar, 2 May 1746, Ozanam, *Diplomacia,* 93; Burnaby Parker to Newcastle, 4 December 1746, NA SP 89/45 f. 158–59.

55. Stanhope to Newcastle, October 21, 1726, NA SP 94/95 f. 90; consul Parker to Delafaye, 10 March 1730 and 8 April 1730, NA SP 94/216; Holloway to Newcastle, 28 February and 6 April 1732, NA SP 94/216, Parker to Delafaye, 12 May 1732, NA SP94/216.

56. Campillo to Valdes, 23 May 1741, AMB, LA/1741, ff. 329–332; *ordenanza,* 4 December 1746, NLS Astorga G. 31.c.1 f. 393ff.

57. Valguarnera to CEIII, 21 August 1741, AST, LM Spagna/70; *Relación Verídica del combate* and *Gaceta de Madrid,* both sent with Stanhope to Craggs, 5 October 1718, NA SP 94/88; *Gaceta,* 22 January 1743; *Gaceta,* 26 January 1745.

58. *Gaceta,* 1 September 1744, *Gaceta,* 19 October 1745; Relación de lo sucedido en el Reyno de Sicilia . . . campo de Villafranca, 26 June 1719, NLS; Relaciones of success of Philip V's troops at Ceuta, NLS, Astorga: G. 25.e.2 (117–119); and *Relación de la Victoria que las armas del Rey, mandadas por el Theniente General Don Juan de Gages, ganaron en Campo Santo . . .* (Madrid: Joseph Texidó, 1743); Fernández Duro, *Armada,* 6:203; Keene to Newcastle, 27 January 1733, NA, SP/94/116; Enciso, "Opinión," 568, 572.

59. *Gaceta,* 25 July 1719; *Gaceta,* 25 Nov. and 9 and 23 Dec. 1720; Mur i Raurell, *Diplomacia Secreta y Paz,* 1:197–99; Rosa Isusi Fagoaga, "Fiestas Regias y Celebraciones Musicales durante el Establecimiento de la Corte de Felipe V en Sevilla (1729–1733)," in Serrano, *Felipe V,* 2:867–81 (at 877); Pérez Samper, *Isabel,* 262; Baudrillart, *Philippe,* 4:117; Philip's order, 6 July 1732, NA, SP 94/216; Arvillars to CEIII, 11 July 1732, AST, LM Spagna/64; consulta of Council of Castile, 10 December 1732, AHN, Consejos, libro 1017 f. 377; Keene to Newcastle, 14 June May 1734, NA, SP 94/119; Pérez Samper, *Isabel,* 279,

285; *Gaceta*, 26 February 1743; *Gaceta*, 31 August, 28 September, 5 and 26 October, 16 November and 14 December 1745; Pérez Samper, *Isabel*, 298; *Gaceta*, 16 June, 14 July, and 4 August 1744, and *Gaceta*, 25 May, 6 July, 3 and 24 August, and 7 and 21 September 1745; Martínez Shaw and Alfonso Mola, *Felipe*, 173; Carvajal to Huéscar, 25 September 1747, Ozanam, *Diplomacia*, 232.

60. Erizzo, *Relazione*, 49; Cappello, *Relazione*, 10–11; Armstrong, *Elisabeth*, 324–25; Carvajal, *Testamento*, 16.

61. Castro, *A la sombra*, 363, 368; Egido López, *Opinión*, 182 and passim; Poyntz to Townshend, 9 June 1728, Coxe, *Memoirs of Walpole*, 2:627–29; Martínez Shaw and Alfonso Mola, *Felipe*, 127–28, 133; Walpole to Marchmont and Whitworth, 16 May 1725, Coxe, *Memoirs of Walpole*, 1:314–16; Chance, *Alliance*, 359, 435; Armstrong, "Bourbon Governments . . . I," 138. Carvajal, *Testamento*, 24; Arvillars to CEIII, 25 January 1732, AST, LM Spagna/64; Fernández Duro, *Armada*, 6:202; Baudrillart, *Philippe V*, 4:461.

62. Mur i Raurell, *Diplomacia Secreta y Paz*, 2:344; Egido López, *Opinión*, 290–92. Arvillars to VAII, 30 August 1728, AST, LM, Spagna/60; Bustanzo to Signori, 11 September 1728, Ciasca, *Istruzione*, 6:130–32; Coxe, *Walpole*, 1:457–59; Baudrillart, *Philippe*, 4:161, 173, and urged the British government to act, exploiting the absence of Spanish troops in Italy; Keene to Newcastle, 7 July 1738, NA, SP 94/131; J. L. Gómez Urdáñez, *Fernando VI*, 21–26, 39–40.

63. Dedieu, "Dinastía," 381–400; Kamen, *War*, 99, 107; González Caizán, "Primer círculo," 177–78; Giovanni Stiffoni, "Un documento inédito sobre los exiliados españoles en los dominios austriacos después de la guerra de sucesión," *Estudis* 17 (1991): 7–56; V. León Sanz, "La oposición a los Borbones españoles: Los austracistas en el exilio," in *Disidencias y exilios en la España Moderna*, ed. Enrique Giménez López and Antonio Mestre Sanchis (Alicante: Universidad de Alicante, 1997), 469–99; Carrasco, *Poder*, 108–10; F. J. Gutierrez Nuñez, "Joaquin Ponce de León Lancaster y Cárdenas, Duque de Arcos (VII)," *Diccionario Biográfico Español, 50 vols. (Madrid: Real Academia de la Historia, 2009–13)*, 41:962–63, for that grandee; Antonio Ramón Peña Izquierdo, *La Casa de Palma: La familia Portocarrero en el gobierno de la Monarquía Hispánica (1665–1700)* (Córdoba: Univesidad de Córdoba, 2004), 377–78; Erizzo, *Relazione*, 46–47 (referring to Medinaceli's loss of Puerto de Santa María); Muñoz Rodríguez, *Séptima Corona*, 294–95, for Murcia, home of Macanaz.

64. Kamen, *War*, 99, 106; Muñoz Rodríguez, *Séptima Corona*, 271–73; Virginia León, "Acuerdos de la Paz de Viena de 1725 sobre los exiliados de la Guerra de Sucesión," *Pedralbes* 12 (1992): 293–312; Amparo Felipo Orts, "La repercusion de la política de confiscaciones de Felipe V, sobre don Juan Basilio de Castellvi, conde de Cervelló y marqués de Villatorcas," *Estudis* 31 (2005): 253–68; Felices de la Fuente, *La nueva nobleza*, 201–12; Ozanam, *Diplomacia*, 9 (for the house of Alba); A. Tedesco, "Juan Francisco Pacheco V Duca di Uceda, uomo politico e mecenate tra Palermo, Roma e Vienna nell'epoca della guerra di successione spagnola," in Álvarez-Ossorio, García García, and León, *Pérdida de Europa*, 491–548. González Mezquita, *Oposición y disidencia*, 104; Pedro Moreno Meyerhoff,

"Los Grandes de España creados por el Archiduque en la Corona de Aragón," in Serrano, *Felipe V,* 2:363–403 (at 397–98).

65. Didier Ozanam, *Les Diplomates espagnols du XVIIIe siècle: Introductión et repertoire biographique (1700–1808)* (Madrid: Casa de Velázquez, 1998); Atienza Hernández, *Aristocracia, poder y riqueza,* 92–93, 110; Dedieu, "Dinastía," 392–93.

66. Atienza Hernández, *Aristocracia, poder y riqueza,* 105–6; Mur i Raurell, *Diplomacia Secreta y Paz,* 2:349; Castro, *A la sombra,* 44. Juan José Iglesias Rodríguez, ed., *Puerto de Santa María 1752, Según las Respuestas del Catastro de Ensenada* (Madrid: Tabapress, 1992), 15–16.

67. Carvajal, *Testamento,* thought Oran should be exchanged for British-occupied Menorca; Delgado Barrado, *Aquiles y Teseos,* 118–20 and passim; Arvillars to CEIII, 13 April and 18 May 1731, AST, LM Spagna/63; Arvillars to CEIII, 28 January and 17 October 1732, AST, LM Spagna/64; Canga Arguelles, *Diccionario,* 2:19–20; Ibáñez Molina, "José del Campillo," 53; the duke of Huéscar to Ensenada, 28–29 June 1747, Ozanam and Téllez Alarcia, *Misión,* 271.

68. Bishop of Oviedo to Carvajal, 18 October 1747, AHN, E/3149/1/145. For a similar ruling in January 1747, see *Novísima Recopilación,* book 4, title 8, law 7, 253. The last ruling of this sort was in July 1717, ibid., book 4, title 3, law 15, 222; Parker to Newcastle, 15 December 1742 and 3 August 1743, NA SP 89/43 f. 182; Parker to Newcastle, 5 April 1743, NA SP 89/43 f. 168; Parker to Newcastle, 15 December 1744 and 23 January 1745, NA SP 89/45 f. 7; Parker to Newcastle, 18 September and 12 October 1745, NA SP 89/45 f. 49, 55.

69. Keene to Newcastle, 12 May and 7 June 1734, NA, SP 94/111, and the end-of-mission relazione of the Venetian ambassador (1735), Armstrong, *Elisabeth,* 323–24; Keene to Newcastle, 2 August 1738, NA SP 94/131; Erizzo, *Relazione* (1730).

70. Pérez Samper, *Isabel,* 400 (claiming that many Spaniards aspired to [restore] a Spanish presence in Italy but giving no reference); Armstrong, *Elisabeth,* 173; Kamen, *Philip V,* 81 (for one pamphlet of 1714 lamenting the loss of Spain's extra-Iberian European territories). Castro, *A la sombra,* 323; Ozanam, *Diplomates espagnols du XVIIIe siècle,* 403.

71. Gómez Urdáñez, "Carvajal–Ensenada," 75; Diego Téllez Alarcia, "El caballero Don Ricardo Wall y la conspiración antiensenadista," in Delgado Barrado and Gómez Urdáñez, *Ministros de Fernando,* 93–138 (at 114); Antonio Mestre Sanchis, "Reflexiones sobre el marco político y cultural de la obra del P. Feijoo," *Bulletin Hispanique* 91 (1989): 295–312, republished in ibid, *Apología y crítica de España en el siglo XVIII* (Madrid: Marcial Pons, 2003) 167–83; Ensenada to Huéscar, 19 April 1747, Ozanam and Téllez Alarcia, *Misión,* 230, Huéscar to Ensenada, Paris, 20 January 1748, *Mision,* 372.

Chapter Five. Foral Spain

Epigraph: Campoflorido, captain general of Valencia, to Castelar, 6 August 1726, proposing the creation of miliria units there, Pradells Nadal, "Reorganización militar de Valencia," 309.

1. J. H. Elliott, "A Europe of Composite Monarchies," *Past and Present* 137 (1992): 48–71; Helmut Koenigsberger, *The Government of Sicily under Philip II of Spain: A Study in the*

Practice of Empire (London: Staples, 1951), 58; J. H. Elliott, *The Revolt of the Catalans: A Study in the Decline of Spain, 1598–1640* (Cambridge: Cambridge University Press, 1963).

2. García Cárcel, *Felipe V,* 114–20; Muñoz Rodríguez, *Séptima Corona;* Joaquim Albareda Salvado, "Felipe V y Cataluña: Balance de un Reinado," in Serrano, *Felipe V,* 2:91–118 (at 99).

3. Coxe, *Memoirs of Kings,* 2:155–56; Instructions for Ripperda, 22 November 1724, Mur i Raurell, *Diplomacia Secreta y Paz,* 287–90; full powers for Ripperda to negotiate and conclude a treaty with Charles VI, 2 April 1725, and with the czarina of Muscovy, 31 July 1725, AHN, E/3369/2, 6; Baudrillart, *Philippe,* 4:169; Grimaldi to Signori, 20 November 1740, Ciasca, *Istruzioni,* 6:251–54. C. Therlinden, "Un grand homme de guerre belge en Italie au XVIIIe siecle: Le comte de Gages," *Bulletin de l'Institut Belge a Rome* 25 (1950–51). In 1739 the Flemish comtesse de Seve was appointed one of the ladies of honour of the bride of the Infante Felipe, Baudrillart, *Philippe,* 4:500–501.

4. Pere Molas Ribalta, "Qué fue de Italia y Flandes?," in Álvarez-Ossorio, García García, and León, *Pérdida de Europa,* 693–715 (at 703); Franco Venturi, *Settecento Riformatore,* vol. 1: *Da Muratori a Beccaria* (Turin: Einaudi, 1969), passim; José Álvarez-Junco, *Spanish Identity;* Bartolomé Yun Casalilla, *Marte contra Minerva: El precio del Imperio español (c. 1450–1600),* (Barcelona: Crítica, 2004), 574.

5. Martínez Shaw and Alfonso Mola, *Felipe,* 58, 296; José María Iñurritegui, *Gobernar la occasón: Preludio político de la Nueva Planta de 1707* (Madrid: Centro de Estudios Políticos y Constitucionales, 2008); Eloy Fernández Clemente and Guillermo Pérez Sarrión, "El siglo XVIII en Aragón: Una economía dependiente," in *España en el siglo XVIII: Homenaje a Josep Fontana,* ed. Roberto Fernández (Barcelona: Crítica, 1985), 565–629; Pedro Ruiz Torres, "El País Valenciano: La transformación de una sociedad agraria en la época del absolutismo," in Fernández, *España en el siglo XVIII,* 132–247; José A. Armillas and María B. Pérez, "La Nueva Planta Borbónica en Aragón," in Serrano, *Felipe V,* 2:257–92; Kamen, *War,* 263–68, 302–5; Castro, *A la sombra,* 161–63; Pedro Voltes Bou, *La Guerra de Sucesión en Valencia* (Valencia: Instituto Valenciano de Estudios Históricos, 1964), 76–78, for the decree; Castro, *A la sombra,* 164; Albareda, *Felipe V y el triunfo,* 89–96; 201–19; Vidal, "El reino de Mallorca," in Serrano, *Felipe V,* 2:151–210. Cowans, *Early Modern Spain,* 204–6, for extracts from the decree of 1716. In 1717 the imperial court hoped to recover Majorca as compensation following the Spanish conquest of Sardinia, Baudrillart, *Philippe,* 2:284.

6. Albareda, *La Guerra de Sucesión en Espana,* (Barcelona, 2010), 419–51; Stiffoni, "Un documento inédito," 7–56; Virginia León Sanz, "Represión borbonica y exilio Austracista al finalizar la Guerra de Sucesión Española," in Álvarez-Ossorio, García García, and León, *Pérdida de Europa,* 567–89; Enrique Giménez López, "El primer Capitán General de Cataluña, marqués de Castel Rodrigo (1715–1721) y el control del Austracismo," in Fernández Albaladejo, *Los Borbones,* 401–20.

7. Morozzo to Victor Amadeus, 29 April 1715, AST, LM Spagna/57; Albareda, *Felipe V y el triunfo,* 89–96; Pablo Fernández Albaladejo, "La Monarquía de los Borbónes" in

ibid., *Fragmentos de Monarquía* (Madrid: Alianza, 1992), 353–454. Venality was not extended to municipal office in Valencia until the fiscal crisis provoked by intervention in the War of the Polish Succession, María del Carmen Irles Vicente, "Política y hacienda: La enajenación de regidurías en los municipios valencianos cabeza de corregimiento," in *Política y Hacienda en el Antiguo Régimen: Actas de la II Reunión científica de la Asociación Española de Historia Moderna*, ed. José Ignacio Fortea Pérez and Carmen María Cremades Griñan, 2 vols. (Murcia: Universidad de Murcia, 1993), 1:323–32.

8. Pradells Nadal, "Reorganización Militar de Valencia," 310; Montserrat Jiménez Sureda, "La política armamentística de los Borbones en Cataluña tras la Guerra de Sucesión," *Investigaciones Históricas* 21 (2001): 103–32; order, 15 December 1730, AGS, SG/4997; Borreguero Beltrán, *Reclutamiento*, 98–99; Andújar Castillo, "Nobleza catalana al servicio de Felipe V: La Compañía de Granaderos Reales," *Pedralbes* 27 (2007): 293–313; Andújar Castillo, *Sonido*, 119–20. The sorteo was not extended to Catalonia until 1770, Joan Mercader, *Els Capitans Generals* (Barcelona: Vicens-Vives, 1956).

9. Victor Amadeus to Arvillars, 8 August 1728 and Arvillars to Victor Amadeus, 30 August and 20 December 1728, AST, LM Spagna/60, and various related documents in AST, Negoziazioni Spagna/7/21; Martínez Shaw, and Alfonso Mola, *Felipe*, 205; Enrique Giménez, "El peligro austracista en tierras valencianas tras la guerra de Sucesion," *Anales Valencianas* 26 (1987): 135–239; Elliott, *Revolt of Catalans*, 63–65, and Henry Kamen, "Public Authority and Popular Crime: Banditry in Valencia, 1660–1714," *Journal of European Economic History* 3 (1974): 654–87; Enrique Giménez López, "Conflicto armado con Francia y guerrilla austracista en Cataluña (1719–1720)," *Hispania* 65/2, 220 (2005): 543–600; Baudrillart, *Philippe*, 2:362, 366–67; Virginia León Sanz, "Los españoles austracistas exiliados y las medidas de Carlos VI," *Revista de Historia Moderna: Anales de la Universidad de Alicante* 10 (1991): 162–73, and "Acuerdos de la Paz de Viena de 1725 sobre los exiliados de la Guerra de Sucesión," *Pedralbes* 12 (1992): 293–312; Baudrillart, *Philippe*, 2:430 and 3:185, 394–95; Orendain to Ripperda, 22 January and 5 and 16 June 1725, Mur i Raurell, *Diplomacia Secreta y Paz*, 1:294–95, 342, 347–48; Armstrong, *Elisabeth*, 279–80. Arvillars thought there would be too great hostility for the proposal to give Aragon to Don Carlos to succeed.

10. Carpintero to Patino, 30 January 1734, AGS, E/5703; Arpe to Patino, 2 March 1734, AGS, E/5511; Ernest Lluch, *Las Españas vencidas del siglo XVIII* (Barcelona: Crítica, 1999); Glimes to Villarías, 6 October 1740, AHN, E/541

11. Poyntz to Addison, 13 August 1717, NA, SP 89/25 f. 148 and enclosures; Lista das Prevencoes . . ., Barcelona, 22 January 1718, NA, SP 89/26 f.; Worsley to Addison, 27 February 1718, NA SP 89/26 f. 13; Armstrong, *Elisabeth*, 240–41; Borré to CEIII, Madrid, 15 March and 12 April 1734, AST, LM Spagna/66. Andújar Castillo, *Sonido*, 117–18; Richmond, *Navy*, 3:165–66. Enrique Giménez López, *Alicante en el siglo XVIII: Economía de una ciudad portuaria del Antiguo Régimen* (Valencia: Institución Alfonso el Magnánimo, 1981), argues that war merely interrupted economic activity and prosperity but focuses on the later eighteenth century.

12. Kamen, "Public Authority," 687. For eighteenth-century Catalonia, see Pierre Vilar, *La Catalogne dans l'Espagne: Recherches sur les fondements économiques des structures nationales*, 3 vols. (Paris: S.E.V.P.E.N., 1962) (and 3:364 for the role of the state); Carlos Martínez Shaw, "La Cataluña del siglo XVIII bajo el signo de la expansión," in Fernández, *España en el siglo XVIII*, 55–131; Pierre Vilar, "Agricultural Progress and the Economic Background in Eighteenth-Century Catalonia," *Economic History*, n.s., 11 (1958): 113–20, Carlos Martínez Shaw, *Cataluña en la carrera de Indias, 1680–1756* (Barcelona: Crítica, 1981); James Thomson, "Explaining the 'Take-off' of the Catalan Cotton Industry," *Economic History Review* 58 (2005): 701–35; Antonio Espino López, *Catalunya durante el reinado de Charles II : Política y guerra en la frontera catalana, 1679–1697* (Bellaterra: Universitat Autónoma de Barcelona, 1999), 307–34; budgets in AGS, SSH/408.

13. Agustin Gónzalez Enciso, "La política industrial en la época de Carvajal a Ensenada, 1698–1754," in Delgado Barrado and Gómez Urdáñez, *Ministros de Fernando VI*, 265; Martínez Shaw, *Cataluña en la carrera*, 88 (for opportunities offered by the siege of Gibraltar in 1727); AGS, SG/Sup/484, cl. 11, 12; Holloway to Newcastle, 28 February and 2 March 1732, and Windsor to Newcastle, 22 June and 25 October 1732, NA, SP 94/216; contract for 200 *azemilas de carga*, or pack mules, and another 140 mules for the artillery train for Italy, Barcelona, 8 November 1733, AGS, SSH/1040; Skinner to Newcastle, 30 January 1733, NA, SP 98/34.

14. Estado de las Embarcaciones . . ., June 1718, NA, SP 89/26 f. 49 (identifying 58 English, 58 Catalan, 35 Genoese, and 18 Irish vessels); *Gaceta*, 22 December 1744 and 31 August and 14 December 1745; Castelar to Ensenada, 26 March 1745, AGS, SG/2145; Castanos to Ensenada, 11 April 1746, AGS, SG/2160; *Gaceta*, passim, for Catalan privateers in the War of the Austrian Succession; Díaz Ordóñez, "Fabricación de jarcia en España," 404

15. Eloy Martín Corrales, "Los Coraleros Catalanes en el Litoral Argelino en el Siglo XVIII," in Martínez Shaw, *Derecho*, 427–56; Gemma García Fuertes, "De la conspiración austracista a la integración de la Nueva Planta: La familia Durán, máximo exponente de la burguesía mercantil barcelonesa en el siglo XVIII," *Espacio, Tiempo y Forma*, ser. 4, 17 (2004): 143–62; María de los Angeles Pérez Samper, "La presencia del rey ausente: Las visitas reales a Cataluña en la época moderna," in *Imagen del rey, imagen de los reinos: Las ceremonias públicas en la España moderna (1500–1814)*, ed. Agustin González Enciso and Jesús María Usunáriz (Pamplona: Ediciones Universidad de Navarra, 1999), 63–116; Martínez Shaw and Alfonso Mola, *Felipe*, 206, 264. For a more negative contextualisation of Don Carlos's reception, see. Lluis Roura I Aulinas, "1731: L'herencia italiana i la relació entre la monarquía borbonica I el principat de Catalunya," *Pedralbes* 18 (1998): 521–30.

16. Valentín Vázquez de Prada, José María Sese, Ana Azcona, and Alfredo Floristán, "Relaciones de Navarra con el Gobierno central en el siglo XVIII: La pugna por el ejercicio del poder legislativo," in *Coloquio Internacional Charles III y su Siglo*, 1:997–1019; Alfredo Floristán Imízcoz, *El reino de Navarra y la conformación de España (1512–1841)* (Madrid: Akal, 2014), 235–59; Rafael Torres Sánchez, "Prólogo: Nuevos retos de la 'hora navarra,'" in

ibid., *Volver,* 9–30; Regina Grafe, *Distant Tyranny: Markets, Power and Backwardness in Spain, 1650–1800* (Princeton: Princeton University Press, 2012), 144–45, 157–58; AGS, TMC/4475/143.

17. Laborda, *Señorío de Vizcaya;* Grafe, *Distant;* Miguel Artola, *La Monarquía de España* (Madrid: Alianza, 1999), 604–14; Fernández Albaladejo, "Monarquía de los Borbones," 390; royal cédula, 24 June 1725, Portugués, *Colección,* 2:635–44: Domingo Ignacio de Egana, *El guipuzcoano instruído en las reales cédulas . . .* (San Sebastián: Imprenta D. Lorenzo Riesgo Montero de Espinosa, 1780), 421. For tensions between the crown and the province of Alava, not least during the War of the Austrian Succession, see Porres Marijuán, "Fueros y Sal," 225–56.

18. Martínez-Radío Garrido, *Guerra de Sucesión y Asturias,* 151–52, 368–69; Gonzalo Anes, "La Asturias preindustrial," in Fernández, *España en el siglo XVIII,* 505–35.

19. Pere Molas Ribalta, "Diversidad en la unidad," in *El Mundo Hispánico en el siglo de las Luces,* 2 vols. (Madrid: Universidad Complutense, 1996), 1:193–206; Bernal, *España, proyecto inacabado,* 33 and passim; Concepción de Castro, *La Revolución Liberal y los municipios españoles* (Madrid: Alianza, 1979), 25–26; Postigo Castellanos, "Monarca frente a Maestre," 309–18.

20. Jorge A. Catalá Sanz, "El coste económico de la política matrimonial de la nobleza valenciana en época moderna, *Estudis* 19 (1993): 165–89 (at 184), for the "Castilianisation" of the Valencian nobility after 1707; Alonso Aguilera, *Conquista,* 67; Andújar Castillo, *Sonido,* 83–85; Martínez Shaw, "Cataluña," 108–9.

Chapter Six. Italy and Identity

Epigraph: Bartolomeo Corsini to cardinal Neri, 1 October 1735, in Caridi, "Dall'investitura al Concordato," 542.

1. "Italy" was, to antedate Metternich's lapidary expression, a geographical expression until the creation of the kingdom of Italy in 1861. All references here to Italy and Italians are thus simply a convenient shorthand, but see the very apposite observations of Carlo Capra, *Gli italiani prima dell'Italia* (Roma: Carocci, 2014), 401–11. Similarly, "Spanish Italy" simply refers to the territories in Italy which had been part of the Spanish Monarchy.

2. James S. Amelang, "Exchanges between Italy and Spain: Culture and Religion," in *Spain in Italy: Politics, Society, and Religion 1500–1700,* ed. Thomas J. Dandelet and John A. Marino (Leiden: Brill, 2007), 433–55; the Montijo family patrimony included Neapolitan saltworks, Paula de Demerson, *María Francisca de Sales Portocarrero (Condesa de Montijo): Una Figura de la Ilustración* (Madrid: Centro de Investigaciones Sociológicas, 1976), 71; Richard Kagan, *Students and Society in Early Modern Spain* (Baltimore: Johns Hopkins University Press, 1974), 33, 65; *Novísima Recopilacion,* lib. 1/18/31; *Gaceta,* 16 July 1743; Maximiliano Barrio Gozalo, *La embajada de España en Roma durante el reinado de Carlos II (1665–1700)* (Valladolid: Universidad de Valladolid, 2013), 235–90; [?] to Campoflorido, Madrid, 29 January 1713, AGS, E/6121/67; Relaciones, 1713, AGS, E/6123/80, 146; Resumen de los

oficiales . . ., 29 September 1713, AGS, E/6123/95; Relacion y reparto . . ., Casas Pintas, 8 November 1713, AGS, E/6123/116; Gros to Victor Amadeus, 20 September 1722, AST, LM Genova/8; Pérez Estévez and González Martínez, *Pretendientes,* and Thomas Dandelet, *Spanish Rome, 1500–1700* (New Haven: Yale University Press, 2001); Mari to Villarias, 23 Jan 1745, AGS, E/5736; A. Spagnoletti, *Principi italiani e Spagna nell'eta barocca* (Milan: Franco Angeli, 1996); Arpe to Patino, 23 March 1734, AGS, E/5511; Edoardo Grendi, *I Balbi: Una famiglia genovese fra Spagna e Impero* (Turin: Einaudi, 1997), for the Balbi in Spain before 1700; Ozanam, *Diplomates espagnols du XVIIIe siècle.*

3. Aurelio Musi, ed., *Alle origini di una nazione: Antispagnolismo e identità italiana* (Milan: Guerini, 2003); Francesca Fausta Gallo, "Italia entre los Habsburgo y los Borbones," in Fernández Albaladejo, *Los Borbones,* 141–62 (at 152–53); Molesworth to Carteret, 23 May 1722, NA, SP 92/31, f. 92

4. Francesco Manconi, "Cerdeña a finales del siglo XVII–principio XVIII: Una larga crisis de casi medio siglo," *Estudis* 33 (2007): 27–44, and ibid., "The Kingdom of Sardinia: A Province in Balance between Catalonia, Castile, and Italy," in Dandelet and Marino, *Spain in Italy,* 45–72; Copia di procura fatta dal Re . . ., 7 April 1701, AST, Sardegna, Materie Politiche/Categoria I/1/1; Jon Arrieta Alberdi, El *Consejo Supremo de la Corona de Aragón (1494–1707)* (Zaragoza: Institución Fernando el Católico, 1994), 218, 225; Alonso Aguilera, *Conquista,* 78–79, 87–88; Pérez Samper, *Isabel,* 122; Hochedlinger, *Austria's Wars,* 194–202.

5. Alonso Aguilera, *Conquista,* 115–20; Pujol Aguado, "España en Cerdeña," 191–214; Mattone, "La cessione del Regno di Sardegna," 5–89; José Luis Bermejo Cabrero, "Un decreto más de Nueva Planta," *Revista de Derecho Político* 5 (1979–80): 130–44; intendant's patent of appointment and instructions, AST, Sardegna Materie Economiche/Impieghi Economici/1/15; Abbad and Ozanam, *Intendants,* 11–12; Rafael Escobedo Romero, "La expansión geográfica de la renta del tabaco," *Estudis* 33 (2007): 193–224.

6. For Philip's appointment of Spaniards to Sardinian episcopal sees, Pierpaolo Merlin, *Il Vicere del Bastione: Filippo Guglielmo Pallavicino di Saint Rémy e il Governo della Sardegna (1720–1727)* (Cagliari: Provincia di Cagliari, 2005), 37; Alonso Aguilera, *Conquista,* 128–29; consultas of royal confessor, AGS, GJ/609.

7. Mattone, "La cessione del Regno di Sardegna," 47–57; Riflessioni suggeriti . . . 1732, and Copia di Real Viglietto . . ., 14 March 1732, AST, Sardegna Materie Politiche/ Categoria. IV/1/25, 26, and the instructions given the new viceroy (1731), marchese Girolamo Falletti di Castagnole, G. Olla Repetto, "Gerolamo Falletti marchese di Castagnole," *Dizionario Biografico,* available online at http://www.treccani.it/enciclopedia/ gerolamo-falletti-marchese-di-castagnole (Dizionario Biografico)/;Pujol Aguado, "España en Cerdeña," 204; G. Quazza, "Giovanni Battista Lorenzo Bogino," *Dizionario Biografico,* available online at http://www.treccani.it/enciclopedia/giovanni-battista-lorenzo-bogino (Dizionario Biografico)/; Merlin, *Vicere,* 10–11, 35, 45, 53, 78–80; Antonello Mattone and Eloisa Mura, "La relazione del reggente la Reale Cancelleria, il conte Filippo Domenico Beraudo di Pralormo, sul governo del Regno di Sardegna (1731)," *Bollettino Storico*

Bibliografico Subalpino III (2013): 459–530 (at 465–71). In 1726 Philip protested following a papal grant to Victor Amadeus that Philip claimed affected his reversionary interest, AST, Sardegna Materie Politiche/Categoria I/2/58.

8. Mattone, "La cessione del Regno di Sardegna," 28–30; José I. Ruiz Rodríguez and Pierluigi Nocella, "Cambio dinástico en los dominios de la Italia del sur y la Guerra de Sucesión," in Edelmayer, León Sanz, and Ruiz Rodríguez, *Hispania-Austria III: Der Spanische Erbfolgekrieg / La Guerra de Sucesión española*, 295–318; A. Álvarez-Ossorio Alvariño, "El final de la Sicilia Española? Fidelidad, familia, y venalidad bajo el virrey marqués de los Balbases (1707–1713)," in Álvarez-Ossorio Alvariño, García García, and León, *Pérdida de Europa*, 857; Javier Sánchez Marquez, "La Fine della Sicilia Espagnola e l'Esperienza Politica di Luigi Reggio, Principe di Campofiorito," *Rivista Storica Italiana* 123 (2011): 537–91; instructions for the marqués de Villamayor, and [?] to Diego Merino de Roxas, *procurador general* of confiscated estates in Sicily, and same to Gaspar de Narbona, and procurador general of the same estates, 30 June 1715, cl. 3, AHN, E/3457/3; Geoffrey Symcox, *Victor Amadeus II: Absolutism in the Savoyard State, 1675–1730* (London: Thames and Hudson, 1983), 171–73; Castro, *A la sombra,* 321. In 1718 a mission to resolve difficulties between the two courts over Modica camouflaged secret negotiations, "Relazioni sulla Corte di Spagna dell'Abate Doria del Maro e del conte Lascaris di Castellar, ministro di Savoia," ed. Domenico Carutti, *Memorie della Reale Accademia delle Scienze di Torino,* ser. 2, 19 (1861): 107–211.

9. Armstrong, *Elisabeth,* 110–12; Mattone, "La cessione del Regno di Sardegna," 31; Andújar Castillo, *Sonido,* 103–4; Victor Amadeus to Cortanze, 19 October 1720, AST, LM Inghilterra/20; Schaub to Stair, Madrid, 8 May 1720, NA, SP 94/89; Elena Papagna, *La Corte di Carlo di Borbone il re "proprio e nazionale"* (Naples: Guida, 2011), 123–24 (for the brothers of the prince of Palagonia); Orendain to Luis Ripperda, 15 January 1726, Mur i Raurell, *Diplomacia Secreta y Paz,* 1:482–83; Merano to Grimaldo, Palermo, 27 February 1724 and 7 April and 28 July 1725, AGS, E/6130.

10. Orendain to Ripperda, 24 July and 5 August 1725, Mur i Raurell, *Diplomacia Secreta y Paz,* 1:378; Roberto Fernández, *Charles III* (Madrid: Arlanza Ediciones, 2001), 57–67; Baudrillart, *Philippe,* 4:104; Franco Angiolini, *I Cavalieri e il Principe: L'Ordine di Santo Stefano e la Società Toscana in Eta Moderna* (Florence: Edifir, 1996).

11. Martínez Shaw and Alfonso Mola, *Felipe,* 148; Bethencourt Massieu, *Relaciones de España,* 161; Bernardo Tanucci, *Epistolario,* vol. 1: *1723–1746,* ed. R. P. Coppini, I. Del Bianco and R. Nieri (Rome: Edizioni di Storia e Letteratura, 1980), 98; Giuseppe Caridi, *Essere Re e Non Essere Re: Carlo di Borbone a Napoli e le Attese Deluse (1734–1738)* (Soveria Mannelli: Rubbettino, 2006), xii. Santisteban's father had served as viceroy of both Naples and Sicily, and he himself had been born in Palermo, Molas Ribalta, "Qué fue?," 710; Ferrer Benimeli, "El Conde de Aranda," 726–27.

12. Baudrillart, *Philippe,* 4:290; Mafrici, *Re delle speranze,* 162–65. (Some of the evacuated troops were sent to Naples); Sandro Landi, *Il governo delle opinioni: Censura e formazione del consenso nella Toscana del Settecento* (Bologna: Il Mulino, 2000), 50–52.

13. Antonio Calabria, *The Cost of Empire: The Finances of the Kingdom of Naples in the Time of Spanish Rule* (Cambridge: Cambridge University Press, 1991), 4–8; Storrs, *Resilience*, 191, 212–22; John Robertson, *The Case for the Enlightenment: Scotland and Naples, 1680–1760* (Cambridge: Cambridge University Press, 2005); Domenico Sella, *Italy in the Seventeenth Century* (Harlow: Longman, 1997), 28; *Il Regno di Napoli nell'età di Filippo IV (1621–1665)*, ed. Giovanni Brancaccio and Aurelio Musi (Milan: Guerini, 2013).

14. Aurelio Musi, *L'Impero dei vicere* (Bologna: Il Mulino, 2013), 250–52; Carla Russo, "Tiberio Carafa," *Dizionario Biografico*, available online at http://www.treccani.it/enciclopedia/tiberio-carafa (Dizionario Biografico)/; Aurelio Musi, "Politica e cultura a Napoli tra il crepusculo del sistema imperial spagnolo e l'avvento degli Asburgo d'Austria (1698–1707)," in Álvarez-Ossorio Alvariño, García García, and León, *Pérdida de Europa*, 785–98; Giuseppe Ricuperati, "L'immagine della Spagna a Napoli nel primo Settecento: Vico, Carafa, Doria e Giannone," in *Alle origini di una nazione: Antispagnolismo e identita italiana*, ed. Aurelio Musi (Milan: Guerini, 2003), 83–118; Antonio Spagnoletti, "Il dibattito politico a Napoli sulla Succesione di Spagna," in Álvarez-Ossorio Alvariño, *Famiglie, nazioni e Monarchia*, 267–310; Coxe, *Memoirs of Kings*, 1:197–98; Philip V to Louis XIV, 28 March, 2 May and 3 and 10 October 1707, in *Las Cortes de Madrid y Versalles en el Año 1707: Estudio Traductológico e Histórico de las correspondencias real y diplomática*, ed. José Manuel de Bernardo Ares and Elena Echeverría Pereda (Madrid: Silex, 2011), 245–46, 262–63, 328–29, 330–31; Instructions, 28 December 1711, AHN, E/3376/2/10, clause 15.

15. Egido López, *Prensa Clandestina Española del Siglo XVIII*, 129, for one contemporary Spanish comparison with that earlier conquest; Tanucci to Laviefville, 4 November 1747, in Tanucci, *Epistolario*, ed. R. Coppini and R. Nieri, 2:326; Hochedlinger, *Austria's Wars*, 208–17; Mafrici, *Re delle speranze*, 125–36; Pérez Samper, *Isabel*, 278–79; Arpe to Patiño, 20 April 1734, AGS, E/5511; Antonio Di Vittorio, *Gli Austriaci e il Regno di Napoli, 1707–1734*, 2 vols. (Naples: Giannini, 1969), vol. 1: *Le Finanze Pubbliche*, 96–100, 103–22 (revenues doubled c. 1707–31); Mafrici, *Re delle speranze*, 50–56; Popoli Caridi of Calabria (Citra and Ultra) to [Philip V], 24 February 1731, AGS, E/6130; [Anon.], "Antonio Carmine Caracciolo," *Dizionario Biografico*, available online at http://www.treccani.it/enciclopedia/antonio-carmine-caracciolo (Dizionario Biografico)/, and Francesco Barbagallo, "Marino Francesco Caracciolo," ibid., availablre online at http://www.treccani.it/enciclopedia/marino-francesco-caracciolo (Dizionario Biografico)/. The latter, prince of Avellino and one of the great feudatories of Naples, was offered a company of Spanish cavalry by Philip V in 1734 as he sought to secure the support of the Neapolitan aristocracy. On the disillusionment of the Neapolitan nobility with the Austrian regime—and much else—see Rafaello Ajello, "Lo Stato e la società degli Austriaci e dei Borboni: La transizione dalla repubblica dei togati all'assolutismo," in De Rosa and Enciso Recio, *Spagna e Mezzogiorno d'Italia*, 1:189–237.

16. Caridi, *Essere Re*, 41–3; Carlos's decree, 14 March 1734, BNM, MSS/12948/37; Fernández, *Charles III*, 68–70, 74; Maximiliano Barrio, ed., *Cartas de Charles III a Tanucci (1759–1763)* (Madrid: Banco Bilbao Vizcaya, 1988), xiii; Sergio Bertelli, ed., *La Vita di Pietro*

Giannone, 2 vols. (Turin: Einaudi, 1977), 2:264–65; Pérez Samper, *Isabel*, 278. Maresca, "Relazione," 701; Russo, "Tiberio Carafa,"; Baudrillart, *Philippe*, 4:236–39. (The brief account of the conquest by Robertson, *Case*, 353, does not make clear the role of Spanish troops or mention Philip's grant); Mafrici, *Re delle speranze*, 125–36; Fernández, *Carlos*, 69–70, ibid., 74. As his father had done in 1701, Don Carlos presented in Rome the annual *hacanea*, or white horse, in recognition that he held Naples as a papal vassal.

17. Luigi De Rosa, "La historiografía italiana sobre Carlos de Borbón," in VV.AA., *Coloquio Internacional Charles III y su Siglo*, 1:173–90; Caridi, *Essere Re*, 42–43; Venturi, *Settecento*, 1:1ff. "Gli 'afrancesados' a Napoli nella prima meta del Settecento: Idee e progetti di sviluppo," in *I Borboni di Napoli e i Borboni di Spagna*, ed. Mario Di Pinto, 2 vols. (Naples: Guida, 1985), 1:185–86; Pérez Samper, *Isabel*, 280; Fernández, *Carlos*, 76; Dino Carpanetto and Giuseppe Ricuperati, *Italy in the Age of Reason, 1685–1789* (Harlow: Longman, 1987), 179–80; Robertson, *Case*, 333, for the young lawyer Giovanni Pallante; Mafrici, *Re delle speranze*, 255–56; McKay and Scott, *Rise of the Great Powers*, 150–51; Fernández, *Charles III*, 75; Vittorio Sciuti Russi, "Bartolomeo Corsini," *Dizionario Biografico*, available online at http://www.treccani.it/enciclopedia/bartolomeo-corsini (Dizionario Biografico)/ (for Corsini's viceroyalty).

18. Fausta Gallo, "Italia," 161–62; Rafaello Ajello, "La vita politica napoletana sotto Carlo di Borbone: La fondazione e il 'tempo eroico' della dinastia," in Luigi Labruna, ed., *Storia di Napoli*, 10 vols. (Naples: Edizioni Scientifiche Italiane, 1971–78), 7:461–717; Ilaria Zilli, *Carlo di Borbone e la rinascita del regno di Napoli: Le finanze pubbliche, 1731–1742* (Naples: Edizioni Scientifiche Italiane, 1990), 182–83, and Mafrici, *Re delle speranze*, 189–200, for the financial, military, and naval dependence of the Neapolitan court on that of Madrid. In 1742 Don Carlos's fleet comprised just 1 warship, 1 frigate, 4 galleys, and 4 *galeotte*. Because of his very different focus, Robertson, *Case*, does not properly reflect this aspect of the Neapolitan experience after 1734.

19. Mafrici, *Re delle speranze*, 161–62, 166–69 172–75, 185; Pérez Samper, *Isabel*, 281–83; Ajello, "Afrancesados," 259–60, for the key role played in Rome by Cardinal Acquaviva in the negotiations with the Roman Curia for the investiture of Don Carlos by the pope; Di Rienzo, "Celestino Galiani," *Dizionario Biografico*, available online at http://www.treccani. it/enciclopedia/celestino-galiani (Dizionario Biografico)/; Montealegre to Cornejo, Naples, 20 August 1737, AHN, E/1679, for the Spanish chargé at Lucerne forwarding to Naples offers of Swiss troops for Don Carlos; María Grazia Maiorini, "Neapolitan Diplomacy in the Eighteenth Century: Policy and the Diplomatic Apparatus," in *Politics and Diplomacy in Early Modern Italy: The Structure of Diplomatic Practice, 1450–1800*, ed. Daniela Frigo (Cambridge: Cambridge University Press, 2000), 176–209; Pérez Samper, *Isabel*, 281; Tanucci, *Epistolario*, 1:57, for Sora, a Spanish loyalist who had lived in exile in Rome until 1734, when he was given a number of senior appointments by Don Carlos, and who received the Golden Fleece from Philip in 1736.; [Anon.], "Antonio Carmine Caracciolo," *Dizionario Biografico*; Bartolini to Venetian Senate, 8 November and 27 December 1740, in *Corrispondenze Diplomatiche Veneziane da Napoli*, vol. 17, ed. Mario Infelise (Rome: Istituto

Poligrafico e Zecca dello Stato, 1992), 196, 207; Giuseppe Caridi, "Una Riforma Borbonica Bloccata: Il Supremo Magistrato di Commercio nel Regno di Napoli (1739–1746)," *Mediterranea ricerche storiche* 21 (2011): 89–124 (at 121).

20. Zilli, *Carlo di Borbone*, 27, 143. Vignola to Senate, Naples, 6 August 1737, *Corrispondenze*, 16:467–69; Caridi, "Dall'Investitura," 551; Venturi, *Settecento*, 1:39; Mafrici, *Re delle speranze*, 195–96; Caridi, *Essere Re*, 45–46, 73–75; [?] to Santistevan, 20 September 1734, AGS, E/5847; Mafrici, "Mezzogiorno," 641; A. V. Migliorini, "I Problemi del Trattato Franco-Napoletano di Navigazione e di Commercio (1740–1766)," *Rivista Storica Italiana* 91 (1979): 180–209 (at 185); Amedeo Sorge, "La Venalita degli uffici nel regno di Napoli: Un tentativo di riforma nel primo decennio borbonico," in Di Pinto, *I Borboni*, 1:291–304.

21. Ajello, "Stato e società," 196, 212 (and passim); Bethencourt, *Relaciones de Espana*, 567; Tanucci, *Epistolario*, 16:112–13; Vittorio Sciuti Russi, "Stabilita ed Autonomia del Ministero Siciliano in un Dibattito del Secolo XVIII," *Rivista Storica Italiana* 87 (1975): 47–90.

22. Santisteban to Patiño, Naples, 30 August 1735, AGS, /E/6349; Santisteban to de la Quadra, 4 February 1738, with Memoria, and 19 August 1738, AHN, E/6349. For Charny, see Tanucci, *Epistolario*, 1:89; for Reggio, ibid., 618. Unfortunately, Giovanni Montroni, "The Court: Power Relations and Forms of Social Life," in Girolamo Imbruglia, ed., *Naples in the Eighteenth Century: The Birth and Death of a Nation State* (Cambridge: Cambridge University Press, 2000), 22–43, focuses on the later period. Philip's first six nominations were the duke of Mirandola, the marqués de San Juan, the duke of Medinaceli, the conde de Montijo, the duke of Gandía, and the marchese Scotti; Huéscar to Carvajal, 29 January 1747, Ozanam, *Diplomacia*, 128–32; Salas to Villarias, Naples, 29 December 1739, AHN, E/6349. Philip had nominated the duke of Veraguas, Medinaceli having died. Another Spanish recipient of the order included the marqués de la Ensenada, Ensenada to corregidor of Burgos, 24 April 1745, AMB, LA/1745 f. 118. On chivalric or military orders and their significance, see Antti Matikkala, *The Orders of Knighthood and the Formation of the British Honours System, 1660–1760* (Woodbridge: Boydell, 2008), and Storrs, *War, Diplomacy*, 193–94.

23. Don Carlos sent Patiño one of the medals struck on the occasion of his coronation, Santisteban to Patiño, 5 July 1735, AGS, E/7732; Keene to Newcastle, 18 March 1737, NA SP 94/127; Instituto "Salazar y Castro," *Elenco de Grandezas y Títulos Nobiliarios Españoles 1995* (Madrid: Ediciones de la Revista Hidalguía, 1995), sub voce; Tanucci, *Epistolario*, 1:45; Fernández Duro, *Armada Española*, 6:206; Andújar Castillo, *Consejo*, 277–78; Vignola to Senate, 10 February 1739, *Corrispondenze*, 16:612–14. In Spain, Philip consulted Santesteban on Neapolitan affairs, Tanucci, *Epistolario*, 1:118.

24. Chamberlayne to Walpole, 20 August 1736 (and enclosure), BL, Add. 73990 f. 174; Keene to Newcastle, 1 April 1737, NA, SP 94/127; Mafrici, *Re delle speranze*, 196; *Gaceta*, 21 April 1744; Sebastián de la Quadra to Torrenueva, 2 March 1737, AGS, SSH/2; Virginia León Sanz, *Carlos VI: El emperador que no pudo ser rey de España* (Madrid: Aguilar, 2003),

345–52; Di Vittorio, *Austriaci*, 1:292. The conde de la Corzana had received the fief of Squillace, which was sequestered by Don Carlos in 1734, Antonio Rodríguez Villa, *Don Diego Hurtado de Mendoza y Sandoval, conde de la Corzana (1650–1720)* (Madrid: Fortanet, 1907), 270.

25. Oficios al Duque de Montemar, 1737; BN, MSS 12950/28; [King] to Leseta, 20 September 1745, AHN, E/libro 361 f. 61; Elena Postigo Castellanos, "El Cisma del Toisón: Dinastía y Orden (1700–1748)," in Fernández Albaladejo, *Los Borbones*, 331–80; Skinner to Newcastle, 28 August 1734, NA, SP 98/34. Philip gave his portrait, mounted in diamonds, to another four Neapolitan nobles. In November 1739, at Don Carlos's request, Philip gave the Golden Fleece to the prince of Avellino, Barbagallo, "Marino Francesco Caracciolo," *Dizionario Biografico*; [Anon], "Antonio Carmine Caracciolo," *Dizionario Biografico*. Another Neapolitan noble who enjoyed Spanish grandeza was the prince of San Severo, Don Carlos's chamberlain, and a member of the Order of San Genaro, Tanucci, *Epistolario*, 1:450; *Gaceta*, 1 January 1743.

26. Fernández, *Carlos*, 79–80. See also Salas to Villarias, Naples, 8 May 1742, AGS, E/5837; Sciuti Russi, "Bartolomeo Corsini"; Charles to Philip and Isabel, 31 December [1738], AHN, E/2760; Caridi, "Una riforma," passim; Migliorini, "Problemi," 190; Santisteban to Patiño, 20 June 1735, AGS, E/7732. The duke of Solferino sought Philip's support in his efforts to obtain the Order of San Genaro, [?] to Salas, January 1739, AHN, E/6349; Vignola to Senate, 26 May 1739, *Corrispondenze*, 16:640–42. (In 1737 Salas had sent his wife to the Spanish court, where she was lady-in-waiting to Isabel, to lobby on his behalf, Vignola to Senate, 15 October 1737, *Corrispondenze*, 16:486); conte di Monasterolo to CEIII, 23 January 1742, AST, LM /Napoli/8. In September 1742 Montealegre threatened to have Madrid intervene in a dispute with Tanucci, Tanucci to Sora, 20 September 1742, *Epistolario*, 1:624–25; relazione del conte Solaro di Monasterolo, 1 September 1742, AST, Negoziazioni Napoli/1/ 4; Mafrici, *Re delle speranze*, 259.

27. Carlo Antonio Broggia, *Trattato de' tributi, delle monete, e dello governo politico della sanità* (Naples: Pietro Palombo, 1743); Venturi, *Settecento*, 1:90; Bartolini to Senate, 26 July 1740, Tonetti, *Corrispondenze*, 17:165–66; John A. Marino. *Becoming Neapolitan: Citizen Culture in Baroque Naples* (Baltimore: Johns Hopkins University Press, 2011), 89 and passim; *Gaceta*, 1743/27; Monasterolo to CEIII, 14 November and 19 December 1741, AST, LM Napoli/8; *Gaceta*, 1 January, 21 May, and 5 November 1743.

28. Caridi, *Essere Re*, 43–44;? to Campillo, 16 July 1734, AGS, SSH/1040; Allen to Newcastle, 26 May 1736, BL, Add. 73990 f. 20; Vignola to Senate, 29 October 1737, in Infelise, *Corrispondenze*, 16:486; Bartolini to Senate, 2 January 1742, Tonetti, *Corrispondenze*, 17:307–8;; Relazione . . . di Monasterolo . . ., 1 September 1742, AST, Negoziazioni Napoli/1/4. For exports in 1748, see Piatti to Senate, 8 October 1748, Tonetti, *Corrispondenze*, 17:790–91; Carmen Martín Gaite, *Macanaz: Otro paciente de la Inquisición* (Barcelona: destinolibro, 1969), 443–44.

29. Fernández, *Charles III,* 100. In 1738 the formation of a military camp in Naples prompted suspicions that the Spanish court intended to seize Tuscany for the Infante

Felipe while Charles VI was preoccupied in Hungary, Mocenigo to Senate, 29 July 1738, in Infelise, *Corrispondenze*, 16:571–72; Anderson, *War of Austrian Succession*, 99; Bartolini to Senate, 7 November 1741, in Tonetti, *Corrispondenze*, 17:294–95; Monasterolo to CEIII, 14 November 1741 and 13 February 1742, AST, LM Napoli/8

30. Mafrici, *Re delle speranze*, 231; Pierluigi Rovito, "Palo Mattia Doria," *Dizionario Biografico*, available online at http://www.treccani.it/enciclopedia/paolo-mattia-doria (Dizionario Biografico)/; Lodovico Bianchini, *Della Storia delle Finanze del Regno di Napoli* (Palermo, 1839), 421–25. For the vulnerability of Don Carlos's regime and the advisability of not pressing his subjects too hard, see Bartolini to Senate, 14 November 1741 and 1 May 1742, Tonetti, *Corrispondenze*, 17:296–97, 338–39; for early disillusion with the Spaniards, see Bagshaw to Newcastle, 7 and 21 October, 18 November 1734, NA, SP 79/17; Anderson, *War of Austrian Succession*, 100; Fernández, *Carlos*, 99; Venturi, *Settecento*, 1:82; Carignani, "Il Partito Austriaco nel Regno di Napoli al 1744," *Archivio Storico per le Provincie Napoletane*, Anno Sesto (1881): 37–73; Tanucci to Corsini, 18 July 1744, in Venturi, *Settecento*, 1:86–87; Wilkinson, *Defence of Piedmont*, 178.

31. Carignani, "Il Partito Austriaco"; F. A. Meschini, "Costantino Grimaldi," Dizionario Biografico, available online at http://www.treccani.it/enciclopedia/costantino-grimaldi_ (Dizionario_Biografico)/; A. Mazzacane, "Gregorio Grimaldi," *Dizionario Biografico*, available online at http://www.treccani.it/enciclopedia/gregorio-grimaldi_(Dizionario_Biografico)/; [Anon.], "María Francesca Afan de Rivera," *Dizionario Biografico*,, available online at http://www.treccani.it/enciclopedia/afan-de-rivera-maria-francesca_(Dizionario_Biografico)/; Anderson, *War of Austrian Succession*, 137; Vignola to Senate, 10 December 1737 and 6 January and 24 February 1739, Infelise, *Corrispondenze* 16:502–6, 603–4, 616–17; and Mocenigo to same, 25 June 1738, ibid., 554–56; P. Villani, *Mezzogiorno tra riforme e rivoluzione* (Rome: Laterza, 1974), 105–53; Fernández, *Charles III*, 112; Caridi, "Una riforma," 123; *Gaceta*, 6, 13, and 20 July, 17 and 24 August, 28 September, 26 October, and 14 December 1745; Richmond, *Navy*, 3:154.

32. S. De Majo, "Giovanni Fogliani Sforza d'Aragona," *Dizionario Biografico*, avaiulable online at http://www.treccani.it/enciclopedia/fogliani-sforza-d-aragona-giovanni_(Dizionario_ Biografico)/; Nicolini, "Troiano Acquaviva d'Aragona," *Dizionario Biografico*, available online at http://www.treccani.it/enciclopedia/fogliani-sforza-d-aragona-giovanni_(Dizionario_ Biografico)/; Carvajal to Huéscar, 13 March 1747, Ozanam, *Diplomacia*, 160–61. For Don Carlos's resentment that the duke of Sora had done homage to Ferdinand VI for his fief of Piombino, see Tonetti, *Corrispondenze*, 17:665, 751. He had earlier (1745) done it to Philip V, *Gaceta*, 18 May 1745; Piatti to Senate, 26 December 1747, Tonetti, *Corrispondenze*, 17:761.

33. Pablo Fernández Albaladejo, "De 'llave de Italia' a 'corazón de la Monarquía': Milan y la Monarquía Católica en el reinado de Felipe III," in Fernández Albaladejo, *Fragmentos*, 185–237; Maffi, *La Cittadella in Armi*; Philip V to Louis XIV, Madrid, 18 July 1707, in Bernardo Ares and Echeverría Pereda, *Las Cortes de Madrid y Versalles*, 298–99. For eighteenth-century Milan, see Domenico Sella and Carlo Capra, *Il Ducato di Milano dal 1535 al 1796* (Turin: UTET, 1984), 153–684; instructions, 28 December 1711, AHN,

E/3376/2/10, clause 15. During the earlier Partition Treaty negotiations, William III had observed that the kingdom of Naples had always been more esteemed than Milan, Tallard to Louis XIV, London, 22 May 1698, in Grimblot, *Letters of William III and Louis XIV,* 1:500–509 (at 504); *Politica, vita religiosa, carità: Milano nel primo settecento,* ed. Marco Bona Castellotti, Edoardo Bressan, and Paola Vismara (Milan: Jaca, 1997), 74; Ripperda to San Felipe, 12 September 1725, Mur i Raurell, *Diplomacia Secreta y Paz,* 2:164; Francisco Andújar Castillo, "Entre la corte y la guerra: Militares italianos al servicio de España en el siglo XVIII," in Bianchi, Maffi, and Stumpo, *Italiani al servizio straniero, 130.*

34. Baudrillart, *Philippe,* 4:165–67; Borré to Ormea, 11 January 1734, AST, LM Spagna/66 (warned about one D. Ignacio [Sevella], a Milanese employed in Spain who was en route to Milan, where his brother was a cleric); Carpintero to Patiño, 30 January and 27 February 1734, AGS, E/5703. Madrid clearly agreed, Fuenclara to Patiño, 1 May 1734, AGS, E/5704; Bethencourt, *Relaciones de España,* 280.

35. Baudrillart, *Philippe,* 5:10–15, 89; Pérez Samper, *Isabel,* 295; Rodríguez Villa, *Marqués de la Ensenada,* 13, for Philip's renunciation; Sella and Capra, *Ducato di Milano,* 276–77; Andrea Merlotti, *L'Enigma delle Nobiltà: Stato e ceti dirigenti nel Piemonte del Settecento* (Florence: Olshi, 2000), 139–63; *Gaceta,* 1 and 16 November 1745.

36. The Spanish occupation of the Milanese has hardly been explored, although the sources to do so exist in Milan, Madrid, and Simancas. Unfortunately, there is no reference to the response of Gabriele Verri, a Milanese patrician, in the study of his more famous son by Carlo Capra, *I Progressi della ragione: Vita di Pietro Verri* (Bologna: Il Mulino, 2002). Alba Tirone, "Giulio Antonio Biancani" *Dizionario Biografico,* available online at http://www.treccani.it/enciclopedia/giulio-antonio-biancani_(Dizionario_Biografico)/; Carlo Capra, "Francesco Melzi d'Eril," *Dizionario Biografico,* available online at http://www.treccani.it/enciclopedia/francesco-melzi_(Dizionario_Biografico)/ (with details of continuing links between the family and Spain well after 1748); Guido Fagioli Vercellone, "Clelia del Grillo Borromeo," *Dizionario Biografico,* available online at http://www.treccani.it/enciclopedia/borromeo-clelia-del-grillo/; Anna M. Serralunga Bardazza, *Clelia Grillo Borromeo Sarese: Vicende private e pubbliche virtù di una nobildonna nell'Italia del Settecento* (Biella: Eventi e Progetti, 2005), 78–99, and (for the later investigation into the contessa's conduct during the occupation) 250–303; Guido Fagioli Vercellone, "Antonio Giuseppe della Torre di Rezzonico," *Dizionario Biografico,* available online at http://www.treccani.it/enciclopedia/della-torre-di-rezzonico-antonio-giuseppe_(Dizionario_Biografico)/Laura Facchin, "L'immagine di Filippo di Borbone e di Elisabetta Farnese nello stato di Milano nel XVIII secolo: Dalla diffusione iconografica all'utilizzo come arma politica," in *La Corte de los Borbones: Crisis del modelo cortesano,* ed. José Martinez Milán, Concepción Camerero Bullón, and Marcello Luzzi Traficante, 3 vols. (Madrid: Polifemo, 2013), 3:1799–1840; Merlotti, *Enigma,* 150.

37. These issues have spawned a substantial literature in recent years. See Álvarez-Junco, *Spanish Identity,* passim; Tamar Herzog, *Defining Nations: Immigrants and Citizens in Early Modern Spain and Spanish America* (New Haven: Yale University Press, 2003); Laborda,

Señorío de Vizcaya, 573–74; Fernández Albaladejo, "Dinastía y comunidad política," 485–532; Torres Sánchez, "Prólogo," *Volver;* Antonio Juan Calvo Maturana and Manuel Amador González Fuertes, "Monarquía, Nación y Guerra de la Independencia: Deber y haber historiográfico en torno a 1808," *Cuadernos de Historia Moderna: Anejos* 7 (2008): 321–77.

38. Álvarez-Ossorio Alvariño, "Introducción," in Álvarez-Ossorio Alvariño and García García, *Monarquía de las naciones*, 29–36; Irving A. A. Thompson, "La Monarquía de España: La invención de un concepto," in *Entre Clio y Casandra: Poder y Sociedad en la Monarquía Hispánica durante la Edad Moderna, Cuadernos del Seminario Floridablanca*, no. 6, ed. Francisco Javier Guillamón Álvarez, Julio D. Muñoz Rodríguez, and Domingo Centenero de Arce (Murcia: Universidad de Murcia, 2005), 31–56; I. A. A. Thompson, "Castile, Spain and the Monarchy: The Political Community from Patria Natural to Patria Nacional," in *Spain, Europe and the Atlantic World: Essays in Honour of John H. Elliott*, ed. Richard Kagan and Geoffrey Parker (Cambridge: Cambridge University Press, 1995), 125–59; Baudrillart, *Philippe*, 4:110.

39. Catia Brilli, "La importancia de hacerse español: La elite mercantile genovesa de Càdiz en el siglo XVIII," in Lobato and Oliva, *El Sistema Comercial Español en la Economía Mundial*, 225–55, for Genoese subjects; Melón Jiménez, "Las fronteras de la Monarquía y las aduanas de Felipe V," 173, 180–82, for Italian financiers as farmers of the Spanish customs (1734–39); Thompson, "Castile, Spain and the Monarchy," 148–50.

40. Kamen, *War*, 66, 330. In 1732 the commander of the Oran expedition, Montemar, summoned from Málaga all those former inhabitants of Oran who had fled to Spain in 1708 and were still there, Holloway to Newcastle, 20 April 1732, NA SP 94/216. See Patiño to Bohorques, 2 September 1732, AGS, SG/Sup/486; Gaspare De Caro, "Giovanni Brancaccio," *Dizionario Biografico*, available online at http://www.treccani.it/enciclopedia/giovanni-brancaccio_(Dizionario-Biografico)/; consultas of Council of State on petitions of Doña Leonor Bonet, 22 September and 6 December 1712 and 27 June and 19 August 1713, AGS, GJ/609.

41. Consulta of Council of State, 26 February 1715, AHN/E/Libro 386 f. 215. On the request of D. Francisco Cobri, previously a senior official in Sicily, for the continuation of his salary, Philip ordered that he be treated the same as others of his grade and rank who had reached Spain, consulta, 15 June 1715, AHN/E/Libro 386 f. 221; María del Carmen Irles Vicente, "Italianos en la administración española del siglo XVIII," *Revista de Historia Moderna* 16 (1997): 157–76; Baudrillart, *Philippe*, 3:115; Relación de las Mrds y Pensiones concedidas por SM . . . [1737], AGS/SSH/408.; petition (1737) of Octavio Giménez Aldeano (above), AGS/SSH/407; Álvarez-Ossorio Alvariño, "El final?," 897–903; Bustanzo to Signori, Madrid, 7 November 1733, Ciasca, *Istruzioni*, 6:179; Arvillars to CEIII, 20 July 1731, AST, LM Spagna/63.

42. Letter sent by the Sicilian noblewoman Caterina Gravina to her husband, the prince of Campofiorito (Campoflorido), and forwarded by him to Philip V's secretary, Grimaldo, Sánchez Marquez, "Fine della Sicilia Spagnola," 567; A. Álvarez-Ossorio

Alvariño, "Naciones mixtas: Los jenízaros en el gobierno de Italia," in Álvarez-Ossorio Alvariño and García García, *Monarquía de las Naciones*, 597–649; José Manuel de Bernardo Ares, "Felipe V: La trasformación de un sistema de gobierno," in Serrano, *Felipe V*, 1:986; Álvarez-Ossorio Alvariño, "Felipe V en Italia," 836; Ozanam, *Diplomates espagnols du XVIIIe siècle*, 215, 217–18; Vargas y Ponce, *Vida de D. Juan Josef Navarro*, 1–11, 367–69, 373–78; O'Donnell y Duque de Estrada, *El primer marqués de la Victoria*, 15, 19–20; Marchena Fernández, "Italianos al servicio," 135–75. The Asturian noble Carlos Ramírez de Jove succeeded (1707) to the title of marqués de San Esteban del Mar on the death of his uncle at the siege of Tortona (Milan), Martínez-Radío Garrido, *Guerra de Sucesión en Asturias*, 171.

43. Ensenada to Huéscar, 30 December 1747, Ozanam and Téllez Alarcia, *Misión*, 362–63; Andrés-Gallego, *El Motín de Esquilache*.

44. On this development, see Thompson, "Castile, Spain, and the Monarchy," although Thompson's approach differs from that suggested here.

Chapter Seven. Spain's Resurgence, 1713–1748

Epigraph: Nuncio Alamanni to Papal Secretary of State, 13 August, 1734, ASV, SS/244A (Cifre)/1734 f. 83ff.

1. Pierre Vilar, "Estado, nación y patria en las conciencias españolas: Historia y actualidad," in ibid., *Hidalgos, Amotinados y Guerrilleros: Pueblos y Poderes en la Historia de España* (Barcelona: Crítica, 1982), 255–78 (at 269); Fernández Albaladejo, "Monarquía de los Borbones," 380.

2. José Luis Hernández Marco, "El colbertismo de Felipe V y Valencia: La industria textil no sedera," *Estudis* 5 (1976): 47–58.

3. Fernández Albaladejo, "Monarquía de los Borbones," 380–85.

4. Juan Rico Giménez, 'Legislar y administrar: El despotismo ilustrado y los gitanos,' in *Coloquio Internacional Carlos III y su Siglo*, 2:151–65.

Note on Sources

1. Armstrong, *Elisabeth*, 322; Delgado Barrado, "La transmisión . . .," 59; Bustanzo to Genoa, 1 January 1735, Ciasca, *Istruzioni*, 6:200–203.

2. See Angel de la Plaza Bores, *Guia del Investigador*, 2d rev. ed. (Madrid: Ministerio de la Cultura, 1980).

3. José A. Martín Fuertes, *Fondo Histórico del Archivo Municipal de Astorga: Catálogo* (León: Institución "Fray Bernardino de Sahagún," 1981).

INDEX